MARYLAND
The Federalist Years

MARYLAND
The
Federalist Years

L. Marx Renzulli, Jr.

Rutherford • Madison • Teaneck
FAIRLEIGH DICKINSON UNIVERSITY PRESS

© 1972 by Associated University Presses, Inc.
Library of Congress Catalogue Card Number: 70-149405

Associated University Presses, Inc.
Cranbury, New Jersey 08512

SBN: 0-8386-7903-X
Printed in the United States of America

To
Russell E. Miller
and
Robert Van Waes
tantum accepi tantulum reddo

Contents

Preface

The Federalist Party in Maryland, as in the nation itself, arose in answer to the need for political and economic stability which the powerless, debt-ridden Confederation government could not provide. Although from their viewpoint the ensuing experiment under the Constitution was a dismal failure, the Maryland Federalists were remarkably successful in achieving fundamental goals. They weathered the struggle to prevent ratification in the state and they helped to transform a pregnant document into a workable, effective instrument of government; they saved their state from the chaos of paper money and economic ruin; they encouraged commerce and financial probity; and they showed that a political party could function without appeals to demagoguery. The Federalists functioned best, moreover, when Maryland was weak, discontented, and practically insolvent.

Ironically, Federalist support was always strongest in the agrarian areas, although the party's appeal was generally directed toward the state's commercial elements. The latter, centered from the beginning in the counties of Baltimore, Anne Arundel, and Harford, inveterately supported the opposition. There were reasons for this—sound ones—but the key to understanding the political battles of the period lies in the fierce contest waged by the Chesapeake counties to wrest control of Maryland politics out of the hands of the dominant Potomac oligarchy.

This was the eye of the conflict, assuredly one of the major reasons for the Federalists' downfall. As the party degenerated into a conservative vehicle of the status quo, it ultimately drove rural Maryland into the arms of the Jeffersonian Republicans. The progressive loss of that stronghold, together with the growing preponderance of Baltimore, Annapolis, and the developing sections along the upper Chesapeake Bay, hastened the inevitable collapse.

There were other reasons. The Federalists ceased offering a positive program to the electorate, for whom they publicly professed distrust. They were not willing to wed Hamiltonian economic theories to the more popular and dynamic philosophy which was the political heritage of the Revolution—a heritage carried to victory by the Jeffersonians in 1800. Possessed with fears of mobocracy should the political balance of power rest with the propertyless, they refused to recruit new leaders from beyond the narrow circle of Maryland's established and aristocratic families, nor would they adopt the devices of mass political organization so successfully used by the opposition. Above all, the party became characterized by genuine fear. There was fear of change and fear of that most democratic of all impulses, the growing application of rule "by the people." Belated attempts at reform failed, largely because the conservatives would not broaden their concepts or abandon their fixed belief in minority rule. Essentially, the Federalists of Maryland and of the nation were not able to meet the new age, to extend their policies toward it, or to understand its meaning. By succumbing to panic, they rushed into extinction.

Acknowledgments

First, I wish to express my appreciation and gratitude to Professors Thomas Perkins Abernethy and Dumas Malone, both of the University of Virginia, under whose direction this study was begun. Their encouragement, criticism, and suggestions have been invaluable, and whatever merit this work may have is primarily owed to them.

I am especially indebted to the Thomas Jefferson Foundation, Charlottesville, Virginia, under whose auspices much of the research was completed and parts of the finishing touches applied.

The search for the essence of the Maryland Federalists must, of course, begin in the Old Line State. At the Maryland Historical Society the great mass of Federalist papers, collections, and other contemporary material were made available to me, and I wish to express my thanks to Mr. P. William Filby, the Librarian and Assistant Director; Miss Hester Rich, Assistant Librarian; Miss Elizabeth Merritt, whose facility with eighteenth-century script was a wonder to behold; Mrs. John Boles, Curator of the Manuscripts Division; Mrs. Lois B. McCauley, Curator of Graphics; and Mr. John Kilbourne, now Curator of the Historical Society of Pennsylvania.

There was much help from other sources in Maryland, Washington, D.C., and Virginia. I am deeply grateful to Miss

Dorothy Brown, Associate Professor of History at Georgetown University, for extensive information and aid on early political struggles and party organization, and for her permission to cite material from her doctoral dissertation, "Party Battles and Beginnings in Maryland." My thanks also go to Mr. Edward C. Carter II, Editor-in-Chief, The Papers of Benjamin Latrobe, for permission to use Latrobe material; to Mr. Morris L. Radoff, Archivist and Records Administrator, the Maryland Hall of Records; and to Mr. William Runge, Curator of the MacGregor Library at the University of Virginia. The staffs of the Virginia Historical Society, the Manuscripts Division of the Library of Congress, the Enoch Pratt Free Library, Baltimore, the Peabody Institute, Baltimore, and the Alderman Library of the University of Virginia have all been generous with their time and assistance.

At the Friendship Library of Fairleigh Dickinson University, Madison, I am under obligation to Mr. James Fraser, Librarian; Mrs. Dorothea Creamer, Circulation Librarian; and to Mrs. Helen Ross, Reference Librarian, for advice and information which has been of great aid to me.

Special permissions to use quoted material were graciously granted by the following publishers and individuals: from The Journal of William Maclay, E. S. Maclay, editor, copyright 1927, by Albert and Charles Boni, Inc.; Democratic-Republican Societies, 1790–1800, by Eugene P. Link, copyright 1942, by Columbia University Press, New York; material reprinted from Freedom's Fetters: The Alien and Sedition Laws and American Civil Liberties. James Morton Smith, © 1956 by Cornell University. Used by permission of Cornell University Press; The Life of Thomas Johnson, by Edward S. Delaplaine, copyright 1927, by F. H. Hitchcock and Company, used by permission of Mr. Delaplaine; History of Maryland, by Matthew Page Andrews, copyright 1929, by Doubleday & Company, Inc.; The Federalist Era, 1789–1801 by John C. Miller, copyright 1960, by Harper and Row, Publishers, Incorporated; A Diplomatic History of the United States, by Samuel Flagg

Acknowledgments

Bemis, copyright 1955, by Holt, Rinehart and Winston, Inc.; *Paper Money in Maryland, 1727–1789,* by Kathryn L. Behrens, copyright 1923, by The Johns Hopkins Press, from *Maryland During and After the Revolution,* by Philip A. Crowl, copyright 1943, by The Johns Hopkins Press, and from *The Adams Federalists,* by Manning J. Dauer, copyright 1953, by The Johns Hopkins Press; *The New Nation During the Confederation, 1781–1789* by Merrill Jensen, copyright 1950, by Alfred A. Knopf, Inc.; *The South in the New Nation 1789–1819,* by Thomas P. Abernethy, copyright 1961, by Louisiana State University Press; *Baltimore on the Chesapeake,* by Hamilton Owens, copyright 1941, used by permission of Mrs. Hamilton Owens; *American Suffrage from Property to Democracy, 1760–1860,* by Chilton Williamson, copyright © 1960, by Princeton University Press; Princeton Paperback, 1968; and *The Power of the Purse,* by E. James Ferguson, copyright 1961, by the University of North Carolina Press for The Institute of Early American History and Culture.

Preparation and completion of the Index was done by Mary Alice Deasey and Thomas H. Cifelli, both of Fairleigh Dickinson University at Madison, and I am most indebted to them for undertaking this difficult task.

Finally, I wish to thank three lovely ladies in my life who have worked long and understandingly with me these many months: my editor, Mrs. Mathilde E. Finch; the Department of History's secretary, Mrs. Elizabeth A. Claus; and my wife, Giuliana. Their patience has been exceeded only by their ability to put me in my place.

1

The Ninety-nine Plagues
of an Empty Purse

DURING the first years of peace following the American Revolution, a spirit of extravagance and love of luxury prevailed throughout the United States and among all classes of the people. Independence having been secured, Americans looked forward to an era of boundless opportunities and equally boundless profits.[1] Commerce—freed at last of the trammels of the English Navigation Acts—found its way back into many old channels and many new ones. Although some old avenues, such as the West India trade, were closed, American products were otherwise carried any place in the world where there was a market.[2] Imports grew large and business was brisk.

Much of America's wealth, as before the Revolution, was

1. Merrill Jensen, *The New Nation A History of the United States During the Confederation, 1781–1789* (New York: Random House, Alfred A. Knopf, Inc., 1950), pp. 177–88.
2. Paul Bentalou Journal, 1784–1813, M.H.S. (Maryland Historical Society), Baltimore, Maryland. See also mercantile accounts of Samuel Smith and Company in the Smith Letterbooks, 1783–1784, M.H.S., *passim,* and numerous references to trade in the Otho Holland Williams Papers, Vol. 4, M.H.S.

in the form of ships, wharves, stores, and goods.[3] But to this there was added new wealth in the form of government debt, of private debts growing out of the war, and of expanding markets both old and new. Paper money and certificates of indebtedness, either State or Continental, were plentiful for use at home.[4] In domestic affairs the federal government was solvent, or nearly so. Requisitions by the Confederation Congress were successful up to a point: they raised almost enough to meet the normal expense of federal administration while the states took care of the interest on the public debt.[5]

The new prosperity was expressed most dramatically in a national buying spree in whose current both aristocrat and mechanic were swept along. Having been deprived of European goods for almost ten years, Americans eagerly bought all that was offered without a thought of where the money was to be obtained.[6] As the war came to a close, United States ports were thrown open to the world, and Dutch, French, Danish, Swedish, and other Europeans set sail for them—in many cases without waiting for legislatures to determine the channels of trade.[7] British vessels appeared everywhere, English merchants being anxious to continue handling the greater share of American commerce and to find a market for their manufactures which had been accumulating during the war. The rush to America, which began upon the cessation of hostilities, continued throughout 1783 and well into 1784.[8]

3. Jensen, *New Nation, ibid.* See also Kathryn L. Behrens, *Paper Money in Maryland, 1727–1789* (Baltimore: The Johns Hopkins Press, 1923), p. 78.
4. Behrens, *Paper Money*, pp. 78–79.
5. E. James Ferguson, *The Power of the Purse* (Chapel Hill: The University of North Carolina Press for the Institute of Early American History and Culture, 1961), pp. 220–22.
6. Jensen, *The New Nation*, pp. 186–88. Behrens, *Paper Money*, chapter 8.
7. Kathryn Sullivan, *Maryland and France, 1774–1789* (Philadelphia: University of Pennsylvania Press, 1936), pp. 133ff.
8. Behrens, *Paper Money*, chapter 8.

But the prosperity hovering over the new republic was more apparent than real. American markets were soon more than adequately supplied. Most of the buying, moreover, which had been accomplished through credit and easy terms, led to an unhealthy spiral of too much buying and too much credit. Mechanics were reported to be buying silk stockings and farmers' daughters buying silks. What little specie there was available in the United States poured back to Europe, so that by 1784 the boom that had started on shaky ground continued in the seaport towns as a credit-supported balloon growing ever larger, ever weaker.[9] The inevitable time arrived when British creditors began to demand the payment of debts which had been incurred both before and since the war. By the spring of 1784, America was in the midst of a severe commercial depression.[10]

Maryland shared fully in both the boom and the bust. It was, in fact, a mirror in which the hopes and disillusionments of the rest of the country were reflected in microcosm. By 1783 the bustling town of Baltimore was no longer a hamlet by Jones' Falls but a thriving port with a population rapidly approaching 14,000.[11] Market Street, its chief thoroughfare, had just been laid with cobblestones, and the town's merchant-fathers went even further by providing for sidewalks and a permanent police force, and by arranging to have the main streets paved and lit at night. The waterfront echoed to the sound of new wharves being built, while in the taverns and coffee houses affluent merchants were planning to improve the harbor, which had an unpleasant way of silting up every

---

9. Jensen, *The New Nation*, p. 187.
10. Sears and Smith to Henry Knox, dated Boston, August 13, 1783; ms. correspondence of Henry Knox, M.H.S. See also Smith Letter-books, 1783–1784, M.H.S.
11. C. P. Gould, "The Economic Causes of the Rise of Baltimore," in *Essays in Colonial History Presented to Charles McLean Andrews by His Students* (New Haven: Yale University Press, 1931), pp. 234–35.

spring and keeping vessels from approaching the numerous wharves in the basin.[12] The marshes surrounding the town were filled in, causeways were built, and the fundamental problem of bettering communications to the north and west by canal or road so as to insure a steady flow of wheat for the city's mills and ships was given that serious attention which any commercial port intent on future growth and competition with other eastern seaports must undertake.[13]

For it was wheat and other grains that were the touchstone of Maryland's economic prosperity between 1781 and 1784. The rapid spread of grain culture on the Eastern Shore, in the Piedmont region of Western Maryland, and in the Susquehanna valley of Pennsylvania, along with the consequent shift away from tobacco, redounded to the benefit of both merchant and farmer. Wheat and corn crops sold for peak prices in the city's marketplaces,[14] and Baltimore's leading merchants—Sam Smith, Paul Bentalou, the Gilmors, Ridgelys, Pattersons, and Ellicotts (to mention but a few)—by and large prospered enough from the commercial opportunities present in the export of grain to provide themselves with manorial country-seats and townhouses despite postwar market fluctuations, interstate tariffs, trade restrictions, the general instability and depreciation of American currency, and the growing dependence on bills of exchange and outright barter to carry on trade.[15]

Because of its phenomenal rise following the war, Baltimore

---

12. Hamilton Owens, *Baltimore on the Chesapeake* (New York: Doubleday, Doran and Co., Inc., 1941), pp. 127–29. Although he is not a professional historian, Owens gives an excellent account of early Baltimore.
13. Owens, *Baltimore*, pp. 128–29.
14. Lewis C. Gray, *History of Agriculture in the Southern United States to 1860.* 2 vols. (Washington: The Carnegie Institute of Washington, 1933) 2:606–10. According to Gray, the Southern States were the "bread states" for a time after the Revolution. See also Sullivan, *Maryland and France, passim,* and C. P. Gould, "Rise of Baltimore," pp. 237ff.
15. Gould, *ibid.* See also Smith Letterbooks, 1783–1784.

became known as "the boom town of the 1780's."[16] But the basis of Maryland's prosperity—as reflected in the development of its leading city—was as unhealthy as that of her sisters. Agriculture and trade grew, but cash disappeared. Overproduction in both grain and tobacco drove prices down. Merchants cut their imports drastically, yet by 1784 ships were reported arriving in London in ballast and carrying only specie, an export which only aggravated the country's depressed economy. It was discovered too late that barter and bills of credit could not substitute for hard money indefinitely. And last, there was the burden of private debts and taxes.[17]

This burden was widely distributed throughout the state and was becoming critical by 1784. Of the several debts owed by the citizens of Maryland, none was more onerous, yet required more delicate attention by the legislature, than the foreign debt held mainly by Great Britain. Large sums were still owed for debts incurred before the war to British mercantile houses whose agents returned after the peace to make good their claims under Article IV of the Peace Treaty.[18] A report prepared by the House of Delegates in January 1787, estimated that the amount thus owed came to about 600,000 pounds sterling, or 1,000,000 pounds current money. The total estimated debt, consisting of debts due to Great Britain since the peace, private domestic debts, debts owed the state on bonds for confiscated property, and tax arrearages owed the state, came to 2,489,586 pounds current money.[19] Assuming that these figures are nearly correct, Marylanders owed slightly more than two-fifths of their total debts in prewar obligations contracted with England.

---

16. Jensen, *The New Nation*, p. 192.
17. *Ibid.*, pp. 187, 236–38. See also Gray, *Agriculture*, 2:610ff.
18. This article expressly provided that "Creditors on either side shall meet with no lawful Impediment to the Recovery of the full value in Sterling Money of all bona fide Debts heretofore contracted." The treaty was ratified by the United States on April 15, 1783.
19. Address of the House of Delegates of Maryland to their Constituents. Dated January 16, 1787. Printed broadside, M.H.S.

The necessity which faced the legislature after 1783 of
bringing some order out of the confusing debt-burden left as
a legacy of the Revolution only served to increase financial
distress among the citizenry and to set into motion a trend of
monetary deflation which made the payment of these debts
still more difficult.[20] To a people harassed by domestic creditors, loaded with a large public debt, and now beginning
to suffer a severe period of deflation, the importunities of
British agents and collectors must have seemed an unwarranted burden indeed. Until recently these men had been
enemies of the state and had given support to the British
government in its war against the United States; now they
returned under the protection of the laws to press Americans
for the payment of debts which many thought the war had
been fought to wipe out. Marylanders naturally asked themselves why their state permitted these men to return when
in the neighboring state of Virginia severe repressive measures
were taken against the returning British factors, which lasted
until the establishment of superior federal courts in 1789.
Maryland lawmakers, on the other hand, were comparatively
lenient in their treatment of these same creditors after 1783.[21]

This tolerance on the part of the legislature was partly
explained by the fact that the problem of British debts was
much less serious in Maryland than in Virginia.[22] But in

20. Behrens, *Paper Money*, pp. 79–87, provides an extended treatment
on this subject.
21. Philip A. Crowl, *Maryland During and After the Revolution* (Baltimore: The Johns Hopkins Press, 1943), pp. 78–80. In May of 1782
the Virginia Assembly passed a law prohibiting the recovery of
any debt due a British merchant in any court in the state. This law
remained in force until the ratification of the Federal Constitution.
In 1787, however, Virginia passed an act repealing all laws prohibiting the recovery of British debts on condition that Britain
should first evacuate the northwest trading posts and make repara-
tions for stolen slaves. Isaac Harrell, *Loyalism in Virginia* (Philadelphia: Duke University Publications, 1926), pp. 125, 140–51.
22. Isaac Harrell, *Loyalism in Virginia* (Philadelphia: 1926), pp. 26ff.
In 1791 British merchants debited almost two and a half million
pounds sterling to Virginia as against only half a million pounds

addition, the state was faced with a peculiar and delicate problem which made her legislators hesitant in taking discriminatory measures against the British creditors. In 1765, under the old proprietary government, funds belonging to the Province had been invested in capital stock of the Bank of England. The stock continued to remain in England after the peace, having been held in trust for the old province by three London merchants, and the state was anxious to make good its claim to it. Negotiations for recovery were begun by Maryland in 1784 with the dispatch of Samuel Chase to London as agent for the state. His efforts met with failure because of adverse claims by Henry Harford, late Proprietor of Maryland, and by Englishmen whose property in the state had been confiscated during the war; and it was not until the various claims had been settled in 1804 that the state was finally able to recover its stock. In the meantime, however, it had been impolitic to antagonize the British government and British merchants too far by imposing heavy restrictions on the collection of prewar debts. Such action might prove costly for the state, and therefore Maryland debtors were enjoined to suffer in silence.[23]

That its position was so forbearing in comparison with other states was owing in large part to the strength of conservative opinion in Maryland. Politically this was expressed in the high property qualifications demanded of councillors, governors, and senators which served to keep the function of government in the hands of a small, considerably wealthy, upper class. These offices rotated within a very narrow circle of men—staunchly conservative, aristocratic, and for the most part sympathetic to the idea of rigid debt collection, or

sterling to Maryland. Jefferson estimated that at least 2,000,000 pounds sterling was owed to British merchants by Virginians.

23. Behrens, *Paper Money*, chapter 9, has an excellent and concise treatment of the bank stock question in detail. Most of the documents relative to the Bank of England Stock are in Papers Relative to the Maryland Stock in the Bank of England, "Rainbow Series," Blue Books II and III, MS, Hall of Records, Annapolis, Maryland.

friendly to returning merchants who had played so important a role in Maryland before the war.[24] Although the difference in background between the members of the Senate and the House of Delegates was one of degree only, the former was consistently conservative and was the seat of resistance to debt reform proposals put forward by the latter. The minimum property requirement for senators was twice as high as that for delegates, while the small size of the Senate produced a cohesiveness and traditionalism impossible in the larger and more unwieldy House. Also, the five-year tenure of the senators helped remove them from popular influence and from the whims of public opinion, a factor of no mean importance in the coming struggle for debtor relief.[25]

Early in 1780 the Senate was instrumental in defeating a bill passed by the House of Delegates permitting debtors whose creditors were not residents of the state to discharge their obligations in depreciated Continental, Colonial, or Con-

---

24. In the decade 1777 to 1787, there were but a few individuals in the Maryland Senate who could be counted as controlling members of that body. These were William Perry, Daniel Carroll, John Smith, George Gale, Edward Lloyd, Samuel Hughes, John Henry, William Hindman, Charles Carroll, Barrister, Robert Goldsborough, William Hemsley, Charles Carroll of Carrollton, Matthew Tilghman, George Plater, and Thomas Stone. They performed the main function for which the Senate had been originally established, which was to act as a conservative check against the more popularly elected House of Delegates, and to safeguard property rights and the interests of the upper economic and social class from attack. *Votes and Proceedings of the General Assembly of the State of Maryland*, Senate, February Session, 1777, to November Session, 1787. See also Bureau of the Census, *A Century of Population Growth, 1790–1900* (Washington: Government Printing Office, 1909), pp. 296–98, for a survey of class structure in Maryland. General O. H. Williams, a Maryland aristocrat, took a much more moderate view toward the debt problem, writing that, because of Article IV of the peace treaty, American debtors should rightfully look to the state for restitution. O. H. Williams to Dr. Philip Thomas, dated Baltimore, July 29, 1789. O. H. Williams Papers, Vol. 5, M.H.S.

25. F. N. Thorpe, *Federal and State Constitutions, Colonial Charters, and Other Organic Laws.* 7 vols. (Washington, D.C.: Government Printing Office, 1909), 1686–1712.

vention currency.[26] Although not specifically stated, this
measure was obviously aimed against British creditors who
had by and large fled the state after the outbreak of war.
Later in 1780, however, the measure was enacted into law,
and debtors hastened to pay off their debts in depreciated
currency at the rate of 40 to 1. Not only was this procedure
extraordinary, since the actual creditors were not consulted,
but it also involved payment at a rate far below the real value
of the debts. Technically, British debts to the value of 144,574
pounds current money were thus paid off by Maryland citizens;
but in sterling terms the payments came to only 86,744
pounds.[27] In addition, the same law provided a moratorium
on prewar debt prosecutions, whose time of grace was eventually extended to January 1, 1784.[28]

Thus, when the Preliminary Articles of Peace were ratified
in the spring of 1783, returning British creditors found themselves in a highly dubious legal position. On the one hand,
large sums had been written off in Maryland by the deposit
of worthless paper money in the state treasury; on the other,
Article IV of the Treaty guaranteed that creditors would meet
with no lawful impediment in the recovery of their money.
Although the moratorium of 1780 was not due to expire for
almost a year, creditors or their agents were already beginning
to return, one even receiving a promise of protection from
the governor himself as long as he conducted his affairs with
propriety.[29]

Spurred on by this pressure, the situation among the debtors
in Maryland grew increasingly desperate. Rumors spread
throughout the state in the spring and summer of 1783 that

26. *Maryland Journal*, January 4, 1780, M.H.S.
27. *Votes and Proceedings*, Senate and House of Delegates, November
    Session, 1785, to March 1786.
28. William Kilty, *The Laws of Maryland*. 2 vols. (Annapolis: 1799),
    April Session, 1782, chapter 55. See also Crowl, *Maryland,* chapter
    3, for a discussion of the debt question.
29. W. H. Browne, ed., *Archives of Maryland*. 57 vols. (Baltimore,
    1883–1940), 48:443.

the legislature would assume responsibility for the difference between the actual sums paid in depreciated currency by the debtors and the true sterling value of their obligations.[30] To a few conservatives, such as Otho Holland Williams, action by the state in aid of debtors was "surely . . . founded in *Justice* if not in law." Bad as the act of 1780 was, added Williams, "it has always been my own opinion that . . . those who complied with it ought to derive all the advantages proposed by it. If any eluded the Spirit of intention and acted fraudulently— prove it and punish *them*."[31] But the great majority of conservative-minded men in Maryland viewed proposed legislative action in this sphere with outspoken alarm. Their fears were voiced by Charles Carroll of Carrollton when he declared that stay laws had a "manifest Tendency to exonerate the Debtors, and to subject the State to this new burthen, already sufficiently loaded with Taxes."[32]

Whatever their hopes may have been, when the General Assembly convened in Annapolis in April of 1783 the Senate was unwilling, either then or later, to aid the debtors by assuming the debt as a public burden. One final measure to impede the designs of the British creditors was enacted: Maryland judges were allowed to disqualify attorneys who were loyalists or British sympathizers during the war. This act was designed to strike at those who might be expected to represent British creditors in prosecuting their suits in the state courts, and thus to hamper the plaintiffs by forcing them to rely on inadequate counsel or none at all.[33] Further the Senate would not go, and when this act expired in 1786 no effort was made to renew it. In 1785, moreover, the Senate rejected a House bill striking off all interest on British debts from April 1775,

---

30. *Maryland Journal,* April 11, 1783.
31. O. H. Williams to Dr. Philip Thomas, dated July 29, 1789. MS in O. H. Williams Papers, Vol. 5, M.H.S.
32. Charles Carroll of Carrollton to ———, dated 1783. MS. in Miscellaneous Collection, M.H.S.
33. *Votes and Proceedings,* Senate, April Session, 1783.

until March 1783.[34] And in the following year the legislature
came full circle when it declared the Treaty of Peace to be
"the supreme law within this state."[35] The conservatives had
scored a notable victory, but rumblings of anti-aristocratic
sentiment and social discontent were heard more frequently
throughout the state.[36]

These murmurings in favor of debtor relief, however, were
mere harbingers of what was to come once the legislature
inaugurated its program of currency deflation on an overall
scale. Having struck at those debtors owing money to British
factors, it next undertook to systematize the collection of
debts due to the state and to provide for their liquidation
within six years. In November 1784, at what was later termed
the "Black Session," the General Assembly passed the Consolidating Act, which provided that all bonds for confiscated
British property payable in specie (taken before June 1, 1785)
be set apart as a sinking fund for the redemption of two
emissions of Revolutionary paper money known as continental
state money and black money,[37] along with other bonds
already pledged for that purpose. By a subsequent act these

34. *Votes and Proceedings,* Senate, 1785 to March 1786.
35. *Ibid.,* November Session, 1786, to April 1787. This by no means
marked the end of impediments to British creditors, however. In
June 1795, the Maryland Court of Appeals, the state's highest court
of appeal, reversed favorable decisions of the General Court when
it decided that in all cases where full payments had been made
into the state treasury under the Act of 1780, the debts had been
legally extinguished. This decision was in turn reversed by the
Supreme Court of the United States in the 1797 case of *Clerke* v.
Harwood, where the Act of 1780 was finally declared void.
36. John Thomas Scharf, *History of Maryland.* 3 vols. (Baltimore:
J. B. Piet, 1879), 2:538–39.
37. *Votes and Proceedings,* November Session, 1784. For a detailed discussion, see Behrens, *Paper Money,* pp. 70, 73, 78–87. Red Money,
which had been issued in 1781, was almost entirely redeemed by
1784. All three issues of Maryland's Revolutionary paper money
had depreciated in value almost immediately after being printed,
but under the terms of the consolidating act would be receivable at
par in payment of all tax arrearages due before March 1, 1784.

two emissions—both issued in 1780—were declared receivable at par with specie for any taxes due before January 1, 1785, and the tax collectors were authorized to exchange specie for either continental or black money at par.[38] In addition, the legislature provided that all confiscated property still unsold, all unreserved bonds for confiscated property, and all tax arrearages be consolidated into a general fund and pledged to the redemption of the state debt by January 1, 1790, with 6 percent interest payable annually in specie until that time. This caused the tax collectors—who had been inclined toward leniency with the people—to call for arrears and to increase their exertions in behalf of the government, at whatever cost to the debtors throughout the state.[39] The result, of course, was immediate deflation, which served only to increase the difficulty in paying debts contracted before and after the war.[40] The enactments of the "Black Session," moreover, struck hardest at the purchasers of confiscated British property— thereby creating yet another discontented minority which agitated for reform.

The widespread purchase of confiscated property in Maryland involved a financial investment amounting to almost 651,000 pounds current money, most of which represented a credit to the state rather than cash outlay at the time of purchase.[41] Buyers, for the most part, had preferred going into debt by giving their bonds to the state rather than making cash payments for the land; the state, in turn, had not only accepted these bonds but had been officially and un-

38. *Ibid.*, November Session, 1785.
39. *Votes and Proceedings*, November Session, 1784. All purchasers of confiscated property who had not given bond were ordered to do so before April 1, 1785, or to face immediate suit for recovery. See also Behrens, *Paper Money*, p. 78.
40. O. H. Williams to Dr. Philip Thomas, dated Baltimore, April 7, 1785. MS in Vol. 3, O. H. Williams Papers, M.H.S. The value of black money and continental state money increased in relation to other commodities, but this lasted less than a year.
41. This figure is cited in Crowl, *Maryland*, p. 60.

officially lenient in suspending executions against purchasers unable to pay and in extending moratoriums up to 1784.[42] Purchasers realized, certainly, that they would eventually have to make good on their bonds, but until the day of reckoning came they lived in happy uncertainty and nourished vague hopes that the legislature would relax its legal claims against them.

Their awakening therefore was all the more rude, and the distress occasioned by the readjustments under the Consolidating Act was keenly felt from 1785 to the middle of 1788. Agitation for paper money and debtor relief flourished in those areas of the state where investments in property had been the heaviest and most widespread—namely, Baltimore and Harford counties—and was led by some of the heaviest speculators in confiscated property—William Paca, Luther Martin, Jeremiah Townley Chase, Charles Ridgely, and Samuel Chase—names and places of utmost significance in analyzing Maryland's stand on the adoption of the federal Constitution.[43] Thus by 1785 the attendant factors of currency deflation, collection of prewar foreign and domestic debts, and the strict collection of tax arrearages combined to force all debtors in the state to turn to the legislature for relief, and at the same time to exploit popular resentment against the men of wealth who occupied such powerful positions in Maryland's aristocratic government.

Demands for a state emission of paper money to remedy the growing scarcity of specie were voiced as early as November 1784,[44] while in December a writer from Baltimore denounced the worthless rhetoric "disgorged by the ARISTO-

---

42. Browne, ed., *et al.*, *Archives of Maryland* 48:250, 443. See also Scharf Papers, MS, M.H.S.
43. Commissioners' Ledger and Journal of Confiscated British Property; Sale Book of Confiscated British Property, 1781–1785, and 1784, Hall of Records, Annapolis. See also State Treasury Ledger A, Hall of Records, Annapolis.
44. *Maryland Journal*, November 26, 1784. M.H.S.

CRATIC FACTION," and added that "if we are in want, we have the means of relief in paper currency."[45] "The quantity . . . of money . . . in circulation is not sufficient for a medium of domestic trade," proclaimed another. "A paper medium is our *dernier* resort; we have no other. . . . Thousands are suffering the ninety-nine plagues of an empty purse."[46] Response to these pronouncements was not slow in forthcoming. Alexander C. Hanson, describing himself as a "warm advocate of public faith," wrote a lengthy pamphlet reminding those who protested against the cost of government that they spent more every year at the theater than they paid in taxes for the salaries of state officials.[47] Dedicating his work to William Paca (a choice which he later admitted was unfortunate, since Paca became an ardent champion of paper money and "persecuted by his speeches every man who did not change as he had done"), Hanson urged him to run for the legislature and lead the fight against any attempts to enact an emission of paper. His thoughts, moreover, showed equal concern for the hectic condition of national affairs:

> My purpose is to point out some of the most material errors of our own government, and to propose such measures as I conceive necessary to revive public credit, to establish a fair national character, and to render government firm, respectable, and happy. . . . Without more harmony between the States, without more zeal, public spirit, and attention in our rulers, without a more vigorous government, without more regard to justice, good faith, honour and gratitude, this great and stupendous revolution will answer no better

---

45. *Ibid.*, December 7, 1784.
46. *Ibid.*, July 9, 1785.
47. *Political Schemes and Calculations, Addressed to the Citizens of Maryland, By A Native Citizen and Servant of the State* (Annapolis, February 1784), M.H.S. This pamphlet, printed by S. and F. Green, was bound in a volume entitled "Hanson's Pamphlets," and contained the various printed works of the author with manuscript notes and addenda by the author in the margins.

purpose than to convince mankind they were never intended to be free.[48]

The measures which Hanson advocated were substantially those passed by the General Assembly in the Consolidating Act, and were outlined again in another pamphlet in which he gave a detailed account of the state debt and the means by which he thought it should be paid. One suggestion provided for a land tax in addition to the five per cent duty on imports recommended by the Confederation Congress in order to pay Maryland's share of the national debt,[49] while in still another tract he outlined for the legislature the text in full of "An Act for the Support of Public Credit, the Relief of Public Debtors, and the Better Regulation of Finance," which he proposed as a solution to the problem of the public debt.[50] Tossing aside Hanson's massive verbiage, Theodoric Bland summed up conservative feelings in general when he scratched in his diary a few lines from Pope's *Essay on Riches*:

> Bless'd Paper credit!—last and best supply,
> That lends corruption lighter wings to fly![51]

Nevertheless, advocates of cheap money as a cure for Maryland's economic sickness became more vociferous in the public prints throughout 1785, and whether the movement was actually democratic in character or whether it originated in the personal desires of a small faction of the ruling oligarchy, it derived nourishment from a sizable body of the distressed

48. *Ibid.* Hanson's main argument was in urging that the confused financial situation of Maryland be relieved by consolidating all state debts, including the bills of credit, into one account which would be equalized by the sale of the confiscated British property and the annual revenue from taxes.
49. *To the General Assembly of Maryland* (Annapolis, 1784), M.H.S.
50. *To the Members of the General Assembly of Maryland* (Annapolis, December 17, 1784), M.H.S.
51. Bland Papers, 1757–1846, M.H.S.

citizenry in the state. It was in the name and in the language of this anonymous group that appeals for reform were made. Hanson's appeals for stable public credit were at once attacked by Daniel of St. Thomas Jenifer, Intendent of the Revenue, who declared in a broadside that his "erroneous . . . OPINIONS may mislead those who have confidence in his abilities and professions."[52] His worthy colleague, concluded Jenifer, would have avoided gross errors "if part of the time . . . had been spent in gaining information of facts." Almost simultaneously with demands for an emission of paper—by now filling the pages of such papers as the *Maryland Journal*[53]—attacks were leveled against the "Black Session" of the General Assembly for enacting class legislation designed to favor the rich and well born when it passed two acts appropriating public funds for the endowment of Washington College and St. John's College.[54] "Only consider . . . that you can't salt your mush without paying a tax for it," a "Planter" from the Eastern Shore wrote, because "you are taxed . . . for the education of gentlemen's children, for gentlemen's children to be educated at the public expense—strange!—yet true!"[55] A correspondent from the Western Shore seconded that "poor men and men of common estates cannot send to the university at all, and yet whether they send or not, they must annually pay the tax."[56] "A dangerous effort in civil society to aggrandize the few and depress the many," an "Old Soldier" declared,[57] while yet another saw in the act the beginning of a scheme "wherein the lordly sons of our future nobility will be trained up, uncontaminated by a mixture with boys of plebeian mould."[58] Petitions addressed to the state authorities made similar complaints. Three hundred and twelve inhabitants of Harford

52. Untitled folio broadside, dated December 24, 1784. M.H.S.
53. *Maryland Journal*, August 1785, *passim*. Also November 22, 1785.
54. *Votes and Proceedings*, November Session, 1784.
55. *Maryland Gazette* (Baltimore), February 11, 1785. M.H.S.
56. *Ibid.*, February 23, 1785.
57. *Ibid.*, April 1, 1785.
58. *Ibid.*, June 17, 1785.

county requested the Governor and Council to delay debt prosecutions and to mitigate the rigors of tax collection until the harvest when they would "enjoy the benefit of their present Crop of wheat," and thus save their property from seizure.[59] Another petition demanded an emission of paper money as "the most eligible plan to relieve . . . our present distress. We are not able to pay the present taxes and satisfy our creditors. We are really in a most deplorable situation."[60]

Attempts to remedy this "deplorable situation" by the emergent paper money faction within the state government were futile. On December 24, 1785, the Senate unanimously rejected a bill passed by the House of Delegates for an emission of credit to be lent out on loan;[61] in its place, it returned a bill for the protection of creditors who found themselves impeded in the collection of their debts by the cumbersome legal machinery of the state.[62] The Delegates treated this measure with equal contempt and killed it by an almost unanimous vote—for which they received a scorching reprimand from their aristocratic colleagues, laying the entire blame for Maryland's financial and economic distress on the extravagance and dissipation of the debtor class.[63] It was clear that a stalemate had been reached. The House replied tersely to the Senate's diatribe in a message scoring "the power of cruel and oppressive creditors," and the legislature adjourned without making any progress whatsoever.[64]

Far from improving during 1786, conditions worsened everywhere. From New York Nathaniel Ramsey wrote that "I . . . am much distressed to find our affairs in such a Situation as makes it more than probable that a very short period will bring about a National Bankruptcy and of course a dissolution of our

---

59. Petition of Sundry Inhabitants of Harford County, MS, M.H.S.
60. "Money! Money! Money!" Broadside, M.H.S.
61. *Votes and Proceedings*, November Session, Senate, 1785.
62. *Ibid.*
63. *Ibid.*, House of Delegates, January 1786, and Senate, February 1786. The vote in the House was 43 to 9.
64. *Votes and Proceedings*, House of Delegates, February 1786.

confederate Union."[65] Congress, he added, was broke, "and
will be under the necessity in the course of a few months to
plainly tell our foreign creditors that they cannot make them
any payment, and that they have neither any money nor a
power to command any." In Maryland, bonds pledged to
redeem the state emissions of 1780 were deferred because of
the scarcity of money, and for the same reason land sold for
debt was almost given away. "My embarrassments are lack
of money," O. H. Williams at length wrote in April, after
admitting that he had been "for ten months destitute of any
surplus cash" and could not "spare a shilling. I will give able
interest for any sum that can be procured upon solid real
security."[66] Interest, however, was twenty-five to thirty percent,[67] and prudent men such as Charles Carroll of Carrollton
announced that it was unsafe to lend at all.[68] Newspaper
columns were filled with notices of insolvency.[69] Red money
and Black money—so recently stabilized by the legislature's
program of currency deflation—had depreciated to former
levels and was as difficult to unload as before. "Pray," wrote
Williams to his friend Philip Thomas, "if you are upon easy
terms with Mr. G. Scott enquire of him if he cannot, or will
not, make an Exchange of some Specie for black State
paper. . . ."[70] Three months later he complained of the "great
difficulty in getting my black money exchanged for Specie,"[71]
and in August added that it "is not all off my hands yet."[72]
Nathaniel Ramsey, meanwhile, informed Williams that he
could not sell his land to pay his debts, and asked his friend

65. Ramsey to O. H. Williams, dated July 1, 1786. MS in O. H. Williams
    Papers, Vol. 4, M.H.S.
66. Williams to Dr. Philip Thomas, dated Baltimore, April 12, 1786.
    MS in O. H. Williams Papers, Vol. 4, M.H.S.
67. *Maryland Gazette* (Baltimore), November 21, 1786.
68. *Maryland Journal*, March 16, 1787.
69. *Maryland Gazette* (Annapolis), 1786, *passim.*
70. Williams to Thomas, dated Baltimore, April 12, 1786. MS in O. H.
    Williams Papers, Vol. 4, M.H.S.
71. Same to same, dated July 22, 1786, Vol. 4.
72. Same to same, dated August 17, 1786, Vol. 4.

if he could exchange "a few pounds of red money" for him.[73] Although times were difficult, gentlemen remained gentlemen, and thus Williams did not hesitate to assure Thomas Johnson that the latter would suffer no "imposition or disadvantage" because he took an assignment of the former's bond; indeed, he pledged his honor that payment would not be made in depreciated paper, but "shall be made in Specie."[74] Slaves were reported being sold for five and six pounds each, a decline due as much to the financial depression as to the transition of Maryland's economy from tobacco to wheat.[75] Of the weed itself, Williams advised Thomas that it "will bring almost nothing nor more at most than 25 cw, it would be throwing it into the Sea to Ship it that's nonsense. Commerce is declining—and the world is in a bustle. Risque nothing, not even a few Hhds of Tobacco."[76]

While efforts to obtain needed reforms were generally confined to the political realm, Maryland did not escape popular outbreaks undertaken by debtors to gain their ends by the use of more direct action. These disturbances, moreover, were serious enough to alarm men of property and wealth in the state. In June of 1786 the Charles County Court was forced by a turbulent multitude of over a hundred men to suspend all civil suits when attempts were made to collect prewar British debts. Although the governor immediately issued a special proclamation denouncing the rioters and enjoining any such disturbances in the future,[77] in Harford county two weeks later the inhabitants resorted to force to prevent anyone from bidding for land that was offered by the sheriff for sale.[78] Organized public boycotts of sheriff's sales took place

73. Ramsey to Williams, dated April 24, 1786, Vol. 4.
74. Williams to Thomas Johnson, dated August 31, 1786. MS in O. H. Williams Papers, Vol. 4, M.H.S.
75. *Maryland Journal*, July 4, 1786. See also Gray, *History of Agriculture* 1:474–78.
76. Williams to Thomas, April 12, 1786, MS in O. H. Williams Papers, Vol. 4, M.H.S.
77. *Maryland Gazette* (Annapolis), July 20, 1786.
78. *Maryland Journal*, June 27, 1786.

in Calvert county, effectively tying the hands of the authorities, and in Cecil county anonymous handbills were circulated threatening violence to any state officer who attempted to seize property for nonpayment of taxes. In most cases the use of law was met with defiance on the part of the populace.[79] "I fear there is a scene of distress and confusion, if not anarchy, not far distant from the State of Maryland," Nathaniel Ramsey wrote to Williams.[80] "What are the present politics of Baltimore?" In reply, Williams probably discussed the county's embroilment in the paper-money issue, whose leader in Baltimore was Samuel Chase, for in his next letter Ramsey wrote at length of the experiments in paper undertaken in Pennsylvania, New York, and Rhode Island.[81] Currency in the latter state, he declared, "is totally damned," while in Pennsylvania "paper . . . is publicly and generally sold at a discount of from 10 to 12%. I find by experience that since it has got into circulation every article which I purchase at market is raised in price." He concluded that since "the rage for a paper currency in Maryland still prevails, I apprehend that it will be necessary to gratify the populace with a small sum this fall to prevent a greater evil. . . ."

Ramsey's "small sum" concession, however, was not shared by others of his class, although more than a few of the landed aristocracy were caught up in the same financial maelstrom that was proving so ruinous to their poorer and less wise neighbors. As his letter pointed out, conditions similar to Maryland's were prevalent in other parts of the country. By 1786 six of the thirteen states had passed laws for the relief of debtors. Unstable conditions in Pennsylvania had led to an armed insurrection as early as 1783,[82] while in Massachu-

79. Archibald Job to Governor William Smallwood, dated December 11, 1786. MS in Miscellaneous Collection, M.H.S.
80. Ramsey to Williams, dated August 7, 1786. MS in O. H. Williams Papers, Vol. 4.
81. Ramsey to Williams, dated August 28, 1786. MS in Vol. 4.
82. Henry Carbery to Williams, dated September 29, 1789. MS in Vol. 5. In June 1783, Carbery had beset the state house in Phila-

setts they led to Shays' Rebellion and in Rhode Island to the
formation of a debtor party which gained control of the state.
Under such circumstances conservatives in Maryland demanded more severity, less leniency. Viewing the Charles
county riots with feelings akin to horror, "Frederick" called
for such severe legislation against the upstart debtors that
even Otho Williams found "his censure of a *Class* of Men . . .
illiberal in the extreme. Rather arrogantly . . . and rather fool-
ishly is it presumed that the same measures are in all cases
equally applicable in the dominions of a Despot and a republic."[83] "In the course of a few years," cautioned John Henry,
"we must expect to be torn to pieces by civil dissentions and
to suffer all the calamities in which uncontrouled passions can
involve the human species." As for "the late insurrection in
Massachusetts," the worst was yet to come:

> There is still a spirit of discontent existing in the minds of
> a great number of the inhabitants of that state which sooner
> or later will break out into a conflagration and may be
> attended with the most fatal consequences. Free govern-
> ments when not in awe of a superior power frequently de-
> generate into licentious ones. The New England states I
> fear will verify this observation, for the genius of the people
> leads them all to be politicians and this genius begets habits
> of idleness destructive to republics.

Separation of "the now nominally United States," declared
Henry, would inevitably occur from a lack of power in the
federal head to regulate its proceedings. "Shallow politician
as I am," he concluded, "I can plainly forsee the events unless
some speedy measures be adopted to impede their progress,
and none are sufficient but the investing Congress with powers

---

delphia with an armed force, which was suppressed. In this letter
to Williams he expressed sorrow for his past activities and requested help to emigrate to France.

83. Williams to Thomas, dated August 17, 1786. MS in O. H. Williams
Papers, Vol. 4.

proportionate to the arduous task."[84] More optimistic, Charles
Carroll expressed the hope to his cousin that the suppression
of Shays' Rebellion by the government of Massachusetts "will
increase its energy, and have a good effect in other states
where similar dispositions might otherwise have occasioned
similar commotions."[85]

Carroll's hopes were grounded on the strength of conservative control throughout the state. While Maryland did not
avoid radical agitation by debtors intent on gaining extralegal
respite, the Charles county riot marked the peak in the use
of violence against both creditors and state officials; hereafter
the issue of debtor relief was confined to the newspapers and
the legislature, where it raged until overshadowed by the
larger issue of the federal Constitution. Various schemes were
proposed in the public prints. "An American" advised the
establishment of a loan office,[86] the *Maryland Gazette* edi-
torialized in favor of the issuance of bank notes because they
were payable on demand,[87] "A Marylander" declared that an
emission of properly funded bills of credit—unsupported by
a tender law—would relieve momentary distress, but asked
that arguments both for and against paper should be given
that people might be better informed,[88] and "A Farmer" advocated the removal of the state government to Baltimore as
the best means of reviving trade and reestablishing overall
confidence in the economy.[89] Alexander Contee Hanson, writing as "Aristides," replied to this seemingly thoughtless proposal with a spirited defense of Annapolis, which he considered "*his* masterpiece, but not *a* masterpiece." He identified
the author as no mere "Farmer," but as Judge Richard

84. John Henry to Robert Goodloe Harper, dated March 6, 1787, MS
    in Harper-Pennington Papers, M.H.S.
85. Charles Carroll of Carrollton to Daniel Carroll of Duddington, dated
    March 13, 1787. MS in Harper-Pennington Papers, M.H.S.
86. *Maryland Gazette* (Baltimore), May 19, 1786.
87. *Ibid.*, May 2, 1786.
88. *Maryland Journal*, June 23–30, 1786.
89. *Maryland Gazette* (Annapolis), January 19, 1786.

Ridgely, relative of Captain Charles Ridgely, political boss of Baltimore county and one of the most powerful merchants in the state.[90] At the time Hanson wrote this pamphlet he was under heavy attack from the Ridgely machine and its spokesmen—Samuel Chase, William Paca, and Luther Martin—leaders in the fight for paper money. When his opponents combined to prevent circulation of his pamphlet in Baltimore, Hanson turned to the newspapers. "They have no thought," he wrote,

> that the people of Annapolis will suffer ... and that a town noted for its grace, beauty, and cosmopolitan atmosphere will decline overnight. Annapolis is and ever has been the seat of elegance, propriety, and refinement of manners. It is here that examples of benevolence and patriotism are shown. No rude mobs have ever disturbed the deliberations of any public body under the present government; in this place there may always be a perfect freedom of debate.

It would reflect lasting disgrace to the legislature and to the state, concluded Hanson, should the capital be removed to satisfy the mercenary instincts of the merchants of Baltimore.[91]

Other articles, mostly anonymous, followed Hanson's. About three-fourths of these were in favor of an emission of paper.[92] As the date for fall elections to the General Assembly drew near, interest in the subject became intense. "A Delegate" ad-

90. Ridgely Papers, MS, M.H.S., *passim*. See also Ridgely Family Papers, M.H.S.
91. *Considerations on the Proposed Removal of the SEAT OF GOVERNMENT, Addressed To the Citizens of Maryland*, by "Aristides" (Annapolis, 1786), M.H.S.
92. See *Maryland Journal, Maryland Gazette* (Baltimore), and *Maryland Gazette* (Annapolis), for July and August 1786, *passim*. Most of the letters asserted than an emission of paper would raise the value of land, enable debtors to discharge their obligations, encourage the building of roads (whose tolls would be used for sinking the money), stimulate manufactures and agriculture, and promote trade and industry in general. Opponents of emission pointed out that the paper would depreciate and cause greater suffering, that it would drive out all specie and eventually increase the number of those indebted to the state.

vised the people that the ultraconservative Senate must be overthrown, and that electors should be chosen who would put in "interested" men,[93] but "A Citizen" reminded voters to think twice before they dismissed a body of worthy and proven men in order to enact a paper money bill.[94] In Anne Arundel county, "A Friend to Paper Money" circulated handbills inciting the people to overthrow the unholy combination of merchants, moneylenders, and wealthy men entrenched in the Senate. "The *rich*," he declaimed, "know not the distresses of the middling rank of men; living in affluence and ease, with every necessary and many of the luxuries of life, they neither *"know, feel,* or *care* for the wants of others. Wealthy men . . . are proud and arrogant, and despise the inferior classes of life."[95] "The wealthy now have their day," added another. "Heaven grant, may it be of short duration."[96]

The result of the October elections was a victory for paper money in the House of Delegates, but defeat in the Senate. The acknowledged spokesman for the debtor class in the lower house of the legislature was Samuel Chase, whose assumption of the role during this period was rather incongruous, to say the least. Long dedicated to the maintenance of upper-class political domination, Chase was anything but democratic in his economic and political affiliations. He had been, in fact, instrumental in the framing of Maryland's highly conservative constitution of 1776 and took great pride in the aristocratic features of that document.[97] His temporary desertion to the ranks of the debtors, therefore, can be explained only by the heavy burden of debt into which he himself had fallen at this time—"the desperate circumstances into which his imprudence, incapacity, and extravagance" had plunged

93. *Maryland Gazette* (Annapolis), August 24, 1786.
94. *Ibid.*, August 17, 1786.
95. *To the Voters of Ann-Arundel County,* September 23, 1786. Broadside, M.H.S.
96. *Maryland Gazette* (Baltimore), October 17, 1786.
97. *Maryland Journal,* November 8, 1785.

him.[98] Chase's debt to the state through speculations in confiscated property amounted to about 3,542 pounds; by 1787 he was in such deep financial difficulties that he petitioned the government for relief.[99] But while he posed as the political champion of the downtrodden, Samuel Chase was absolutely silent on the question of legislative relief to the debtors of British merchants. In this connection silence was indeed golden, for his commission as Maryland's agent in negotiations for the Bank of England stock had been set by the legislature at four percent of the net sum received upon settlement.[100] Provocation of the British government in this sphere, therefore, was a direct threat to his own financial interest.

Opposition to Chase and his faction centered in the Senate and was led by Charles Carroll of Carrollton, long recognized as the strongest bulwark against popular radicalism in the legislature. Their enmity was both personal and political, extending back to 1777 when Chase accused Carroll of being "the advocate of the disaffected tories and refugees" because "he opposed the confiscation of British property, and insolently and falsely imputed my maintaining the propriety of the measure to base and interested motives."[101] On his side, Carroll replied that Chase was out to slander the Senate:

His suspicions of his being hated or envied by the Senate are truly ridiculous, if well founded, he must be either a bad and dangerous citizen, or the late Senate was a tyran-

---

98. *Maryland Gazette* (Baltimore), September 28, 1787. Chase had invested, in his own name, 6,367 pounds in British property, and also had an eighth share of the investments of Charles Ridgely and Co. The latter amounted to over 40,000 pounds. See Ridgely Papers, M.H.S., and also Sale Book of Confiscated British Property, 1781–1785, Hall of Records, Annapolis.
99. *Votes and Proceedings*, Senate, April Session, 1787.
100. *Votes and Proceedings*, House, April Session, 1783.
101. *Maryland Gazette* (Annapolis), August 23, 1781. See also issues for August 30, September 27, October 11, 1781, and February 28, 1782.

nical or corrupt body, willing to oppress the infallible and
virtuous Mr. Chase, or awed by, & consequently jealous of
the great abilities of so . . . intrepid a patriot.[102]

The hostility between the two men became public in 1781
when Chase, writing under the name of "CENSOR," denied
charges that he had used his position as a delegate to Congress in 1778 for the purpose of lining his own pockets and
denounced Carroll as the author of a resolution passed in the
General Assembly in 1779 reprimanding him and containing
an official declaration of his guilt.[103] Carroll at once responded
and the battle was joined, the paper money controversy eventually being enmeshed within the general background of the
quarrel.[104] From then on it became Chase's goal to wreak
vengeance on the lord of Doughoregan Manor, but try as he
might to ruin him politically, Carroll was easily reelected to

---

102. Carroll Papers, Vol. 8, 1781–1833, MS collection at M.H.S.
103. *Maryland Gazette* (Annapolis), June 30, 1781. The accusation was
    first made by Alexander Hamilton who, writing under the name of
    "Publius," charged Chase in 1778 with conspiring to buy up all the
    rye, wheat, and flour in Maryland on secret knowledge that Con-
    gress intended to purchase large supplies of wheat. The grain would
    then be sold to the government for top prices. See Jensen, *New Na-
    tion*, p. 182. The ensuing scandal induced the Maryland legislature
    to declare merchants ineligible in the future to represent that state
    in Congress.
104. *Maryland Gazette* (Annapolis), June 21 and August 23, 1781. Car-
    roll published all the evidence available to prove that Chase was
    guilty of malfeasance, declaring that "a Black gown sometimes
    covers a scoundrel . . . and the garb of patriotism frequently con-
    ceals a traitor." He accused Chase of "betraying the secrets of
    Congress . . . to his own private emolument, to the great injury of
    his country." However, Carroll did not wish to air the dispute in
    the newspapers, and on January 25, 1782, he wrote Chase suggest-
    ing a private settlement of the quarrel. Chase replied on the 28th
    that "whether our controversy shall be continued in the public pa-
    pers remains with you. . . . I can and will vindicate my character."
    But on February 3, 1782, he wrote Carroll that he would "drop all
    further publications respecting the . . . controversy between us," and
    on the 11th declared that the matter was at a close although he
    would always consider Carroll the "aggressor." Carroll Papers, Vol.
    8, M.H.S.

the Senate in 1786 and the upper house remained as firm as before in its resistance to monetary inflation.[105]

When the legislature reconvened in November of 1786, Chase lost little time in introducing a measure for an emission of bills of credit to the amount of 350,000 pounds current money. This brought on a lively debate which, as recorded in verse by a bemused and poetic delegate, was not without its lighter moments:

> In the Delegates' House a debate was brought on,
>   and fully contested and quibbled
> Twixt Jenings and Chase was bandied about
>   'till old Cockey Dye was bedevilled
> To order he called, yet Chase still bawl'd on
>   and pledg'd for the good of the Measure,
> *Reputation* (he'd gain'd by Life without blame)
>   *to a Farthing* with infinite pleasure.
> Here Jenings reply'd the Bet must be just,
>   in every chance of the Nation,
> *a Farthing* 'tis true, is *a very small sum,*
>   but equal to Sam's *Reputation!*[106]

Nevertheless, on December 15 the House passed its second emission bill by a vote of 37 to 25. Fifteen days later the Senate unanimously rejected it, together with a House bill designed to ameliorate the rigors of imprisonment for debt. The House thereupon determined to adjourn and appeal to the people to force the Senate to capitulate. Tempers were again at the straining point and it was obvious that nothing

---

105. *Votes and Proceedings*, Senate, November Session, 1786.
106. Daniel Dulany to George Fitzhugh, January 27, 1787. MS in Dulany Papers, 1659–1799, M.H.S. In the debate, Chase declared he would stake his reputation to a farthing on the "propriety" of the bill, to which Jenings retorted that he thought it "an equal bet." Thomas Cockey Dye of Baltimore County was Speaker of the House of Delegates.

would be accomplished for the rest of the session but the Senate vigorously opposed adjournment.[107] It wished to give immediate attention to the request respecting an appointment of delegates to the Philadelphia convention, which the legislature had received on December 16, in the midst of debate on the currency bill.[108] Recess at this critical moment would not only delay the appointment of deputies to revise the tottering Confederation, but would also force the Senate to face a popular referendum on the matter of emission. The House, however, was eager for vindication of its position. Shelving the question of appointments to Philadelphia until March, it ignored a last minute appeal from the Senate and repeated its determination to close the session at once. On January 20 the Senate acquiesced and the issue was carried to the people.[109]

Upon adjournment of the legislature, the Senate immediately reconvened at Mann's Tavern where its members decided on a plan of campaign. A declaration was drawn up which the Senators signed and circulated throughout the state:

We the subscribers, attached to the present form of government, and esteeming it proper and necessary to preserve every part of it, are of opinion that each branch of the legislature ought to be free and have full liberty to exercise

---

107. *Votes and Proceedings*, November Session, 1786, House of Delegates and Senate. See also *Maryland Gazette* (Annapolis), January 11, 25, 1787. O. H. Williams corresponded with Chase during this session, trying to get the legislature to keep its promise to the Maryland Line of land in the western part of the state. He wanted this to be safe from speculators and illegal settlers, but such was the assembly's concern on the question of paper that his efforts were fruitless. Williams to Samuel Chase, dated December 27, 1786. MS in O. H. Williams Papers, Vol. 4.
108. *Ibid.*, Senate, December 1786.
109. *Ibid.*, House of Delegates, January 1787. In its message the Senate declared that "appeals to the people . . . are unprecedented. In consequence of such appeals . . . the senate will be deprived of that freedom of debate and decision, which the constitution meant to secure to that branch." The action was, moreover, contrary to the 11th article of the Constitution.

their judgment upon all public measures proposed by one to the other.[110]

The Senators protested, moreover, that the time for consulting the people was too short to allow a fair canvass of the state by the upper house, whereas the Delegates had the advantage of numbers. The latter were not to be outdone by their intransigent colleagues; shortly before the legislature adjourned, the Delegates had prepared an address to their constituents explaining away the objections made by the Senate on the proposed currency bill. This of course declared that the construction placed on the bill by the Senate was entirely wrong, and added that the upper house should not interfere with the established privilege of the Delegates to originate all money matters. It further explained:

> By our plan the money was *first* to circulate *on loan,* and every man, having land in fee, would have an opportunity of borrowing. By the proposal of the Senate, the money was only to be taken out by the holders of the continental depreciated securities, and every person wanting this money for taxes could only borrow from them. It appeared to us, that acceding to the scheme of emission to purchase final settlements, though it might greatly benefit the *adventurers* in these securities, would not answer any great *public* purpose. . . . The APPEAL . . . is *now* made to you as to the propriety and necessity of an emission of *paper money circulated on loan for the purpose of enabling you to pay the heavy but necessary taxes for the support of your own and the federal government;* and we wish you to express your sentiments to both branches of your legislature.

The address concluded that, unless such a measure were enacted, "you would compare us to the Egyptian taskmasters who compelled the Israelites to make bricks without straw."[111]

---

110. *Maryland Journal,* April 6, 1787.
111. *An Address of the House of Delegates of Maryland to their Constituents,* undated broadside, Ridgely Papers, Box II, M.H.S.

The campaign to the voters became increasingly bitter. The Senate was accused of being independent of all control and of harboring designs to overthrow the government.[112] One extremist proposed "to compel them by arms to acquiesce or leave the Courts of Justice shut,"[113] while another asked, "If we are to be made slaves to a few designing rich men . . . will the people be quiet under it? If this is to be our situation . . . decided measures will be necessary to relieve us from such alarming evils."[114] Charles Carroll's opposition was attacked because he did not want to "lose part of his immense and dearly beloved wealth" by having his many loans repaid in paper, and he was accused at the same time of buying votes in the Senate.[115] Carroll replied by denouncing the writer, generally believed to have been Sam Chase, as having completely "deviated from truth and honesty."[116] Under his own name Chase addressed an article "To the Independent Citizens of Maryland," in which he admitted that the contest was more than an emission of paper—it was the right of the people to instruct the Senate.[117] The constitutional implications of this doctrine produced such inflamed discussion in the public prints that attention was diverted to some extent from the more immediate issue of paper money and debtor relief.

Conservatives, frankly alarmed, put forth a more serious effort to sway public opinion than at any time previously. Alexander Contee Hanson, writing as "Aristides," turned once more to his pen to remind the people that the Senate was neither a dangerous nor a useless body, and that in the previous election "the gentlemen most distinguished for opposi-

---

112. *Maryland Journal*, February 13, 1787.
113. *Maryland Gazette* (Baltimore), January 30, 1787.
114. *Ibid.*, March 6, 1787.
115. *Maryland Journal*, March 2, 3, 6, 9, and 16, 1787.
116. *Ibid.*, March 16, 1787.
117. "To the Independent Citizens of Maryland," MS in hand of Samuel Chase, Samuel Chase Letters, M.H.S. Chase stated that he did not believe emission would have either the benefits promised by its advocates or the consequences guaranteed by its opponents.

tion to paper were honoured with almost every suffrage." He continued:

> It will be strange indeed if you can now be persuaded that the new Senate has perverted the ends of government by declining an expedient rejected by the old, and by two successive houses of delegates. The mode of appointing your senate is esteemed by wise men the most admirable institution in all the United States. . . . It has been continually acquiring the esteem and confidence of the people, whilst other senates have fallen in repute. The difference arises from the different modes of election. It is not a man's popularity in a single county or district, it is his general good character and his real dignity and importance that confer on him this honor. The suffrage of the electors is a tribute paid to worth.

"Bills of credit," Hanson added, "not being from their nature ready cash, if the people do not think them so, there is nothing which can make them so." The loud clamors for an emission were coming "almost entirely from speculators and debtors," and it was they who spread the popular delusion that the projected paper would answer all the purposes of specie. But in fact, he concluded, the opposite would happen:

> I assert positively that the paper, in the course of six months after an emission, would depreciate more than thirty-three and one third per cent, and were my life depending on the truth of my prediction, I should feel no more concern than if it depended on the old Chesapeake's keeping to its channel. . . . We are now, from the signal interposition of Heaven, a free independent people. We are on a footing with other nations, and specie will find its level amongst us as with them. In the name of common sense and common justice, for the sake of your neighbors, yourselves, your posterity, your country, reflect on all these things and bestow on this scheme, the sure instrument of your destruction, such decisive marks of disapprobation as shall forever deter its advocates, demonstrate your good sense, retrieve the national

character, and make rapid advances to that grand consummation of policy—the RESTORATION OF PUBLIC AND PRIVATE FAITH.[118]

The effect of Hanson's pamphlet was almost overwhelming.[119] In Annapolis the people signed instructions approving the conduct of the Senate and declared that, even if they disapproved, they had no right to interfere with its deliberations or to instruct the legislators in the interim between elections.[120] The same sentiment prevailed in Montgomery, Talbot, Somerset, and St. Mary's counties, and on the entire Eastern Shore.[121] Citizens in Frederick County organized a troop of horse to defend the Senate against possible violence,[122] while in Frederick-town voters in town meeting directed their delegates in the legislature to oppose an emission of paper.[123] At an assembly in Washington county the people were reported to be ten to one against paper;[124] inhabitants there drew up a petition to the General Assembly lamenting "the imprudence of some of the Citizens . . . which appear[s] calculated to create apprehensions of an attempt on our Government." A paper medium, it declared, "would banish the coin now among us . . . and would eventually lead to disappointment and disgrace."[125]

---

118. REMARKS on the Proposed Plan of an EMISSION of PAPER, and on the Means of Effecting It, Addressed to the Citizens of Maryland, by "Aristides." Annapolis, 1786. M.H.S.
119. It was published in both the Maryland Journal, April 13, May 18, June 22, July 13, August 3, 14, and 31, 1787, and in the Maryland Gazette (Annapolis), May 17, 1787. The article brought forth a great deal of debate.
120. Maryland Journal, February 9, 1787.
121. Maryland Gazette (Annapolis), March 22 and 29, April 26, 1787. Maryland Journal, April 19 and February 9, 1787. The grand juries of these counties, and of the Eastern Shore, endorsed the views of the Senate and declared their opposition to paper money, moves which probably had a great deal of influence in the state.
122. Maryland Journal, March 2 and 30, 1787.
123. Maryland Journal, February 20 and March 6, 1787.
124. Ibid., March 30, 1787.
125. "To the Delegates of Washington County in the Maryland House of Delegates," from the Inhabitants of Washington County. MS in

"If any dependence can be placed in reports," Charles Carroll predicted, "a majority of the people will be against an emission on loan."[126]

Carroll's prediction was correct. Conservative opinion in Maryland was too strong, and the radical attack fizzled out under the weight of superior opposition. When the General Assembly met in the spring of 1787 the House of Delegates was compelled to retreat. No further effort to introduce a paper money bill was made.[127] Early in the session the legislature turned to the problem of appointing delegates to the forthcoming Philadelphia convention. However, most of the eligible candidates declined to be considered, and four of the five men chosen to represent the state resigned for reasons unnamed.[128] Their refusal to serve was not based on indifference but on the very real fear that the paper faction would utilize their absence to renew agitation at home. When the epoch-making convention got underway, Maryland's best statesmen were not present.

Thus the controversy—whether genuinely democratic or merely a struggle for power among the mighty—was not dead. Its bitterness was absorbed and carried into the contest for the adoption of the Constitution. Without some knowledge of the political, economic, and social conflicts which divided Maryland during these interim years, that contest cannot be understood.

O. H. Williams Papers, Vol. 9, M.H.S. Williams owned a great deal of land in Washington County, and the petition was written in his hand.

126. Charles Carroll to Daniel Carroll, dated March 13, 1787. MS in Harper-Pennington Papers, M.H.S.

127. *Votes and Proceedings*, House of Delegates, April Session, 1787. See also *Maryland Gazette* (Baltimore), April 24, 1787.

128. *Votes and Proceedings*, House of Delegates and Senate, April Session, 1787. Among those conservatives who resigned or refused to serve were Charles Carroll, Thomas Johnson, Governor Smallwood, Thomas Sim Lee, John Henry, George Gale, Robert Hanson Harrison, and Thomas Stone. Of the debtor faction, Samuel Chase and William Paca also refused to serve.

2

The Seventh Pillar

O N September 17, 1787, the new Federal Constitution was signed and forwarded to Congress with the recommendation that it be submitted to a convention of delegates in each state, and be adopted as the frame of government for the United States as soon as nine should ratify. Eight days later Marylanders read the text of the new plan of government for the first time in the *Maryland Journal*, and for seven months thereafter political attention in the state centered on the question of ratification. Matters of local interest were almost completely pushed aside.[1] In many respects the battle was a continuation of the old paper-money fight, with the parties aligned as formerly; but although the conflict was renewed in the struggle over the Constitution, the issues were not altogether identical. In 1788 they were much more involved.

---

1. *Maryland Journal*, September 25, 1787. The Maryland delegation, as finally chosen by the General Assembly, consisted of Luther Martin, John Francis Mercer, Daniel Carroll, James McHenry, and Daniel of St. Thomas Jenifer. Of these five, only the latter three stayed to the end of the meeting and signed the completed document. Except for Martin's important role at the convention, which was primarily negative, none of the other members of the Maryland delegation took an active part in the debates, nor did they have any noticeable influence on the formation of the Constitution.

The Constitution was a complex document with wide and varied economic and political connotations, and therefore reaction to it in Maryland did not correspond exactly to previously expressed attitudes toward debtor relief and cheap currency. However, the opposing political leaders were the same in both instances, and the appeals which they addressed to the people for support rested on much the same grounds. Further than this, the parallel cannot be carried with complete consistency.

Considerable interest had been shown throughout the state while the convention was meeting in Philadelphia. In April 1787, the grand jury of St. Mary's county declared in its report that a "cheerful co-operation" among the states at the ensuing federal convention would "restore public credit and give the United States . . . a rank and consequence in Europe that will be admired by all such as have witnessed the past exertions of patriotism and virtue which so eminently distinguished our glorious revolution."[2] Charles Carroll felt that the time was ripe for drastic revision of both the confederation government and of the individual state governments. Unless the latter were reorganized, he wrote, "I am confident the federal Govt., however perfect it may appear in Theory, will always be found very defective in practice."[3] "A Federalist" added that it would be better to have either the Senate or a body of electors appoint members to the ratifying convention, since the people would undoubtedly elect uneducated men.[4] The Maryland press was filled with articles on the question of revising the Confederation; but while most of the contributions leaned to the Federalist side, arguments opposing the new frame of government received equal attention.[5] From Fred-

2. *Maryland Gazette* (Annapolis), April 26, 1797.
3. "Outlines for a Plan of Government for the United States, and Amendments to the Constitutions of the Several States of this Union," by Charles Carroll of Carrollton. MS in Carroll Papers, Vol. 8, 1781–1833, M.H.S.
4. *Maryland Gazette* (Annapolis), October 9 and 25, November 8, 22, 1787.
5. *Maryland Journal,* April 17, June 5, and September 1787.

ericktown Dr. Philip Thomas contributed his thoughts on the proposed convention in a piece which his Baltimore friend, Otho Holland Williams, found "sensible, plain, and pertinent, but . . . deficient in composition notwithstanding. It wants *acrimony, scurrility* and *vulgarity* to give it rank with the fashionable controversial pages of abuse, and therefore . . . will be read and considered only by the few whose reason and discretion triumph over prejudice and sycophancy." However, added Williams, "*your* patriotism appears to be governed by precaution; and the moderation of your arguments appeals to the deliberate judgment of your readers."[6] Another correspondent declared that the confederation was merely a tent and that a more durable framework must soon be erected before it was rent asunder.[7]

By the fall of 1787 the question of calling a state ratifying convention had become the uppermost issue of the day. As such it was put before the voters in the October elections to the House of Delegates. Opposition to unconditional ratification—the stand of the emergent Antifederalist party—was directed by the same group who were the leaders in the struggle for paper money. As he had been formerly, Samuel Chase remained the acknowledged leader of this discontented faction in Maryland's body politic.[8] Running as a candidate for the legislature from Baltimore, Chase judiciously avoided committing himself too definitely on the subject of the Constitution. Enthusiasm for the new frame of government was strong among the mercantile and shipping elements of Baltimore, and Chase was politically acute enough to foresee the reaction which an outspoken opposition to ratification

---

6. Williams to Thomas, April 4 and 10, 1787. MS in O. H. Williams Papers, Vol. 4, M.H.S. Williams added that almost all of his friends who praised the article were enemies of Chase, "and you know that I am his friend."

7. *Maryland Journal*, July 3, 1787.

8. Other members included William Paca, the Ridgelys, John Francis Mercer, and Luther Martin. Martin was not a commanding figure in Maryland politics at this time.

would produce.[9] But although he acted with circumspection, his criticism of the Constitution was by no means subdued. In a speech given at Fells Point in September, he declared that he was uncertain whether to support the call for a state convention and warned his audience not to hastily relinquish the present form of government, "under which we have lived happily for more than ten years."[10] Several days later in an address delivered to a "numerous and respectable body of citizens" at the courthouse, he asserted that the proposed Constitution would modify the constitution of Maryland and therefore the legislature must act on it in the same way as on any other constitutional amendment, namely, by passing the measure at two successive sessions of the General Assembly. Chase added that he was not opposed to the Union but had always maintained the necessity of it and "the increase of powers in Congress":

> I think the federal government must be greatly altered. I have not formed my opinion, whether the plan proposed ought to be accepted, as it stands, without any amendment or alteration. The subject is very momentous and involves the greatest consequences. If elected, I will vote for and use my endeavors to procure a recommendation by the Legislature to call a convention, as soon as it can conveniently be done, unless otherwise directed by this town.[11]

This was followed up by a letter to the *Maryland Journal* in which Chase again stated that he meant to advocate the call of a convention "to consider and decide upon the Constitution . . . as soon as the convenience of the people will permit. I further beg leave to add as my opinion, that the election

9. Extract from a letter from Baltimore dated December 12, 1787, printed in the *Massachusetts Gazette* of January 4, 1788. Cited in O. J. Libby, *The Geographical Distribution of the Vote of the Thirteen States on the Federal Constitution, 1787–88* (Madison, Wis.: The University of Wisconsin Press, 1894), p. 33.
10. *Maryland Journal,* September 25, 1787.
11. *Ibid.,* September 28, 1787.

of delegates to the Convention ought to be as early in the spring as may be."[12]

There is no doubt that the foregoing pronouncements had much to do with Chase's majority in the ensuing election. Over three-fourths of the votes cast in Baltimore were in favor of the Constitution. Once elected, however, Chase became bolder and threw his great influence against ratification. Scarcely had the balloting ended than a letter written by him and signed "Caution" appeared in the Baltimore press. Addressed to the "Inhabitants of Baltimore Town," it warned them that "an attempt to surprise you into any public measure ought to meet your indignation and contempt." The letter went on to tell the people that such an important step in the future of the country should not be taken without "a free and full examination of the subject and all its consequences." In particular, "Caution" urged the voters not to sign a current petition calling for a ratifying convention which signified "your entire approbation of the New Federal Constitution and your desire that it should be adopted and confirmed by this State, as it now stands, without any amendment or alteration." At least three months should elapse, the author concluded, before the question of a state convention should be finally decided. During this time both sides could be heard and conclusive opinions respecting the Constitution held in abeyance; otherwise Marylanders would unwittingly find themselves drawn "into a declaration in favor of *the whole system,*" bound hereafter to support it, "which you must do, or allege deception or surprise."[13]

While Chase's strategy was clearly to prevent unconditional ratification unless amendments were first added, Federalists on the other hand threw their wholehearted support in favor of the proposed Constitution in its entirety. This group was composed of those conservatives in the state government who had so recently thwarted the debtor faction in their demand

12. *Maryland Journal,* October 5, 1787.
13. *Maryland Journal,* October 11, 1787.

for cheap money, and it counted in its ranks such notables as Charles and Daniel Carroll, James McHenry, Thomas Johnson, Edward Lloyd, George Plater, Robert Goldsborough, Thomas Sim Lee, Daniel of St. Thomas Jenifer, and Alexander Contee Hanson. Johnson and Lee, together with Richard Potts, had been elected to the House of Delegates from Frederick County on the basis of forwarding the call for a state convention,[14] while Charles Carroll's activities on behalf of a stronger federal government included an outline plan revising the Confederation and active campaigning as the Federalist candidate for the ratifying convention from Anne Arundel county.[15] Daniel Carroll took up his pen to publicly refute Chase's "Caution" letter by urging the citizens of Baltimore to sign the petition for a convention in order that the General Assembly "may have the authority of the largest and most promising and manufacturing town in the state to countenance so important a recommendation." The state convention, he declared, will meet to ratify the Constitution, not to "propose amendments or alterations." Since the document was generally approved by the people, Carroll found the Baltimore petition to be in every way necessary as an inducement to the legislature to proceed at once with the calling of a state convention.[16]

But by far the most articulate Federalist in the state was Alexander Contee Hanson. Writing again under the name of "Aristides," he supported the Constitution with all the zeal he could command. His pamphlet was the most able and exhaustive political tract published in Maryland, and was, moreover, the only one in the country noticed by the English reviewers. Dedicating his work to George Washington, a

14. *Maryland Gazette* (Baltimore), October 16, 1787. Daniel Carroll's exhaustive correspondence with James Madison kept the Virginia Federalists posted on the progress of events in Maryland. See Madison Papers, MS, Vol. 8, Library of Congress.
15. "Outlines for a Plan of Government," MS in Carroll Papers, Vol. 8, 1781–1833, M.H.S. *Maryland Journal*, April 18, 1788.
16. *Maryland Journal*, October 16, 1787.

laborer "in the same common cause," Hanson's essay was essentially a detailed examination of the Constitution and a thorough refutation of Antifederalist arguments. For Americans to view the most illustrious assemblage of minds in the country with suspicion and distrust was absolute folly, he said; unless order were at once restored throughout the United States the people would submit to the very evils which they had intended to prevent—"the increase and abuse of authority." The Framers also had the evils of big government in mind, for they created a federal system of checks and balances, thereby giving the states the benefits of a single government without its attendant misfortunes. "There is nothing in their plan like the cloathing of individuals with power, for their own gratification. Every delegation, and every advantage that may be derived to individuals, has a strict reference to the general good." The best compromises, Hanson felt, had been made on the delicate question of representation:

> I apprehended, in particular, that the dispute about representation would be the rock on which the vessel containing all our hopes would be dashed. But when . . . I discerned that equitable compromise between the larger and lesser states, my anxiety was instantly removed and my soul enlightened by a sudden ray. Had an angel been the umpire, he could propose no expedient more equitable and more politic, not only as a compromise, but to establish such a detailed difference between the two branches of Congress as will make them indeed two distinct bodies.

A bill of rights, however, Hanson did not find necessary or desirable since the federal government was one of delegated powers and therefore could not "exert any power not expressly, or by *necessary* implication, conferred by the compact." He concluded with an eloquent appeal to the people to join in the country's future glory by embracing "those blessings which Providence is ready to shower on us. . . . To acquit themselves like men when visible danger assails; and, when it is repelled, to sink like savages into indolence, is said to be the characteristic of Americans. I wish only . . . to rouse every man from that supineness."[17]

Although Aristides' tone was in some respects overbearing ("The judge," commented Williams, "betrays an Egotism which the generality of mankind cannot feel"[18]), still it represented the best Federalist effort in Maryland. Newspapers throughout the state carried it in serial form, together with other numerous articles defending or attacking the Constitution. Intense interest was manifested in the proceedings in other states, while in Baltimore a local controversy raged as to whether Chase should be instructed to vote for a state convention or left to his own discretion in the matter.[19]

When the General Assembly met in November of 1787 it turned almost immediately to the question of ratification. On the 29th the delegates to the Philadelphia convention were

---

17. REMARKS on the PROPOSED PLAN of a FEDERAL GOVERN-MENT, Addressed to the Citizens of the UNITED STATES OF AMERICA, and Particularly to the People of MARYLAND, by Aristides (Annapolis, December 1787), bound in with "Hanson's Pamphlets," M.H.S. Hanson wrote later that he was accused of "mean, designing adulation" for writing this pamphlet, but felt that it was of more value than The Federalist in recommending the Constitution, since the latter "was not completed until almost every state in the Union had decided on the constitution."

18. Williams to Thomas, dated April 4, 1787. MS in Vol. 4, O. H. Williams Papers, M.H.S. Williams added that "few, I believe almost none, think him wrong, or insincere, but some except to his vanity in speaking and writing so decisively on points of the greatest importance which, they observe, may justify the charge of arrogance with others who are less acquainted with his merits." See also Same to Same, dated March 19, 1787, Vol. 4, and Feb. 2, 1791, Vol. 6, for private discussions of Hanson.

19. A Plan of the New Federal Government, Broadside, Ridgely Papers, Box II, M.H.S. See also Maryland Journal for October 30, and November 2, 6, and 9, 1787; Maryland Gazette (Baltimore), October 5, 9, and 12, November 2, 6, 16, and 20, 1787.

summoned before the House to give testimony and information concerning the proceedings of the previous summer.[20] McHenry's testimony stressed the advantages that would be gained under the new framework of government to the state's commercial and manufacturing interests, especially those centered in Baltimore, with which he himself was so intimately connected. Although couched in legal and political terms, Federalists did not miss the promise implicit in McHenry's discussion of greater concrete benefits, materially speaking, to be acquired through a workable federal system capable of regulating commerce and collecting taxes.

Luther Martin was also called to testify before the House. Reverting to the opposite extreme, he delivered a diatribe against the Constitution which was reported in full in the *Maryland Gazette* and which he later expanded into a pamphlet entitled *The Genuine Information Relative to the Philadelphia Convention.*[21] Martin's argument was basically the same one he had used at the convention itself, namely, that its action was altogether illegal and would result in destruction of the independence of the smaller states. He also alleged that many of the delegates were monarchists "covertly endeavouring to carry into effect" a monarchical system of government "which they well knew openly and avowedly could not be accomplished." Should the Constitution be adopted, Martin warned, the country would soon find itself under the rule of a king thinly disguised as a president.[22]

Upon the close of hearings the Assembly resolved that an

---

20. *Votes and Proceedings,* November Session, House of Delegates, 1787.

21. *Ibid.* See also the *Maryland Gazette* (Baltimore), December 28, 1787, to February 26, 1788.

22. Luther Martin, *The Genuine Information, delivered to the Legislature of the State of Maryland, Relative to the Proceedings of the General Convention, Lately Held at Philadelphia,* in Jonathan Elliot, *The Debates in the Several State Conventions, on the Adoption of the Federal Constitution as Recommended by the General Convention at Philadelphia in 1787* 5 Vols. (Philadelphia: J. B. Lippincott Co., 1896), 1:344–89.

election be held on the first Monday in April 1788, to choose
delegates to a "convention of the people" at the state capital
on April 21; there the Constitution would be submitted "for
their full and free investigation and decision." Four deputies
were to be chosen from each county, and two each from the
towns of Baltimore and Annapolis, by those citizens entitled
to vote in elections for the General Assembly.[23] The Senate,
however, expressed dissatisfaction with the House resolutions.
A committee composed of George Gale, Charles Carroll, John
Hall, and Daniel Carroll reported in favor of holding elections
in January and the convention itself in March; moreover, in
order that a decision as to ratification should be made quickly
and should rest with men of property, it advised that the
Constitution be submitted to the deputies only "for their
assent and ratification," and that a property qualification of
five hundred pounds be imposed on the convention members.[24]
But to these stipulations the House vigorously objected.
Under the influence of Chase and his supporters its decision
to postpone the convention until April was reaffirmed by a
vote of 24 to 23, and the property qualification was voted
down at the same time.[25] Federalists regarded this action as
unfriendly to the Constitution, even though Philip Key's resolution providing that the convention need not be unanimous
in its approval of the Constitution was passed in the House
by a vote of 28 to 21.[26] Still, the insistence of the House on
"full and free investigation" together with postponement
worked to the advantage of the Chase faction, for it precluded the Federalists' desire for quick, unconditional ratification while granting Antifederalists the opportunity to attack
the Constitution without completely opposing it. On December
1 the Senate agreed to withdraw its resolutions in favor of

23. *Votes and Proceedings*, November Session, House of Delegates, 1787.
24. *Ibid.*, Senate, November Session, 1787.
25. *Votes and Proceedings*, House, November Session, 1787. See also
    Maryland Gazette (Annapolis), December 6, 1787.
26. *Ibid.*, House, November Session, 1787. The words "if approved of
    by them or a majority of them" were inserted instead.

those passed by the House; it had no desire to prolong the session by useless debate causing even greater delay in reaching a final settlement. Two thousand copies of the Constitution were ordered to be printed and circulated throughout the state, and the legislature adjourned to gird itself for battle within the week.[27]

That battle was waged in both press and pamphlet during the next four months. As soon as it was determined that a convention would be called, "A Marylander" wrote on the importance of choosing the proper men. The convention, he declared, should be made impartial by rejecting salaried officers, senators, delegates, and holders of public certificates in order that it could not later be reproached with having consulted personal pecuniary interests over the preservation of the public good.[28] "A Letter from Baltimore" stated that the mercantile interest in the town, together with a majority of the people of Maryland were in favor of the new federal plan—"yet, like the state of New York, it will be strongly opposed by some men of great influence and very leading characters in the state. For which opposition, 'tis said, they are actuated by a dread of the loss of their own popularity."[29] "An American" and "A Federalist" laughed outright at Luther Martin's charge that a conspiracy existed between George Washington and Benjamin Franklin "to subvert the liberties of the United States,"[30] but "A Farmer" intimated in an attack on "Aristides" that the new plan was indeed a conspiracy to satisfy the designs of a few ambitious men for power and office.[31] Both sides closely watched and alternately praised or

---

27. *Ibid.*, House and Senate, November Session, 1787. Three hundred copies were ordered to be printed in German for distribution in Baltimore, Washington, and Frederick Counties.
28. *Maryland Gazette* (Baltimore), December 4, 1787.
29. Extract of a letter from Baltimore, dated December 12, 1787, printed in the *Massachusetts Gazette* of January 4, 1788. Cited in Libby, *Geographical Distribution*, p. 33.
30. *Maryland Gazette* (Baltimore), December 28, 1787; January 11, 15, and 22, 1788.
31. *Maryland Gazette* (Baltimore), February 15, 1788.

blamed the conduct of Pennsylvania, Connecticut, Massachusetts, and Georgia,[32] while rumors of a plot in New York to buy up Antifederalist votes found ready circulation in Maryland's public prints.[33] "An Annapolitan" denied that the new government, controlled by the people, would become an aristocracy, but admitted that in every county there were disaffected men "exerting their whole power and putting every engine in motion to defeat, as they allege, the deep concerted scheme of a few aspiring, wealthy, and well born." Maryland would gain rather than lose by adoption, he concluded, since most internal matters would be left in control of the state while Annapolis might even become the seat of the future federal government.[34] "Civis" informed the people that the Philadelphia Convention was an "august assembly, consisting of men of the most distinguished abilities, integrity, and virtue" who produced a plan of government "universally admired by those of impartial political erudition and which, upon candid examination . . . is found to be fully calculated to promote the liberty, happiness, and prosperity of all the States in the Union."[35] To this "A Clergyman" added that without immediate and effectual union the country would be invaded by European nations seeking payment of debts.[36] Another correspondent advised voters to select men of "property, character, and abilities" to the forthcoming convention rather than those in desperate or embarrassed circumstances who had lately been in favor of paper money.[37] Defective as the

---

32. *Ibid.*, January 4, 18, 19, 22, 25, and 29 and February 1, and 5, 1788. Writing from New York, John Eager Howard revealed that "the Assembly of this State are now sitting at Poughkeepsie; nothing yet has been done relative to the Government—The Convention of the Massachusetts are now sitting, but as there is great opposition it is not certain that they will adopt it." Howard to William Smallwood, dated New York, January 27, 1788. MS in McHenry Family Papers, M.H.S.
33. *Ibid.*, February 19, 1788.
34. *Maryland Gazette* (Annapolis), January 31, 1788.
35. *Maryland Journal*, February 1, 1788.
36. *Maryland Gazette* (Baltimore), February 12, 1788.
37. *Ibid.*, January 4, 1788.

Constitution may be, Otho Williams wrote in the *Maryland Journal,* "it is better and safer than none. We have it in our choice to accept, and make it what we want it, or reject it, and commit ourselves to chance. . . . Democracy, Aristocracy, Oligarchy, Monarchy &c &c seldom fail when artfully used, to create jealousies; and Characature [*sic*] any form of Government that is intended to be represented as tyrannical or Wicked."[38] The little care and thought necessary to understand the subject, he felt, "gives great advantage to the opposition, and it is truly disgusting to hear many argue and clamor about the business who never read or even heard the constitution read, and who are totally deceived by those whose opinions they have imbibed."[39] Beliefs that the "new constitution is pregnant with despotism and even that it is dreadful to liberty," Daniel Carroll cautioned, "have been chiefly propagated in Maryland by men whose interests would be deeply affected by any change of government, especially for the better, and those to whose embarrassed circumstances regularity and order would be exceedingly inconvenient."[40]

As tempers and pens were activated into fever pitch during the winter of 1788, "Aristides" emerged as the most controversial figure in the state. His interpretation of the Constitution was heavily attacked by Luther Martin, who remarked that if the federal judiciary system was too complex for "Aristides'" understanding, it was too intricate a system for common people also. If accepted unamended, he warned, the

---

38. O. H. Williams Papers, Vol. 4. Dated March 20, 1788, and signed "A Marylander." M.H.S.
39. O. H. Williams Papers, Vol. 4, M.H.S. Williams felt that delegates to the ratifying convention should be allowed full freedom of debate, but that decisions must be made quickly, for "delay renders every day more critical." It was necessary for a strong government extending to the most remote corners of the union that would provide for a return of justice and equity, the curtailment of unhealthy credit, the end of public and private speculation, and the restoration of property. "All hopes of prosperity under the present confederation have subsided . . . it is abandoned, and given up."
40. *Maryland Journal,* January 8, 1788.

Constitution would reduce the people to "mere beasts of the burden . . . to a level with your own slaves, with this aggravating distinction, that you once tasted the blessings of freedom." State rights and individual rights would be no more, because state governments would be annihilated. "Peaceably, quietly, and orderly to give this system of slavery your negative is all that is asked by the advocates of freedom," Martin finished.[41] Rejoinders came from both within and without the state. Oliver Ellsworth of Connecticut, writing as "Land Holder," answered Martin's objections point for point,[42] "Grateful" responded with satire,[43] "Countryman" asked "Aristides" to write in detail whether the Constitution would override state laws,[44] "Sidney" reminded voters that "we common people are more properly citizens of America, than any particular State,"[45] and an unnamed correspondent wrote that "the most inveterate opponent will not pretend that the Articles of Confederation can establish our safety."[46] "Hamden" exhorted the people to adopt the frame of government created by "so many eminent and learned personages . . . men of candour, sense, and integrity, and also profound politicians." Defending the provisions concerning a strong executive, he declared that the Constitution was the best possible compromise between "a republican form of government and that of a limited monarchy." Only "desperate men, lost to love of country," could oppose such a union when the country's foreign trade and public and private security were in jeopardy.[47] "An Elector," in reality Dr. Philip Thomas of Fredericktown, suggested to "Aristides" that he compromise on his opposition to a bill of rights, for "there *really* are situations in which it *appears* to

41. *Maryland Journal*, January 18, February 29, March 7 and 18, 1788.
42. *Ibid.*, March 21, 28; April 14, 1788.
43. *Maryland Gazette* (Baltimore), February 15, 1788.
44. *Ibid.*, March 11, 1788.
45. *Maryland Journal*, February 29, 1788.
46. *Maryland Gazette* (Annapolis), January 31, 1788.
47. *Maryland Journal*, March 14, 1788. See also *Maryland Gazette* (Annapolis), April 15, 1788.

. . . be *necessary* for a man to conciliate &c. Wherein it is at least proper, if not necessary for him to forbear from creating Enemies; especially when it is not possible for him to serve friends."[48] Williams, too, agreed that "the members of the Convention were not unmindful of the popular prepossession in favor of a declaration, or *Bill of Rights*."[49] But "Aristides" compromised with neither friends nor enemies,[50] and although he responded to his detractors through occasional letters in the press,[51] for the most part his defense was taken up by "Plebeian," who engaged in a battle of wits with Hanson's former and most bitter opponent, "A Farmer." Complaining that there was too little general interest in the coming convention, "Plebeian" urged voters to elect and instruct their delegates and to inquire, "with the strictest scrutiny, into the sentiments and abilities of those who solicit our favor." He defended the provision for a standing army and the omission of a bill of rights,[52] and together with "Decided Federalist,"[53] condemned the use of bribery by the opposition and the supineness of Baltimore town and county. The latter reminded voters that "a rich intriguing Anti-Federalist character" (none other than Charles Ridgely) would send what delegates he pleased to the ratifying convention by means of the numerous hands he employed and the inhabitants of the precincts, "a

48. Williams to Thomas, dated Baltimore, March 29, 1788. MS in Williams Papers, Vol. 4, M.H.S.
49. Williams to the Editor of the *Maryland Journal*, dated March 20, 1788. MS in Williams Papers, Vol. 4.
50. "He has a foible in his nature which all his reason cannot cure," wrote Williams in 1791. "He cannot tolerate an opinion . . . which is contrary to his own judgment." Williams to Thomas, February 2, 1791. MS in Williams Papers, Vol. 6.
51. *Maryland Gazette* (Annapolis), April 3, 1788. Hanson admitted that he was wrong in imputing original jurisdiction of the U.S. Supreme Court in cases between a state and its own citizens. To increase the jurisdiction of the federal courts, he felt, would only increase the number of its enemies.
52. *Maryland Gazette* (Baltimore), March 7 and April 4, 15, and 18, 1788.
53. *Maryland Journal*, March 14, 1788.

knot always under his command." "A Farmer," on the other
hand, sneered at the Federalists as imitators of England. He
insisted that a majority of Americans wanted to maintain a
confederacy of "independent states," and that a federal government on the model outlined at Philadelphia would imperil
civil and religious liberty, overturn trial by jury, institute
controls on the press, and result in a Senate composed of
an oligarchy of aristocrats who would engross all powers of
government.[54] Particularly bitter over the absence of a bill of
rights, "A Farmer" brought much knowledge of history to
his argument on the need for such guaranties. He received
support from "Caveto" and from "Neckar," who also argued
vigorously against arbitrary power while maintaining that
"every stipulation should be previous to adoption."[55] "Tully,"
"Fabius," and "Insolvent" responded with fresh arguments
in support of the Constitution, and so the battle over ratification waxed undiminished.[56] Resort was even had to bits of
poor poetry, Federalist writers bursting forth with a rhyme
entitled "The Raising for Federal Mechanics":

Huzza, my brave boys our work is complete,
The world shall admire Columbia's fair seat . . .
Whilst we drain the deep Bowl, our Toast still shall be
Our Government firm and our Citizens Free.[57]

To which the "Anti's" replied in equally bad verse:

All such important high pretensions
Weigh well, ye ensuing State Conventions

---

54. *Maryland Journal,* March 4 and 14, 1788; *Maryland Gazette* (Baltimore), February 15 and 29, March 4, 7, 18, 21 and 25, April 1, 4,
11, 15, 22, and 25, 1788.
55. *Maryland Gazette* (Baltimore), February 26, March 25, and April
11, 1788.
56. *Maryland Gazette* (Baltimore), April 22, 1788. *Maryland Journal,*
April 1 and 22, 1788.
57. *Maryland Gazette* (Baltimore), February 19, 1788.

If selfish should they prove, or fain,
Subverting concord's sacred fane,
Reject the whole impious band,
Ere discord curse the guilty land.[58]

Although most of the argument for and against ratification
of the Constitution was expressed in terms of political theory
and eighteenth century concepts of natural law, penetration
to the heart of the conflict in Maryland reveals important
economic issues at stake. These issues were more often than
not defined in terms of class interests. Opponents of unconditional ratification denounced the Constitution as an aristocratic
plot and predicted that its adoption would result in monarchy
or at least in perpetual rule by the rich and well-born. Supporters, conversely, did not hesitate to proclaim the emergence
of popular democracy, social dissolution, or even general
anarchy should the new government fail to be accepted. Notwithstanding certain discrepancies, the paper money issue was
the most integral part of the struggle in Maryland. Appeals
by both parties were addressed to the voters on the same
basis as they had been in the contest for debtor relief, thus
providing an underlying continuity between the conflict of
1785–86 and that of 1787–88. The same leaders employed the
same tactics of exploiting class antagonisms and anti-aristocratic feeling to gain their desired ends, while all sides realized
that the fate of currency inflation and debtor relief was completely bound up with the outcome of the present momentous
conflict. From the tone of the charges and accusations hurled
back and forth during this period it is clear that cheap paper
money still occupied a position of paramount importance in
the state.

Federalists declared from the outset of debate that opposition to the Constitution came primarily from speculators and
debtors who wanted paper money and cancellation of both
British and domestic debts, "men in desperate and em-

58. *Maryland Journal,* February 15, 1788.

barrassed circumstances who may have been advocates for . . .
the truck bill, or insolvent act; and who may expect to escape
in the general ruin of the country."[59] It was predicted in
more ominous tones that the total dissolution of civil society
would take place:

> Should it be flatly rejected . . . it will be next to impossible
> ever again to collect these states under any regular govern-
> ment. Anarchy and discord will speedily ensue. The hands
> of the son will be imbrued in the blood of his father and
> nearest relations. CIVIL COMMOTION, with all her
> hideous train! will ride triumphant . . . over disunited
> America.[60]

"Real Federalists" joined in the prediction of anarchy and
warned the voters that the majority of the House of Delegates
were "needy men" who had voted in favor of currency inflation. Such men, especially the insolvent debtors, should neither
be trusted nor chosen as deputies to the convention for they
were slaves to their creditors and liable to be bribed.[61] Choose
instead "the rich and the great," added "A Countryman" as he
advised voters to scorn the anti-aristocratic propaganda, because "the knowing man who has studied law and politics is the
most suitable . . . and deserves the confidence of the people."[62]
"Aratus" urged the people not to become "dupes to demagogues,"[63] while another begged them to awake from their
lethargy and "exert every nerve to prevent such men from
being . . . elected to the ensuing Convention, and such as
already have been pointed out to your particular aversion,
I mean the advocates for paper money . . . and the authors
of the insolvent act."[64] A letter to the "Country People of

59. *Maryland Journal,* February 1, 1788.
60. *Ibid.*
61. *Ibid.,* March 21, April 4 and 25, 1788.
62. *Maryland Gazette* (Baltimore), March 6, 1788.
63. *To the People of Maryland,* Broadside, M.H.S.
64. *Maryland Journal,* March 14, 1786.

Maryland" assured those who had fallen upon lean days that
federal taxation would be no burden to them since it would
be raised through excises upon imported luxuries rather than
from the landed interest.[65] The *Pennsylvania Gazette*, meanwhile, reported the following economic analysis of antifederal
feelings in the state:

> Baltimore and Harford counties alone are clearly Anti-
> Federal, in which are many powerful and popular men
> who have speculated deeply in British confiscated property
> and for that reason are alarmed at shutting the door against
> state paper money. The same men, their relations and par-
> ticular friends are more violently Anti-Federal because they
> paid considerable sums into the treasury in depreciated
> continental currency and are scared at the sweeping clause
> . . . which may bring about a due execution of the treaty
> between Great Britain and America, to their loss. All these
> men are unanimous against the Federal government; they
> are here called the Black List, by way of emphatical dis-
> tinction. . . . Mr. Chase is an Anti-Federal, both from ambi-
> tion, because he cannot expect to be so powerful in the
> general government as he is in the state and because his
> shattered circumstances render him interested in discord
> and civil war.[66]

To a large extent these accusations were more than justified.
Antifederalist leaders in Maryland had not only speculated in
confiscated property, but had supported paper money and
debtor relief, had gone into debt to British merchants, and
had attempted to cancel these debts with depreciated currency.[67] It was precisely against any such future threats in

---

65. *Maryland Gazette* (Baltimore), March 4 and April 4, 1788.
66. *Pennsylvania Gazette*, April 30, 1788. Dated Baltimore, April 24,
    1788. Cited in Libby, *Geographical Distribution*, pp. 65–66. "De-
    cided Federalist" declared that "Federalists should keep out all in-
    solvents on the Black List", *Maryland Journal*, March 14, 1788.
67. See chapter 1. Sam Chase, William Paca, and Charles Ridgely, op-
    ponents of unconditional ratification, were heavy speculators in
    confiscated property and were leaders in the fight for paper money.
    Luther Martin and Jeremiah Townley Chase were also large inves-

Maryland and elsewhere that the Philadelphia Convention provided by declaring in Article I, Section 10 of the Constitution that "No State shall coin money; emit Bills of Credit; make any Thing but gold and silver Coin a Tender in Payment of Debts," pass ex post facto laws, or laws impairing the obligation of contracts. Federalists such as Alexander Contee Hanson recognized in this clause a degree of security for property rights long absent in his state, and he did not fail to publicize this fact in his offering as "Aristides":

> Too long have we sustained evils resulting from injudicious emissions of paper and from the operation of tender laws. To bills of credit . . . may we impute the entire loss of confidence between men. Hence it is that specie has in a great degree ceased its proper offices, and been confined to speculations. Hence chiefly are the bankruptcies throughout America, and the disreputable ruinous state of our commerce. Hence it is principally that America hath lost its credit abroad, and American faith become a proverb. The convention plainly saw that nothing short of a renunciation of the right to emit bills of credit could produce that grand consummation of policy, the RESTORATION OF PUBLIC AND PRIVATE FAITH.[68]

While such control of runaway inflation undoubtedly appealed to the propertied classes, it was also desired by many of those in less affluent circumstances. This was expressed rather poignantly in an address "To the Working People of Maryland":

> The interest of money here is said to be 25 per cent. No

---

tors in confiscated property. Many of the Ridgelys were obligated for prewar debts to British merchants and had written them off by payment of depreciated currency into the state treasury. If the Constitution were adopted, *full sterling* value would have to be repaid. Sale Book of Confiscated British Property, 1781–1785, Hall of Records, Annapolis. See also Ridgely Papers, and Ridgely Family Papers, M.H.S.

68. *REMARKS on the PROPOSED PLAN of a FEDERAL GOVERNMENT,* by "Aristides," bound in with "Hanson's Pamphlets," M.H.S.

man can afford to borrow at that rate, to pay debts contracted at 6 per cent. To save bread for his children he
had better go to jail. Were the land, which maintains
children, now seized and sold, the few monied men here
would get it all, for a little indeed; because in Europe,
where money is so plenty that the highest interest is 5 per
cent, the people there say that we make bad laws and too
many of them, and they cannot trust themselves or their
money among us, though they are pinched for land there.
I think the Constitution will heal this grievous sore, and
enable us to borrow money in other countries on reasonable
terms to pay workmen for improving our lands and houses
that we may make better crops. . . . Taxes, too, are to be
everywhere equal. . . . Taxes on imported goods . . . can
distress none but the rich. . . . We shall be freed from tax
gatherers.[69]

Antifederalists based most of their opposition to the Constitution on the grounds that it was an aristocratic plot that
precluded future resort to paper money as a solution to the
problems of economic depression. In *The Genuine Information,* Luther Martin condemned this prohibition and declared
that the country had benefited from paper money in the past,
that it would be a necessary and useful measure in the future,
and that legislative alteration of contracts was often unavoidable for "the times have been such as to render regulations of
this kind necessary in *most* or *all* of the states, to prevent the
wealthy creditor and the moneyed man from totally destroying
the poor, though industrious debtor. Such times may again
arrive. . . . I apprehend, sir, the principal cause of complaint
among the people at large is the public and private debt
with which they are oppressed, and which, in the present
scarcity of cash, threatens them with destruction. . . ."[70] This

---

69. *Pennsylvania Gazette,* April 2, 1788. Originally dated February 27,
1788. Cited in Libby, *Geographical Distribution,* pp. 33–34.
70. Luther Martin, *The Genuine Information,* in Jonathan Elliot, *Debates in the Several State Conventions on the Adoption of the Federal Constitution,* p. 376.

was followed in 1789 by John Francis Mercer's lengthy pamphlet defending the legality of payments made into the Maryland treasury in full cancellation of prewar debts to British merchants. Although it is not known whether Mercer himself had incurred obligations of this nature in either Maryland or Virginia, his outspoken opposition to their payment would lead one to believe that he had. "The unjust authors of our calamities," he declared, should share equally in the burden of debt payments.[71]

In the same vein, spokesmen in favor of paper money attempted to excite opposition to the Constitution by stirring up class antagonisms once again. Besides alleging that those who supported the new frame of government were all monarchists at heart, Luther Martin asserted that the net result of the whole system would be to debase and impoverish the great bulk of the country's population:

This government proposal . . . so far from removing, will greatly increase those complaints, since, grasping in its all-powerful hand the citizens of the respective states, it will, by the imposition of the variety of taxes, imposts, stamps, excises, and other duties, squeeze from them the little money they may acquire, the hard earnings of their industry, as you would squeeze the juice from an orange, till not a drop more can be extracted; and then let loose upon them their private creditors, to whose mercy it consigns them, by whom their property is to be seized upon and sold, in this *scarcity of specie,* at a *sheriff's sale,* where nothing but ready cash can be received, *for a tenth part of its value,* and themselves and their families to be consigned to indigence and distress . . . without a moment's indulgence.[72]

---

71. John F. Mercer, *An Introductory Discourse to an Argument in Support of the Payments made of the British Debts into the Treasury of Maryland during the late War* (Annapolis, 1789).
72. Luther Martin, *The Genuine Information,* in Elliot, *Debates,* 1:376–77.

"A Farmer and Planter" added that adoption of the Constitution would certainly bring loss of liberty. Urging his fellows to read the document, he declared, "I have done so, and can find that we are to receive but little good and a great deal of evil—Aristocracy, or government in the hands of a very few nobles or RICH MEN, is therein concealed in the most artful plan that ever was formed to entrap a free people." As for the excise, people were warned not to believe that this would be solely the burden of the rich. If, on the other hand, citizens refused to pay the federal poll tax, the militia of Philadelphia and Boston would come and force them to do so. Only the wealthy, he proclaimed, were in favor of the Constitution, and as proof disclosed that the four richest men in Anne Arundel county had been nominated for the ratifying convention. In conclusion Marylanders were advised to "be wise, be virtuous, and catch the precious moment as it passes to refuse this new-fangled government," and thereby extricate themselves and their posterity "from tyranny, oppression, aristocratical or monarchical government."[73] "Betsey Cornstalk" lent added support in a more comical vein,[74] as did several other would-be humorists.[75]

While it is clear that the economic issue of paper money and prewar debt obligations formed an integral part of the fight over the Constitution, there were also specific economic interests that stood to gain by ratification. The power given to Congress to regulate commerce among the states and with foreign nations, and to collect duties, imposts, and excises,[76] was of immeasurable importance to the trading, shipping, and manufacturing interests of Maryland. If exercised by the new government, this power would grant security and protection which neither the individual states nor the Articles of Confederation had been able to bestow. That such was the hope

---

73. *Maryland Journal*, April 1 and 18, 1788.
74. *Maryland Gazette* (Baltimore), March 7, 1788.
75. *Ibid.*, March 18, April 11, 15, and 25, 1788.
76. Article I, Section 8, Constitution of the United States.

of many residents of Baltimore can be seen in a petition signed by tradesmen, mechanics, and others to the first Congress of the United States in April, 1789:

> The happy period having now arrived when the United States are placed in a new situation; when the adoption of the General Government gives one sovereign Legislature the sole and exclusive power of laying duties upon imports; your petitioners rejoice at the prospect this affords them, that America, freed from the commercial shackles which have so long bound her, will see and pursue her true interest, becoming independent in fact as well as in name; and they confidently hope, that the encouragement and protection of American manufactures will claim the earliest attention of the supreme Legislature of the nation.[77]

The new government, moreover, would certainly discharge the debts accumulated by Congress since the Revolution. Government certificates which had depreciated steadily since that time would thus be redeemed in full or part value, and men who had fought in the army, who loaned the government money or sold it supplies or performed other services of a military or civil nature, and above all, speculators who had bought up large quantities of these certificates, fully understood the advantage of a strong national government which would honor its obligations.[78]

The climax of the six months' fight over ratification came during the first weeks of April. Although little is known of the campaign in the counties, accounts of the elections in a few of them were reported in the public prints. In Montgomery

---

77. *American State Papers, Finance,* 1: 5. The petition was dated April 11, 1789, and was signed with over 700 names. Specifically, it asked protection for such products as ships, hardware, cordage, furniture, clothing, leather goods, paper, soap, etc., that were manufactured in Maryland.

78. Charles A. Beard, *An Economic Interpretation of the Constitution of the United States* (New York: The Macmillan Co., 1913), pp. 32–33, 150; chapter 5.

county Federalist enthusiasm was whipped up by the able speeches of William Dorsey in support of the Constitution, and despite Antifederalist rebuttal given by John Mason of Virginia, the vote was three to one in favor of the Federal candidates.[79] Washington county, in the extreme west of the state, was overwhelmingly Federal and elected its four delegates to the state convention by a vote of 657 to 84.[80] While at least token opposition had been presented there, in Frederick county no Antifederalist ticket appeared in any form,[81] and if any candidates ran against the Federalists in Annapolis, or in the counties of Calvert, Caroline, Cecil, Charles, Dorchester, Kent, Prince George's, Queen Anne's, St. Mary's, Somerset, Talbot, and Worcester, the fact was not made known in the newspapers.

Antifederalist candidates were returned in the three counties of Baltimore, Anne Arundel, and Harford—the very same counties that had sent paper money delegates to the General Assembly and where large areas of British land had been confiscated and sold on credit. In Baltimore county the four Federalist candidates were defeated by a majority of 447 votes, although it was asserted at first that they had been elected.[82] Their opponents immediately charged that at one of the polling places, town men, some of them "apprentice boys, servants, and slaves having no property in the world," were encouraged to vote the Federal ticket.[83] "Solon" declared, however, that the Constitution was being adopted by "the people of the United States," voting in a state of nature, and that therefore the Maryland legislature had no right to

79. *Maryland Journal*, March 28, April 4 and 13, 1788. The majority in favor of the Federalists was 583.
80. *Ibid.*, April 13, 1788.
81. *Ibid.*, April 11, 1788.
82. *Maryland Gazette* (Baltimore), April 11, 1788. The Federalist candidates were Harry Dorsey Gough, John Cradock, James Gittings, and John Eager Howard. Their victorious opponents were Captain Charles Ridgely, his cousin, Charles Ridgely of William, Nathan Cromwell, and Edward Cockey.
83. *Ibid.*, Signed by "Casca," April 18, 1788.

dictate the method of election of delegates.[84] But the matter
was soon clarified and those candidates running in opposition
to unconditional ratification were declared duly elected.[85] In
Harford county three nonresidents were elected in spite of the
legislature's stipulation that members to the convention should
reside in the county of their election.[86] And in Anne Arundel
county the victory of the Antifederalist candidates came as a
distinct shock to the friends of the Constitution. There had
been no sign of organized opposition to the Federalist ticket
of Charles Carroll of Carrollton, James Carroll, Brice Worthington, and John Hall until four days before the election when
the Antifederalists, under the leadership of the redoubtable
Samuel Chase, conducted a whirlwind campaign which succeeded in winning a majority of the voters to their support.
Jeremiah Townley Chase and John Francis Mercer signed and
distributed a handbill which declared that the French interest
was actually behind the promotion of the Constitution, and
that the Philadelphia Convention wished to do away with
trial by jury.[87] Sam Chase immediately left Baltimore for an
electioneering trip through Elkridge and Annapolis, while
J. T. Chase, Mercer, and Benjamin Harrison, the fourth Antifederalist candidate, did the same in other sections of the
county.[88] There was some criticism of Chase being chosen as

84. *Ibid.*, April 25, 1788. "Solon" felt that people should be allowed to
   vote for delegates to the convention at the place where they happened to be on election day.
85. *Maryland Gazette* (Baltimore), April 15, 1788.
86. See *Maryland Gazette* (Annapolis), April 10, 1788. The three Antifederalists elected in this county were Luther Martin of Baltimore,
   William Paca of Queen Anne's county, and William Pinkney, who
   was then serving as a law clerk in the office of Samuel Chase.
87. *Maryland Gazette* (Annapolis), April 18, 1788.
88. *Maryland Journal,* April 18, 1788. Samuel Chase was apparently
   proposed as a candidate without his knowledge, the Antifederalists
   having unsuccessfully approached Governor William Smallwood.
   The *Pennsylvania Gazette* of April 30, 1788 reported that "Anne
   Arundel county, though naturally Federal, have elected four Anti-
   Federalists, owing to the popular electioneering talents of Mr.
   Chase, who has represented them for twenty years." See Libby,
   Geographical Distribution, pp. 65–66.

an Antifederalist from one of the counties while he was still a member of the House of Delegates from the Federalist town of Baltimore, but his friends responded that the so-called Antifederalists were the true Federalists, and that those who now called themselves Federalists were really Nationalists in disguise.[89] Nevertheless, despite charges that party labels were clearly misleading, the decision in Anne Arundel county went to those who opposed ratification of the Constitution without amendments.

In Baltimore town, where two delegates were chosen, the elections were even more exciting and the details were reported in full in the newspapers. On the first day the hustings were opened only two candidates, Samuel Sterett and David M'Mechen, presented themselves to the people. Since their position on the controversial subject of amendments was not entirely clear to some of the voters, a delegation was dispatched from Starck's Tavern to determine whether they would support the Constitution "without alteration or making amendments a previous condition of adoption?"[90] The replies being reported unsatisfactory, Federalists actively bestirred themselves to urge the freemen of the town to choose two pledged men, preferably members of the Philadelphia Convention itself. Conditional ratification was deprecated since this would, in fact, amount "to an entire rejection of the whole, because there is no provision made for taking up such a proposal or rendering it of any effect. . . . We who are Federalists should vote for and support with all our might two able upright Federalists, whom we know to be decidedly Federal, upon the most permanent and fixed principles."[91] Shortly thereafter James McHenry and Dr. John Coulter were nominated to the Federalist ticket, and although this did not take place

---

89. *Maryland Gazette*, (Annapolis), April 22, 1788.
90. *Maryland Journal*, February 19, 1788.
91. *Ibid.* See also issue of March 14, 1788. It was declared that Baltimore should not be permitted to be the only seaport in Maryland to disgrace the convention by sending anti-Federal representatives.

until the second day of the election, they were successful in defeating the two original candidates by a majority of over six hundred votes.[92] The victorious party declared that never had any election shown "greater unanimity," and that "the general suffrages of their fellow-citizens" had been obtained because the people were "of the opinion that the ratification of the Constitution ought to precede any amendments" for "it would be injurious to our common interests to delay its ratification in the hope of obtaining them in any other manner than prescribed by the Constitution."[93] After the election a procession of shipbuilders, "tradesmen concerned in navigation," merchants, manufacturers, and upwards of one thousand inhabitants marched through the town preceded by the United States flag and by a group of sailors carrying a small decorated ship named the *Federalist*, symbol of the prosperous era envisioned under the aegis of the new Constitution.[94]

The Antifederalists did not succumb quietly, however. They charged at once that commissioners of election permitted all freemen over twenty-one to vote, ballots thereby being cast by men who were strangers on the town and by others who were not naturalized Americans. The commissioners, moreover, had not been sworn in as judges of election, and had adjourned the election when they desired. It was also charged that on the second day of the three-day election peaceable German citizens were prevented from voting by a group of men, including foreign sailors and servants armed with bludgeons, who forcibly took possession of the polls. Although the Antifederalists admitted that over 250 illegal votes were cast for their candidate, they asserted that almost 800 fraudulent ballots were cast for the Federalist standard-bearer, McHenry. By the time this most important of elections was over, reports declared that of the 1047 legal voters in Baltimore 671 did

---

92. *Maryland Gazette* (Baltimore), April 18 and 25, 1788. *Maryland Journal*, April 11, 1788.
93. *Maryland Gazette* (Baltimore), April 11, 1788.
94. *Maryland Journal*, April 11, 1788.

not vote but 1050 votes were recorded. Both sides were clearly guilty of malpractice in varying degrees, but the losers did not make an issue of the matter when the long-awaited convention met in April.[95]

Defeat for the Maryland Antifederalists had indeed been overwhelming. The *Pennsylvania Gazette* of April 30 reported that if the elected candidates carried out the pledges made at the hustings, "sixty-four Federalists are elected out of a total of seventy-six."[96] There were, nevertheless, alternative measures left open to the opponents of the Constitution that held some promise of ultimate victory. One was to assent to ratification only upon the condition that amendments be added, thereby necessitating the calling of a second convention of the states to agree upon the specific changes required. Then the Constitution could be pruned of objectionable features, a bill of rights added, or the new framework might be emasculated altogether.[97] Another avenue of escape—and one infinitely preferred by those Antifederalists totally opposed to the Constitution—was to persuade the Annapolis Convention to adjourn pending the decision of the Virginia convention in June. This plan, if successfully executed, might well have been the death knell of the entire Federalist cause, and thus Maryland's course of action was fully appreciated by her sister states at the time. By April of 1788 six of the states had already ratified the Constitution, but the issue was in grave doubt in North and South Carolina, Virginia, New York, Rhode Island, and New Hampshire. Virginia was the keystone to the entire structure; if her delegates rejected the new form of government there could be little hope for a favorable decision in those states where Antifederalist sentiment was predominant. Writing to Otho Williams from New York, Henry Knox confided to his wartime friend that

95. *Maryland Gazette* (Baltimore) April 15 and 22, 1788. See also *Maryland Journal* April 11, 15 and 18, 1788 for final outcome of the election in Maryland.
96. Cited in Libby, *Geographical Distribution*, p. 86.
97. *Maryland Gazette* (Annapolis), May 1, 15 and 22, 1788.

the antifederal interest is so powerful as to give them a
majority of 45 or 46 out of 66. They are obstinate and artful.
They will not probably have the hardihood to openly reject
the constitution should Virginia adopt it, but they will adjourn to a distant day. They will in the meantime consult
on the conduct which will best promote their policy. Everything rests on the decision of Virginia—If she will adopt the
constitution all things will be easy notwithstanding the
crooked policy of this State and Rhode Island.[98]

If Maryland refused to ratify, or if the Annapolis Convention
adjourned without final action, the forces of opposition in the
doubtful states would be greatly encouraged. And in Virginia,
the decision in Maryland might well be the determining factor
in the outcome of the Richmond convention, for adjournment
in Maryland could be interpreted as tantamount to rejection
of the Constitution. Virginia Federalists would thus be hard
put to overcome the tactical advantages gained by their opponents, while the outcome of the May convention in South
Carolina might be no less seriously affected by the proceedings
in Maryland. On April 10 James Madison warned Daniel
Carroll and James McHenry of "the critical importance of a
right decision there to a favorable one here,"[99] and on the
20th McHenry appealed to Washington himself to exert his
influence upon the delegates then assembling at Annapolis:

Our opposition intend to push for an adjournment under the
pretext of a conference with yours respecting amendments.
As I look upon such a step to amount to a rejection in both
States I shall do everything in my power to prevent it. Your
sentiments may be useful. You will be kind enough there-

---

98. Henry Knox to Otho Holland Williams, dated New York, June 11,
    1788. MSS in O. H. Williams Papers, Vol. 4, M.H.S.
99. Madison to Washington, dated April 10, 1788. Cited in A. H. Allen,
    ed., Documentary History of the Constitution of the United
    States. 5 vols. (Washington: Government Printing Office, 1905),
    4:575. The letters were dispatched to Washington first, for his
    approval.

fore if you have leisure to write to me at Annapolis. . . .[100]

Although McHenry's appeal was timely, Washington had already acted. On the very same day, he had dispatched a plea to Thomas Johnson to guard against any flank attacks by the opposition, reminding him that adjournment in Maryland meant rejection in Virginia and in the nation.[101] Arriving in the midst of debate at Annapolis, Washington's letter was promptly circulated among the delegates and undoubtedly served to inject new vigor into the Federalist cause.[102]

Thus, in an atmosphere of increasing doubt and uncertainty, the Annapolis convention assembled on April 21. The first day was taken up with routine business only. George Plater of St. Mary's county was unanimously elected president, other officials were chosen, and a committee of elections consisting of five men (four of whom were Federalists) was appointed.[103] Forty-seven of the seventy-six members attended the first meeting. Two delegates, both Federalists, were unable to attend at all because of sickness, while most of the Eastern Shore delegates, together with those from Baltimore and Harford county, did not arrive until the 24th. These absentees, surprisingly, included the principal Antifederalist leaders. Although the Ridgelys, Jeremiah T. Chase, Mercer, and Benjamin Harrison appeared and took their seats on the first two days, William Paca, Samuel Chase, and Luther Martin did not present themselves until the fourth day of the convention. As they formed the spearhead of the opposition to ratification, their absence was certainly a grave error in strategy. It allowed the Federalists a free field for their maneuvers, and for three

---

100. *Ibid.*, 4: 580. McHenry to Washington, dated April 20, 1788.
101. *Ibid.*, 4: 581. Washington to Thomas Johnson, dated April 20, 1788.
102. Thomas Johnson to Washington, dated October 10, 1788. Cited in Edward S. Delaplaine, *The Life of Thomas Johnson* (New York: F. H. Hitchcock & Co., 1927), pp. 458–60.
103. The Federalists were Thomas Johnson, Col. Richard Barnes, John Done, and Abraham Faw. The single Antifederalist member was Jeremiah Townley Chase. Allen, ed., *Documentary History*, 2: 97–122.

days they were able to work unimpeded by the dilatory tactics of the popular and powerful Antifederalist triumvirate.[104]

Since the great danger to ratification lay in delay, the Federalists resolved upon a program of quick, decisive action. On the morning of the 21st, before the convention met, they caucused and agreed

> that they and their constituents had enjoyed abundant leisure and opportunity for considering the proposed system of a Federal government, that it was not probable any new lights could be thrown on the subject, that (even if it were) the main question had already, in effect, been decided by the people in the respective counties, that, as each delegate was under a sacred obligation to vote conformably to the sentiments of his constituents, they ought to complete that single transaction for which they were convened, as speedily as was consistent with decorum. A prompt determination in this State, they conceived, might have a happy influence in other States and they expressed a desire that all argument in favor of an indispensable measure might be omitted. In short they esteemed nothing wanting except the mere forms of a ratification.[105]

Every proposition to bring about discussion by parts was therefore to be rejected. Indeed, haste was of such importance that when the committee of elections made its report on Tuesday the Federalists did not choose to delay the proceedings long enough to contest the election of Martin, Chase, Paca, and William Pinkney, who had been chosen from counties in which they did not reside. The majority clearly felt that their power was too limited and the crisis was too dangerous to devote precious hours to the luxury of useless haggling.

---

104. *Ibid.* See also *Maryland Journal,* April 11, 15, and 18, 1788. The two Federalist absentees were Robert Goldsborough, Sr., of Dorchester County, and Jeremiah Baining, of Talbot County.
105. Alexander C. Hanson, "An Address to the People of Maryland," cited in Allen, ed., *Documentary History,* 4: 650. See also *Maryland Gazette* (Annapolis), April 24, 1788, May 1, 8, 15, and 22, 1788.

On Wednesday the proposed constitution was read for the first time, after which the convention resolved that it would "not enter into any Resolution, upon any Particular Part of the proposed plan of Federal Government . . . but that the whole thereof shall be read the second time, after which the Subject may be fully debated and considered." On the "grand question," however, it was "clearly understood" that each member would be free to speak as often as he should think proper. "And then the President shall put the Question, that this Convention do assent and ratify the same Constitution, on which Question the Yeas and Nays shall be taken."[106] The Constitution was then read for the second time and the convention adjourned. Without doubt, the Federalists had scored an important victory; by preventing examination and debate over the separate clauses of the Constitution they literally stole the dilatory oratorical thunder—a major piece of Antifederalist strategy—from the very mouths of the opposition.

By Thursday only the main question needed to be put before the delegates to complete the business of the session. It was at this juncture that Chase and Martin finally arrived, and their presence added fresh life to the diminishing hopes of the minority. Chase at once arose and stated his many objections to ratification in an eloquent and lengthy speech which, he declared, would be continued on the following day.[107] Mercer and Martin thereupon carried on, but when they concluded, the Federalists declined to reply and studiously avoided a rebuttal. As no other speaker arose, the convention adjourned for dinner. When the delegates reconvened at 4:30, William Paca appeared and took his seat. With the Antifederalist forces now complete, he arose and informed the convention that he had "a variety of great objections to

106. Allen, ed., *Documentary History*, 2: 102–3.
107. *Ibid.*, 4: 651. See also William Smith to Otho H. Williams, dated April 28, 1788. MS in O. H. Williams Papers, Vol. 4, M.H.S. Chase argued that amendments should be forced now, when it could be done by five states, rather than later, when it would require the votes of nine states.

the Constitution in its present form, and that, although he did
not expect amendments to be made the condition of ratification, he wished them to accompany it." Because he had just
arrived, however, the several amendments which Paca wished
to propose for the consideration of the members were as yet
unprepared, and he requested permission of the house to delay
submitting them until the following day.[108] Thomas Johnson
at once moved to adjourn until the next morning, declaring
that "the request was candid and reasonable and that the
gentleman ought to be indulged." Although Johnson's fellow
Federalists were not a little taken aback by this gesture, his
motion was seconded and the delegates unanimously agreed
to adjourn.[109]

The majority was now thrown into a state of confusion.
Thomas Johnson had hitherto been considered unquestionably
safe in his views on the Constitution. As first governor of the
state of Maryland, and as Washington's acknowledged spokesman in the convention, he was a man of enormous prestige
and influence whom the Federalist majority could ill afford to
lose. Although he maintained that his action was merely a
courtesy extended from the first governor to the third governor, rumors soon arose that the real reason lay in his resentment at the impertinent tone of Washington's April 20 letter.
This seems rather unlikely, and would certainly be of little
use in explaining Johnson's conciliatory attitude toward the
opposition. In December of 1787 he had written Washington
to express his hope "that the plan recommended will be
adopted in twelve of the thirteen States without condition
sine qua non,"[110] and his basic position in this respect did
not change in the succeeding months. In due course the rumor
wafted its way up the Potomac to Mount Vernon, prompting
Washington to inquire

---

108. Allen, ed., *Documentary History*, 4: 651–52. See also Elliot, *Debates*,
2: 548ff.
109. *Ibid.*
110. Johnson to Washington, dated Annapolis, December 11, 1787. Cited
in Delaplaine, *Life of Thomas Johnson*, pp. 431–33.

what foundation there is for so much of the following . . .
as relates to the officious light in which my conduct was
viewed for having written the letter alluded to. . . . If the
letter which I wrote to you at Annapolis . . . was so considered, I have only to regret that it ever escaped me. My
motives were declared. Having such proofs as were satisfactory to me, that the intention of the leaders of opposition
was to effect an adjournment of your Convention (if a direct
attack should be found unlikely to succeed) I conceived
that a hint of it, thereof could not be displeasing to the
supporters of the proposed Constitution.[111]

On his part, Johnson vehemently denied the mounting gossip.
But while protesting his sincere friendship, he took occasion
to explain his conduct in the following letter:

instead of being displeased I thought myself much obliged
by the Letter you wrote me in the Time of our Convention.
—To strengthen the Friends of the new Constitution and
expedite its Adoption I showed that, and other Letters, containing much the same Information and Sentim^{ts}, to some
Gent. and mentioned them to others—a strange Conduct
had I been under the Impressions suggested! Nor do I recollect any Conduct of mine which can be called active to
bring about any Amendments—I was not well pleased at the
manner of our breaking up, I thought it to our discredit
and should be better pleased with the Constitution with
some Alterations but I am very far from wishing all that
were proposed to take place.[112]

One may thus conjecture that Johnson's accommodation of
Paca represented more than a mere desire to pour oil on the
troubled waters of the convention. But if such were the case,
he probably wished to add nothing save amendments in the

---

111. Washington to Johnson, dated Mount Vernon, August 31, 1788.
    Cited in *Ibid.*, pp. 458–59.
112. Johnson to Washington, dated Frederick, October 10, 1788. Cited
    in Delaplaine, *Thomas Johnson,* pp. 459–60.

nature of a bill of rights—guaranties which were equally desired by other Federalists throughout the country.[113]

When the delegates reconvened on Friday, however, the Federalists had regained their composure and rallied their forces. Before Paca had a chance to present his amendments, one member from each of the eleven Federalist counties and one each from the city of Annapolis and the town of Baltimore arose and declared that they "were under an obligation to vote for the Government" as quickly as possible and to do no more, that after the ratification their power ceased, and that they did not consider themselves authorized to consider amendments. Paca then arose to offer his amendments, only to be interrupted by George Gale who declared that he was out of order inasmuch as the main question ("that this convention do assent and ratify the proposed constitution") was still before the house.[114] Although Paca remonstrated warmly against the alleged indecency of treatment being accorded him, his protests went unheeded. Plater, who on the day before had granted Paca's request for time to submit his amendments, sustained the point of order. Technically the Federalist position was correct: the convention had not given Paca express permission to read his amendments, as the resolution of the preceding day to adjourn had not specifically authorized him to submit them. Still, Johnson's motion for adjournment had been put for the clear and express purpose

---

113. Delaplaine maintains that Johnson's action was simply in the nature of a friendly gesture toward Paca, and that his wish for changes in the Constitution was groundless. In view of Johnson's October 10 letter to Washington, however, this position seems unlikely. See *ibid.*, pp. 457ff.

114. Allen, ed., *Documentary History*, 4: 653. Gale, a Federalist member from Somerset county, had been absent the preceding afternoon and supposed Paca to be out of order, which he technically was. One wonders, however, whether Gale was entirely ignorant of what had taken place before his arrival on the scene, and whether his absence and subsequent presence did not provide a convenient method for the Federalists to "dump" Paca and go back on their vote of the day before without losing face.

of giving Paca time to prepare to introduce them, and that motion had passed without a division. The Antifederalists clung to this interpretation, but the Federalist majority were already dizzy with the taste of imminent victory. This had nearly been snatched from them once, and they were certainly not going to loosen their grasp now.[115]

The opposition continued their protests and objections throughout the rest of the day and all Saturday morning, the Federalists repeatedly being called upon by Chase and Luther Martin to respond. They refused to answer the arguments, however, defending their inflexible silence by saying that they were instructed to vote for the Constitution while their colleagues were equally instructed to vote against it. By Saturday afternoon the Antifederalists had talked themselves dry, and when the main question was put before the house the Constitution was adopted by a vote of 63 to 11, all the delegates from Anne Arundel, Baltimore, and Harford counties, except one, voting in the negative. This lone vote in the Antifederalist camp belonged to Paca, who cast his lot with the majority in spite of the cavalier treatment accorded to him and his amendments.[116]

With ratification an accomplished fact, the Federalists at last permitted Paca to read the amendments he had prepared. He prefaced his remarks by declaring that he had voted for the Constitution "only . . . under the firm persuasion . . . that

---

115. Elliot, ed., *Debates*, 2: 548; Allen, ed., *Documentary History*, 4: 597–607.
116. Allen, ed., *Documentary History*, 4: 597. See also William Smith to Otho H. Williams, dated Baltimore, April 28, 1788. MS in O. H. Williams Papers, Vol. 4, M.H.S. Smith wrote that when the question was put, "two federals, R. Goldsborough and a Mr. Cramton [Thomas Cramphin], Absent, which were the only absentees of the whole body . . . . Martin had a sore throat which disqualified him from holding forth, and saved a great deal of time and money to the state. It seems the federals agreed to hear the minority patiently all they had to say but declined making any reply . . . . We always counted on 12 Antifederals in convention, the converted member not yet certain, but Supposed to be our late Gov. P."

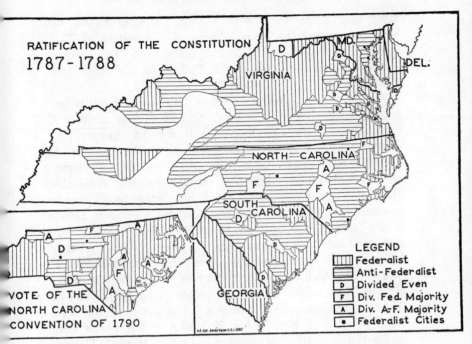

RATIFICATION OF THE CONSTITUTION
1787-1788

VOTE OF THE
NORTH CAROLINA
CONVENTION OF 1790

LEGEND
Federalist
Anti-Federalist
D Divided Even
F Div. Fed. Majority
A Div. A.-F. Majority
• Federalist Cities

... amendments would be peaceably obtained, so as to enable the people to live happily under the government, that the people of the county he represented ... would support the government with such amendments, but without them his constituents would firmly oppose it, he believed even with arms."[117] A resolution was then offered authorizing a committee to consider the amendments and to report to the house on Monday next "a draught of such ... as may be thought necessary in the proposed constitution ... to be recommended to the consideration of the whole people of the State if approved by this Convention."[118] The resolution was adopted by a vote of 66 to 7, but had the delegates foreseen the entangle-

117. Elliot, *Debates*, 2: 549ff. See also Allen, ed., *Documentary History*, 4: 654.
118. Elliot, *Debates*, 2: 549.

ment into which they were falling, the vote would not have been nearly so overwhelming. A Committee of Thirteen was appointed under the chairmanship of Paca, its composition otherwise including nine Federalists and three Antifederalists.[119]

For the second time in as many days the Federalists had granted concessions to the opposition by a large number of votes. Although these concessions were at best temporary, they merit consideration as to the motives of the majority in awarding them at all. Having conjectured on Johnson's change of course in the convention—a change that was noticeable albeit slight—one might recall that his motion to adjourn to accommodate Paca was supported without a division. Hence it may be supposed that many of the Federalist delegates were interested in Paca's amendments, or, going further, that they believed such amendments necessary for the protection of Maryland as well as for the protection of the liberties of her citizens. And while the vote appointing the Committee of Thirteen was not quite unanimous, it was nearly so and must have included all but the few Federalist diehards who were under the leadership of Alexander Contee Hanson. Despite his judgment that the majority "did not deem the proposed amendments necessary to perfect the constitution," many Federalists took the view that as private citizens they could make certain recommendations to the people as against proposing them in their official or conventional capacity. Hanson did not relish this novel distinction and declared it entirely false, while expressing regret at the "embarrassment into which the Convention was thrown." Consideration of amendments, he felt, would be construed by Antifederalists in other states as proof that the new Constitution was extremely defective and needed sweeping changes. His colleagues, on the other hand,

---

119. The Federalist members of the Committee of Thirteen were Thomas Johnson, Thomas Sim Lee, Richard Potts, James Tilghman, William Tilghman, Robert Goldsborough, George Gale, James McHenry, and A. C. Hanson. In addition to Paca, the three Antifederalists included John Francis Mercer, Jeremiah T. Chase, and Samuel Chase.

feared that Maryland Antifederalists might emulate those of Pennsylvania and incite discontented elements within the state into determined opposition to the convention's decision. Indeed, such action in Maryland was firmly predicted by Paca unless concessions were made. If, however, the convention followed the example of Massachusetts by recommending that amendments be added to the Constitution, the minority might be persuaded to accept defeat in good grace and work toward that end upon the organization of the new government. According to Hanson, it was only this desire to keep peace, and not a real conviction that amendments were necessary, that induced the Federalists to give them consideration. Whether or not a proportion of the majority, in line with Thomas Johnson, favored some amendments for reasons of necessity must remain speculative.[120]

The Committee of Thirteen assembled on Sunday morning to begin consideration of Paca's amendments. It got off to a bad start almost at once and as an instrument of reconciliation left much to be desired, although thirteen amendments were proposed and agreed upon, "most of them by a great majority."[121] The first of these declared that Congress should exercise no powers except those expressly delegated by the Constitution while the following twelve comprised a bill of rights.[122] Fifteen other reservations, designed chiefly to protect

120. Allen, ed., *Documentary History*, 4: 656.
121. Elliot, ed., *Debates*, 2: 549–53.
122. *Ibid.* These twelve amendments guaranteed jury trial, gave Federal and State courts concurrent jurisdiction in matters *ex contractu*, limited the jurisdiction of inferior Federal courts, gave State and inferior Federal courts concurrent jurisdiction in matters *ex delicto*, prevented Federal courts from acquiring jurisdiction by collusion, prevented Federal judges from receiving the profits of any other public position during their terms of office, forbade the issuance of warrants without oath or general warrants of search and seizure, restricted the period of military service to four years in times of peace, forbade the quartering of soldiers in private homes during peacetime without consent of the owners, limited the duration of mutiny bills to two years, preserved freedom of the press, and confined the jurisdiction of martial law over the state militia to times of war, invasion, or rebellion.

the states from infringement by the national government,[123] were proposed but rejected by the majority of the committee.

After the first two amendments had been approved, however, Hanson's distrust and suspicion of the minority erupted openly to frustrate any further progress. Declaring that he would agree to no more than the two proposals already acceded to "except *sub modo*," he requested that the members do likewise by sustaining their work as the act of private individuals. He also asserted that no other amendments should be proposed in the convention except those recommended by the committee itself.[124] Although no direct answer was made to this, Samuel Chase stated that if the committee could not agree on all the amendments "which the Constitution requires," every member was at liberty "to take in the convention, or any other place, the part he might think proper."[125]

On Monday, when the committee held its second and final meeting, the expected denouement took place. Relations were already strained, and they rapidly worsened when the Federal-

---

123. *Ibid.* The fifteen rejected amendments were intended to restrain the federal government from ordering the State militia beyond its own borders without the consent of the governor or the legislature, to prevent changes in the time, place, or manner of holding elections for members of Congress, to give the states full opportunity to collect any direct federal taxes, to prohibit the President from commanding the army in person without the consent of Congress, to prevent the maintenance of a standing army during peacetime without a two-thirds vote of Congress, to make members of Congress ineligible to any other federal office, to place all duties and imposts to the credit of the State in which they were collected, to prohibit a federal poll tax, to prevent any treaty from repealing any provision of a State constitution, and to guarantee full religious liberty. One of the amendments, "that no regulations of commerce, or navigation act, shall be made, unless with the consent of two-thirds of the members of each branch of Congress" was designed to protect the agricultural South from the machinations of the Eastern commercial states. Another boldly proclaimed the right of revolution with a concomitant denial of the "absurd, slavish and destructive" doctrine of nonresistance.

124. Elliot, ed., *Debates,* 2: 552ff. Hanson voted against all subsequent amendments.

125. *Ibid.*

ists added stipulations to the thirteen amendments agreed upon by the members for submission to the convention. Fearful lest the minority attempt to put forth its entire program, including the fifteen amendments which had been rejected, the Federalists agreed to report back the first thirteen propositions and to support them "both in their public and private characters, until they should become a part of the general government," only on condition that none of the rejected amendments or any others be laid before the convention. They further stipulated that the accepted amendments be accompanied with an address to the people—ostensibly prepared by some of the Federalist committee members but probably written by Hanson—which would make clear that in offering amendments the convention was not motivated by the idea that the Constitution could be improved or that the amendments submitted were necessary or even adequate, but that the delegates desired only "to quiet the apprehensions of those who think additional security is needed." The Federalists, in brief, wished to make it thoroughly clear that the amendments should not be taken too seriously.[126]

Although neither condition was acceptable to the minority, who alleged that "all the members who voted for the ratification declared . . . they would engage themselves, under every tie of honor, to support the amendments they had agreed to,"[127] with a deadlock imminent they promised not to push for additional changes either in the convention or without if the Federalists would accept, in addition to the thirteen amendments already assented to, the first three of the fifteen rejected propositions. These concerned elections of members for Congress, the collection of direct federal taxes by the states, and state control over the use of the militia. When again put to a vote,

126. Elliot, ed., Debates, 2: 550–53. See also Delaplaine, Thomas Johnson, pp. 449–51.
127. Samuel Chase, however, felt that the address was a matter of little importance, provided it was so worded as to give no offense and cast no reflection. His only objection was that it was not agreed upon beforehand.

however, the disputed articles were defeated by a vote of eight to five—Paca, Samuel Chase, J. T. Chase, Mercer, and the Federalist Thomas Johnson voting in the affirmative. The dissenters then asked permission to take the sense of the whole convention upon the three disputed propositions, and agreed to hold themselves bound by the decision of that body. This was rejected. At the same time the majority insisted that no amendments be reported back to the house unless accompanied by their address, stating that they would never have agreed to amendments in the first place had they not believed the address would be submitted with them. This stand was indeed questionable; most of the amendments had been voted upon the preceding day, whereas the Federalist address had not been mentioned—and might not have been prepared—until sometime on Monday. In a final effort to salvage part of their work, the minority declared that "as the Committee had agreed to a number of propositions," they, at least, ought to be signed and reported. To this the majority replied that "if any member had voted on a misconception of the footing on which the propositions were to go to the people, he should, on finding his mistake, have an opportunity of retracting and the propositions ought to be reconsidered." This effectually terminated negotiations, but it was left to the minority to have the last word; upon the committee's dissolution Samuel Chase averred that he thought himself at liberty, since the committee was making no report, "to propose to the Convention whatever he might esteem proper."[128]

The convention, meanwhile, had resolved not to consider any amendments except those submitted by the committee. While impatiently waiting and repeatedly calling for the return of the thirteen members, the main body adopted a resolution delivering the proceedings of the convention, together with the ratification of the new federal government, to the governor of Maryland for subsequent transmission to the United States Congress. It appears that this motion was passed

128. Elliot, ed., *Debates*, 2: 550ff.

so that any amendments reported by Paca's committee and adopted by the convention would not be passed on to Congress or the other states, but to the people of Maryland alone. As the majority of the committee retracted their original assent to the thirteen propositions, however, there was no official report and therefore no further business. On returning to the convention Paca related what had passed, and in so doing used this opportunity to present the thirteen amendments which had been adopted as well as the first three of those rejected. A motion that the delegates consider the amendments just read was spurned by a determined and tired majority. Instead, a motion of adjournment was passed by a vote of 47 to 27. Although in the final count fifteen Federalists defected to the minority, which voted solidly against adjournment, the Constitution was signed by all sixty-three members who had voted for ratification three days previously, and by May 1 was on its way to Congress.[129]

Celebrations took place throughout the state upon news of the Federalist victory. In Annapolis an "elegant entertainment" was given the delegates at Mann's Tavern, followed by thirteen toasts, each accompanied by a discharge of thirteen cannon. The fifth toast, significantly, was to General Washington, already talked of as the first president under the new government. This was followed by a ball in the Assembly Room, while outside there was a great illumination of fireworks in which all the citizenry participated.[130] The celebration in the capital, however, was austere in comparison with the festivities that took place in Baltimore. There, great hopes for commercial prosperity and a revival of trade were assured upon acceptance of the Constitution. Manufacturers looked toward a uniform duty on foreign goods, shippers toward a federal navigation act, and the commercial class toward increased

---

129. Allen, ed., *Documentary History*, 2: 662ff. See also *Maryland Journal*, May 2, 1788; *Maryland Gazette* (Annapolis), May 15 and 24, 1788; and *Maryland Gazette* (Baltimore), May 12, 1788.
130. *Maryland Gazette* (Annapolis), May 1 and 8, 1788; *Maryland Journal*, May 2, 1788.

credit and the permanent removal of the threat of inflation. In
their joy and gratitude the mechanics and merchants of Baltimore prepared a parade in which an estimated three thousand
men marched from Philpott's Hill to Fells Point. Each trade
marched together, displaying slogans which clearly reflected
the reasons for their enthusiasm over the new frame of government. Typical sentiments called for increased trade and more
industry, and for protection from foreign goods as noted by the
silversmiths in their banner, "No Importations, and we shall
live!" Eleven of the "Virtuous Sixty-three" who had signed
the ratification brought up the rear, while interspersed throughout were floats and figures representing the various trades in
the state. Captain Joshua Barney contributed his miniature
ship, the *Federalist,* for the grand occasion, after which it was
launched on the bay and navigated to Mount Vernon where it
was bestowed upon Washington as a memento of the town's
esteem. The procession terminated at Federal Hill, a site
specially named for the occasion, where the participants were
seated at a circular table of 3,600 feet and treated to an
"elegantly disposed" repast consisting of "50 Gammons of
Bacon, as many Rounds of beef, bbls of Country beer &ca,"
the whole prepared as "a cold collation."[131] Perhaps the general
sentiment of the people was most vividly expressed by the
Maryland Journal, which declared ecstatically that

Maryland has erected the seventh pillar upon which will be
reared the glorious fabric of American greatness, in which
fabric the rights of Mankind will be concentered as to their
native home. O, may the happy moment soon arrive when
the august Temple of Freedom shall be supported by thirteen pillars, with its gates unfolded to every part of Creation,

---

131. William Smith to Otho H. Williams, dated Baltimore, April 28, 1788.
MS. in O. H. Williams Papers, Vol. 4, M.H.S. See also *Maryland
Journal,* May 6, 8, and 9, 1788; and *Maryland Gazette* (Baltimore),
May 6, 1788. For record of other celebrations in the state, see
Maryland Journal, May 16 and 30; July 1 and 15, 1788.

may its duration be as permanent as Time and its period engulfed only in the bosom of Eternity![132]

News of Maryland's ratification was not long in reaching the other states, and the importance of its action in support of the Federalist cause was not lost upon Virginia and South Carolina. In the latter state a delegate to its convention asserted that he had opposed the Constitution but would now vote for it since the voice of Maryland had been decisive in its adoption;[133] ratification took place there on May 23 by a vote of 149 to 73. In Virginia, Washington expressed his hope that

> The Unanimity of the Agricultural State of Maryland in general . . . will not (I persuade myself) be without due Efficacy on the Minds of their Neighbours, who, in many instances, are intimately connected . . . by . . . the habits of Life. Under these circumstances, I cannot entertain an Idea that the Voice of the Convention of this State which is now in Session, will be dissonant from that of her nearly-allied Sister, who is only separated by the Patowmack.[134]

The force of Federalism was too strong to be overcome by the Virginia Antifederalists. Without Maryland and South Carolina there could be no Southern confederacy, and the Old Dominion chose union by a vote of 89 to 79. Had the opposition received six more votes the Constitution would have

---

132. *Maryland Journal*, May 16, 1788. The *Maryland Gazette* (Baltimore), in a somewhat less effusive but more practical vein, declared that "the unanimity in the Convention suppressed the necessity of debate and . . . has saved to the public the sum of £ 4000." See issue of May 9, 1788.
133. *Maryland Journal*, June 6, 1788.
134. *Ibid.*, June 24, 1788. In line with this statement, "An American" prophesied that Virginia would certainly lose its Eastern Shore to Maryland if it failed to ratify. See *Maryland Gazette* (Annapolis), June 12, 1788.

been rejected, a shift which Maryland's decision might well have prevented.[135]

Five days after the adjournment of the Maryland convention, the Antifederalists published an address to the people entitled, "A Fragment of Facts Disclosing the Conduct of the Maryland Convention on the Adoption of the Federal Constitution." This contained a list of the amendments rejected by the Committee of Thirteen, together with a statement of the reasons for the minority's dissent. It attracted little attention, so little in fact that Alexander Hanson, who prepared an elaborate rebuttal, decided not to publish it because the Federalists were "doubtful as to the propriety of answering a narrative which they conceived had made little impression on the people."[136] Several Antifederalist articles also continued to appear in the public prints throughout the summer, gradually disappearing in the wake of ratifications by Maryland's sister states.[137] For the most part these articles contended that ratification in Maryland was not final since it altered the state constitution and therefore needed the sanction of two successive General Assemblies, that amendments were needed before the Constitution could be accepted, and that the new form of government was a plot put over by the aristocracy to keep the "common class" in perpetual debt. Others denounced the framers of the Constitution as "vile conspirators" and urged

---

135. Elliot, ed., *Debates*, 3: 338. For an account of the celebrations in New York and Philadelphia pursuant to Maryland's ratification, see Otho H. Williams to Dr. Philip Thomas, dated May 14, 1788. MS. in O. H. Williams Papers, Vol. 4, M.H.S. Williams, visiting in New York at the time, reported that "ringing of Bells—firing of great Guns . . . testified the joy they felt on the news . . . . All my old acquaintances received me with pleasure and many who knew me not before seized and shook my hand as a Patriot Citizen of a Patriotic State."

136. Elliot, ed., *Debates*, 2: 547–56. See also Allen, ed., *Documentary History*, 4: 645; and *Maryland Gazette* (Annapolis), May 1, 15, and 22, 1788.

137. *Maryland Gazette* (Annapolis), May 15, and 22, 1788; *Maryland Gazette* (Baltimore), May 9 and July 11, 1788; *Maryland Journal*, May 16 and 20, 1788.

the people to choose, as delegates to the coming legislature, men who had opposed the adoption of the new government and who would thus vote to amend the Constitution.[138] Federalist replies to these sporadic attacks were few and brief—victory was theirs and they were already looking ahead to more important matters.[139]

What were the reasons that lay behind the Federalist success in Maryland? Why, in other words, was the passage of the Constitution strongly favored by most of the people throughout the state? In the first place, ratification was given much support by the great majority of the ruling gentry—that small element of the population who dominated Maryland politics and who assumed the yoke of government as a matter of course. The Constitution was backed by intelligent propaganda, especially designed to appeal to the interests of the upper class, and it enjoyed the sanction of Washington himself, whose personal influence in Maryland politics was enormous. Moreover, the delegates to the ratifying convention, by exercising the natural influence with which their wealth, power, and family connections endowed them, were in a large measure responsible for the success of the Federalist cause in the state. Thus it might be said that their victory was to a considerable extent a matter of personal leadership.[140]

It was this, of course, and more. The new government promised certain clear and definite economic advantages to many Marylanders, especially in the highly important areas of trade and agriculture. Well before the outbreak of the Revolution, depleted lands in the tidewater sections of the

---

138. *Maryland Journal*, May 20, 1788. *Maryland Gazette* (Baltimore), June 3 and 27, 1788.
139. *Maryland Journal*, May 9 and June 10, 1788. *Maryland Gazette* (Baltimore), May 23 and 27, 1788.
140. Libby, *Geographical Distribution*, pp. 32–33. See also Bureau of the Census, *A Century of Population Growth, 1790–1900* (Washington: Government Printing Office, 1909), pp. 296–98. This gives some approximation of the distribution of wealth in Maryland during this period.

state forced a change in Maryland's economy from tobacco to wheat. Thereafter the recovery of tobacco culture was never more than modest, and between 1770 and 1800 prices on the weed rose and fell continuously. Wheat, which could be grown in leaner soil, supplanted tobacco and gradually became the principal product of the eastern shore as well as the transmontane region. However, tobacco continued to dominate the economies of several western shore counties, retaining a notable foothold in those which cast their votes against the Constitution.[141]

The agricultural transition from tobacco to wheat was a timely one, but its effect on the state's domestic and foreign commerce in turn produced a rather complex political situation. A great deal of Maryland's wheat was shipped to the other states, an arrangement by no means ideal in a Confederation noted for its barriers to trade between state and state. Trade came down the Susquehanna River from Pennsylvania to Baltimore, and down the Potomac to Chesapeake Bay. While the Potomac was entirely subject to the jurisdiction of Maryland, the Capes giving access to Chesapeake Bay were both in Virginia, creating problems which led to the calling of the Annapolis Convention of 1786 and ultimately the Philadelphia Convention of 1787. As the eastern shore was closer to Delaware and Virginia than it was to the rest of Maryland, practically all the peninsula's trade had to cross state lines. Little wonder therefore that Maryland's wheat growers and merchants, anxious to escape the economic magnetism of growing urban neighbors offering easier credit and better handling of goods, were irresistibly drawn to that clause in the Constitution giving the federal government control over foreign and interstate commerce. Proposals along this line had been made

141. Avery Craven, *Soil Exhaustion as a Factor in the Agricultural History of Virginia and Maryland, 1606–1860* (Urbana, Ill.: University of Illinois Press, 1926), pp. 72–73, 84, 86. See also Gray, *History of Agriculture*, 2: 602–8, 908ff., and Arthur H. Cole, *Wholesale Commodity Prices in the United States, 1700–1861, Statistical Supplement* (Boston: Harvard University Press, 1938), pp. 100, 120–23.

by Maryland's delegates in Congress as early as 1783.[142] More-over, the unrest in Europe at this time created an unusual demand and a high price for wheat. A strong federal govern-ment would protect and encourage such lucrative foreign trade far more effectively than thirteen powerless and some-what disunited states, and would also be of immeasurable value in reopening the equally profitable West Indies trade.[143] The latter—for which Baltimore and Norfolk were the largest Southern outlets—had provided a market for American beef, pork, and wheat, and its closure by Great Britain after the Revolution presented a serious problem with which the indi-vidual states were unable to cope.[144] With few exceptions, on the other hand, tobacco planters were generally not inclined toward Federalism. Adequate transportation to the ports of Virginia and Maryland was within access of their tidewater farms, and as most of their product found its market in England, where heavy duties had to be paid on it, a strong central government was considered unnecessary and of little benefit in changing the situation.[145] The manipulations carried on by Robert Morris in 1786–87, however, which resulted in falling tobacco prices, might well have weakened resistance to the Constitution among planters by hastening the shift to wheat in hopes of bettering their already uncomfortable economic position.[146]

142. Gray, *Agriculture*, 2: 601–6. See also Jensen, *The New Nation*, pp. 337–38, 401–2; and Thomas P. Abernethy, *The South in the New Nation 1789–1819* (Baton Rouge: Louisiana State University Press, 1961), pp. 20–26.
143. Abernethy, *South in the New Nation*, pp. 20–41. See also Craven, *Soil Exhaustion*, pp. 83–86; and Gray, *Agriculture*, 2: 602–9.
144. Adam Seybert, *Statistical Annals of the United States of America* (Philadelphia: Thomas Dobson and Son, 1818), p. 276; Owens, *Baltimore*, pp. 138–39; Abernethy, *South In New Nation*, pp. 22–23.
145. Abernethy, *South in New Nation*, p. 23. See also Joseph C. Robert, *The Tobacco Kingdom* (Durham, N. C.: Duke University Press, 1938), pp. 120ff.
146. Robert Morris to Robert Gilmor and Company, dated Philadelphia, July 9, 1786. MSS in Bordley-Calvert Manuscripts, 1720–1828, M.H.S. It is evident from this letter that Morris was actively work-

While transportation to markets in tidewater Maryland was more than adequate for purposes of trade, conditions were exactly opposite in the western part of the state. The difficulties of overland trade were hopelessly pointed out to Otho H. Williams in the following letter from the backcountry:

I don't recollect that a single Waggon [sic] has been able to reach Baltimore since you left us nor is it possible for any number to come to this markett [sic], Unless during a hard frost, & even that is too hazardous to risque for a Long Journey. Unless something can be done for the Roads to the Westward, we must inevitably loose [sic] all that trade which will perhaps be a loss in revenue to the State nearly equal to the expence of making and Keeping those roads in repair.[147]

With overland communication between the transmontane area and the Baltimore market so abysmally bad, wheat farmers in Maryland's fertile Shenandoah and Potomac Valleys naturally had an acute interest in the development and improvement of satisfactory trade routes to the eastern ports. Washington himself considered this of utmost importance in keeping the west aligned with the east, believing that without prompt improvements the majority of western trade and ultimately western political allegiance would go down the Mississippi River to Spanish New Orleans. At least part of this area might be retained, however, if the waters of the Ohio could be connected

---

ing to drive tobacco prices down. In 1787, moreover, a dispute arose between the agents of Morris and those of the French Farmers-General, "in consequence of which the funds that were ordered to London to meet Morris's drafts to a very considerable amount, are stopped. His Agent who resides in London is returned to America, and his bills of course protested. This circumstance has alarmed the merchants here, and I believe nearly all his notes that were in circulation at this place are sent to Philadelphia for payment." Letter from Daniel Delozier to Otho Williams, dated Baltimore, July 4, 1787. MSS in O. H. Williams Papers, Vol. 4, M.H.S.

147. William Smith to O. H. Williams, dated January 2, 1786. MS in O. H. Williams Papers, Vol. 4, M.H.S.

with those of the Potomac.[148] The outcome of Washington's
interest was the incorporation of the Potomac Company by
Virginia, which had vast land claims to the west, in 1784–
85.[149] Thus western Maryland's strong support of the Constitution was probably influenced a great deal by its belief that
a federal government would be instrumental in aiding the
development of navigation along the Potomac.[150]

For the same reason it has been suggested that merchants
residing in the counties surrounding Baltimore[151] withheld
their support from the Constitution for fear that river trade on
an improved Potomac would eventually wind up in Alexandria
or Georgetown, thereby undercutting the land route to Baltimore or completely bypassing that city. However this may be,
one must beware of fully applying the doctrine of economic
determinism in explaining the motives of men. Those who
supported ratification in Maryland had varied and often con-
flicting economic interests. Otho Holland Williams, for example, gave his complete support to the new government. Yet
he was both debtor and creditor, having bought up confiscated
Tory property for purposes of speculation.[152] In Virginia, moreover, tidewater planters who owed pre-Revolutionary debts to
British merchants (collection of which would be facilitated by
adoption of the Constitution) actually voted against their

---

148. Thomas P. Abernethy, *Western Lands and the American Revolution*
(New York: Russell & Russell, Inc., 1937), p. 295. See also Kilty,
Laws of Maryland, 1, chapter 33. See also Delaplaine, *Thomas
Johnson*, pp. 384–99.
149. Jensen, *The New Nation*, pp. 342–43.
150. Libby, *Geographical Distribution*, pp. 46–48.
151. Specifically Baltimore, Harford, and Anne Arundel counties. See
Irving Brant, *James Madison*. 3 vols. (Indianapolis: The Bobbs-
Merrill Company, 1941–50), 2: 366ff.
152. State of Maryland, John Rogers, Chancellor, to O. H. Williams.
Dated April, 1787. Two bills of sale giving Williams title to Lots
31 and 32 of Monococy Manor, confiscated Loyalist property up
for sale by the state commissioners. MS in Williams Papers, Vol. 4,
M.H.S. See also Williams to Dr. Philip Thomas, dated June 24,
1789, Vol. 5, in which he discusses purchases and speculations in
confiscated property with Thomas Johnson.

economic interests in that section of the state.[153] The Constitution itself could not possibly resolve all these conflicts.

Last, one must consider the unsettled political scene in both Maryland and the Confederation during the 1780s. Characterizing the period as one of "internal debility," Theodorick Bland declared that the country was "sustained only by a feeble set of political institutions, the powers of which dropped into total disregard with the subsiding of . . . the revolutionary struggle,"[154] while as early as 1783 Washington warned that without "a supreme power to regulate and govern the general concerns of the Confederated Republic . . . the Union cannot be of long duration, and everything must very rapidly tend to anarchy and confusion."[155] Edmund Randolph stated the case even more bluntly when he declared at the Philadelphia Convention that "our chief danger arises from the democratic parts of our constitutions. None of the constitutions have provided a sufficient check against the democracy. The feeble sentiment of Virginia is a phantom. Maryland has a more powerful senate, but the late distractions in that state have discovered that it is not powerful enough."[156] Thus, economic motivations aside, it appears that a major reason for the Federalist success in Maryland can be found in the desire for stability and in the horrors of unchecked democracy.

Yet the reverse does not hold true for the Antifederalists in the state. Luther Martin excepted, none are known to have been political democrats. Indeed, Samuel Chase was to emerge in the coming years as a pillar of the Federalist Party and as its most fanatical spokesman against the purported "mob rule" of Jeffersonian democracy. Their opposition to the Constitu-

---

153. Libby, *Geographical Distribution*, pp. 18–26, and 66–67; Charles Beard, *An Economic Interpretation of the Constitution of the United States* (New York: The Macmillan Company, 1913), pp. 282–91, 318.
154. "A Tabular Digest of the Constitutions of the United States," n.p., n.d., MS in Bland Papers, 1757–1846, M.H.S.
155. *Maryland Gazette* (Annapolis), July 11, 1783.
156. Cited in Jensen, *The New Nation*, p. 426.

tion in 1787, therefore, cannot be attributed to fundamental differences over philosophies of government. Rather, the reasons must be sought in the bitter political struggles for personal power and paper money that rocked Maryland on the eve of the new nation's birth.[157]

157. As late as 1808, by which time Martin had been characterized as the "bull dog of Federalism," he was still upholding the Maryland Insolvency Law of 1787 in favor of debtor relief. See Opinions of Walter Dorsey and Luther Martin, dated March 21, 1808. MSS in Cornelius Howard Papers, 1727-1844, at M.H.S. In this instance Martin declared that a debtor's widow who had inherited property could not have the property taken away by her husband's former creditors in payment of the deceased man's debts. By 1790, on the other hand, none other than Alexander Contee Hanson wrote that Samuel Chase "has been the mover of almost everything this state has to boast of . . . . Without him how very seldom would anything good have passed the legislature." See MS note in Samuel Chase Letters, July 25, 1790, M.H.S.

3

The "Great Experiment" Begins

HAVING emerged from the battle to ratify the Constitution relatively unscarred and with their forces still intact, Federalists in Maryland and elsewhere looked toward the consolidation of their victory in a new era of union, peace, and prosperity. Although the Federalists were well aware of the magnitude of the undertaking upon which they had embarked, happily for them there were a goodly number of factors working for the success of the newborn government. By 1789 the country was on the way toward recovering from the effects of the postwar depression. Commerce and shipbuilding were reviving, American agricultural products were finding larger outlets in Europe, and the return of confidence in public and private enterprise was beginning to show its effects. Those conditions which had produced truck bills, stay laws, tender acts, and other forms of debtor legislation were disappearing. With them disappeared the political conflicts and factionalisms which had kept the states in turmoil during the period of the Confederation. While such conflicts of interest and ideas were to continue to dominate American politics, the chief battles would be fought within the confines of the federal structure (and the emergent machinery of a nationwide party system) rather than within the states.[1]

As the old government was quietly slipping into limbo, Federalists throughout the country turned their attention to the coming elections which would inaugurate the new one. Activity in Maryland in this respect was energetic, though by no means feverish. Federalists in the state were apparently content to rely upon their recent victory in the contest over ratification as a guarantee that the electorate would not change political horses in midstream. Voters were warned to take care, in the forthcoming October elections to the House of Delegates, not to elect any candidate who had shown Antifederalist sympathies.[2] Chase and his party, on the other hand, made it clear during the summer that the fight had only just begun. Federalist delegates to the ratifying convention were accused of conspiring to suppress publication of the convention's proceedings so that the people would be kept in ignorance of the illegal system being forced upon them.[3] This argument actually did have some merit. The debates at Annapolis had been covered by Thomas Lloyd, whose expenses had been paid by several Federalists and whose notes were, in fact, never published.[4] Seizing upon this evidence, the Antifederalists penned an indictment against Lloyd in the Maryland press:

Mr. Lloyd, a warm and decided friend to the *new* constitution, *frequently* expressed his *concern* at the silence of the majority, and declared that it would never do to publish the objections and arguments against the constitution, without any answer.—After the convention was dissolved, the *majority* made a collection for Mr. Lloyd, to defray his *ex-*

---

1. John C. Miller, *The Federalist Era 1789–1801* (New York: Harper and Brothers, 1960), pp. 2–5.
2. *Maryland Journal*, May 9, 1788. Signed "Federalism."
3. *Ibid.*, May 20, 1788.
4. Marion Tinling, "Thomas Lloyd's Reports of the First Federal Congress," *William and Mary Quarterly*, 18 (October 1961): 526.

penses; and he declared his intention *not to publish* what he had taken down. It is observable, that Mr. Lloyd has *hitherto* only published the speeches of two gentlemen of the Pennsylvania convention in favour of the government.[5]

Although a Federalist replied that "it was agreed among the members of the majority not to waste time or protract the decision by arguments in favor of the system,"[6] the opposition followed up this attack by other equally strong accusations.[7] At the same time they demanded immediate publication of the proceedings, that the voters might know how rashly the majority had acted.[8] The general Federalist response, however, was one of silence. This attitude was expressed by "A Private Citizen" when he wrote that "the charge, however vile, was too contemptible to be honoured by the notice of any member of the convention."[9]

Denunciations by the Antifederalists increased in bitterness as Marylanders turned their attention toward the autumn elections to the House of Delegates. Heading the opposition's ticket in Baltimore, Samuel Chase and David McMechen defined their stand by campaigning on the promise to sponsor amendments to the Constitution. This was a position that the Federalists, under the leadership of James McHenry and John Coulter, found utterly absurd; they declared, as one of them put it, that the friends of the Constitution would "no more think of calling in enemies to amend it, than they would submit their locks and keys to the file of an artist who had at-

---

5. *Maryland Gazette* (Annapolis), May 22, 1788.
6. *Maryland Journal*, July 25, 1788.
7. See *Maryland Journal*, May 23 and August 1, 1788; and *Maryland Gazette* (Baltimore), June 6, 27, and July 11, 1788. See also *Maryland Gazette* (Annapolis), June 19, 1788.
8. *Maryland Journal*, May 23, 1788; *Maryland Gazette* (Baltimore), June 3 and 27, 1788.
9. *Maryland Journal*, July 25, 1788. It is more likely that there were not enough subscribers to warrant publication.

tempted to rob them, or trust their lives to a physician who thirsted to drink their blood."[10]

The campaign was an exciting one and appears to have been marked by more than a little violence. Writing to his friend Robert Carter on September 16, Robert Lemmon confided that "our town has been in great confusion these several days upon electioneering, the parties run extremely high and little business attended to. The opposition is to Mr. S. Chase, and he has his friends; many fights have taken place and sometimes general engagements seemed near."[11] Lemmon was undoubtedly referring to the Gay Street riot of September 5, an altercation which developed when a peaceful political rally held by one of the parties suddenly found itself set upon by a gang of toughs who turned the meeting into a lively free-for-all. Although both sides claimed not to have started the tumult,[12] the Federalists neither forgot nor forgave the incident. Several weeks later they retaliated by assaulting an Antifederalist rally near the Court House, then moved on to Chase's house where both stones and epithets were hurled at the candidate and his windows.[13] Little wonder that Nathaniel Ramsey expressed his regret to Otho Williams on hearing "of the violence with which your citizens carry on their politics. They will thereby much destroy the influence they might have in the State if they were unanimous."[14] Williams, in turn, informed Dr. Philip Thomas that "we have had the devil to pay here for a few days past. . . . Don't you see our daily papers how they teem with invectives, epithets, censure, and all the

10. *Maryland Journal*, August 10, 1788.
11. Robert Lemmon to Robert Carter, dated Baltimore, September 16, 1788. MS in Carter Papers, M.H.S.
12. *Maryland Journal*, September 12, 1788.
13. *Ibid.*, September 23, 1788.
14. Nathaniel Ramsey to Otho H. Williams, dated Carpenter Point (Cecil County,) September 24, 1788. MS in O. H. Williams Papers, Vol. 4, M.H.S. Of Chase, Ramsey declared that "amongst all the crimes he has been charged with, that of being unfaithfull to those who confided in him, cannot be alledged."

elegant ingredients of explicit calumny? The spirit of controversy prevails, and nothing like good humour would be looked at."[15]

In addition to their specific opposition of the Constitution, the Antifederalists found it profitable to revive the issues of the recent paper money conflict. Emphasizing the still smoldering class antagonisms between debtors and creditors in the state, the candidates persistently accused the Federalists of economic coercion of the voters while at the same time describing themselves as friends of the poor.[16] It was hoped in this way to win the votes of the various minority groups in the city, especially the large German and Irish elements whose ballots might determine the contest.[17] In support of this aim, Chase published a broadside to the Catholic voters of Baltimore shortly before the election; this was intended to refute charges that he was anti-Catholic because he had supported a bill which resulted in the confiscation of property belonging to the Church.[18]

The Federalists angrily hurled accusations of their affiliation with upper-class rule back into the face of the opposition. Neither Chase nor McMechen, they declared, had ever been sympathetic toward the plight of poor taxpayers in the state; at least their respective voting records in the General Assembly did not show this to be so. Chase's speculative activities,

---

15. Williams to Dr. Philip Thomas, dated Baltimore, September 20, 1788. MS in O. H. Williams Papers, Vol. 4, M.H.S. In his own quiet way Thomas himself appears to have been active in support of the Federalist cause. An article written by him and signed "Elector," appeared in the *American Museum* and other public prints, leading Williams to comment that "kissing goes by favor. . . . I shall think of you as I do of the federal printers of Pennsylvania—anything that comes from their friends, or which is on their side of the question, is selected and approved . . . . A little 'redundancy' of words when a man is scarce of ideas is not so miserable."
16. *Maryland Journal,* September 5 and 30, 1788.
17. *Ibid.* See also *Maryland Gazette* (Baltimore), September 22, 1788.
18. "To the Roman Catholic Voters of Baltimore," broadside signed by Samuel Chase and dated October 4, 1788, M.H.S.

moreover, were publicized in order to show that his attitude toward wealth had certainly never been one of disdain. Rather, his activities in attempting to corner the Maryland flour market during the Revolution proved that he was not only a mercenary opportunist in business but a scoundrel as well.[19] Thus insult was traded for insult as the bitter and highly personal campaign in Baltimore neared its close.

The "warmth" induced by frequent meetings of the opposing parties, Otho Williams wrote, resulted in "threats of a town meeting" by the "Antis" to answer Federalist charges. But when Chase failed to carry out his promise, the Federalists under the leadership of Robert Smith seized the initiative and caught the opposition almost totally unawares:

> The Federal Champion, irritated by a thousand threats, *dared* to come forward, boldly called a town meeting—gave his name to the public, and Saturday last, in spite of intimidations, appeared at the hustings, mounted the tub, and exhibited in bold, eloquent language a catalogue of charges —papers &c which took up the whole day. He used great freedom of speech, and, in quoting of law, mentioned *lashes* with a degree of emphasis that cut to the quick. Some took great offence—then applauded the orator.[20]

On Monday, Williams continued, Chase "mounted the tub and with Superior Eloquence made his defence":

> He did not spare "His Public Enemy." Great Expectations were formed of the event. . . . At night, two great bodies were several times at the point beyond which nothing could have prevented a dreadful conflict. The principal men on both sides exerted themselves, and happily the multitude were separated. Not a few got broken heads, and one of the

---

19. *Maryland Gazette* (Baltimore), September 26, 1788; *Maryland Journal*, September 5 and 30, 1788.
20. Williams to Philip Thomas, dated Baltimore, September 20, 1788. MS in Williams Papers, Vol. 4, M.H.S.

Principals had his windows demolished. How it will end I don't know.[21]

On October 3, with the election only three days away, Chase and McMechen issued a broadside attacking the Federalists for refusing to permit the ratifying convention to submit amendments to the Constitution for approval by the electorate. They also accused their opponents of refusing to make proper arrangements for voting in the election, and asked that all citizens be forbidden to come to the polls or walk in the streets with weapons, colors, fifes, or drums. Sea captains were asked to keep their sailors aboard ship, justices of the peace were requested to be in constant attendance at the polls, and permission was asked for three friends of each candidate to be present during voting as observers.[22]

The Federalists, however, had learned from experience to distrust the reliability of Chase and his party. In reply to these latest accusations, they scattered handbills throughout the state publicizing the stand of the party that had voted against the Constitution. "Caveto" declared that Chase was planning a large demonstration during the election and that liberty caps, fifes and drums, and other republican regalia were being readied for this purpose.[23] But it was the Federalists and not the Antis who climaxed the campaign by entertaining Baltimore with a lively parade similar to the one which had taken place upon news of Maryland's ratification months earlier. A miniature ship and pilot boat were carried through the town

21. Williams to Thomas, dated Baltimore, September 20, 1788. MS in Williams Papers, Vol. 4, M.H.S.

22. "To the Voters of Baltimore-Town," broadside signed by Samuel Chase and David McMechen and dated October 3, 1788, M.H.S. See also Bernard C. Steiner, *The Life and Correspondence of James McHenry* (Cleveland: Burrows Brothers Company, 1907), p. 114.

23. John Thomas Scharf, *History of Baltimore City and County* (Philadelphia: L. H. Everts, 1881), p. 116. See also *Maryland Journal*, October 4 and 7, 1788.

to the accompaniment of flying colors and fifes and drums. Doubtless this spectacle was intended to serve as a vivid reminder of those festivities of the previous May, when the benefits to be derived from the Constitution had been portrayed.[24]

Violence broke out on the very first day of balloting, but although it is difficult to place the blame at its proper source, it appears that both sides were guilty of excesses. Each accused the other of being the first to seize control of the polls in order forcefully to prevent opponents from voting, but it is clear that each party at one time or another during the next four days took possession of the polls until driven off by mobs of the opposing group. Likewise, charges of fraudulent voting, of plying the electorate with gin, and of outright beatings, were also exchanged in the public prints during the following weeks. Chase, moreover, charged that Federalists had distributed handbills threatening to name those who had voted for him and McMechen as "enemies to the new federal government." The one constant in all the charges and countercharges that filled the air was the fact that the Federalists were in control of the polls on the second day of the election, after having beaten off an attack by the Antifederalist forces.[25]

In spite of the opposition's resort to force and its appeal to class interests, or perhaps because of these tactics, McHenry and Coulter received 635 and 622 votes respectively in comparison to Chase's 505 and McMechen's 494. The Federalist success in Baltimore was repeated elsewhere throughout the state, with the exception of Baltimore, Anne Arundel, and Harford counties. In these three tidewater counties, notable previously for their support of paper money and their opposition

---

24. Scharf, *Baltimore*, p. 116.
25. Dorothy Brown, "Party Battles and Beginnings in Maryland" (Ph.D. dissertation, Georgetown University), pp. 46–48. Miss Brown carefully considers both sides of the election controversy, citing the *Maryland Journal* of October 14, 17, and 24, 1788, and the *Maryland Gazette* (Baltimore), of November 28, 1788, and concludes with the present author that both parties were at fault in their seizure of the polls.

to the Constitution, Antifederalist delegates were returned to the legislature. Still, this did not alter the reality that the opposition had received a statewide beating at the polls, and when the General Assembly met on November 4 the Federalists were in firm control of both the Senate and the House of Delegates. On November 10 Thomas Johnson was chosen to succeed William Smallwood as governor. But Johnson was reluctant to resume public life, and upon his refusal of the office John Eager Howard of Baltimore was selected as the fifth executive of the state. Federalist ascendency in all branches of the government was now complete.[26]

Although the Antis had been soundly whipped, defeat was a word not in their vocabulary. Five days after the election an Antifederalist meeting in Baltimore declared that the electoral count in the city was incorrect since Federalists had resorted to violence, intimidation, and fraud to overcome the true political sentiments of the people.[27] A petition was thereupon presented to the legislature praying that the election be declared void. Aside from charges of outright force, it accused one of the Federalist candidates of subscribing a large sum of money to the party's campaign fund in order to insure his election. On November 6 the House decided by a vote of 31 to 24 to read the petition for a second time the following week, and at the same time gave notice that the parties concerned should call witnesses in their behalf.[28] The Antis concentrated most of their attack upon McHenry and Coulter, and when the latter agreed to bear the expenses of a hearing, their opponents published a broadside charging that the money was really coming

---

26. Steiner, *James McHenry*, pp. 114ff; Delaplaine, *Thomas Johnson,* pp. 460–61; *Votes and Proceedings,* November Session, 1788, House of Delegates and Senate.
27. *Maryland Journal,* October 14, 1788.
28. By the much narrower margin of 29 to 26 it was also determined that the contestants need not specify with certainty and under specific heads the particular facts they meant to prove in support of the various charges.

from a slush fund subscribed by "Tories" who had recently emigrated from Great Britain and who were not yet citizens.[29]

The hearings began on November 14 and continued until the 21st. They were then postponed until the 25th, and appear to have been dropped altogether after that time. In December the delegates voted that the costs, amounting to sixty-one pounds, should be paid by the respective parties involved.[30] Just why the Antis accepted stalemate at this juncture is not clear, but aside from the fact that the Federalists dominated the House and thus controlled the proceedings to their advantage, it seems probable that everyone's attention had now turned toward the more important issue of the first national elections. In this respect the Antifederalists were to fare no better than before.

Having disposed of the machinations devised by Chase and his party, the General Assembly devoted itself to the consideration of Maryland's new relations with the federal government. In this respect the most important question to be determined was the method of electing congressmen, for upon the settlement of this issue hung the Federalists' opportunity to wipe out lingering Antifederalist resistance in Anne Arundel, Baltimore, and Harford counties. Thus, when the committee to which the matter had been referred reported that the state be divided into two districts—the western shore to elect four members and the eastern shore two—the Federalist majority for obvious reasons refused to concur. Maryland was instead divided into six districts, with a congressional representative from each. Although candidates had to be residents of the district they were to represent, voters in the state could choose all six (that is, one from each district) by general ticket. By this means Federalists throughout the entire state could throw the combined weight of their votes against the last Anti-

---

29. *Votes and Proceedings*, November Session, 1788, House of Delegates. See also Steiner, *James McHenry*, p. 115.
30. *Ibid.*, November Session, 1788, House of Delegates.

federalist strongholds.[31] Presidential electors, meanwhile, were apportioned in the ratio of five to the western shore and three to the eastern.[32]

On December 3 the House of Delegates resolved to take the oath to support the federal Constitution, following which debate began as to the method of selecting candidates for the United States Senate. The upper house proposed that the senators be elected by a joint ballot of both houses, and that a majority vote of the attending members should determine the choice. After considerable discussion the Delegates agreed upon this method, which was further elucidated on December 9 by a joint resolution declaring that one senator should be a resident of the western shore and the other of the eastern shore. Balloting took place on the same day, Charles Carroll of Carrollton and Uriah Forrest being nominated to represent the western shore, and John Henry and George Gale for the eastern shore. Each candidate received forty-one votes on the first ballot except Carroll, who received forty. On the second ballot Henry received forty-two votes and was chosen, but Carroll and Forrest were tied at forty-one. The legislature then adjourned for the day, and it can be assumed that much politicking was carried on before the two houses reassembled on the 10th. At that time Carroll was elected as Maryland's second senator, receiving forty-two votes to Forrest's thirty-nine. Thus, and not surprisingly, two eminent Federalists had been selected to represent Maryland in the first Senate of the United States.[33] On the 19th the General Assembly voted to

---

31. *Votes and Proceedings,* November Session, 1788, House of Delegates. The 1st district was composed of St. Mary's, Charles, and Calvert counties; the 2nd of Kent, Talbot, Cecil, and Queen Ann's counties; the 3rd of Anne Arundel and Prince George's counties and the town of Annapolis; the 4th of Baltimore and Harford counties and the city of Baltimore; the 5th of Somerset, Dorchester, Worcester, and Caroline counties; and the 6th of Frederick, Washington, and Montgomery counties.
32. *Ibid.*
33. *Votes and Proceedings,* November Session, 1788, Senate and House of Delegates. See also *Laws of Maryland,* 1788, chapter 44. In

petition congress for amendments to the Constitution, and on December 22 it adjourned to prepare for the campaign.[34]

The issues dividing the parties in the first national election were precisely those which dominated the foregoing contests on the state level. If party divisions were intensified at this time, which they generally were, the reason can be found in the importance of the election and in the introduction of party tickets to ensure regularity throughout the state.[35] The Antifederalists again came forth as the defenders of the debtor class against the "aristocratical influence and spirit" so "dangerous to public liberty." Religious persecution, foreign intervention, compulsory military service, outrageous taxes, and the reestablishment of monarchy were but a few of the ominous predictions with which the electorate were overwhelmed by the Antis. While the Federalists avoided being pushed into the defensive by their opponents, they do not appear to have indulged in the orgy of charges and countercharges so characteristic of previous election campaigns. Instead, they quietly asked for another victory to bury both the lies and the liars in the Antis' very own dung-heap.[36]

Although the use of party tickets in the campaign secured a greater degree of cohesiveness on both sides, the new device also created confusion to no small extent. Party alignments were in some instances actually weakened by such discrepancies in the tickets as the listing of a candidate's name on both the Federalist and the Antifederalist slates. William Tilghman, for example, was listed as the choice of both parties for presidential elector from the eastern shore, while

---

drawing for the short and long terms, Carroll drew for two years and Henry for six years.

34. *Votes and Proceedings,* November Session, 1788, Senate and House of Delegates.

35. "The Federal Ticket," "Friends to Amendments," and "No Party" broadsides, dated 1789, M.H.S.

36. *Maryland Gazette* (Annapolis), January 1, 1789. Brown, "Party Battles and Beginnings," p. 50, summarizes the main Antifederalist charges.

Joshua Seney received the same double backing for the position of representative to Congress from the second congressional district. Moses Rawlings, who found himself placed on the wrong slate for presidential elector from the western shore, hastily wrote to Otho Williams to explain "how I suppose my name came to appear on what is call'd the anti ticket." After placing the blame squarely on the shoulders of the Antifederalist Abraham Faw, whom he accused of purposely tampering with the ticket in order to confuse the voters, Rawlings promised to "remove any bad suspicion that the people may have Taken up" by publishing his correct party affiliation in the public prints.[37] Confusion was also intensified by the distribution of Antifederalist broadsides which differed noticeably in the pairing of candidates with the districts they were supposed to represent.[38]

37. Moses Rawlings to Otho Holland Williams, dated Hagers Town, January 8, 1789. MS in O. H. Williams Papers, Vol. 5, M.H.S. The *Maryland Gazette* (Baltimore), listed the following Federalist and Antifederalist tickets in its December 30, 1788 issue:
    Representatives to Congress:

Federalist		*Antifederalist*
1st Dist.	Michael Jenifer Stone	George Dent
2nd "	Joshua Seney	Joshua Seney
3rd "	Benjamin Contee	John Francis Mercer
4th "	William Smith	Samuel Sterett
5th "	George Gale	William Vans Murray
6th "	Daniel Carroll	Abraham Faw

    Presidential Electors, Western Shore:

Federalist	*Antifederalist*
George Plater	George Thomas
Alexander C. Hanson	Lawrence Oneale
John Rogers	Moses Rawlings
Robert Smith	Charles Ridgely of William
Dr. Philip Thomas	Jeremiah Townley Chase

    Presidential Electors, Eastern Shore:

Federalist	*Antifederalist*
Dr. William Matthews	John Seney
Col. William Richardson	James Shaw
William Tilghman	William Tilghman

38. Broadsides entitled "Friends to Amendments," and "No Party," M.H.S., presented differing slates in an obvious effort to confuse the electorate.

In addition to these devisive tactics by the opposition, the Federalists were weakened internally at this time by developing factionalism within the party itself. Late in September Nathaniel Ramsey offered his services to the Federalists "as a deligate [*sic*] in the new Congress,"[39] and it appears that his name was duly recorded on the Federal ticket as a candidate for the second district. Two months later, however, Ramsey wrote Otho Williams to complain that his name had been stricken from the slate by the "Committee of the Assembly" in favor of Joshua Seney. Although his friends were prepared to back him despite the committee's decision, and indeed insisted upon his "standing a poll," Ramsey doubted that his supporters were strong enough throughout Maryland to override the ticket agreed upon by the party leaders. Williams being one of the latter, and "on this occasion a much better Judge than I am," Ramsey earnestly sought his advice and promised to abide by it.[40] Seney remained on the Federalist ticket, thus giving an indication of Williams's reply.[41]

The Federalists did not hesitate during the campaign to revive the economic issue of prewar British debts in their effort to discredit the opposition's charges of aristocratic exploitation. Nowhere was the debt question used with more telling effect than in the fourth congressional district, comprehending two (Baltimore and Harford) of the three counties in Maryland most heavily involved in British debt obligations and speculation in confiscated loyalist property. Here, declared a broadside addressed to the "Freemen of Baltimore Town," were to be found those men comprising the "black list" who had opposed the federal government in order to avoid the payment of debts. Their candidate, Samuel Sterett, was backed by none other than Charles Ridgely who, together with

---

39. Nathaniel Ramsey to O. H. Williams, dated September 24, 1788. MS in O. H. Williams Papers, Vol. 4, M.H.S.
40. Same to same, dated December 29, 1788. Williams Papers, Vol. 4, M.H.S.
41. I have found no record of Williams's reply to Ramsey.

Sterett's father, had deposited state paper in the treasury to pay off a combined debt amounting to more than 10,000 pounds sterling. Marylanders were cautioned to think twice before installing a spokesman of the Ridgely machine in the halls of Congress.[42]

As campaigning ended and hustings were opened throughout the state, it appeared certain that the Federalists would be swept into office by large majorities. From Frederick, Richard Pindell recounted to Otho Williams "the pleasing prospect of seeing the Federal Tickett [sic] prevail by a great Majority . . . we are all anxious & have pledged ourselves . . . that every exertion shall be made to bring in Votes & to . . . counteract the Dark & Villainous designs of the Anti's." Pindell went on to relate the activities of "Doct. Cruz," an Antifederalist from Baltimore, who had been circulating "infamous falsehoods against the Federalists" since his arrival in Frederick. Pointing out a favored aspect of Antifederalist political policy, he concluded:

It appears that they wish to raise a Distinction between the Germans & Americans & to create Animosities among us— he made his appearance yesterday evening at Beltzhover's when his designs were soon fathomed, and it was hinted that a Coat of Tar & Feathers would be given him as a reward for his services if he did not quickly make his Escape, which he accordingly did altho it was dark & very Cold.[43]

Heartening as this report was, advance information sent to Otho Williams from Washington county was yet more favor-

---

42. Broadside entitled "To the Freemen of Baltimore Town and the Fourth District," M.H.S. Ridgely was accused of paying a debt amounting to 3,273 pounds sterling with 23 pounds of Maryland state paper. Sterett's father paid 48 pounds paper money on a debt of 6,937 pounds sterling. See also Ridgely Papers, M.H.S.

43. Richard Pindell to Otho Williams, dated January 6, 1789. MS in Williams Papers, Vol. 5, M.H.S. Pindell added that he was also writing to the "big Captains" in his vicinity to request their exertions in bringing out the vote.

able to the Federal cause. Writing from this westernmost area of Maryland, John Stull related that "our powls [sic] stand in this manner, 809 on the Federal ticket and not a man has Even opened his jaws on the other side. . . . I thinck [sic] before 12 o'clock this knight [sic] we Shall Get at Least 3 or 4 hundred more which will make our number 1000 or 1200."[44] Williams's delighted remark that "our victory is compleat," scratched at the bottom of Stull's letter, was not proven rash in the light of his correspondent's final report two days afterward. "Eleven hundred & Sixty Seven with federal tickets not a man with any other sort not a singel [sic] anti," exultantly proclaimed Stull in language both spontaneous and crude. The Antis did not fail from lack of trying, however. Several days after his hasty departure from Frederick, Pindell's "Doct. Cruz" hopefully wended his way into Washington county to repeat those tactics—with the same degree of success—that he had tried to initiate in other parts of the state. With tongue in cheek, Stull chastised Williams over the appearance of the luckless Antifederalist. "If ever you send any more Baltimorans [sic] here to Dicktate and breed Contension a munckst the Good people of W County thay [sic] will not be so gently handeled [sic] as Cruse was," he warned. "I was the only man saved his ticket but I suppose he will Give me no Credet [sic]. But Credet from such a feller as him is not Desired by me Know [sic] Sir."[45]

It would have taken much more than Stull's meager efforts to save the Antis' ticket, however, for as the county returns were made known it was clear that the Federalists had won a sweeping victory throughout Maryland. The greatest majorities were secured in Washington, Montgomery, Caroline, Cecil, Dorchester, Frederick, and Somerset counties—areas de-

44. John Stull to O. H. Williams, dated January 9, 1789. MS in Williams Papers, Vol. 5, M.H.S. "15 Light boys" were being sent out "to scower the County" and bring in the vote. Williamsport sent "150 men in one body" to vote the Federal ticket.
45. Stull to Williams, dated January 11, 1789. MS in Williams Papers, Vol. 5, M.H.S.

pendent upon the exportation of wheat, domestic and foreign markets, and interior commercial development.[46] In addition to the election of all six congressional representatives, the Federalists also carried the eight presidential electors allotted to Maryland. When the latter group met to ballot, the state's votes were cast unanimously for George Washington for President and Chief Justice Robert Hanson Harrison for Vice-President, each man receiving eight votes.[47]

A deceptive calm settled over the new nation as the great experiment got under way. Washington's popularity,[48] together with the gradual return of prosperity, created a favorable atmosphere which tended to reconcile many Antifederalists to the new government.[49] All of the Southern states except Vir-

---

46. *Maryland Journal,* January 13, 1789. See also Scharf, *Maryland,* 2:550.

47. Scharf, *Maryland,* 2:549.

48. Washington's candidacy for President was being urged by such Maryland friends as Thomas Johnson and Otho Williams throughout 1788. He certainly stood at the head of the Federalists in Maryland. See Delaplaine, *Thomas Johnson,* pp. 460–62, and Otho Williams to Col. David Humphries, dated April 5, 1789, in Vol. 5, Williams Papers, M.H.S. In this letter Williams discusses "the universal wish and demand that G. Washington shall be the Prest. of the new Govt."

49. On December 22, 1789, for instance, Washington tendered William Paca a temporary appointment as United States Judge for the district of Maryland. A permanent appointment confirmed by the Senate followed on February 13, 1790. See George Washington to William Paca, dated February 13, 1790, Vertical File, Nos. 39–41, MS at M.H.S. Samuel Chase also made his peace with the Federalists during the Washington administrations. In 1790 Alexander C. Hanson anointed the renegade Chase by declaring that "he has been the mover of almost everything this state has to boast of. . . . Without him how very seldom would anything good have passed the legislature. . . . I have viewed him with admiration and with . . . kindness." MS notes by A. C. Hanson on the activities of Samuel Chase, in Samuel Chase Letters, M.H.S. Dated July 25, 1790. Chase's supposed belief in political democracy, always rather doubtful, was questioned by William Wirt as early as 1810. In a letter from Wirt to Chase, dated Richmond, January 18, 1810, Wirt discussed the latter's opinion toward Patrick Henry, which was clearly not favorable. See William Wirt Letterbooks, 1806–1816, MSS at M.H.S.

ginia[50] sent Federalist majorities to Congress, thus apparently deciding sectional differences over the Constitution. In Maryland, however, the political consequences of the constitutional settlement were both ironic and unusual. While defeat at the polls certainly weakened the Antifederalist's *raison d'être*, throwing that party into a period of decline, Federalist success destroyed any unity which had existed in the state. Hereafter, division within the Federalist ranks took place on almost every issue. But while most of these disagreements only weakened their political solidarity, one—the location of the federal capital —rocked the emergent Federalist party structure to its very foundations and resulted in the creation of two factions which struggled during the ensuing years for political control of the state.

Splits within the Federalist camp occurred almost at once over Alexander Hamilton's financial program. As Secretary of the Treasury, Hamilton placed the reestablishment of the country's economic stature both at home and abroad in the forefront of a more grandiose political program upon which the present and future stability of the new nation would rest. His aim, generally, was to win the undeviating support of the country's creditors and upper class by measures designed to promote their confidence in the government by offering them a rather large stake in its success. The program rested on three comprehensive but highly controversial policies which bore the stamp of fiscal probity if not outright genius—funding of the foreign and domestic debt at par, assumption of state debts incurred during the Revolution, and the creation of a national bank along the lines of the Bank of England. A fourth policy called for the enactment of protective tariffs, an issue on which Hamilton was somewhat less adamant. Enmeshed and entwined in the entire scheme—at once a part of it and yet distinctly separate—lay the thorny and emotion-charged issue of

---

50. *Annals of Congress*, 1st Congress, 1st Session, p. 381. Richard Henry Lee and William Grayson, Senators from Virginia, were both Antifederalists.

the permanent location of the new federal government. Clearly recognizing this potent factor, Hamilton used the issue as a political lever to award his supporters the economic balance of power.

Maryland's delegates in Congress disagreed at the outset on each of the proposals which lay at the heart of Hamilton's well-integrated program. In the House of Representatives, Michael Stone, William Smith, and Joshua Seney threw their support to James Madison, Representative from Virginia and leader of the opposition against Hamilton's sound but "unjust" fiscal measures. George Gale and Daniel Carroll, on the other hand, were generally in favor of the program, although Carroll almost bolted over the question of assumption. Likewise, the administration could usually count on the support of Maryland's delegates to the Senate, John Henry and Charles Carroll of Carrollton.[51]

Stone voiced the objections of his fellow Marylanders to the funding plan when debate on that bill began in the House, declaring that it would give the nation a "capacity to run into debt with the utmost facility."[52] He was supported by Fisher Ames of Massachusetts, who held the bill to be an arbitrary act of power which would destroy the essential rights of the people and eventually terminate in a dissolution of the social compact.[53] Opinion within Maryland, however, was not nearly so negative as that expressed by Stone. As early as 1789, Elie Williams, brother of the Baltimore Federalist leader, Otho Williams, had written to Alexander Hamilton in support of reviving the public credit. "It is of the greatest consequence," Williams declared, "that our credit should find the support which we endeavour to merit by our exertions. . . . We rely confidently on you for that support which is consistent with public justice, and which your own disposition will be inclined

---

51. *Annals of Congress*, House of Representatives, 1st Congress, 1st Session, p. 1216; and Senate, 1st Congress, 2nd Session, 1:1028.
52. *Annals of Congress*, House of Representatives, p. 1216.
53. *Ibid.*, p. 1195. Ames preferred assumption without funding.

to afford."[54] Several months later a writer signing himself *Public Credit* defended the Funding Act in the public prints. Merchants, he argued, should be pleased with the bill since funding would stimulate industry and commerce and thereby add millions to the capital of the nation. Similarly, landholders and manufacturers should favor the act because funding would instantly "convert forty millions of dollars into circulating medium," and they too would benefit by this plentiful supply of money.[55] The Maryland General Assembly also favored this aspect of Hamilton's plan, and recommended to creditors in the state that they subscribe to the loan authorized by Congress to raise a fund in maintenance of the Act.[56]

But why did a man such as William Smith, staunch Baltimore Federalist representing Maryland's fourth district in Congress, vote against the funding bill? From the voluminous correspondence which he conducted with his son-in-law, Otho Williams, it appears that they—along with other leading Federalists—were extremely interested in the speculative gains to be made by the passage of the act. In January, 1790, Williams was advised by a New York correspondent to purchase "finals" and "indents" at once, for "the most prevailing opinion here is papers will rise still higher . . . before Funding."[57] Although

---

54. Elie Williams to Alexander Hamilton, dated October 10, 1789. MS in O. H. Williams Papers, Vol. 5, M.H.S.
55. *Maryland Journal*, February 16, 1790.
56. Kilty, ed., *Laws of Maryland*, November Session, 1790, p. 29.
57. Kingsmill Davan to O. H. Williams, dated January 17, 1790. MS in O. H. Williams Papers, Vol. 5, M.H.S. Davan added that many expected finals and indents to be funded at 4 per cent interest. According to Ferguson, *The Power of the Purse*, while the funding debate was in progress, "everything connected with securities speculation quivered in suspense. Speculators did not know where to turn. They plunged this way and that, took their money out of one type of security and put it into another. . . . Every man interpreted the course of events according to his own temper. In a spirit of optimism, he could view the delay in funding as a fortuitous opportunity to pick up securities before they rose in value. . . . The situation did not afford a certain basis for judgment—all was conjecture." See pp. 326–28.

Smith also related "that continental securities will rather rise than fall,"[58] he was hesitant to speculate so soon, because "public securities fluctuate . . . and *yet* are governed by public opinion *only*. But I question if it will soon exceed 10/ on the principal, & you had best in the first Instance draw y^r Interest to Jany 1788."[59] A close study of Smith's correspondence throughout 1790, however, reveals that he gradually overcame his reluctance regarding speculation and began to indulge in "this lucrative business"[60] as feverishly as other creditors in the

---

Indents, or certificates of interest, were incorporated by Congress early in 1784 in that part of requisitions levied to service the public debt. The system was pursued to the end of the Confederation. "Ideally," writes Ferguson, "the indents would be retired by taxation within a year and a new series issued to bring the interest another step forward." But, once unleashed on the economy, indents became objects of speculation as they were cheap and plentiful, and "few people expected Congress to fund them on equal terms with the principal." *Power of the Purse,* pp. 223–24; 269–70. Finals, or final settlement certificates, were created by an act of Congress in February, 1782, and at first consisted only of balances due on loan certificates issued to cover war expenses. On loan certificates, finals amounted to over $3,700,000. In 1783 Congress took over the claims of the Continental army, and in the adjustment of army accounts, another $11,000,000 in final settlement certificates were issued to the troops. Most of these securities (also known as Pierce's notes) were sold soon after issuance, and came to form the bulk of the large speculative holdings. A third (and last) group of finals was issued by Congress to settle the accounts of officials who had handled public money or property during the war. Consolidated, the three issues of finals comprised the public debt, the principal of which by 1790 was about $27,400,000, and the accumulated interest $13,000,000. Loan certificates, which persisted throughout the Confederation, eventually came to the amount of $11,000,000, and drew the highest market price from speculators. See *Ibid.,* pp. 179–80, 251–53.

58. William Smith to O. H. Williams, dated January 17, 1790. MS in O. H. Williams Papers, Vol. 5, M.H.S.

59. Smith to Williams, dated January 24, 1790. MS in O. H. Williams Papers, Vol. 5, M.H.S.

60. Williams to Dr. Philip Thomas, dated January 26, 1790. MS in O. H. Williams Papers, Vol. 5, M.H.S.

nation.[61] By the very nature of his financial activities during this period Smith was committed to support the public credit, and his defection from Hamilton's program must be sought on grounds other than disaffection with funding of the public debt.[62]

---

61. The change was noticeable as early as January 28, when Smith wrote Williams that "I am inclined to believe . . . a very great majority in this house are favorably disposed to support Public credit." On February 9 Smith happily confided that the House appeared "decidedly in favor of funding the public debt, *Without discrimination.*" Discrimination, which Smith condemned as impractical, formed the main topic in letters written on February 14, 16, 17, and 22, while mention was also made of the likelihood of funding at 6%. On March 11 Smith again reported that perhaps "two thirds of the Principal shall be funded at Six p cent," and on April 11 added that "the value of . . . military . . . Certificates may perhaps in some measure depend on the assⁿ or non assumption of the State Debts." The drop in finals from 11/ to 7/ caused Smith some worry, which he explained (March 21) as being caused by speculators who bought on credit and who are now "obliged to sell to raise the money to comply with their engagements." At any rate, Smith was not pulling out, and on March 28 he advised Williams to buy up continental paper in Baltimore, "if there is still any of it to be purchased it would *perhaps* be a better speculation than *Finals.*" Also, continental loan office certificates were recommended, as they are "liquidated here, by the Congress scale, *none lower than forty for one,*" with "specie registered certificates given in exche." Williams must, however, purchase by the "State scales" if he wished to make large profits. On December 16 Smith reported that "funded 6 p cent certificates *now sell* at 15/ p. Pound. . . . I therefore conclude not to dispose of my Maryᵈ. depreciation certificates." By December 23, with continental securities bringing between 16/ and 20/ in the pound, Smith gleefully wrote that "it won't do to sell *mine* at any price." And on January 31, 1791, he advised Williams to exchange and reexchange their State paper "for that of the U. S. as often as you find it profitable & convenient so to do." O. H. Williams Papers, Vols. 5 and 6, M.H.S.

62. Otho Williams, to whom Smith's letters were written, delayed not an instant in transmitting the news on speculation to his close friend, Dr. Philip Thomas. "Send me your money," he urged on January 26. "I'll make what I can on't. There's no danger of loss." But time was of the essence, since "the opportunity of making great bargains in Speculation upon public paper is almost, if not altogether,

Two factors might account for Smith's change of position. Both are relevant in considering not only the actions of individual Federalists in Maryland—for which purpose Smith's collected letters provide an excellent case study—but also as an explanation of the state's ambivalent attitude toward the Secretary's financial scheme in its coordinate whole. The first factor was the incorporation of the assumption clause into the funding bill. This was no sooner introduced than Smith declared that "I would be glad, *occasionaly* [sic] to hear the Sentiments of my fellow Citizens on the principal points in the Sec^ys. Report. The consolidating of State debts, I apprehend, will not be acceptable."[63] At this stage Smith appeared indecisive and certainly was not willing to commit himself until the political winds had wafted Baltimore's sentiment northward. "I expected at least an outcry," he wrote on February 16. "But I have been hitherto disappointed, not even in the Baltimore papers do I see a single Politician step forth for or against."[64] On February 22, while again seeking some "opinion from our State on this head," Smith discussed for the first time the major reason for his lack of enthusiasm over funding and assumption. Although bitter, it was undeniably valid:

---

over. . . . The holders of certificates . . . will part with them only in cases of necessity. . . . The State *funded* paper long since arrived at its Zenith. The paper of . . . the greatest expectation is the Unfunded Certificates of the United States." On February 23 Williams wrote to assure Thomas that, although speculation was precarious it was still worthwhile, and "if I make any purchases I shall not exceed double the sum you have in my hands and we will jointly abide the issue." O. H. Williams Papers, Vols. 5 and 6, M.H.S.

63. Smith to Williams, dated January 28, 1790. MS in O. H. Williams Papers, Vol. 5, M.H.S.
64. Smith to Williams, dated February 16, 1790. MS in O. H. Williams Papers, Vol. 5, M.H.S. A further plea was made on February 25, when Smith wrote that "the Represent^s. from Maryland are totally in the dark on this subject. . . . I believe however we will be unanimous in the Negative. Virginia will concur with us." O. H. Williams Papers, Vol. 6.

Those Politicians, who prevented the Maryland Assembly from complying With the requisitions of Congress, made in 1787, whereby Indents were made receivable for the respective quotas of each State's *interest* due the U.S. have done an irreparable injury to us. And that finally we will be obliged to make good that deficiency, in Specie. This will give a great advantage to those States who were so Judicious as to comply.[65]

The second factor governing Smith's action on this measure was his disillusionment over the bargain which resulted in the creation of a permanent national capital on the Potomac instead of at Baltimore. But while funding and assumption eventually meshed with Jefferson's desire for a national capital in Virginia, thus producing one of the better-known incidents of

---

65. Smith to Williams, dated February 22, 1790. Vol. 6. In other letters Smith bolstered his main objection to the assumption measure by rather vague reasons, some of which point out his fear that "many members would give up the *whole*, if thwarted in their favorite scheme," and thus wreck the entire funding bill. On February 25 he declared that "my objection to the plan, is that it is very Unexpected in the different States, may alarm their fears, & give rise to groundless apprehensions. . . . Such of the State creditors, who choose to exch^e. their securities for that of the U.S. shall have their debt funded by the U.S. *equally with all other creditors of the U.S.* only no provision is to be made for payment of *their* Interest before 1792. . . . I am convinced the business is premature & am fearfull it will be attended with injurious consequences which a delay might prevent." See also letters of March 9 and 11. On March 14, Smith foresaw "great frauds" if assumption were adopted, and again put his "Curse" on those Maryland politicians who did not comply with the requisitions of 1787. Assumption was once more the topic of criticism in letters dated April 11, 12, 18, and 27, June 15, August 1, in O. H. Williams Papers, Vol. 6, and letter of April 4, 1790 in Robert Gilmor Jr. Papers, Vol. 3, Division III, at M.H.S. In the latter letter Smith rejoiced that the friends of assumption "seem afraid to let it come forward, & have by various means hitherto prevented a decision. I believe they begin to despair of success. . . ."

backstage negotiations in American politics, each had its separate impact upon Maryland politics.[66]

Smith's opinion on the assumption clause was generally shared in Maryland, but there were important exceptions which tended to divide the Federalists both at home and in Congress. Maryland had taken action on assumption of the public debt as early as 1782, though on a lesser scale. Its citizens were invited to exchange their securities for state notes bearing 6 percent interest, the state government thereby assuming over $200,000 in this way. This assumption, however, had been confined to loan certificates issued in Maryland and currently owned by its citizens. While the state stood to lose should federal assumption take place, its loss would neverthe-

---

66. There might also have been a third factor in regard to Smith's conduct, pertaining to the individual himself. This was his thorough disgust, as expressed in a letter to Williams on June 15, 1790, with the low interest provided on the funded principal. "The Senate," he wrote, "has this day passed a Bill, *14 to 12*, for assuming the State debts. . . . That house has also changed the face of our funding Bill, by striking out all the alternatives, & giving 4 p cent interest *only*." O. H. Williams Papers, Vol. 6. Hamilton's decision to fund at 4 per cent, according to Ferguson, "was not distinctly favorable to the creditors, some of whom may have purchased securities at as high as 50c on the dollar." The Senate "also disapproved of funding indents or interest on equal terms with the principal, that is, at 4 percent; the Senate bill put indents at 3 percent. In subsequent negotiations the House attempted to restore 4 percent on indents, but the final act followed the Senate bill in this as well as other major details." But while public creditors complained over this aspect of Hamilton's bill, they were "much more in earnest in objecting to the assumption of state debts. . . . The majority . . . would doubtless have preferred that the government commit its revenues to the public debt and let the state debts alone. . . . They were well aware that the reduction of interest was linked with the assumption, which they denounced as rash, adventurous, and unconstitutional. The additional load of the state debts might prove too much to handle and bring on a general default in interest payment which would impair the value of all securities." Ferguson, *The Power of the Purse*, pp. 326, 296–97, 304. See also letter from "A Republican Citizen," in *Maryland Journal*, March 23, 1790.

less be considerably smaller than that of New York or Virginia.[67]

Maryland's midway position in the line-up over assumption was clearly reflected by the various stands taken among the Federalists. Otho Williams declared that he did "not admire so much the *perfection* of the plan before Congress, as . . . the Capacity of the Author of it—His talents are unquestionably of the first rate." Although assumption was somewhat objectionable to Williams, the dose was a mild one so long as "creditors . . . find their claims." He concluded:

It is the same thing to Maryland whether her debt be paid to A.B.C. or to Congress. . . . Would not the opportunity of making U.S. debtor for the debt contracted in Holland, counterbalance any probable disadvantage to this State? . . . Governments may be so circumstanced as to make a departure from the established maxims of justice and morality not only expedient, but indispensably necessary. . . . While I anticipate, with delight, the resplendent figure which our Country is to make in the group of Nations, I am not unwilling to overlook the few inconveniencies that must, unavoidably, attend the measures necessary to the glorious effect.[68]

But Philip Thomas, to whom the foregoing thoughts were offered, did not share in Williams's admiration for either Hamil-

---

67. *Votes and Proceedings,* House of Delegates, November Session, 1782, 1787, and 1790. See also *Address of the Maryland House of Delegates to their Constituents,* 1787, in Broadside Collection, Portfolio 28, No. 24, Rare Books Division, Library of Congress. By 1790 Maryland's holdings, through later investments, amounted to $661,000.

68. Otho Williams to Dr. Philip Thomas, dated February 12, 1790. MS in O. H. Williams Papers, Vol. 5, M.H.S. The debt contracted between Maryland and Holland, known as Vanstaphorst's debt, was the subject of a letter from Smith to Williams on January 28, 1790. To Smith, payment of this debt was the only benefit Maryland would gain by assumption.

ton or his plan,[69] finding rather that "the plan of the Secretary was not consistent with his professed principles."[70] At Smith's urging, however, both men committed their opinions to print in hopes of stimulating further comments which would acquaint the congressman with sentiment in Maryland.[71] Williams's piece eventually appeared in the New York Daily Gazette,[72] while Thomas's critical, "copious . . . closely reasoned" essay drew a spirited response from Charles Carroll of Carrollton.[73] Carroll, author of the Senate's Assumption bill, naturally supported the measure in Congress and in the press.

Federalist division over funding and assumption, argued in press and post, was even more noticeable in the legislative halls of Annapolis and New York. On December 16, 1790, three resolutions condemning the assumption clause were introduced in the House of Delegates. The first resolution de-

---

69. Although Williams begged Thomas, on February 12, to "look back—for a moment reflect on the irreparable injustice suffered by the most meritorious class of public creditors from the imperfections of the Union," his own opinion changed when it appeared likely that assumption might drive down the funded principal from 6 percent to 4 percent. On April 8, 1790, he wrote Thomas that "I am pleased to find . . . the Secretary's plan is attacked and reprobated by . . . some . . . sensible writers who concur in sentiment with the Republican Citizen, whom I have not yet seen in the prints. . . . There is a hope that the friends to the adoption of the State debts by the U. States will not succeed in that measure." O. H. Williams Papers, Vol. 6, M.H.S. "A Republican Citizen" had demanded sincerity and justice to creditors at 6 percent, and no assumption. The former preserved sanctity of contract while the latter was unconstitutional. Maryland Journal, March 23, 1790.

70. Cited by Williams in a letter to Thomas, dated March 17, 1790. MS in O. H. Williams Papers, Vol. 6, M.H.S.

71. Williams to Thomas, dated March 17, 1790. MS in O. H. Williams Papers, Vol. 6, M.H.S.

72. Same to Same, March 17, 1790. See also Smith to Williams, dated March 7, 1790. Smith was quite surprised that his son-in-law did "not touch on . . . the assumption of the state debts."

73. Williams to Thomas, dated April 18, 1790. Here Williams stated that Carroll's article "contradicted you pre-emptorily," since his sentiments "were in part opposite to yours." O. H. Williams Papers, Vol. 6, M.H.S.

clared assumption to be "a measure dangerous in its consequences to the governments of the several States," the second held it "particularly injurious to this State," while the third resolution formally proclaimed the measure "Unconstitutional." The first and second resolutions were adopted by a narrow margin which clearly reflected a major party split. The third resolve failed of passage altogether.[74] A week later, however, another resolution was introduced rescinding the two condemnatory resolutions. This resulted in a tie vote of 26–26, which was broken when Speaker of the House, George Dent, decided in favor of repealing the former resolves.[75] The change of heart on the part of the Delegates cannot be easily explained, debate not being recorded in the proceedings of the legislature. Nor do the Maryland newspapers illuminate the reason for the inconstancy of the House. Although "Inquisitive" demanded a satisfactory explanation in the public prints, it appears that he got none. His assertion that it was unconstitutional for the legislature to pass and rescind resolves during the same session only provoked a legal controversy over procedure, but there was no elucidation as to intent.[76] Another correspondent made known his apprehension that the states would be reduced to a position of servile dependency should they be forbidden from contracting debts without the consent of Congress. This, he declared, was the real significance of assumption.[77]

There were those speculators in Maryland, however, who stood to profit handsomely by both the funding and assumption provisions in Hamilton's scheme, and herein may lie the answers so vainly sought in the press. As public securities had become scarcer and more expensive, state debts had correspondingly emerged as the only remaining low values that

74. *Votes and Proceedings,* House of Delegates, November Session, 1790. The first resolution passed the House by a vote of 32–26, and the second passed by 30–28.
75. *Ibid.*
76. *Maryland Journal,* January 8, 1791.
77. *Ibid.*

promised sensational profits. By 1790, $900,000 in both public securities and unassumed state debts was held by Maryland speculators who had ranged outside of their own state in quest of the now certainly lucrative state securities. Assumption by Maryland, moreover, had never been complete.[78] Of this $900,000, over half was owned by sixteen individuals, while 11 percent of the total was held by the politically prominent firm of Benjamin Stoddert and Uriah Forrest. The influence of such speculators as a factor in the legislature's swift reversal of position on the assumption clause—albeit this position was rather extreme for Maryland in the first place—must certainly be taken into consideration.[79]

In Congress, Michael Jenifer Stone stood forth as the most vociferous opponent of assumption from Maryland. In addition to questioning the constitutional validity of the measure, Stone voiced his fear that assumption would result in an autocratic, "impregnable" national government which, by paying all the debts, would gain complete control over the revenue and hence unlimited power over the states. The latter, he concluded, would dwindle in usefulness while the various legislatures, unable to attract men of ability, would become mere debating societies concerned only with trivia. As the states were reduced to puppetry the federal government would grow correspondingly stronger, until there would be no doubt "whether a confederated government remains, when the General Government possesses the power of the purse."[80]

---

78. As indicated, it had been confined to loan certificates issued in Maryland and currently owned by its citizens. See *Votes and Proceedings,* House of Delegates, November Sessions, 1782, 1787, and 1790.

79. Ferguson, *The Power of the Purse,* pp. 270–77. The author points out that of the $900,000 held in Maryland, almost none of it was in original holdings. "The rate of transfer for the entire debt subscribed in Maryland was 81 percent." Also, 63 percent of loan certificates had been transferred, 82 percent of the army certificates, and 95 percent of the indents.

80. *Annals of Congress,* 1st Congress, 1st Session, pp. 1365, 1375. Stone admitted that the assumption measure was "convenient," but

On April 12 the opponents of assumption in the House of Representatives were at last successful in deleting that clause from the funding bill by the vote of 31 to 29.[81] But, as William Smith reported, the members "were so equally divided on this question that one vote more in favor of the proposition would have carried it."[82] Further attempts, notably on April 18 and 27, were made to reintroduce the measure as an amendment to other propositions, but the majority against it remained solid and a funding bill without assumption was finally completed and sent to the Senate. All but one of Maryland's representatives voted with the majority at this time. Daniel Carroll, struck by the opposition to the measure, temporarily abandoned assumption and sided with its opponents. This left only George Gale as the lone delegate from Maryland in sympathy with the controversial clause.[83]

The funding bill reached the Senate at the same time that a bill to establish the residence of Congress came up for consideration, thereby setting the stage for a behind-the-scenes compromise. Here, too, the delegates from Maryland were divided. John Henry, formerly a supporter of Hamilton's financial program, turned against the assumption plan in disgust over the intrigues taking place between the opportunistic Secretary and the equally ambitious delegates from Virginia. He complained to Pennsylvania Senator William Maclay that Charles Carroll of Carrollton, chairman of the committee on assumption and author of the bill in the Senate, had secured

---

"for a people who have parted with their liberty the most convenient government is an arbitrary one." His final objections to assumption were set forth in a speech made on February 26, 1790. See Ibid., pp. 1415–16.

81. Annals of Congress, 2:1480, 1513, 1525–26.
82. Smith to Williams, dated April 12, 1790. MS in O. H. Williams Papers, Vol. 6, M.H.S.
83. Same to Same, dated April 18 and 27, 1790. O. H. Williams Papers, Vol. 6. See also Annals of Congress, 2:1544–46, 1588–90, and 1629. Carroll's change was based on his fear that continued debate over assumption might well result in the defeat of funding also. See Ibid., 1396, 1409–10, 1478.

unanimous approval of the measure by writing in the votes of the committee's seven members before they even met. Henry's sad conclusion that "all great governments resolve themselves into cabals," brought a rejoinder from the equally irritated Maclay, who noted that "we did not need this demonstration to prove . . . the whole business was prearranged."[84]

Nevertheless, whether a seamy bargain or just practical politics, once the required votes were secured, assumption passed the Senate on June 15 by the narrow margin of 14 to 12.[85] A month later, on July 26, the measure went through the House after having been made somewhat more palatable by lopping off $3,500,000 from the estimated $25,000,000 in state debts which Hamilton proposed taking over.[86] The majority of Maryland's representatives continued to vote in the negative, their antipathy against assumption in general now being augmented by bitter disappointment at the selection of the Potomac site as the permanent capital. For the same reason, Daniel Carroll again switched his vote to favor the assumption clause. He was one of four men who owned the property to be used for the capital, and it was thus in his interest to approve the bargain. For this ultimate loyalty, Washington appointed Carroll one of the commissioners to lay off "The Territory of Columbia." George Gale, a steadfast supporter of Hamilton's measures from beginning to end, was similarly rewarded by appointment to the lucrative government position of Collector of Internal Revenue for the state of Maryland.[87]

84. *Annals of Congress*, 2:1055. E. S. Maclay, ed., *The Journal of William Maclay* (New York: Albert & Charles Boni, 1927), pp. 319–28.
85. Smith to Williams, dated June 15, 1790. MS in O. H. Williams Papers, Vol. 6, M.H.S. Virginia Senators Alexander White and Richard Bland Lee were induced to change their vote, thereby purchasing the permanent capital for their state. See Ferguson, *The Power of the Purse*, pp. 319–21.
86. Ferguson, *The Power of the Purse*, p. 321. See also Smith to Williams, dated August 1, 1790. MS in O. H. Williams Papers, Vol. 6, M.H.S.
87. *Annals of Congress*, 2:1755. See also Smith to Williams, dated January 24, 1791. MS in O. H. Williams Papers, Vol. 6, M.H.S.

On August 1 William Smith wrote his son-in-law of the settlement, informing him that "assumption, tis said, is given in consequence of a bargain for the temporary & permanent residence, which produced a coalition of two or three different parties, & *interests*." This would seem to indicate that Smith, at least, was among the unenlightened, but if so it is hard to believe.[88] The Maryland delegation in Congress was certainly aware of the negotiations taking place, for they had been among the most insistent in pressing the claims of their state as the ideal site for the nation's capital.

These claims were put forward, with no small expectation of success, on the basis of Maryland's central geographic position. Annapolis, Georgetown, and Baltimore had at various times been proposed, but of the three cities, Baltimore was most determined to wear the crown. As early as 1788, Otho Holland Williams was dispatching letters to Congress asking, "is there not some thing evidently partial and inimical to the genl. interest, in the wish to fix the new Govt. at New York?" If, perchance, Baltimore must be sacrificed, then "ultimately some spot on Potowmac [*sic*] must be determined upon, as the seat of Continental Government, *where* Virginia and Maryland may unite in a cession of territory." At least this would place the capital within a day's post of Baltimore and Annapolis.[89] It was not until 1789, however, that concerted efforts took place among Baltimore merchants and politicians to locate the national capital in the South's fastest growing city. In February a provisional loan was subscribed to erect a building in which Congress might meet, together with "other proper buildings for the great offices of the United States."[90] Hopes of securing Washington's sympathy, if not his outright support,

---

See also Charles A. Beard, *Economic Origins of Jeffersonian Democracy* (New York: The Macmillan Company, 1915), p. 178.
88. Smith to Williams, dated August 1, 1790. MS in O. H. Williams Papers, Vol. 6, M.H.S.
89. O. H. Williams to David Ross, Congress, dated September 1, 1788. MS in O. H. Williams Papers, Vol. 6, M.H.S.
90. *Maryland Journal*, February 10, 1789.

for Baltimore's candidacy doubtless formed part of the motive behind Otho Williams's request that the new president "take this place in his route to Congress and . . . remain a day here."[91] No opportunities were to remain unassailed.[92]

From Congress, meanwhile, William Smith penned reports of the active logrolling which had begun taking place almost at once. While the House of Representatives was "still busy organizing," he informed Williams that "I have reason to believe . . . it is in contemplation by the Pennsilvanians [sic] immediately after the President is Announced to make a motion to adjourn to Phila . . . & proceed to business." Smith found his fellow legislators "much disatisfied" [sic] with New York, for "boarding is very high & by no means so good as at Phila. or Baltimore, nor do I think this the proper place for the permanent residence of Congress on many accounts."[93] Four months later, while writing that "from every information I have been able to collect, Potomack bids fairest for the preference of the Permanent seat of Congress,"[94] he concluded:

If Maryland & Virginia could Unite on a spot, I think it more probable, they would succeed than any other connection, because it is more the interest of the U.S. that some place between the Susquehanah & Potomack should be the spot, than Any other, *the Western country being taken into the Account.* Fort Cumberland, & the mouth of Canogocheague are seriously talked of by many, Harrisburg,

91. Williams to Col. David Humphries, dated April 5, 1789. MS in O. H. Williams Papers, Vol. 5, M.H.S.
92. Williams to Philip Thomas, dated April 8, 1789. MS in O. H. Williams Papers, Vol. 5, M.H.S. Williams remarked that "we anticipate *muttering* and *censure* for assuming to speak for the town."
93. Smith to Williams, dated April 6, 1789. MS in O. H. Williams Papers, Vol. 5, M.H.S.
94. Smith to Williams, dated August 17, 1789, Vol. 5. See also Smith's letter of August 3, which describes the dickering between New York, Philadelphia, Trenton, Susquehanna, and the Potomac (Virginia) interests. Smith was certain the Pennsylvanians preferred even New York "to any other place South of their metropolis."

Wright's Ferry, & Havre de Grace by others; Baltimore, Annapolis, & Geo. Town are spoke of, but have not many friends.[95]

Although Smith clearly favored Baltimore for either the temporary or permanent location, he was not unwilling to bargain so long as Maryland came out on top. Besides plumping for his own city, therefore, he also supported a site on the Susquehanna, for "if the seat of Congress is fixed on that river, the navigation will be cleared to its source & pour into the Chesapeake an immense wealth & consequently Maryland will become the emporium of America." If, on the other hand, a site on the Potomac should be selected, "Virginia will be the gainer."[96] Eastern Shore delegate Joshua Seney likewise favored the Susquehanna location,[97] but the other Maryland representatives were divided on the issue. Debate over the merits of the Susquehanna continued on an up-and-down, now-yes-and-now-no basis, until the close of the session at the end of September.[98] Shortly before Congress adjourned, the House

95. Same to Same, dated August 23, 1789, Vol. 5. In this letter Smith reports on the rumor that New York and Pennsylvania had compromised on Trenton as the permanent seat in exchange for a nine-year tenure by New York, but he felt that this bargain would "end in smoke."

96. Smith to Williams, dated August 31, 1789. MS in O. H. Williams Papers, Vol. 5, M.H.S.

97. *Annals of Congress*, 1:880.

98. Smith's letters to Williams contain a wealth of material on this subject. On September 4, 1789, he wrote with mounting hopes that a majority of the House was in favor of the Susquehanna location, but that he would hold out "for the West side of the river, which I think will be material for Baltimore." Opinion in the Senate, however, was still uncertain. Smith's hopes were borne out on the 7th, when he reported that after three days of debate the Susquehanna was finally "agreed to in a committee of the whole house, about 33 for Susqh. & 21 for Potomac," but the eastern states were determined not to go further than the eastern bank of the river. A note of dejection appeared on the 14th: "I am not sure but it will end in wind for the present session," for the Pennsylvania members took alarm at an anmendment offered providing for navigation of the river "being opened to Chesapeake." Indeed, Smith

adopted the site by a vote of 31 to 17. The measure then went
to the Senate where, in Smith's words,

> the bill was warmly debated . . . and on a motion made to
> Strike out Susquehana. & insert Germantown, that house
> was equally divided, when the Vice President decided in
> favor of German town. The consequence, I expect, will be
> the loss of the bill in our house, although . . . there is such
> jobbing & bargaining on this subject, that it is impossible to
> say what will be the vote of tomorrow.[99]

His prediction was correct. As soon as Congress reconvened
in January, 1790, a joint committee of both houses reported
that "all the business . . . was done away, & must be taken
up de novo."[100] While this was certainly no victory for Maryland, it was a mortal blow for the Pennsylvanians.[101]

declared, they "would rather lose the bill than consent thereto."
He believed at this juncture that a coalition in favor of Delaware
would be formed, "for Potomack has no chance. The Philadelphians
are not quite satisfied with Susquehanna, the Virginians much opposed to it & the eastern men luke warm, think they have consented to go too far." Tempers exploded on the 18th when a clause
was introduced obliging Pennsylvania and Maryland "to make such
provision as may be satisfactory to the President of the U.S. for
the removal of the obstructions in the river below the federal
Town. . . . This clause so alarmed the Philadelphians, that they
declared the bill should not pass. If they vote against it, it will
be lost." Smith hoped his son-in-law was by now convinced "that
it is not only the interest of Maryland in genl. but Balt. in Particular . . . that the permanent seat shall be on Susquehannah."
But in any event, he would rather see the location go to the
Potomac interests than give up the clause respecting the navigation of the river, or the creation of the federal town on the
western side of the Susquehanna. By the 21st it appeared that
indecision still reigned, but "the friends to Delaware are not without their hopes, & great interest is still making for that place."
O. H. Williams Papers, Vol. 5, M.H.S.

99. Smith to Williams, dated September 25, 1789. MS in O. H. Williams Papers, Vol. 5, M.H.S.

100. Same to Same, dated January 24, 1790. Vol. 5.

101. The Pennsylvania delegation wished to take advantage of their
favorable position and push the Germantown site through to a

During the ensuing months, however, the House took little action on the matter, so preoccupied were the congressmen with the thorny funding and assumption bill. It was not until May, when Hamilton's program finally made its contentious appearance in the Senate, that the location problem was revived from its dormant state and offered up in exchange for the assumption clause. The effect on at least one Maryland Senator was immediate, for Maclay wrote that "Carroll of Carrollton seemed to be the leading spirit to get the residence of the capital to Baltimore, and when he could not do this he turned and joined Jefferson, Madison, Hamilton, and Washington."[102]

But Baltimore had no intention of giving up so easily. Inhabitants subscribed over 20,000 pounds during May in a frantic two weeks of fund raising to attract the support of congressional politicians.[103] Had more unity existed among Maryland's delegates these exertions might have met with success, for in revealing the selection of Philadelphia as the temporary capital, Smith reported that he had "offered Baltimore as a substitute for that City, which was supported by a respectable Number of friends, but Unfortunately for Poor Baltimore, the representatives from Maryland were divided . . . & so the question was lost."[104] Hard upon this missive, however, came the heartening news that Baltimore was still "spoken of in the Senate for the Permanent seat," offering "a

quick conclusion before the arrival of the majority of the southern representatives. Because "the Southern States were thinly represented," Smith wrote, the Pennsylvanians "could with great ease have fixed on Germantown." Smith to Williams, dated January 24, 1790. MS in O. H. Williams Papers, Vol. 5.

102. Maclay, ed., *Journal of William Maclay*, p. 328.
103. John Thomas Scharf, *The Chronicles of Baltimore* (Baltimore: Turnbull Brothers, 1874), p. 260.
104. Smith to Williams, dated May 31, 1790. MS in O. H. Williams Papers, Vol. 6, M.H.S. Joshua Seney, Smith, and Michael Jenifer Stone voted for Baltimore; Daniel Carroll, Benjamin Contee, and George Gale voted for Philadelphia. After his resolution was lost, Smith, too, voted in favor of Philadelphia.

distant hope that betwixt two great contending rival Cities, something may turn up in our favor."[105] This hope was becoming, of course, more distant each day, and on July 15 Smith painfully acknowledged that "the permanent seat of the government . . . is fixed by law on the Banks of Potomac, *at the mouth of Canogocheague.*" Philadelphia, he added would be the seat of government for the next ten years, "from whence some think it will be extremely difficult, if not impossible to remove it after so long possession."[106]

Once the jockeying was over and the bargain made, Maryland's delegates in Congress hastened to explain themselves to their disappointed fellow Federalists and constituents back home. Seney maintained that their division was merely a reflection of the national confusion, while Stone reasoned that—all loyalty to his own state aside—the best permanent seat for the government was the Potomac.[107] Charles Carroll expanded on this argument, explaining that Baltimore had really gained by the Potomac choice since its chances for winning the honor had always been slim. The many advantages, he pointed out, were obvious:

> Maryland will be greatly benefited by having the permanent seat of the Govt. within its limits; this seat of Govt. of the U.S. will give a consequence and opulence to our State, which will put it on a par with either of its neighbors, and being more compact and more united it will enjoy advantages superior to those of any other State in the Union.

As a matter of fact, Carroll concluded, Baltimore's main contribution had been to act as a lever against those interests

---

105. Same to Same, dated June 4, 1790. MS in Vol. 6. The rival cities were New York and Philadelphia.
106. Smith to Williams, dated July 15, 1790. MS in O. H. Williams Papers, Vol. 6. The underscoring by Smith is important, which is why Williams was "anxious to learn" of the final settlement. Williams owned a rather large amount of land in the area selected for the capital.
107. *Annals of Congress,* 2:785, 1164.

wishing to keep the capital in either New York or Philadelphia.[108]

Smith did not subscribe to these rationalizations, but continued to view the entire affair as a real loss for Maryland. Although "the Federal buildings . . . must be on the Mary^d. side of the Potowmac," he wrote, "if the present Views are accomplished . . . the buildings will be so situated as to give Virginia all the Advantages."[109] His anger at the bargain boiled over in a letter to his son-in-law in which he declared that "almost all men form their opinions by their interest, without always knowing the governing principal [sic] of their motives or actions . . . not that I believe interest had the smallest influence on the Chief magistrate in this decision."[110]

This contempt might very well have been directed at Williams himself, for he—anxious to maintain his position within the new federal government—had already written to Washington with a proposal that the Maryland legislature "pass an act to appropriate to Congress a district of ten miles square within either of the counties bounding on the river potowmack . . . and to condemn and grant to Congress ——— acres of land anywhere within the said district . . . for public edifices, and building a city."[111] At the same time he added that, although not in favor of the government's policy of soliciting "*private* contributions," he would most willingly consent to grant, "without expectation of compensation," as much of his own land in that area as the government deemed necessary for public buildings. Whether due to Williams's influence or not, the state legislature concurred with his proposal and by a vote of 37 to 30 the House of Delegates appropriated $72,000 in three

---

108. Charles Carroll to Mary Caton, dated July 11, 1790. MS in Carroll-McTavish Papers, M.H.S.
109. Smith to Williams, dated January 24, 1791. MS in O. H. Williams Papers, Vol. 6, M.H.S.
110. Same to Same, dated February 3, 1791. MS in Vol. 6.
111. Williams to George Washington, dated November 1, 1790. MS in O. H. Williams Papers, Vol. 6. The blank space concerning the number of acres to be given was in the original manuscript.

annual payments for buildings in the new federal city. Laws were passed ceding land "in full and absolute right, and exclusive jurisdiction," to the federal government, thus bringing to a close the protracted issue of the capital's location.[112] But the effects in Maryland were yet to be felt.

Division within Maryland's Federalist ranks was notable in one other[113] important national measure forming an integral part of Hamilton's program—the establishment of a national bank. In this respect Maryland's attitude reflected that of the South as a whole. Dominated by agricultural interests, the southern states opposed the proposal to charter a Bank of the United States which would inevitably be controlled by the mercantile northeast. In the House, Michael Stone declared that the doctrine of implied powers put forward by the nationalists was an unconstitutional usurpation of power intended to deceive the people. He was supported in this stand by William Smith, Daniel Carroll, George Gale, and Benjamin Contee, but when Stone moved to recommit the bank bill back to committee the motion was defeated by a vote of 23 to 34. On February 8 the bill passed the House, but of the twenty votes cast against it, nineteen were those of Southern members and no Southern state had a majority in its favor. Even Charles Carroll, a strong supporter of administration measures in the Senate, consistently voted against the establishment of a national bank.[114]

Again, the correspondence between William Smith and Otho Williams sheds much light on the reasons for Federalist disunity over a measure which should have generally appealed to their conservative natures. Certainly the majority of Federalists in Maryland were in favor of a strong, financially

---

112. *Votes and Proceedings*, House of Delegates, November Session, 1790.

113. Maryland's delegates were also divided on the lesser issue of a protective tariff, a division especially evident between the members of the Eastern and Western Shores. See Brown, "Party Battles," p. 58.

114. *Annals of Congress*, 1st Congress, 3rd Session, 2:1830–36, 2012.

sound government, but in Hamilton's proposal for a Bank of the United States they saw a direct conflict with their own interests in Maryland itself. This conflict centered around the Bank of Maryland, an institution in which such leading Federalists as William and Samuel Smith, Otho Williams, and Robert Gilmor were directors or important stockholders. William Smith cogently summed up their very real fears when he wrote that "the law for incorporating the subscribers to the National Bank . . . will probably swallow up all the State Banks, & the subscribers to that of Mary^d. may think it their interest to abandon their own, & become subscribers to the other."[115] Although this did not prove to be the case, Federalists in the state remained disquieted, and as late as 1792 Alexander Hamilton found it necessary to reassure Williams that the national bank was a necessary institution which would "lend its aid boldly . . . to the whole system of public Credit and Finance," and that "the Bank of Maryland need not fear in this instance to extend its operations on the score of the establishment of a Branch of the National Bank. . . . My forbearance will . . . render the extension in this instance without danger to them."[116]

In 1789, while on a trip to New York, Williams wrote Dr. Philip Thomas of affairs in Congress, commenting that he "was surprised to find so few divested of State Politics—so very few who considered the general interest or who had comprehensive ideas of Continental Systems."[117] The observation was astute and, of course, correct. But intentionally or not, Williams's criticism applied in large degree to Mary-

---

115. Smith to Williams, dated February 5 and 23, 1791. MSS in O. H. Williams Papers, Vol. 6, M.H.S. See also letter of February 13, 1791.
116. Alexander Hamilton to O. H. Williams, dated March 28, 1792. MS in O. H. Williams Papers, Vol. 7, M.H.S. See also Williams to Hamilton, dated April 5, 1792; and Williams to Philip Thomas, dated May 16, 1793, in Vol. 8.
117. Williams to Thomas, dated June 7, 1789. MS in O. H. Williams Papers, Vol. 5, M.H.S.

land's Federalist politicians both in and out of the government, for by their very division on all of the major proposals of this period they had shown themselves to be not exempt from the charge. Clearly their disunity had been motivated by the immediate dictates of local or even self interest, and the cohesion which might have been provided by common attachment to the Federalist "party," or cause, was almost entirely absent. It was the hope of strengthening Federalist unity and party support throughout Maryland that led the Washington Administration, between 1789–1793, to make generous use of its chief reward—Federal patronage. The extent of its application in the state can be viewed best through Williams's own voluminous correspondence, which during these years served as a clearing-house for information, requests, and appointments between the government and local party affiliates.

The first request for a position under the new government came from Williams himself. Finding his former position as state customs collector now nonexistent, he informed Thomas in June, 1788, that "the main chance will have my most particular attention."[118] Having set his sights upon the post of Collector of the port of Baltimore,[119] Williams thereupon deluged influential politicians with pleas for support. Early in 1789 he asked Henry Lee, Jr., to intercede on his behalf with Senator William Lee of Virginia,[120] and at the same time

118. Williams to Philip Thomas, dated June 25, 1788. MS in O. H. Williams Papers, Vol. 4, M.H.S.
119. Baltimore was at this time the most rapidly growing city in the United States, and was the fifth largest city in the nation in 1790. It was the center for ships which came down the Susquehanna, and from all the shores of Chesapeake Bay. Plans were even made for digging a canal to connect the Chesapeake with Delaware Bay. See *Maryland Gazette* (Baltimore), June 3, 1790, August 25, 1791, November 22, 1792, and September 15, 1796. See also Kilty, *Laws of Maryland,* I, chapter 23, and II, chapters 16, 23, and 68. See also Scharf, *Chronicles of Baltimore,* pp. 209, 277–78, 280–92; and Owens, *Baltimore,* pp. 128–38, 142–44. Also consult Seybert, *Statistical Annals,* pp. 45–47.
120. Williams to Henry Lee, Jr., dated January 3, 1789. MS in O. H.

wrote Robert Morris that he had "had the honor of some small
share in the revolution. . . . The appropriation of my time
in the early part of life, will involve me in a dependence upon
Congress."[121] While awaiting replies from these indirect feel-
ers, Williams in turn received a request from William Jackson
for aid in securing the post of secretary of the Senate.[122] To
this he responded that "we must render what mutual services
may be within our power. You know that I mean to be at
the head of the Customs in Mary. The new system of Gover.
cancels my office under the State, and I *must* be provided
for."[123] But when letters to Senators James Gunn[124] and John
Henry[125] produced nothing in the way of tangible results,
Williams at length took the bull by the horns and wrote
Washington himself. "I rest my hopes," he persisted, "upon
my experience and knowledge of the business; and upon a
character for assiduity and integrity, which, I flatter myself,

---

Williams Papers, Vol. 5, M.H.S. Lee responded on February 17,
1789 (Vol. 5), that "you may rely on my best exertions."

121. Williams to Robert Morris, dated January 3, 1789. MS in O. H.
Williams Papers, Vol. 5. Morris replied on March 1, 1789 (Vol. 5),
but the tone of his letter was not nearly so satisfactory as Lee's.
Morris declared that "I have laid it down as a fixed rule to make
no promises, but to preserve my independence."

122. William Jackson to O. H. Williams, dated January 20, 1789. MS
in O. H. Williams Papers, Vol. 5, M.H.S. Jackson particularly
wanted Williams to use his influence with Senators Charles Carroll
and John Henry.

123. Williams to Jackson, dated February 2, 1789. MS in O. H. Williams
Papers, Vol. 5. Williams reminded his friend that "your confidence
. . . is justly placed, but your opinion of the *weight* of my recommendation may possibly be a little magnified by your partiality
for me." He then asked Jackson to "take opportunities to inculcate
a favorable opinion of me in your Senators."

124. Williams to Senator James Gunn, dated March 4, 1789. MS in O. H.
Williams Papers, Vol. 5. "I am involved in a dependence upon the
Senate and Solicit your favorable attention. . . ."

125. John Henry to Williams, dated March 5, 1789. MS in O. H. Williams
Papers, Vol. 5. Henry promised that it would give him "the highest
satisfaction to contribute in any degree to your Interest or Happiness."

I have been fortunate enough to establish."[126] Such determination could not go unrewarded, and shortly thereafter Williams was appointed to the coveted position.[127]

Encouraged by his own success in securing an appointment under the new government, Williams became actively involved in seeking patronage for other Federalists in the state. Judging from the many memorandums which passed between the Baltimore political leader and the President, it is evident that Washington came to look upon his former companion-in-arms as the best source of discriminating and reliable knowledge respecting the qualifications (and political loyalty) of the numerous applicants for federal posts from Maryland.[128] James McHenry, who had petitioned in vain

---

126. Williams to George Washington, dated April 16, 1789. MS in O. H. Williams Papers, Vol. 5.

127. A Commission from George Washington, President of the United States of America, to Otho Holland Williams, as Collector of the Port of Baltimore in the State of Maryland. Dated August 4, 1789. MS in O. H. Williams Papers, Vol. 5, M.H.S. Before actually receiving his appointment, Williams was given cause for alarm by a series of letters from his father-in-law in Congress. In June Smith informed Williams that the Senate had determined to consider Washington's nominations for office "by Ballot only. This move . . . will afford an opportunity to Cabal, & thwart the president . . . by negativing as many of those nominated as they may choose to set aside, to make room for friends and Dependents." Appointment to office, he concluded, "will probably be made by bargain & sale." In another communication Smith advised that "it may perhaps be usefull, for you to correspond with as many members of the senate as you can with propriety. You may depend, the balloting business is intended to throw into their hands the appointment of officers." Smith accused Col. Richard Henry Lee of being "at the head of this scheme . . . . You are I believe on Such terms with him as to afford . . . corresponding. He is very open to flattery, as is most men." Still later, Smith told Williams to forget about applying for "the secretaryship of the Treasury office," as "you will only be Disatisfied [sic] with the revenue business." See letters from William Smith to O. H. Williams, dated June 8, 15, 17, 18, and 21, and July 10, 1789, in O. H. Williams Papers, Vol. 5, M.H.S.

128. In "A List of Applications for Appointments from the State of Maryland," dated Headquarters, 1789, Washington presented Williams with the names of 14 men together with the offices they desired in

for a diplomatic post in Paris or London, also served in this capacity.[129] Annoyed when Federalists Thomas Johnson, Alexander C. Hanson, and Robert Hanson Harrison turned down appointments for the position of federal district judge, Washington appealed to McHenry and Williams for additional nominees, asserting at the same time that he would not appoint another Maryland judge unless assured of his acceptance beforehand. Williams put forth his friend Robert Smith, "a Gentleman eminently qualified. . . . He is much esteemed as a Gentleman and a Citizen."[130] The President,

---

the federal government. Most of the positions dealt with the customs service, or with appointments as naval officers, federal clerks, judiciary posts, or just "nothing specified." Williams replied in seven memorandums discussing the qualifications of the applicants named. He noted, for instance, that one Robert Young, "a Merchant in the London trade before the War . . . was averse from the plan of the revolution—remained neuter until the peace took place—and then recommenced business." James Kelso had not been "conspicuous" in his patriotism, and had insolently opposed the Constitution of 1787, while Gustavus Scott had "no just pretensions to the office of a Judge under the Government of the United States. As a Citizen, his duplicity and his enmity to the States were notorious . . . ." Others, such as James Lingan, Alexander C. Hanson, and Captain Joshua Barney, received Williams's hearty endorsement. On July 5, 1789, Williams wrote Washington that "the inclosed papers contain the best information that I have been able to collect, and my impartial opinion respecting each of the persons named on your List." On July 14, Williams despatched more evaluations to New York, together with two private memorandums for the President's use. In the meantime, Williams wrote his father-in-law in Congress to take up the promotion of Hanson's appointment for circuit court judge, to which Smith responded that Charles Carroll "will Serve him if he can, & he will probably be consulted on the Appointments to fill the Judiciary." Smith to Williams, July 27, 1789. On August 3 Smith wrote of impending appointments which the President was recommending in conjunction with the Maryland delegates in Congress. See O. H. Williams Papers, Vol. 5, M.H.S.

129. Steiner, *James McHenry*, pp. 123–24, 130–31. There was no question as to McHenry's value to the Federalist party. In fact, he was too valuable, and for this reason neither Hamilton nor Washington felt he could be spared abroad. McHenry instead went into the Maryland Senate in 1791.

130. Williams to Washington, dated October 10, 1789. MS in O. H.

however, was unmoved, and replied that as "the World will look for a character and reputation founded on service and experience, I cannot conceive that the appointment of so young & inexperienced a Man as Mr. Smith would be considered as a judicious choice by the community in general."[131] McHenry sagaciously suggested a foray into the enemy camp by recommending the Antifederalist William Paca, who accepted the post when it was offered.[132] Robert Purviance and Joshua Barney also owed their positions in the new government to McHenry's influence, and it is probable that either he or Williams was responsible for the appointment of Nathaniel Ramsey as United States Marshal, and Richard Potts as United States Attorney for Maryland.[133] On the whole, Federalists in the state could not complain over the bestowal of patronage in which they so liberally shared.

But despite these rewards on the part of the administration, Federalist unity in Maryland was not immediately attained.

Williams Papers, Vol. 5, M.H.S. Williams declared that Smith had been "principally instrumental in composing the political differences in this town in consequence of which the late election here was determined without a contest."

131. Washington to Williams, dated November 22, 1789. MS in O. H. Williams Papers, Vol. 5, M.H.S.

132. Steiner, *James McHenry*, p. 124. McHenry wrote that Paca would "carry much respectability and legal dignity into the office . . . . I believe also that the appointment will be highly gratifying to him and, I think, it may have good political consequences." See also Brown, "Party Battles," p. 70. See also George Washington to William Paca, dated February 13, 1790. MS in Vertical File, Nos. 39–41, M.H.S. In this letter Washington confirmed Paca's appointment, which had originally been a recess appointment made on December 22, 1789.

133. "A List of Applications for Appointments from the State of Maryland," dated Headquarters, 1789. MS in O. H. Williams Papers, Vol. 5, M.H.S. In this, McHenry appealed to the President on behalf of three friends, while in a separate, undated Memorandum (O. H. Williams Papers, Vol. 5), Williams informed Washington that several petitioners for office "have the advantage of so respectable an advocate that I might be silent respecting them." He was clearly referring to McHenry. See also James McHenry to John Henry, dated May 3, 1789. MS in McHenry Papers, M.H.S.

That the results did not measure up to expectations was made strikingly clear in the disappearance of the Federalists and Antifederalists in the congressional elections of 1790, and the rise instead of two new factions containing elements of both.[134] Geographically oriented, the alignments which emerged at this time were not so much engaged in disputes over constitutional principles and national issues as in carrying out a personal feud over the loss of Baltimore as the site of the national capital. Organizing the "Chesapeake Ticket," Baltimore's revenge-seeking politicians temporarily laid aside former differences in concerted determination to punish their own congressmen—Federalists notwithstanding—who had supported the Potomac location. The division was not one of party, but of intrastate loyalty to the growing and highly competitive Chesapeake and Potomac areas.[135]

Indications of the developing estrangement were apparent early in 1789 when Otho Williams first criticized former Governor William Smallwood, organizer and leader of what was to become the "Potomac Ticket." His "low ambition," Williams wrote Dr. Philip Thomas, "to be the idol of Sycophants—and the meanness of his resentments—first taught me the useful Lesson That Enemies, in some sense, are excellent friends."[136] In another missive Williams summed up his own

134. I am greatly indebted to Professor Dorothy Brown of Georgetown University for much information on the 1790 elections. Her dissertation, "Party Battles and Beginnings in Maryland," provides thorough coverage of the Antifederalists in the state, and the treatment of the Chesapeake and Potomac alignments in 1790 is especially detailed.

135. In 1793, for instance, it was expected that imports to the port of Baltimore would average "about 3,500,000 dollars annually," exports "about 2,500,000 dollars annually." Baltimore also claimed 138 vessels totaling 19,100 tons "burthen," which were "employed to foreign ports, and upward of one hundred sail of Sloops and Schooners employed in the coasting trade." See "Estimate of Imports, Exports &c" for Baltimore, 1793, signed by Daniel Delozier. MS in O. H. Williams Papers, Vol. 8, M.H.S.

136. Williams to Thomas, dated March 24, 1789. MS in O. H. Williams Papers, Vol. 5, M.H.S.

opinion of the Potomac faction when he exclaimed that "pity and contempt are indeed all the passions they ought to excite."[137] But while these would have sufficed for Williams,[138] neither silent pity nor passive contempt satisfied the disappointed Chesapeake politicians. Their plans to chastise the Potomac supporters were at length outlined in the public prints by "Marylander." After recalling the tremendous Federalist majority turned in by Washington and Frederick counties in 1789, which had shown that under Maryland's system of voting a few areas acting together could control an entire ticket, the writer observed that "if Baltimore-town and county, Harford and Anne-Arundel move together with the same unanimity . . . they are certainly more numerous, and can effectively show their resentment to such of their servants as are opposed to their interest." Those large counties tied commercially to Chesapeake Bay and the port of Baltimore could then forcibly express their displeasure at the creation of a Potomac capital which might become Maryland's entrepôt for Western trade.[139]

---

137. Same to Same, dated July 29, 1789. MS in Vol. 5. As shown below, Williams meant his remark to be taken literally, for his interests were about equally divided between the two opposing groups.

138. It is difficult to categorize Williams's behavior over the capital-site issue and the ensuing factional division in Maryland. On the one hand he appears to have favored Baltimore, although he stood to gain financially by the selection of the Potomac site because of the lands he owned in that area. At any rate, he settled for the Potomac location rather quickly, and by his actions did not seem dismayed over Baltimore's loss. On the other hand, his party leadership and influence, together with his new position as Collector of the Port of Baltimore, tied him politically and economically to the Chesapeake group, with whom he generally sided. Evidently embarrassed by this duality of interests, however, Williams tended to follow a middle-of-the-road approach, and tried to bring both factions together in compromise. But this policy on his part was somewhat less than successful, merely earning him the distrust of both sides.

139. *Maryland Gazette* (Baltimore), June 25, 1790. Cited in Brown, "Party Battles," p. 64. The Federalist majority in Western Maryland in the elections of 1789 was 1,167 votes. See also Williams to Thomas, dated July 29, 1789. MS in O. H. Williams Papers, Vol. 5, M.H.S.

The resultant contest cast strange political bedfellows together in a rather impetuous alliance, indicating the crucial position which this issue had come to assume. Paper-money advocates Samuel Chase, William Pinkney, and Samuel Sterett now found themselves united in common cause with moderate Federalists Joshua Seney, Robert and Samuel Smith, and William Smith, and such arch-conservatives as Alexander Contee Hanson and Philip B. Key. Hanson, who had formerly looked upon Chase "with horror . . . and detestation," revised his opinion drastically. Indeed, he now disclosed that his old antagonist was the essence of kindness—a man of "good understanding" who filled him "with admiration."[140] A letter signed by these uneasy allies was sent to Eastern Shore leader William Vans Murray begging his "strenuous exertions . . . in favor of the Chesapeak [sic] Ticket," Murray's name being diplomatically included on the slate in hopes of guaranteeing support from his stronghold. The Potomac forces, meanwhile, came forward with an equally incongruous mixture composed for the most part of incumbents who had supported Hamilton's bargain on the location of the capital. This faction, too, appealed to Eastern Shore votes by including James Tilghman on their ticket, while Samuel Sterett, running from the fourth district under Chesapeake auspices, also made an appearance on the Potomac slate as their candidate from the fifth district.[141]

---

140. MS notes written by Alexander C. Hanson, dated July 25, 1790. Samuel Chase Letters, M.H.S.
141. Letter signed by Engelhard Yeiser, Samuel Smith, Robert Smith, Samuel Chase, et. al., to William Vans Murray, dated September 24, 1790. MS in Miscellaneous Collection, M.H.S. See also the *Maryland Gazette* (Baltimore), September 24, 1790, cited in Brown, "Party Battles," p. 65; and the *Maryland Journal*, September 28, 1790. As drawn up by district, the slates were as follows:

Chesapeake Ticket		*Potomac Ticket*
1st. Dist.	Philip Key	Michael Jenifer Stone
2nd. Dist.	Joshua Seney	James Tilghman
3rd. Dist.	William Pinkney	Benjamin Contee
4th. Dist.	Samuel Sterret	George Gale
5th. Dist.	William Vans Murray	Samuel Sterret
6th. Dist.	Upton Sheredine	Daniel Carroll

Balloting was heavy but orderly, and resulted in an over-whelming victory for the Chesapeake alignment. Ninety-nine percent of the electorate in Baltimore turned out at the polls to cast an unprecedented 3,048 votes, only twelve of which supported the Potomac candidates. In Baltimore and Harford counties, over fifty percent of the electorate appeared at the hustings to cast 2,486 and 1,281 votes respectively in favor of the Chesapeake renegades. Although the Potomac-oriented counties in southern and western Maryland balloted in sizable and almost unanimous numbers in support of their geographic interests, inroads were yet made in these areas by the Chesa-peake party,[142] most notably by William Pinkney.[143] Response on the Eastern Shore was generally mixed. Dorchester County, home of William Vans Murray, gave overwhelming support to the Chesapeake ticket, but neighboring Worcester county went just as strongly for the Potomac group. Caroline county, however, gave six hundred votes to Pinkney, who emerged as the second most popular candidate in the election. The honor for first place went to Samuel Sterett who, backed by both sides, pulled in over 16,000 votes.[144]

The success of the Chesapeake rebellion thoroughly

---

142. O. H. Williams to Dr. Philip Thomas, dated October 16, 1790. MS in O. H. Williams Papers, Vol. 6, M.H.S. In this letter, Williams discussed Chesapeake successes in Frederick, Montgomery, and Washington counties, and included the tale that President Wash-ington, "on the 2d day of the Election, had sent an express to Fredk. with the state of the Poll for Balt. town and County," in hopes of spurring the Potomac party to bring out a larger vote. Sam Smith declared this to be "a d——d lie."

143. Pinkney picked up support in Potomac-dominated Calvert, St. Mary's, and Somerset counties. His election as representative of Maryland's third district was later challenged by Governor Howard on the basis of the state's residence requirements, and Pinkney eventually resigned. John Francis Mercer was selected for the vacancy. Henry Wheaton, *Some Account of the Life, Writings, and Speeches of William Pinkney* (New York: E. Bliss and E. White, 1826), pp. 7–8. See also Brown, "Party Battles," p. 66

144. Brown, "Party Battles," p. 66. See also J. R. Pole, "Constitutional Reform and Election Statistics in Maryland, 1790–1812," *Maryland Historical Magazine*, 55 (December, 1960): 277, 285.

alarmed Maryland's county-based, rural oligarchy. Long having wielded almost absolute power in state politics, the conservative Potomac forces were at last experiencing their nightmare realization of future sovereignty resting in the hands of the three mighty Chesapeake Bay counties—Baltimore, Harford, and Anne Arundel. It had been these same counties which had led in the struggle to enact paper-money bills and debtor-relief laws; likewise, the Chesapeake area had been most vociferous in opposing the adoption of the Constitution. Still insecure from these very recent demonstrations of the political potential inherent in the massed suffrage of the common man, the Potomac conservatives again marshalled their forces to destroy the new alignment.[145]

There was only one road left open through which the power of the three Chesapeake counties could be broken. This lay in the General Assembly, a body elected by separate county vote and dominated by Maryland's conservative rural element. Accordingly, on December 19, 1790, the House of Delegates altered the law governing congressional elections so that electors voted only for candidates of their own districts. Both candidates and voters had to be residents of their districts in order to qualify—a stipulation intended to prohibit the all-too-frequent use of migratory voters by opposing factions in tenuous areas, and to prevent the use of popular vote-

---

145. One such conservative, Michael Taney, father of Roger Brooke, did not go along with his fellow Potomac colleagues, however. Later noted for his introduction of a suffrage reform bill in the Maryland legislature, Taney at this time was so outspoken against the choice of Michael Jenifer Stone as the Potomac candidate for the 1st district that a presentment was exhibited against him which resulted in his being fined at the Calvert County Court. Taney wrote on this occasion that "I have not a doubt myself, but my opposition to Mr. Stone's Congress elections, and the freedom with which I gave my sentiments respecting the man, drew on me his utmost resentment, and the first opportunity he had he made use of his power—which has more fully proved to me the judgement I had formed of the man was not founded in error." Michael Taney to Capt. John Kelty, dated October 24, 1791. MS in Taney Papers, M.H.S. For election of 1790, see Scharf, *Maryland*, 2: 572–73.

getters (such as Sterett and Pinkney) in each party's weakest districts.[146] By this change the ballots of Baltimore city and county would all go toward the election of a single congressman, Harford county would be tied with politically conservative Cecil and Kent, while the third member of the Chesapeake hub—Anne Arundel—would be similarly detached and thrown in with the Potomac-dominated area of Prince George and Annapolis. The electoral vote, however, would remain on a statewide basis, and in the event of a tie for Congress or the electoral college, the winning candidate would be chosen by the governor and his council.[147]

Ripped apart at its core, the nascent Chesapeake "party" disappeared. Perhaps no one was happier than Otho Williams, who had regretted the division in the first place and who was now paying the price of the peacemaker in politics. Writing to Thomas, he lamented:

My conduct in the late Election for representatives to Congress has been misconstrued by both parties. While I was writing to the friends of Potomac . . . with a view to prevent, or eradicate, prejudices against the people of Baltimore, those very people were entertaining the most jealous suspicions of my conduct towards them. . . . My INTEREST was no where involved in the contest. My affections certainly were not, for there was not a man in the poll even of my *particular* acquaintance. . . . I yet believe that the Gauntlet was thrown by the junto at Georgetown. . . . You must forgive me, Thomas, for writing so gravely the subject of the late Election. If, like me, you had thought the matter of controversy so little subject to be influenced by either party, and that both were likely to counter act the interest of this State by a conduct exactly correspondent to the Wishes of the Pennsylvanians, you, like me, would have

146. Scharf, *Maryland,* 2: 573.
147. *Ibid.* Five of the presidential electors were to be residents of the Western Shore, and three of the Eastern Shore. See also Brown, "Party Battles," p. 67, especially footnote 1.

blamed both parties. Political contests and political contingencies have learnt me to reject every occasion of difference among my Country men and friends. A little time makes a succession of great men: and a *very little* time makes great men small. Two days ago I put two Dollars, as a Charity, into a hand that signed the Declaration of Independence, 4 July 1776. Providence has chastened a fellow creature of ours; perhaps for his errors—perhaps to teach us humility.[148]

But while the Chesapeake Ticket was not to reemerge in Maryland contests, the political pattern established by the Chesapeake-Potomac division was to linger on indefinitely. Opposition by the minority continued to center in the Bay area as it had throughout the 1780s. While southern and western Maryland remained more firmly attached to Federalism, the northeast registered increasing sympathy with the emergent policies of Jefferson and Madison.

Encouraged by near success in 1790, the geographic alignment of the Chesapeake counties again made its force felt in the elections of 1792. Despite vigorous campaigning against a rather fragmented opposition, the Potomac-led Federalists lost two of the state's eight congressional seats, while a third was later lost when the victor cast his lot in Congress with the Antifederalists.[149] In Maryland's second district, composed of Anne Arundel, Prince George, and Annapolis, opposition candidate John Francis Mercer defeated Federalist John Thomas by over four hundred votes.[150] Antifederalist Gabriel Christie carried the sixth district (Harford, Cecil, and Kent) by eight hundred votes, easily defeating his Potomac-backed rival William Matthews.[151] Western Maryland's traditionally

---

148. Williams to Dr. Philip Thomas, dated October 16, 1790. MS in O. H. Williams Papers, Vol. 6, M.H.S. See also Same to Same, dated September 23, 1790, in Vol. 6.

149. William Smith to Williams, dated October 8, 1792. MS in O. H. Williams Papers, Vol. 7, M.H.S.

150. *Maryland Gazette* (Annapolis), September 20, 1792. See also Steiner, *James McHenry*, pp. 136–38.

151. Brown, "Party Battles," p. 75.

Federalist fourth district, consisting of that part of Frederick county west of the Monocacy River, returned Thomas Sprigg unopposed. A moderate who did not follow Potomac dictates, Sprigg was elected largely on the basis of his personal appeal with the voters. In Congress he soon wandered over to the Jeffersonian camp, a move which many erstwhile Federalists were to make in the next eight years. Potomac leaders were not elated by the results in other districts either. Their candidate for the upper district on the Eastern Shore was defeated, even though a Federalist was returned by the electorate.[152] Ever-doubtful Baltimore returned Samuel Smith, former leader of the Chesapeake Ticket and a moderate who was also beginning to regard Jefferson with admiration.[153] However, this contest was mild in comparison with the bitter fight which took place over Baltimore's seat in the House of Delegates. It was indeed ironic that the Potomac leaders had only Samuel Chase to thank for the victory of Federalist David McMechen, who triumphed by a slim ten votes, "& those," reported William Smith, "not fairly obtained":

---

152. Steiner, *James McHenry*, pp. 133, 136. The Federalist candidate in this district (Queen Anne, Caroline, and Talbot counties) was William Hindman, who accepted the nomination after it had been declined by his brother-in-law, William Perry. The Potomac candidate was James Tilghman.

153. Steiner, *James McHenry*, pp. 137–38. Hamilton was so concerned about Smith's political loyalty that McHenry wrote in his defense: "Samuel Smith is not . . . a friend to a further assumption. He is however a good federalist." Smith's opponent, Charles Ridgely, provides one of the best examples of the political flux of this period. A former Antifederalist, Ridgely held enough of the Maryland debt to warrant his support of "a further assumption." This aspect of Hamilton's program suited his economic position completely, yet Ridgely ran on the anomalous opposition ticket, a factor which makes sense only if one considers the district from which he ran and the difficulty of changing political horses in mid-stream. In October, McHenry wrote Washington that Smith would probably win, though the vote would be small. By the last day of the election only one half of the town and not a fourth of the county had voted. See also William Smith to O. H. Williams, dated August 16, 1792. MS in O. H. Williams Papers, Vol. 7, M.H.S.

Chase tis said Acted in the most arbitrary & Outragious [sic] manner as a Judge of the Election, so glaringly so that a powerful party of the Mechanics, at the close of the Poll had provided a Chair & were determined to hurtle him into it & carry him to the Dock & there leave him to find his way out the best way he could; they were however prevented by some prudent persons.[154]

Even Charles Carroll of Carrollton had become infected by the politics of Jefferson and Madison, an attachment which, though purely temporary, was not overlooked by the Antifederalists in their attempt to divide Maryland's ten electoral votes for president and vice president.[155] Hoping to influence Federalist votes away from John Adams, the opposition suggested Carroll's name for the second spot on the ballot. Carroll immediately announced that he would not serve if elected,[156] and when the electors met on December 5 the state's votes were cast unanimously for Washington and Adams.[157] Although there had been no real challenge to Federalist supremacy in this sphere, it was obvious that only Washington's name at the head of the ticket assured this victory. In all other respects the hold of the Potomac Federalist forces in the state had been considerably weakened by an opposition

---

154. William Smith to Williams, dated October 8, 1792. MS in O. H. Williams Papers, Vol. 7, M.H.S. It does not appear that Chase actually changed his political affiliation in favor of the Potomac Federalists; at least Steiner does not think so. See *James McHenry,* p. 137. Yet it is clear that Chase at this time was also finding his position within the Antifederalist ranks as somewhat of an anomaly, for it certainly did not accord with his basic views respecting the masses, who were vilified as the "rabble" and the "mobocracy," nor was Antifederalism consistent with his changing economic outlook. At heart, Chase was never a democrat, and his entrance into the Federalist ranks during the 1790s put him where he really always belonged. He is again indicative of the political flux and the emerging new alignments of this period.

155. Steiner, *James McHenry,* p. 136.

156. *Maryland Journal,* October 23, 1792.

157. Thomas Sim Lee to Richard Potts, dated December 3, 1792. MS in Potts Papers, 1774–1803, M.H.S.

which had the benefit of neither federal patronage nor national leadership.

The reasons for this upset in Maryland must be sought in the broad, changing nature of American political organization during these early years. The campaign conducted by the now anomalous Antifederalist party is most illustrative in revealing the structural reorientation taking place in the political arena of the nation between 1789 and 1792. For in this contest which saw opposition candidates such as Sprigg triumph largely on the basis of personal popularity alone, the Antifederalists nevertheless effected a complete departure from their previous stand regarding the Constitution. No longer did they come forth as being unalterably opposed to it. Declaring instead their support and friendship toward the new framework of government, they centered their attack on Hamilton's financial policies and the wild speculation which resulted from them. The choice was a sound one, for Marylanders were still suffering from the reverberations of a recent stock panic caused by the fiscal machinations of William Duer and Robert Livingston. As late as April, 1792, Nicholas Low was writing that "stocks have fluctuated so much . . . that it is difficult to quote any price for them to be relied on, but the Failure of Some and other Dealers stopping payment occasions an extreme demand for money during the Pressure, which will probably continue."[158] The opposition candidates were swept into office on the wave of this speculative bust.

Thus, despite the fact that Hamilton's objective was to promote the unity and national power of the United States, his program reshaped both Federalist and Antifederalist policies and led to the creation of two political parties representing the two dominant economic groups in the country: the planting-small farmer interest and the mercantile-financial interest. But successful as it was in the election of 1792, the Antifederalist party in Maryland never reemerged after the cam-

---

158. Nicholas Low to O. H. Williams, dated March 27, 1792, and April 8, 1792. MS in O. H. Williams Papers, Vol. 7, M.H.S.

paign. Henceforth Hamilton's opponents were blended together into an effective new party that was more than just a state of mind.[159] Calling themselves "Republicans," they vigorously denied that their political organization was Antifederalism revived, although they could not deny that it had been largely built on the ruins of the Antifederalists. As Antifederalists, the opposition in Maryland had seriously challenged the power of the conservative Potomac oligarchy; as Republicans, they almost destroyed it.

159. Miller, *The Federalist Era*, pp. 101-3.

4

Emergent Democracy

THE years between 1792 and 1800 witnessed the fruition of party organization and political reorientation which had been steadily yet nebulously taking shape since the adoption of the Constitution. During this period structural cleavages between Federalists and Republicans solidified, and opposing philosophies were deepened and complicated by the force of world-shaking events. Of these events, none had greater impact than the French Revolution and its consequences. As a divisive force in American politics, the upheavals in Europe cut a deeper swath than did the Hamiltonian financial program. Diplomatically, the United States preserved a tenuous neutrality. Politically, Americans could not remain neutral to so momentous a conflict, and in the ensuing line-up each party took ideologically opposite sides. The Republicans came forth as the spokesmen of liberty, agrarian democracy, and the common man. Maintaining a "grass roots" philosophy, the Jeffersonians were easily identified with the ideals of the French Revolution, if not with the excesses by which these ideals were attained. The Federalists represented themselves as the party of law and order, the guardians of the rights of property who had saved the country from "chaos" in 1787 and 1788. The anarchy engulfing France was in their eyes in no way analogous to that earlier struggle which resulted in the creation of the American Republic. Rather, it affirmed their belief that in an unbridled democracy the normal course of events was from disaster to catastrophe. Under the impact of the shattering events of the 1790s the Federalists increasingly looked toward Great Britain's ideal system of "mixed government" as the world's last, best hope for security and order. Their general conservatism was therefore heightened until, as expressed in the arch-conservative Alien and Sedition Acts, the party stood forth as the champion of reaction. For a moment, a very brief moment, the country united behind the High Federalists in the wake of the XYZ affair. But following the reestablishment of better relations with France, Americans rapidly abandoned the party of "the rich, the wise, and the well born" when its clearly illiberal measures could no longer be justified or tolerated. By 1800 the innovators of 1788 had become the dedicated spokesmen of things as they were. Because of this, they were swept out of office by a nation unwilling to forgo its experiment in popular sovereignty.[1]

At the outset, almost all Americans rejoiced in the French Revolution. The country was still too close to its own revolution not to feel a spiritual affinity and sympathy for a people struggling against despotism. Washington's receipt of the key to the Bastille symbolized the relationship felt by Americans toward France. "The liberty of the whole earth was depending on the issue of the contest," Jefferson wrote,[2] and Charles Carroll of Carrollton, no believer in political democracy, agreed that "on the success of the Revolution in that country not only the happiness of France, but the rest of Europe, and perhaps our own depends."[3] So too thought Otho H. Williams, who early espoused "a disposition friendly to the cause of

---

1. Miller, *The Federalist Era*, pp. 99–125, gives a superb account of the nature of Federalism and the emergence of political parties during this period.
2. Miller, *The Federalist Era*, cited on p. 127.
3. Charles Carroll of Carrollton to Thomas Jefferson, dated April 10, 1791. MS in Jefferson Papers, Vol. 63, Library of Congress.

France . . . that gallant Nation."[4] Writing to the French
Patriots of Baltimore, Williams affirmed that "the rights of
Man formed the first distinct political sentiment with which
my mind was inspired, and it has been my ruling social principle from my Youth up."[5] In Maryland as in other states
Democratic Societies were organized that drew their support,
at first, from both Republicans and moderate Federalists who
believed in the ideals of the French Revolution. These Francophiles were mostly young men who accepted the philosophy
of Rousseau and declared themselves in favor of liberty and
equality.[6] Indeed, espousal of things French became a popular
pastime for the majority of Americans, regardless of their
political affiliations at home.[7]

The Reign of Terror, however, dampened American enthusiasm for the French Revolution, and when, in 1793, France
proclaimed itself a republic and declared war upon Great
Britain, disaffection spread quickly.[8] Politically it was a time
for Federalists and emergent Republicans to stand up and be

---

4. O. H. Williams to Citizen Edmund Genet, dated May 16, 1793.
   MS in O. H. Williams Papers, Vol. 8, M.H.S. By this time, Williams's "friendly disposition" was primarily aimed at securing a
   contract for the sale of flour to Genet for the use of France.
5. Williams to the French Patriots of Baltimore, dated January 22,
   1794. MS in O. H. Williams Papers, Vol. 8, M.H.S.
6. Specifically, the Societies advocated manhood suffrage, proportional
   representation, and the right of the people to assemble, to discuss,
   and to instruct their representatives. The more radical advocated
   rotation in office and objected to the appointment or indirect election of public officials. Their general aim was majority rule. See
   Eugene P. Link, Democratic-Republican Societies, 1790–1800 (New
   York: Columbia University Press, 1942), pp. 9–13, 103ff and 163.
7. Ibid., pp. 87–99. It was at this time that unpowdered cropped hair,
   "pudding bag" cravats, short-waisted, high-collared coats, and
   loose-flapping pantaloons came into style.
8. After the recall of Genet and the collapse of his military program
   most of the Democratic Societies ceased to exist. Genet's connection
   with the Parisian abolitionist group known as the Amis des Noirs
   had an even more telling effect upon the Southern societies, for it
   was this organization which had first stirred up the Negro revolt in
   Santo Domingo in 1793. The society in Baltimore, known as the
   Republican Society, continued to function however. See Link,
   Democratic-Republican Societies, pp. 184–86.

Baltimore from Howard's Park, *ca.* 1796
From the Collections of the Maryland Historical Society

Maryland Federalists

Daniel of St. Thomas Jenifer (1723–1790)
From the Collections of the Maryland Historical Society

Daniel Carroll (1730–1796)
From the Collections of the Maryland Historical Society

Charles Carroll of Carrollton (1737–1832)
From the Collections of the Maryland Historical Society

Samuel Chase (1741–1811)
From the Collections of the Maryland Historical Society

Luther Martin (1748?–1826)
From the Collections of the Maryland Historical Society

Alexander Contee Hanson (1749–1806)
Courtesy Library of Congress

Alexander Contee Hanson (the younger) (1786–1819)
Courtesy Library of Congress

Otho Holland Williams (1749–1794)
From the Collections of the Maryland Historical Society

Benjamin Stoddert (1751–1813)
Courtesy Library of Congress

James McHenry (1753–1816)
From the Collections of the Maryland Historical Society

Philip Barton Key (1757–1815)
From the Collections of the Maryland Historical Society

Robert Goodloe Harper (1765–1825)
From the Collections of the Maryland Historical Society

Roger Brooke Taney (1777–1864)
From the Collections of the Maryland Historical Society

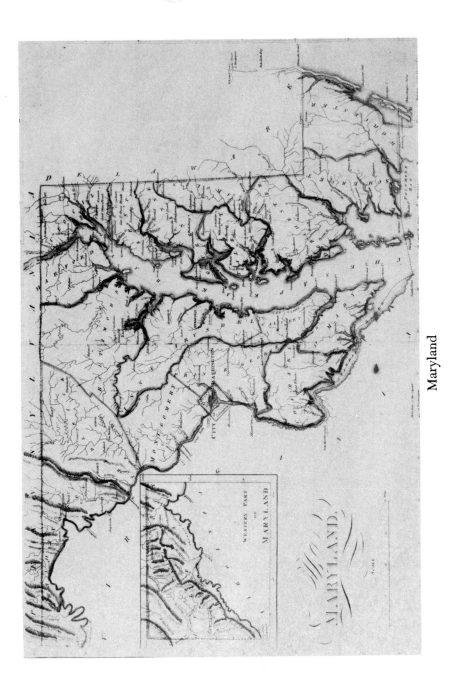

Maryland

Virginia, Maryland and Delaware

counted, but from the start both sides were as one in their determination to adhere to a policy of neutrality. In this respect partisan division was basically absent, and American foreign policy during the next nineteen years was an honest attempt to avoid entanglement with Europe—no matter which party was in control or where the actual sympathies of its leaders might lay. Marked differences there were, but they arose not over the maintenance of neutrality so much as to how this objective could be best achieved.[9]

Political conflict thus centered upon the actual implementation of accepted policy, and it is in this light that divisions and action in Maryland throughout this period must be viewed. It is difficult, however, to categorize the political disposition existing in Maryland, for voting patterns and sentiment did not always follow party lines. Federalist measures appeared to enjoy unprecedented popularity, but Republican successes at the polls steadily increased. This phenomenon was most notable in commercially minded Baltimore, whose citizens became increasingly pro-French although the city's merchants derived much of their business from trade with Great Britain.

With but few exceptions, opinion in the state was very favorable to administration measures, foreign and domestic, during Washington's second term. The president's Proclamation of Neutrality was given warm support, especially by those shipping interests acutely sensitive to any decision affecting commerce. The House of Delegates adopted a resolution by unanimous vote approving the proclamation, and memorials of approbation from the citizens of Annapolis and Baltimore were forwarded to the Chief Executive. To one of these Washington responded, reiterating the unquestionable benefits of peace. "The present flourishing situation of our affairs," he counseled, "and the prosperity we enjoy, must be obvious to the good citizens of the United States; it remains, therefore, for them to

---

9. The most notable protagonists were Jefferson and Hamilton, who disagreed intensely over the pursuance of the neutrality policy which both men wished to preserve. See Miller, *The Federalist Era*, pp. 126–39.

pursue such a line of conduct, as will insure these blessings, by averting the calamities of war."[10]

Marylanders took the advice to heart, but, even so, divisions occurred which cannot be satisfactorily explained as merely partisan. When, for instance, Great Britain's Order in Council of December, 1793, closed American shipping with the French West Indies,[11] resulting in Madison's introduction in Congress of retaliatory "Commercial Propositions,"[12] Republican sympathizer Samuel Smith opposed the measures while Republican Gabriel Christie and Eastern Shore Federalist William Hindman supported them.[13] Representing Chesapeake shipping interests, and a merchant who was himself actively engaged in shipping, Smith felt that this was not the time to risk a war. "Many, very many serious Consequences would arise from a stopping of Trade," he wrote to Federalist leader O. H. Williams.[14] "I would go to War but—I fear we are not able—

10. George Washington to the Citizens of Annapolis, dated September 18, 1793. Cited in John C. Fitzpatrick, ed., *The Writings of George Washington From the Original Manuscript Sources, 1745–1799* (Washington: Government Printing Office, 1937), 33: 90–91. See also Washington to the Mechanical Society of Baltimore, dated June 7, 1793, 32: 490, and Washington to the Merchants and Traders of Baltimore, dated May 23, 1793, 32: 477.

11. The Order in Council was dated November 6, 1793, but was not activated until December. It was aimed at excluding the American merchant marine, the principal carrier of provisions to the French West Indies, from participating in that trade. A British fleet and army were sent to the islands to conquer them, and commanders of British ships were ordered to seize and bring into British ports all neutral vessels engaged in carrying provisions to, or transporting the produce of those islands. About 250 unarmed American ships were thus seized. See Miller, *The Federalist Era*, pp. 140–44.

12. These "Propositions" called for retaliatory duties upon British ships and merchandise, their purpose being to end the "dangerous" dependence of the United States upon British markets and credits. "In essentials, Madison was proposing an American mercantilist system oriented in favor of France." See Miller, *The Federalist Era*, pp. 142–43. See also *Annals of Congress*, House of Representatives, 3rd Congress, 2nd Session, pp. 212–29.

13. *Annals of Congress*, 3: 229–30, 382–83, 399.

14. Samuel Smith to O. H. Williams, dated December 18, 1793, MS in O. H. Williams Papers, Vol. 8, M.H.S.

We have no Money & no Protection to our Trade. . . . We have not the power to chastise them."[15] Both men agreed that "the *audacity* of the British Nation" was hard to bear ("What infamous means does that infamous Nation adopt to revenge the loss of America?" asked Williams), but felt that diplomatic methods rather than economic retaliation would bring the best solution.[16] It seems clear that Smith acted in the best interests of his fellow merchants regardless of his growing political attachment to Jefferson and Madison. Christie and Hindman, however, also represented mercantile areas along the Chesapeake, yet they supported Madison's proposals for varying reasons of their own. Christie admitted that it was Anglophobia rather than his attachment to Jefferson which determined his stand, asserting that, as Maryland's delegates were divided anyway, any measure to humiliate "iniquitous" England would win his vote.[17] Hindman, on the other hand, was perhaps not so much concerned with the state's shipping interests as with the loss of Eastern Shore wheat markets in the French West Indies.[18]

Madison's "Commercial Propositions" were set aside by Congress in the spring of 1794, and the Republicans turned their attention instead to a more drastic bill providing for non-intercourse with Great Britain. This move had come in the wake of British confiscations of American neutral shipping in the Caribbean, reports of which had not been known earlier. Passing the House of Representatives, the Non-Intercourse Bill was defeated in the Senate by the casting vote of Vice President Adams; in its place the government announced a thirty day embargo upon American shipping. Smith gave this mea-

---

15. Samuel Smith to O. H. Williams, dated January 28, 1794, February 25, 1794, March 6 and 20, 1794. MS in O. H. Williams Papers, Vol. 8, M.H.S.

16. O. H. Williams to Dr. Philip Thomas, dated December 14, 1793. MS in O. H. Williams Papers, Vol. 8, M.H.S.

17. Gabriel Christie to Roger Boyce, dated January 26, 1794. MS in Mackubin Papers, M.H.S.

18. This is purely conjecture, but would seem to be the most plausible explanation of Hindman's stand on the Madison proposals.

sure his support, it being the mildest form of economic coercion possible, and in a letter to Williams expressed his hope that the merchants and farmers of Baltimore city and county would understand the necessity for the act.[19] In this respect Smith had little cause to worry, for both Federalists and Republicans in Baltimore had been active in the formation of a Volunteer Corps of Militia to defend the city in the event of British attack—"a proof," chided Williams, "that national defence has not been neglected among us. . . . We have, in the present eventful & critical period, without waiting the command of our Country, assumed the character of Soldiers."[20] These remarks were no doubt intended to score the conduct of affairs by the Republican faction in Congress, which, though eager

---

19. Samuel Smith to O. H. Williams, dated March 6 and March 20, 1794. MS in O. H. Williams Papers, Vol. 8, M.H.S. See also Andrew Buchanan to Williams, dated March 27, 1794, in Vol. 9. Buchanan, a merchant, was one of the few who opposed the measure. He felt it might bring England "to reason, but would we not in the meantime greatly distress ourselves?" As for the measure's other intent, "It cannot be said that it would be to the Interest of America in its present state to go generally into Manufactures—it is too thinly Peopled—labor is too high, and we must manufacture to great disadvantage—also pay double prices for many articles . . . . We had better pay for cultivating the soil, as long as we can find a Market for its produce." On March 24 and 26, 1794, Williams received letters from a very worried Dr. Thomas, conveying power of attorney for the disposition of Thomas's twenty shares of stock in the Bank of Maryland. Thomas was certain that specie, produce, and land "must infallibly fall in value . . . if a War takes place," but "if forced into it to defend our rights I trust we shall 'strike home' with one consent. May God grant us peace." O. H. Williams Papers, Vol. 9, M.H.S.

20. O. H. Williams to the Baltimore Volunteer Corps of Militia, dated December 3, 1793. MS in O. H. Williams Papers, Vol. 8, M.H.S. See also Williams to Governor Thomas Sim Lee, dated December 5, 1793, in O. H. Williams Papers, Vol. 8. See also Henry Knox to Williams, dated April 2, 1794, Vol. 9, regarding organization of the Baltimore militia and defense of the harbor; Williams to Governor Thomas Sim Lee, dated April 2, 1794, Vol. 9, concerning organization of volunteers; Williams to Secretary of War Knox, dated April 4, 1794, Vol. 9; and Christopher Richmond to Williams, dated April 15, 1794, Vol. 9, M.H.S.

to force an economic showdown with Great Britain, vehemently opposed every effort to strengthen the country's defenses. But the expected attacks upon Baltimore did not materialize; indeed, the only violence that took place occurred when the government allowed the purely temporary measure to expire. Disgusted at what appeared to be an abandonment of anti-British policy, several men at Fells Point lowered the flag to half-mast. Riots ensued, coats of tar and feathers were indiscriminately administered, and at length the culprits were brought to trial before Judge Samuel Chase. He demanded a conviction, but was instead censured for his extremism by a jury all too willing to set the defendants free. At this point Chase asked Governor Thomas Sim Lee for the protection of the state militia, Baltimore's troops being unable or unwilling to uphold the law. "In what case," he asked, "can the public (that is, the majority of the people of this state) be considered the supreme tribunal? When the government is dissolved, and in no other case. Alas! Poor Yorick."[21]

21. Samuel Chase to the *Baltimore Daily Intelligencer*, dated August 4, 1794. MS in Samuel Chase Letters, M.H.S. See also Scharf, *History of Maryland*, 2: 590–91. High Federalists James McHenry and William Vans Murray were evidently very favorably impressed by Chase's forceful handling of this challenge to the judiciary, for it was through their recommendations that he was appointed to the United States Supreme Court by Washington. On June 14, 1795, McHenry wrote Washington to propose Chase for a position on the federal bench (without his knowledge), asserting, "Chase and I are on neither good nor bad terms, neither friends nor enemies. To profound knowledge, he adds a valuable stock of political science and information." On December 24 Murray wrote McHenry that "I *have* several times brought up Mr. Chase to view while the official wheel was in motion. I have taken pains to place his and Martin's politics in the true point of view—as yet no consequence has follow'd except perhaps a *preparation*." Washington responded on January 20, 1796, asking McHenry to inquire if Chase would accept a seat on the Supreme Court. McHenry replied (January 21 and 24) that "Chase will accept . . . you have made an old veteran very proud and happy." On January 28 Washington wrote that Chase's name had been put in nomination before the Senate, and promptly confirmed. Steiner, *James McHenry*, pp. 159–68; Scharf, *Maryland*, 2: 594–95.

Though regrettable, the violence with which anti-British feeling was expressed at this time was not unusual. Anglophobia—heightened in the present crisis—had been the prevailing mood in America since independence, and to a large extent the nationalism which existed during these early years was based as much on hatred of Great Britain as on love of country. This was certainly true of Baltimore, whose heavy German and Irish population showed their distaste for England by swelling the ranks of the local Republican Society.[22] In addition to this organization the city boasted a Society of French Patriots composed of ardent Francophiles and French refugees from the strife-torn island of Santo Domingo. About fifteen hundred of these exiles arrived in Baltimore in July of 1793. The majority were royalists who had little love for the Revolution which had been responsible for the Negro insurrection in the French colony, but neither were they favorably disposed toward the British, who now proposed to conquer the French West Indies altogether.[23] Nor were the Chesapeake merchants inclined to view Britain's latest policy with equanimity. Though anxious to maintain peace and resume trade with England, they were at the same time active in furnishing privateers to cruise against British commerce; by 1795 almost fifty vessels had left Baltimore under the French flag.[24] Moreover, of the two hundred and fifty American ships captured in Caribbean waters under Britain's Order in Council of 1793, many were en route from Baltimore laden with wheat for the French West Indies.[25] With both ships and market gone, it

---

22. Scharf, *History of Maryland*, 2: 11–21, 53–67, 551–57.
23. *Ibid.*, 2: 575–80. See also Miller, *The Federalist Era*, p. 141.
24. *Maryland Gazette* (Annapolis), April 10, 1795. Letters of marque were issued by Genet beginning in 1793.
25. John Stricker to O. H. Williams, dated May 17, 1794. MS in O. H. Williams Papers, Vol. 9, M.H.S. After discussing various seizures, including the capture of Captain Joshua Barney's ship, Stricker remarked that "they continue to do us all the mischief they can," but "not withstanding the injuries we have received, there are enough willing to forget them" in order to resume trade. See also

is not difficult to understand why the owners of those vessels and the inhabitants of Baltimore who manned them made common cause for redress.

Tension lessened after the appointment of John Jay as minister plenipotentiary to Great Britain, but by this time the storm center was already shifting from the foreign to the domestic scene with the outbreak of the Whiskey Rebellion in western Pennsylvania. The cause of this insurrection lay in Hamilton's excise tax of 1791 upon domestic distilled whiskey. Republicans as well as Federalists had voted for the measure, which immediately became highly unpopular in the West where whiskey served as a medium of exchange and where its distillation was the only feasible way of moving grain to market. Rumblings of discontent against the oppressively high duties were heard as early as 1792, and in the summer of 1794 open revolts took place to prevent their collection.[26] Although the duties were equally unpopular in transmontane Maryland and with Baltimore distillers, they occasioned little more than criticism, grumbling, and petitions for their repeal, and when rebellion erupted sentiment in the state appeared overwhelmingly in favor of the forceful measures taken by the administration to suppress it.[27] All factions seemed united in this respect. Following Washington's call upon the states for 12,900 men to take the field, Samuel Smith took command of Maryland's militia and marched westward to rendezvous with the Virginia forces.[28] The House of Delegates unanimously commended the use of the state militia in the

---

Scharf, *History of Maryland*, 2: 589–90; and Miller, *The Federalist Era*, pp. 141ff.

26. Miller, *The Federalist Era*, pp. 155–57. The duties were 25 percent of the net price of a gallon of whiskey.

27. *Annals of Congress*, House of Representatives, 2nd Congress, 2nd Session, pp. 790–94, Petition of Baltimore Distillers, November 11, 1791. See also the *Baltimore Daily Intelligencer*, August 6, 1794, and September 8, 1794; and Scharf, *History of Maryland*, 2: 583–89.

28. Scharf, *Maryland*, 2: 583–86.

crisis,[29] while the Republican Society of Baltimore passed resolutions approving the conduct of the administration in snuffing out the insurrection.[30]

But in the light of Maryland's favorable response to the foreign and domestic policies of the Washington administration, the elections of 1794 appear both confusing and inconsistent; one looks in vain for that sweeping approval of Federalist measures which by all indications should have been forthcoming from the electorate. On the whole, Republican strength increased in the center of the state, in those counties bordering Chesapeake Bay, while the southern and eastern fringes remained more steadfastly Federalist. Western Maryland, moreover, showed decided tendencies in favor of Republicanism.

Local issues seemed to have predominated throughout, so much so that little or no use was made of statewide tickets by either Federalists or Republicans. The Federalists in Baltimore, for example, confined their attacks to the "subversive" activities of the local Republican Society, despite the society's support of the administration in the late insurrection, its commendation of Washington in the Fourth of July celebrations of 1794, and its nomination of merchant-General Samuel Smith for reelection to Congress. William Vans Murray's letter to James McHenry expressed these accusations as follows:

The impression of the whiskey insurrection aided in smoothing down every asperity. It has been deep, & effective, it is to be hoped. The roots of the cause however are perhaps to be looked for if any where existing in the remnant of the Democratic clubs. These will I am convinced still go on. They assume a ground so plausible in a free country that they will still flourish & ocassionally produce convulsions, or rather prepare the public mind for them. The present time however is certainly propitious to a sober examination of their tendency, & perhaps of their *Objects*. Every thing is

29. *Votes and Proceedings*, Senate, November Session, 1794.
30. *Baltimore Daily Intelligencer*, September 4, 1794.

to be hoped for from the good sense of the public when so lately roused into reflexion.[31]

Nevertheless, Smith appears to have been acceptable to all groups in Baltimore, for he ran unopposed and avoided the use of party labels in a campaign whose outcome was a foregone conclusion. The same may be said of Alexander McKim and James Winchester, Republican Society nominees for the House of Delegates, who were likewise unopposed in Baltimore. In Harford, Cecil, and Kent counties, Republican incumbent Gabriel Christie was returned to the House of Representatives in a contest which pitted him against fellow Republican Robert Wright. Western Maryland reelected Republican sympathizer Thomas Sprigg, in evident protest over the whiskey tax, but Southern Maryland and the Eastern Shore returned conservative, Potomac-dominated Federalists with virtually no opposition from the Jeffersonians.[32]

The first crack in that almost unanimous support which Maryland had given to the Washington administration became visible in the congressional debates over the controversial Jay Treaty of 1795. As the price of Anglo-American harmony, Jay had in effect accepted Britain's concept of belligerents' rights by renouncing the American principle of freedom of the seas. In exchange for this and other concessions, the British government promised to surrender the Northwest posts by June of 1796. Although the terms of the treaty were to be kept secret until the Senate had been given an opportunity to act, its text soon found its way into Benjamin Bache's Philadelphia

31. Williams Vans Murray to James McHenry, dated December 16, 1794. Cited in Steiner, *James McHenry*, pp. 155–56.

32. *Baltimore Daily Intelligencer*, July 7, 1794, September 4, 1794, and October 6, 1794. See also Steiner, *James McHenry*, pp. 145, 156; and Miller, *The Federalist Era*, pp. 162–63. Incumbent congressman Sprigg was a moderate Federalist until 1794. Elected largely on the basis of personal popularity, he had broken earlier with the Potomac faction and was now to do the same with the Federalist Party. He was subsequently elected as a Republican representative from the same district.

Aurora, where it came as a nasty shock to those Americans accustomed to viewing Great Britain as the country's eternal enemy. Overnight John Jay became the most hated man in the land, and, when the president at length signed the treaty, much of the disgust directed at Jay was unleashed upon Washington himself. From a political standpoint, therefore, the treaty proved very costly to the Federalists, for it not only exposed them to the charge of having abandoned American neutral rights, but it forced Washington into the center of partisan turmoil and into a position he had always tried to avoid—that of the leader of a political party. Moreover, in the ensuing struggle over ratification, the emergent, still amorphous Republicans were provided with a platform and a structural cohesiveness which hastened their growth into a full-fledged party. As Washington's stature shrank, Jefferson's grew, and by 1796 the Republicans were knocking on the door of the presidency itself.[33]

After striking out Article XII, the obnoxious, self-denying commercial ordinance relating to the West Indian trade, the Senate ratified Jay's Treaty on June 24, 1795, by a vote of twenty to ten, this being barely the two-thirds majority necessary for favorable action. Voting was on sectional lines, with almost all of the Southern senators in the opposition while all but two of New England's senators voted in the majority.[34] The treaty's obvious appeal to the mercantile interests could not be denied. It was this appeal which determined Maryland's course, for John Henry and Richard Potts, in marked contrast to their Southern colleagues, voted consistently Federalist in both the debates and final ratification. Their action vividly underscored Maryland's unique borderline position between North and South: culturally it belonged to the latter section;

---

33. Samuel Flagg Bemis, *A Diplomatic History of the United States* (New York: Henry Holt and Company, 1955), pp. 101–4; Miller, *The Federalist Era,* pp. 164ff.
34. *Annals of Congress,* 3rd Congress, 2nd Session, pp. 859–63.

economically, the growing importance of commerce was tying it to the Northeast.[35]

But while the mercantile interests of Chesapeake Maryland were a force to be reckoned with, they by no means represented the entire force of public opinion. Indeed, within the same Chesapeake area, and in transmontane Maryland, there existed an equally strong sentiment against ratification on the part of the business community (especially manufacturers), and among farmers, artisans, and those others who are so often lumped together as the common class. No sooner had the Senate ratified the treaty than public meetings were held by these groups to make formal protests against it. At a meeting held at the court house in Baltimore on July 27, a committee was appointed to address the president against ratification, but it did little good; on August 18, Washington, after much hesitation, signed the treaty. Unhappily for the Federalists, however, this did not put an end to the controversy. Sentiment was still highly critical, and the Republican leaders, thus emboldened by the knowledge that they had a large amount of public backing, resolved to kill the treaty in the House of Representatives.[36]

It was in the House, which had to appropriate money to implement the treaty, that the real struggle occurred. Maryland's role in this struggle centered around the actions of Chesapeake Representative Samuel Smith, who shifted in the

---

35. *Annals of Congress,* 3rd Congress, 2nd Session. See also Joshua Johnson to Silvanus Bourne, United States Consul at Amsterdam, dated May 23, 1795. MS in Bourne Papers, M.H.S. "It is impossible to say what Mr. Jay's Treaty is or is not," Johnson declared, but unless Maryland commerce wished to suffer continued seizures by England the treaty had better be ratified.

36. Scharf, *Maryland,* 2: 591–92. See also Beard, *Economic Origins of Jeffersonian Democracy,* pp. 268, 282–83. Miller, *The Federalist Era,* p. 174, contends that the defection of the business community to Federalism did not originate over disgust with Jay's Treaty, "but with the narrow and exclusive policies pursued by Federalist banks and the Federalist-dominated state legislatures."

treaty debate to the Republican camp but who voted with the Federalists in the final count. His inconsistency cost Smith the future support of his fellow merchants and the Chesapeake politicos, but it cannot be argued that he was unaware of the sentiments of his constituents. At the end of 1795 the General Assembly unanimously passed a declaration of confidence, introduced by William Pinkney, which expressed its "unabated reliance on the integrity, judgment and patriotism of the President of the United States," and denounced the assaults based upon "misplaced suspicion and ill-founded jealousy" which Washington now suffered from an ungrateful people.[37] The merchants and shippers of Baltimore, moreover, led by none other than former Republican Society candidate James Winchester, met when the treaty came up in the House and demanded that Smith support it.[38]

But Smith preferred to cast his lot with what appears to have been a large element in Baltimore who were clearly opposed to the implementation of Jay's Treaty, and his response to the aforementioned instructions took the form of a counter-petition in which he defended his stand in the House debates. This was introduced in the House on April 25, and reputedly represented the opinion and approbation of over four hundred Baltimoreans, although it contained but the signatures of the chairman and clerk of a Baltimore society of manufacturers. For this reason the Federalists voted the peti-

---

37. *Votes and Proceedings,* Senate and House of Delegates, November Session, 1795. See also Steiner, *McHenry,* p. 162. Washington responded in two letters of thanks, but perhaps his real response to this vote of confidence by Federalist Maryland was his offer a few days later, on December 5, of the office of Secretary of War to James McHenry. McHenry accepted the cabinet post on January 24, 1796. The president had previously offered the office of Secretary of State to Thomas Johnson, upon Edmund Randolph's resignation in the wake of the Fauchet affair, but Johnson refused because of his advanced age. Subsequently, Timothy Pickering of Pennsylvania was appointed. See Scharf, *Maryland,* 2: 592–95.

38. Steiner, *James McHenry,* p. 167. See also "Maryland Politics in 1796—McHenry Letters," *Publications of the Southern Historical Association* 9 (September, 1905): 374–78.

tion down, ignoring Madison's argument that such a procedure was not at all uncommon. On the 28th, however, Smith submitted another petition containing instructions from ninety-seven of his constituents to implement the treaty. It was these instructions which he finally followed, but the about face came too late for Smith to win back the alienated merchants. This was made clear in a letter from Winchester to James McHenry. "It may be politic," he wrote, "for him to count on *numbers* since he has so openly relinquished all claim to support from orderly and responsible Citizens."[39]

On April 30, when a roll-call vote was at last taken, Jay's Treaty passed the House by the narrow margin of fifty-one to forty-eight. Only four representatives from the states south of Maryland voted in the affirmative, and of Maryland's eight districts only the fourth, composed of the transmontane area represented by Thomas Sprigg, voted in the negative. But the matter was not yet closed. In a final attempt to prevent passage, Congressman Henry Dearborn of Massachusetts introduced an amendment which declared that the treaty was "highly objectionable and may prove injurious to the United States." Samuel Smith at once attacked the amendment, not because he disagreed with it, but because he found it too strong. Upon his recommendation the foregoing phrase was deleted save for the word "objectionable," after which the amendment itself was defeated by a vote of fifty to forty-nine. Maryland's delegates shifted positions in the line-up on the vote. Sprigg, who voted against the treaty, voted against the amendment. His action appears inexplicable, but one may surmise that he either found the watered-down amendment too weak or else rejected the qualifying precedent being established by the House. Sixth-district representative Gabriel

---

39. *Annals of Congress*, House of Representatives, 4th Congress, 1st Session, pp. 1171, 1228. Reference was also made to another set of instructions signed by 197 persons, but no mention was made of what these instructions contained. See also James Winchester to James McHenry, dated May 1, 1796, *Publications of the Southern Historical Association*, 9: 376-77.

Christie, however, voted for the treaty and for the amendment also. He was the only delegate from Maryland to favor the Dearborn proposal.[40]

Why did Smith and Christie act as they did? Both men were representatives of Maryland's Chesapeake counties, both voted in favor of the treaty, and yet both opposed it in varying degrees during its consideration by the House. Both men, moreover, attempted to explain their ambiguous positions, and it is to these explanations that one must turn for a partial understanding of their motives. In his speech before the House, Samuel Smith declared that while "the great majority of the people of Maryland" disliked the treaty, they felt that "less evils will grow out of its adoption than may be apprehended from its rejection." Although he had not been of a similar opinion, the bitter contest now taking place convinced him that adoption "would tend to restore harmony and unanimity to our public measures," for, Smith concluded, "a House so nearly divided against itself could never thrive."[41] This was probably the major reason for his change of position, but other factors might have included Fisher Ames's highly emotional speech in favor of the treaty, and Chairman Frederick Muhlenberg's affirmative tie-breaking vote to carry it into execution when the question came before the Committee of the Whole House on April 29. It was the latter move—a costly desertion from Republicanism on the part of Muhlenberg—which really proved decisive in securing passage.[42] The same reasons might

---

40. *Annals of Congress,* House of Representatives, 4th Congress, 1st Session, pp. 1279–90, 1291. Dearborn was a Republican from one of the Maine districts of Massachusetts. Congressman Gabriel Duvall had resigned in March, and was replaced by Richard Sprigg, Jr., in May of 1796. This left Maryland with only seven representatives at the time of the vote. See also Upton Scott to Charles Carroll of Carrollton, undated MS letter in Carroll Papers, 8: 1781–1833, M.H.S., in which the House's consideration of the Jay Treaty is thoroughly discussed.

41. *Annals of Congress,* House of Representatives, 4th Congress, 1st Session, pp. 1154–58.

42. *Ibid.,* pp. 1279–82. A few days after he broke the deadlock Muhlen-

apply to Christie, who avowed the treaty to be "a bad bargain," but certainly "not . . . pregnant with all the evils which had been ascribed to it." Since his constituents wished it carried into effect, Christie declared himself bound to lay aside his own opinion and act according to their will, but this did not prevent him from supporting Dearborn's amendment for personal beliefs, nor from comparing Ames's oration to "something like the tale of 'Rawhead and Bloodybones' to frighten children."[43]

Next to Jay himself, no person suffered more abuse during this period than Washington. Sick of politics, wounded by the envenomed shafts of Republican journalists, and eager to retire from the "splended misery of the Presidency" to the solitude of Mount Vernon after a public service of more than twenty years, he decided at the close of the stormy congressional session of 1796 not to stand for a third term. Before taking leave of the people, however, Washington wished to prepare a political testament for their guidance in the form of a Farewell Address. This was drawn up in the summer, with the aid of Hamilton and Jay, and in September it appeared in newspapers throughout the country. There is little need to summarize the Farewell Address here. Every point made in it had been enunciated earlier by Washington and Hamilton; it contained, in brief, the essence of the political philosophy of Federalism.[44]

Republicans everywhere greeted the Address with approval, wishing the President a speedy departure back to the farm so that they might have a turn at the reins of government.

---

berg was stabbed by his brother-in-law, a rabid Republican. He also failed of reelection to the House in the next election. Miller, *The Federalist Era*, pp. 175–76.

43. *Annals of Congress*, House, 4th Congress, 1st Session, p. 1280.

44. Miller, *The Federalist Era*, p. 196. Fear of Washington's retirement was part of the subject of discussion in an undated letter from Upton Scott to Charles Carroll of Carrollton, MS in Carroll Papers, 8: 1781–1833, M.H.S. Both men looked with dread to "the approach of those Infirmities & decline of vigour resulting from his advanced years."

Benjamin Bache's Philadelphia *Aurora,* for instance, pronounced Washington to be "the source of all the misfortunes of our country. . . . If ever there was a period for rejoicing," it continued, "this is the moment. Every heart . . . ought to beat high with exultation that the name of Washington from this day ceases to give a currency to political iniquity and to legalized corruption."[45] The Maryland press, however, did not give vent to such rancorous diatribes. Instead, there appeared an upsurge of enthusiasm throughout the state for the Washington administration, a feeling which was largely unshared among the other Southern states, permanently lost to the Federalist Party in the wake of Jay's Treaty. The public prints expressed the people's "most sensible grief" upon hearing that "the best, the most virtuous, and the greatest man in the world" was leaving the councils of government.[46] Secretary of War McHenry wrote Washington that "many tears were shed. . . . I sincerely believe that no nation ever felt a more ardent attachment to its chief and 'tis certain that history cannot furnish an example, such as you have given."[47] In December these sentiments were capped by a unanimous resolution of the General Assembly praising the President in the highest terms for "his wise and steady administration of the general government, promptness in suppressing domestic insurrection, firmness in defeating improper exertions of foreign influence, and perseverance in the system of neutrality."[48] There could be little doubt after this as to the strength of Federalism in Maryland.

Yet that strength, to a large degree, had been artificially maintained and never effectively challenged as long as Washington stood at the head of the Federalist Party in the state.

---

45. Philadelphia *Aurora,* March 6, 1796. This editorial was printed upon Washington's retirement from office.
46. *Maryland Journal,* September 17, 1796.
47. James McHenry to Washington, dated September 25, 1796. Cited in Steiner, *James McHenry,* pp. 193–94.
48. *Votes and Proceedings,* Senate and House of Delegates, November Session, 1796. See also Scharf, *Maryland,* 2: 596–97.

His forthcoming retirement in 1797 therefore, would provide the first real party test in a presidential campaign. In the ensuing contest structural lines were tightened, party spirit reached new heights, and the present two-party system became established as an integral part of American life. For the first time the opposition could come out swinging—completely unfettered in a no-holds-barred fight for that highest office which had up to now been above politics and partisan exploitation. Unfortunately, the contest was to be overly influenced by foreign meddling, thus sapping its vitality by perverting it toward ends that were not in the genuine interests of the United States.

Such meddling was not a new factor in 1796, and France was the most perennially guilty offender. Although Citizen Genet had been replaced by Citizen Adet as minister to the United States, there had been no change in the practice of attempting to direct American domestic concerns for the benefit of the First Republic. It was Adet who arranged for the publication of Jay's Treaty in the *Aurora,* who exhorted the Republicans in Congress to fight it to the bitter end, and who, upon news of Washington's retirement, worked feverishly to secure the election of Thomas Jefferson to the Presidency. In this effort he appealed to the American people through the press to vote for the friend of France by publishing, in November, 1796, four proclamations which cast the entire blame for the breakdown in Franco-American relations upon the Federalist administration. Secretary of State Pickering immediately replied in kind, and the battle was joined. Picked up and publicized by the press, the campaign soon took on the character of a contest between British and French factions rather than between the Federalist and Republican parties.[49]

Nor did the Federalists themselves present a truly solid front in the election of 1796. Intrigue within their own party was as bad as, if not worse than, that being practiced by

49. Miller, *The Federalist Era,* pp. 192–200; Bemis, *Diplomatic History,* pp. 107–10.

France. The most natural choice for the Presidency was John Adams, the vice-president and heir apparent, who had been personally anointed by Washington in March. But Adams was unacceptable to the Hamiltonian wing of the party, and it was determined to keep him buried in the political graveyard of the vice-presidency while ostensibly supporting him for the top position. There were several reasons behind this lack of support for Adams, the most important being that Hamilton, the acknowledged leader of the High Federalists, could not hope to control the moderate but ornery Bostonian whose independence in matters of policy brought accusations that he had wandered into the Federalist Party purely by accident. In 1796 John Adams was in no-man's-land—a "Half-Federalist" who stood midway between the Hamiltonians and the Jeffersonians. His support was derived mainly from the agrarian wing of the party, and his interests were certainly not oriented toward the commercial, shipping, merchandising, and banking groups who dominated orthodox Federalist policy. Neither did he fall in line with the extreme pro-British faction. Indeed, so distrusted was he by the Hamiltonians that they tried to undermine his candidacy for vice-president in 1789; their suspicions were greatly heightened when Adams broke with the Massachusetts Federalists of the Essex Junto in 1794. On the other hand, he was close enough to the Republicans for Jefferson to support his candidacy for a second term as vice-president in 1792, and to recommend him to the Virginia electors. With virtually all of Adams's economic conceptions together with much of his practical politics thus unacceptable to the High Federalists, Hamilton began to cast about in September of 1796 for a more pliable man to warm the presidential chair. Both John Jay and Patrick Henry were considered, but upon the recommendation of Rufus King, attention was fixed on Thomas Pinckney of South Carolina. The idea met with Hamilton's favor, as Pinckney had the combined merits of being a Southerner and of having just negotiated an excellent treaty with Spain, and his candidacy was accordingly launched.

Much has been surmised about the resultant "Pinckney Plot," but it essentially boiled down to this: the Hamiltonians would support Pinckney for the vice-presidency while privately urging his qualifications for the top position. Insistence was placed upon an equal electoral vote for Adams and Pinckney in the states above the Potomac; below that river it was assumed the votes would naturally gravitate to Pinckney and Jefferson because of the latter's popularity in the South. Since Adams would receive little, if any, Southern support, Northern and Southern electors, in casting their second ballots for Pinckney, would unwittingly elect him President. The entire Machiavellian scheme rested upon the instillation of party regularity as a necessity in the minds of New Englanders who wished the presidency for their favorite son. In effect, Hamilton was risking the breakup of his own party by insisting on that regularity which would bring Pinckney out on top.[50]

Adet's attack on the administration occasioned spirited reaction among Maryland's Federalist leaders, but as usual they were divided in their response. In a letter to James McHenry, William Vans Murray observed that the proclamations were "a curious circumstance in diplomatic business . . . pretty much the *Spargere Voces inter vulgus*, in Genet's way of appeal. I hope no answer will be given to *it*—public or private. . . . He wd. love a newspaper dispute."[51] Samuel Chase and Charles Carroll, however, disagreed with Murray. "I think the Printer ought to be indicted for a false & base *Libel* on our Government," Chase thundered. "I see no difference between Genet and Adet. . . . You may be assured there is but one opinion in Maryland out of this Town."[52] From Annapolis, Carroll informed McHenry that "Adet's note . . . is not at all relished with us," and inquired of the Secretary:

50. Manning J. Dauer, *The Adams Federalists* (Baltimore: The Johns Hopkins Press, 1953), pp. 18–111.
51. Steiner, *James McHenry*. William Vans Murray to James McHenry, dated November 9, 1796. P. 201.
52. *Ibid*. Samuel Chase to James McHenry, dated December 4, 1796. P. 203.

does our Govt. mean to answer his last note, *wh* Includes an appeal from The Governt. to the People? We suspect that ye enemies of ye present administration have Stimulated Adet to this measure, to have an influence on the elections of electors of a Presdt. & Vice Presdt. the timing of this note gives room for the conjecture. I hope the Legislature, in imitation of the Jersey Assembly, will pass some resolves highly approving the Presdt's. address to the People, & perhaps some occasion may be taken, besides the one already mentioned, of reprobating the interference of foreign Ministers with our Govt.[53]

Far from letting Carroll down, the Maryland legislature went a good deal beyond what even he anticipated. In addition to unanimously praising Washington's Address, both Houses resolved that it should be published with the laws of the session and that copies should be printed and distributed throughout the state. Governor Stone, moreover, delivered an address to the assembly containing indirect references to Adet's proclamations, a theme on which the joint answer of the legislators elaborated by discussing the meddling, improper conduct of foreign agents in America's internal affairs.[54] But Federalist delegate Philip Barton Key felt that these utterances were not strong enough. In November McHenry had written Key of "the communications made by Mr. Adet to our government,"[55] and Key seized the opportunity to introduce a series of resolutions condemning the French Minister which

---

53. Steiner, *James McHenry*. Charles Carroll to James McHenry, dated November 28, 1796. Pp. 202–3.
54. *Votes and Proceedings,* Senate and House of Delegates, November Session, 1796. See also Chase to McHenry, dated December 10, 1796, in Steiner, *James McHenry,* pp. 205–6. Chase wrote that about eight or ten delegates objected to this part of the reply.
55. McHenry to Philip Barton Key, cited in *Ibid.,* p. 202. Concerning Adet, Key wrote that "he has lost all character and irretrievably diminished that good will felt for his Government & the people of France by most people here."

passed the legislature early the following month.[56] Chase hailed the resolutions as expressive of "the Real Sentiments of the People of Maryland,"[57] but Carroll complained that they went too far. "The Individual States as Such are not known to foreign powers," he reminded McHenry. "We have nothing to do with them, nor they with us. Should we pointedly notice & disapprove of Adet's proceeding, might we not be accused of reaching in upon the boundary & province of another Legislature Solely entrusted with the management of our external relations?"[58] McHenry's tacit approval of the Key resolutions, however, was evidence enough that he did not share Carroll's fears of state encroachments in the sphere reserved for the federal government.[59]

The contest in Maryland was bitter. Jefferson was attacked as being too democratic, too theoretical, and lacking in firmness. Old charges that he had deserted his post while Governor of Virginia were raked up and publicized, and to these were added accusations that he had abandoned the cabinet as Secretary of State because he did not wish to be associated with Hamilton's unpopular excise taxes. One anonymous writer prophesied the end of prosperity should Jefferson be elected; another surprisingly pronounced the Virginian to be "an advocate for Despotism and Monarchy." It appeared that the Republicans were on the defensive to stay.[60]

Nevertheless, Federalist leaders in the state were determined

56. *Votes and Proceedings*, Senate and House of Delegates, November Session, 1796.
57. Steiner, *James McHenry*, pp. 205–6. Samuel Chase to James McHenry, dated December 10, 1796.
58. *Ibid.*, pp. 204–5. Charles Carroll to James McHenry, dated December 5, 1796.
59. Steiner, *James McHenry*, pp. 206–7. Charles Carroll to James McHenry, dated December 12, 1796, and Philip Key to James McHenry, dated December 13, 1796.
60. *Maryland Journal*, October 8 and 27, 1796. *Federal Gazette and Baltimore Daily Advertiser*, October 25 and November 8, 1796. *Gazette of the United States*, November 9, 11, 16, 24, and 30, 1796.

not to rest on past laurels—one gets the distinct impression that they were "running scared" but refused to admit it. "God send us a Federal Successor," agonized William Hindman. "I wish not to anticipate Evil, I cannot however help dreading the Consequence."[61] Charles Carroll was even more blunt. "I fear Jefferson will be elected Presdt.," he wrote McHenry. "May the good Genius of America avert from us so great an evil & may ye event prove these conjectures groundless."[62] Unity within the party appears to have been Murray's chief concern. Early in September he warned McHenry (a Hamiltonian through and through) that "the timing of the exertions of the Fedd party seems to me very important. This will come from you & Mr. W. & Col. P., for a party dispersed act without concert, unless a rallying point is understood among them."[63] A month later he wrote again, urging that "no effort . . . be omitted let what will come of it. No man ever Saved himself from drowning if instead of swimming he . . . trusted to the tide."[64]

As the Federalist schism deepened and the "Pinckney Plot" thickened, Adams came under heavy attack from his own party and Murray emerged as his strongest defender in Maryland. "A Federalist" declared that Jefferson was too democratic and Adams too much a monarchist for either to warrant the people's support; Pinckney, he concluded, presented the most satisfactory choice between these two extremes. "Safety" ac-

---

61. Steiner, *James McHenry*, pp. 199–200. William Hindman to James McHenry, dated October 13, 1796.

62. Steiner, *James McHenry*, pp. 202–3. Charles Carroll to James McHenry, dated November 28, 1796. On December 5 Carroll wrote again, declaring that "the friends of the Government dread the election of Jefferson; they fear he will pursue a very different line of conduct from the present President . . . there are, no doubt, many in all the States wishing for a revolution & war, but I am confident the great body of the people are attached to the Governt., approve its measures, & wish to remain at peace with the nation." See *ibid.*, p. 205.

63. *Ibid.*, p. 197. Murray to McHenry, dated September 9, 1796.

64. Murray to McHenry, dated November 15, 1796, *Publications of the Southern Historical Association*, 9:382–84.

cused Adams of taking a leading part in the scheme to dump
Washington as supreme commander during the Revolution,
and the most extreme Federalists asserted that the Vice-President in matters of finance was no better than Jefferson. In this
respect it was murmured that Adams lacked the confidence
of the government and especially of those connected with the
Treasury. The most persistent charges, however, centered on
Adams's *Defense of the American Constitutions of Government*, published in 1787 at the time of the Philadelphia Convention. Both Republicans and Federalists intimated that this
work vividly illustrated the author's monarchist sentiments and
his pro-British proclivities. If anything, his opponents insisted,
the *Defense* certainly established Adams's unfitness to lead a
republic.[65]

Murray's response to these accusations was immediate. Writing under the pseudonym of "Union" and "Eastern Shore," he
pointed to the danger of party division in the coming election
and urged all Federalists in Maryland to support Adams.
Early in November he began writing *A Short Vindication of
Mr. Adams' Defense of American Constitutions*, which appeared at first as a serial in the *Gazette of the United States*
and was subsequently published in pamphlet form.[66] Other
correspondents, notably "Union Among Federalists," "Thousands," "Amicus," and "A Freeholder" also defended Adams,
warning traitors within the party that should their efforts result in his defeat it would be not Pinckney but Jefferson who
would emerge on top.[67] As the contest drew to a close, Murray
appeared encouraged. With tongue in cheek he advised Mc-
Henry to "get a Georgetown paper . . . if you like *unions*. . . .
I sent several (I *think* signed Union) particularly on Mr. A's

65. *Gazette of the United States,* November 15 and 25, 1796. *The Federal Gazette and Baltimore Daily Advertiser,* October 29 and November 1, 1796.
66. *Gazette of the United States,* November 5, 16, 19, 24, and 26 and
December 5 and 6, 1796. *Maryland Journal,* October 19, 1796.
67. *Gazette of the United States,* November 19 and 26 and December
2, 1796. *The Federal Gazette,* October 29, 1796.

Dutch Services & a little upon his book. . . . I thought it important, in Speaking of *the man*, to associate him with *Revolution Services* as most unquestioned & most splendid & *long past*."[68] In another series of letters Murray predicted that the Eastern Shore would choose "excellent & trusty Electors . . . the worst come to the worst."[69] Chastising McHenry, he admitted that while the Western Shore might desert, "no Vice is yet mentioned here. . . . In this county, I think I never knew an election so much of *principles*. . . . Our choice is a party question, not a personal matter—this, for a Southern election, is a pleasing feature of the People's goodness."[70] Such ebullience continued unabated during the election, and upon the close of the polls Murray jubilantly but incorrectly reported that "the Jefferson candidate got *one* vote. The Adams candidate 582—no riots—noise or seduction. The farmers came in without leaders to support government, they said, by voting for a Fedl. man as Presdt. I assure you I never saw an election before, in which real good sense appeared unmixed."[71]

But the same could not be said for the rest of Maryland, and by the end of November Murray was forced to admit (again incorrectly) that "we shall be, to my mortification, half and half, a punster would say quite drunk, as we shall be 5 for A. and 5 for J."[72] Charles Carroll was also mortified by the state's mongrelized returns—he suffered defeat as an electoral candidate and his efforts on behalf of Pinckney likewise fell through.[73]

---

68. Cited in Steiner, *James McHenry* (n.d.), pp. 201–2.
69. *Ibid.*, pp. 196–97. Murray to McHenry, dated August 21, September 9, September 24, 1796.
70. Cited in Steiner, *James McHenry,* pp. 198–201. Murray to McHenry, dated October 2 and 9, and November 2, 1796.
71. *Ibid.*, p. 201. Murray to McHenry, dated November 9, 1796.
72. *Ibid.*, pp. 201–2. Same to Same, dated November 15 and 22, 1796.
73. Steiner, *James McHenry,* pp. 202–5. Carroll to McHenry, dated November 28 and December 5, 1796. Dauer, *The Adams Federalists,* pp. 109–10, maintains that Carroll supported Adams in the election. However, on December 12, 1796, Carroll wrote the following to McHenry in this respect: "It is conjectured with us that Mr.

With the exception of one area, however, the pattern of Maryland's electoral returns was not unusual. As expected, the electors from the Eastern Shore remained loyal to Adams, together with the electors from the Western counties, while those from the Chesapeake counties—Anne Arundel, Baltimore, Harford, and the upper counties of Kent and Cecil—voted for Jefferson. The exception was normally Federalist Southern Maryland, composed of Charles, Calvert, and St. Mary's counties, whose elector inexplicably cast one vote for Adams and one for Jefferson.[74]

If the presidential contest left the Federalists somewhat abashed, they could not but rejoice at their success on the state and congressional level. The Maryland Senate was overwhelmingly Federal, and the roster of those selected for the term of five years included such party notables as Charles Carroll, John Eager Howard, James Lloyd, William Perry, and Uriah Forrest.[75] In the congressional election the Federalists secured a safe 6–2 majority as compared to the almost even balance which existed previously. Murray, who had declined to run, was succeeded by a Federalist, the former delegate John Dennis; William Hindman trounced Republican Robert Wright in Caroline and Talbot counties on the Eastern Shore; and Chesapeake congressman Gabriel Christie, representing Maryland's maverick sixth district, was defeated by

---

Pinckney will be elected President; if the eastern electors have generally voted for him, the conjecture may be realized. Some think this event would be a fortunate one, as his administration would be less opposed than that of Mr. Adams's . . . not so much the man as measures occasioned opposition." See Steiner, *James McHenry*, p. 206.

74. *Ibid.*, pp. 204–5. Charles Carroll to James McHenry, dated December 5, 1796. In the overall vote by the Maryland electors, Adams received 7 votes, Jefferson 4, Pinckney 4, Aaron Burr 3, and John Henry 2 votes. The electors were: John Roberts, John Done, John Eccleston, John Lynn, George Murdock, Francis Deakins, Gabriel Duvall, John Archer, John Gilpin, and John Plater. See also Dauer, *The Adams Federalists*, p. 106.

75. *The Federal Gazette*, September 23, 1796. See also Steiner, *James McHenry*, p. 197. Murray to McHenry, dated September 24, 1796.

Federalist William Matthews—"a better member all hollow," commented Murray. The most debated contest took place over Thomas Sprigg's vacated seat in the Western counties of Washington, Allegany, and Frederick, where Federalist candidate George Baer, Jr., triumphed against independent Samuel Ringold. Republican Samuel Smith of Baltimore was returned unopposed, as was Republican Richard Sprigg, Jr., second district candidate from Anne Arundel and Prince George's counties. Montgomery county and Frederick county east of the Monocacy River returned Federalist William Craik, while Southern Maryland's first district (St. Mary's, Charles, and Calvert counties) returned George Dent, a Federalist whose attachment to the party was nominal at best. Once in Congress, Dent would pursue an independent course, often allying himself with Republicans Smith and Sprigg.[76]

With the Federalists thoroughly dominant in the General Assembly, there was no question but that Maryland's Senators in the Fifth Congress would be of the same party. In December of 1796 John Eager Howard, recently elected to the state Senate, was chosen by his fellow legislators to complete the unexpired term of Senator Richard Potts. A year later another vacancy occurred when John Henry resigned his seat to accept the governorship of Maryland. Although a Federalist, Governor Henry nourished a deep-seated Anglophobia, and in his address to the legislature he suggested that his replacement in the Senate be a person capable of resisting the growing wave of British influence sweeping the country in 1797. This advice was further embellished by public statements in defense of Jefferson's attitude toward England. Thoroughly alarmed, the upper house at once ceased its consideration of a more moderate candidate and selected instead James Lloyd to fill the vacancy. "He is as strictly governmental as it is possible,"

---

76. Steiner, *James McHenry*, pp. 196–206. Murray to McHenry, dated October 2 and 13, 1796. William Hindman to McHenry, dated October 13, 1796. See also Dauer, *The Adams Federalists*, pp. 288–300.

Uriah Forrest wrote McHenry, "a man of nice honor and pretty good judgement, slow, and heavy."[77]

As Samuel Chase had predicted during the contest of 1796, his "old friend the Vice President" had come out on top,[78] and as those Federalists who had remained loyal to Adams also predicted, the result of the "Pinckney Plot" skirted disaster by sweeping Jefferson into second place in the electoral poll. Had the Virginian garnered three more votes, Hamilton's intrigue would have brought the Federalists to ruin. In the eyes of the French, however, the United States had now compounded its crime of ratifying Jay's Treaty by electing John Adams President, and in retaliation the Directory stepped up the seizure of American vessels and the confiscation of neutral cargoes. Upon Monroe's recall from France a warm farewell party was given the impolitic minister. At the same time Monroe's successor, Charles Cotesworth Pinckney, was ordered to leave the country, and the Directory declared it would not receive another American minister until French grievances had been redressed. Consequently, on Adams's inauguration diplomatic relations between the former allies were severed.[79]

At length, after much soul searching, Adams determined to send a special mission to France which, to underscore the proper weight the Federalists attached to peaceful relations with that country, would consist of three distinguished public men: C. C. Pinckney, already in Europe, John Marshall, and Elbridge Gerry. Opposition to the mission was at once forthcoming from the cabinet, especially from Secretary of War McHenry, who condemned the entire concept as an expensive delay which "will please nobody, not even those that may be nominated, and will not ensure the United States against a

---

77. Steiner, *James McHenry*, pp. 206, 202, 305–7. Uriah Forrest to McHenry, dated December 6, 1797; James Winchester to McHenry, dated April 18, 1798. The other candidate being considered was Levin Winder. Lloyd was most notable for his introduction of the Sedition Act in the Senate in June, 1798.

78. *Ibid.*, pp. 205–6. Chase to McHenry, dated December 10, 1796.

79. Miller, *The Federalist Era*, pp. 200–206.

single possible evil, nor create to government one additional friend." McHenry particularly distrusted Gerry, about whom he remarked that "if . . . it was a desirable thing to distract the mission, a fitter person could not perhaps be found."[80] Secretary of State Timothy Pickering, and Secretary of the Treasury Oliver Wolcott were in complete agreement with McHenry. High Federalists all, and accustomed to consult with Hamilton on important matters of policy, the three officials followed the advice of the man who was the recognized leader of the Federalist Party rather than the President under whom they were serving.[81]

What finally caused a change of the cabinet's opinion was Hamilton's support of the mission as a means of assuring public support for whatever defense measures might have to be taken. As a matter of fact, he had favored the proposal since the beginning, but had been unable to overcome the opposition on the part of McHenry and Wolcott. Writing each secretary, Hamilton informed them of the necessity to learn "pliancy" in order to avoid policies which would outstrip public opinion. "Take my ideas and weigh them," he counseled McHenry, "of a proper course of conduct for our administration on the present juncture." A "*special extraordinary* mission . . . is at least necessary to know what measure of redress will satisfy, if any is due," and should France refuse to negotiate, Hamilton concluded, "still the great advantage results of showing in the most glaring light to our people her unreasonableness, of disarming a party of the plea that all has not been done which might be done, of refuting completely the charge that the

---

80. Steiner, *James McHenry*, pp. 224–42. From Holland, whither he had gone as American minister, William Vans Murray added the rejoinder that Gerry was "the least qualified to play a part in Paris, either among the men or the women. He is too virtuous for the last, too little acquainted with the world and with himself for the first." Murray to McHenry, June 22, 1797.

81. Steiner, *James McHenry*, pp. 212–22. See also Dauer, *The Adams Federalists*, pp. 120–28.

actual administration desires war with France."[82] By such pressure the original opposition of the cabinet was abandoned, and by the time Adams requested each secretary's opinion as to recommendations he should make to the special session of Congress, called for May 15, they agreed on the propriety of the measure if the country were at the same time put in a proper state of defense. To this the President agreed and the breach was seemingly healed.[83]

But McHenry continued to send copies of Adams's queries to Hamilton, which were answered in detailed letters outlining the policies that the secretary should recommend. Although most of these were acceptable to the President and followed by him without knowledge as to their true source, from this time onward Adams became increasingly aware of the disloyalty within his cabinet. Certainly after the intrigue in 1798, over naming Hamilton second in command to Washington because of the crisis with France, he no longer doubted but that McHenry was acting against him.[84] The only loyal member of the cabinet appears to have been Benjamin Stoddert, a Maryland Federalist who was appointed Secretary of the Navy after the creation of that department in May of 1798. It was Stoddert who ultimately warned Adams that the cabinet was trying to defeat the latter's plan of a peace mission to France in 1799; subsequently Pickering and McHenry were dismissed, but Wolcott succeeded in deceiving the President to the end.[85]

Six months after their arrival in France, the American envoys notified Adams of the collapse of negotiations. On

82. *Ibid.*, pp. 212–24. Hamilton to McHenry, n.d., and Same to Same, dated April 26 and 29, 1797.
83. Dauer, *The Adams Federalists*, p. 127. Miller, *The Federalist Era*, p. 206.
84. Steiner, *James McHenry*, pp. 212–28, 290–96. Hamilton to McHenry, n.d., and Same to Same, dated April 29, 1797; McHenry to Pickering, dated May 28, 1797, and February 23, 1811.
85. Dauer, *The Adams Federalists*, pp. 123–24.

March 19, 1798, the President informed Congress that through no fault of Pinckney, Marshall, and Gerry, the Directory had refused to accept the mission. Nothing remained but to prepare measures of defense. However, fearing the effect on the envoys (who were still in France), Adams decided not to communicate their dispatches. Federalists regarded this information as announcing a situation virtually equivalent to war, but to suspicious Republicans the President's message without the dispatches was considered an insufficient explanation. Feeling certain that conditions were not as bleak as pictured by the administration, they demanded that the entire correspondence be transmitted to Congress. The Federalists at first resisted this proposal, but as news of the insulting treatment to the envoys spread, they became convinced that relations with France were worse than Adams indicated. Upon considering the effect the correspondence would have upon waverers in Congress and the American public at large, both High Federalists and party moderates joined with Republicans in clamoring for the dispatches. It was somewhat ironic that by this action the Federalists completely reversed themselves from their earlier negative stand when Congress called for the papers relating to Jay's Treaty. However, the present vote was not along party lines; of Maryland's eight representatives, for instance, only Eastern Shore Federalist William Hindman voted in the negative.[86]

The ensuing uproar over the "XYZ Papers"[87] electrified the country. Federalists everywhere rejoiced in the national revulsion against France. The champion of national rights against foreign aggression, the party now reaped the reward for its long crusade against the French Revolution as it found new friends and supporters among all classes. John Adams, who

---

86. *Annals of Congress*, House of Representatives, 5th Congress, 2nd Session, pp. 1200–1371.
87. Transmitted to Congress on April 3, the papers were so designated because Adams gave the letters X, Y, and Z in place of the actual names of Talleyrand's agents, which were deleted from the correspondence. See Miller, *The Federalist Era*, p. 210.

had never been permitted to forget that he was "President by three votes," was suddenly raised to the pinnacle of popularity with the American people. Complimentary addresses poured into his office, all of which Adams answered with a virulence worthy of such extremists as Pickering or Wolcott. Thanks to Talleyrand and the Directory, the President and his party had been given a new lease on life.[88]

Federalist leaders in Maryland echoed the sentiment sweeping America. Even before the affair became public, William Vans Murray informed McHenry that "the passions of the people . . . must be set completely against the French or our independence will fall"; the collapse of negotiations, he predicted, would be of positive benefit for Federalism as "the national mind will become truly National."[89] Upon hearing of the mission's failure, Murray again observed that "if a proper use be made of the late event in Paris I should suppose the eyes of many, certainly not all, in America might be opened. . . . Our worthy citizens would no longer be the dupes of the most . . . vicious nation under the sun."[90] From Baltimore William Hindman wrote that "a considerable change of Sentiment has taken Place here towards the French, I wish it was universal throughout the United States, as I believe Them to be a perfidious and abominable Nation, whose Object appears to be to lord it over the rest of the World."[91]

Such feelings were heightened in the following months. Proclaiming that France's "face of Hypocrisy" was now known to the world, the Maryland House of Delegates urged all citizens to awaken from "the delirium of unsuspecting friendship" and "rally round the government of their adoption." Temporarily forgetting his fear that "British influence was

---

88. Miller, *The Federalist Era,* pp. 210–14; Dauer, *The Adams Federalists,* pp. 142–43.
89. Steiner, *James McHenry,* pp. 233–34. Murray to McHenry, dated The Hague, July 14, 1797.
90. *Ibid.,* pp. 275–85. Murray to McHenry, n.d.
91. *Ibid.,* pp. 249–50. William Hindman to McHenry, dated May 7, 1797.

about to overwhelm us," Governor John Henry joined with the General Assembly in this demand for solidarity by encouraging the people to place themselves in a posture of defense.[92] Residents of Annapolis appointed a committee of five to collect subscriptions for the purpose, while at a public meeting organized at the Exchange by the merchants of Baltimore, over $40,000 was subscribed in one evening toward the construction of two sloops of war.[93] Volunteer militia units were organized, and the state militia was readied to ward off an expected French invasion. Some of the volunteer units were formed along party lines, the Federalists being disinclined to serve with or under men who might be of the "French Party." As John Hanson Thomas asserted, "At any other period I should deem it of little consequence who were my commanders; but . . . from a strong desire to avoid being under the command of democratic officers . . . in the present situation of parties I cannot think of putting it in the power of an unprincipled Jacobin to direct me to any place his malice might point out."[94] In mounting excitement, meetings commending Adams and the measures taken by him were held throughout the state,[95] capped by a General Assembly resolution in December expressing Maryland's "entire and cordial approbation of the . . . administration."[96]

The same attitude of preparedness was taken by Maryland's

---

92. *Votes and Proceedings,* House of Delegates and Senate, November Session, 1798; Governor John Henry to the General Assembly, November 1798, in Executive Letterbook, Annapolis Hall of Records; Steiner, *James McHenry,* p. 306.
93. Scharf, *Maryland,* 2:598–600.
94. John Hanson Thomas to William Potts, Jr., dated May 29, 1799. MS in Edwin Thomas Papers, M.H.S.
95. Steiner, *James McHenry,* pp. 305–7. James Winchester to McHenry, dated April 18, 1798. Discussing the "French Party," Winchester wrote: "They dare not face us. But they keep alive the spirit of the party in favor of France, tho' they are ashamed to avow it. They had rather sacrifice their Country, its honor, & national character, than their individual popularity." See also Scharf, *Maryland,* 2:600.
96. *Votes and Proceedings,* Senate and House of Delegates, November Session, 1798.

national representatives. Secretary of the Navy Stoddert pressed for the immediate construction of additional capital ships, while Secretary of War McHenry warned Congress that "to forbear . . . from taking naval and military measures to secure our trade, defend our territory in case of invasion, and prevent, or suppress domestic insurrection, would be to offer up the United States a certain prey to Europe and exhibit to the world a sad spectacle of national degradation and imbecility."[97] In the House, Maryland's representatives of both parties cooperated to a great extent in voting for defensive legislation even though Eastern Shore Federalist John Dennis complained that Congress was not acting fast enough or going far enough in view of the immediacy of the crisis, and Republican Samuel Smith in this respect departed from his expressions of doubt in 1797 as to the truth of the Directory's refusal to receive C. C. Pinckney.[98] Moreover, Smith thought it rather unwise to push France into open hostilities when she had the power to destroy American trade. He thus voted to increase the size of the army but would not sanction offensive military preparations or the passage of discriminatory measures against France. Republican Richard Sprigg, Jr., agreed with the Baltimore congressman.[99]

The justification for strengthening American defenses was the imminent danger in which the country presumably stood of a French invasion. This threat was constantly played up by the Federalist press, so much so that, while war with France stubbornly refused to burst into flame, domestic passions seethed on the verge of explosion.[100] It was not only

97. Steiner, *James McHenry,* p. 304. Summary of McHenry's report to the House of Representatives, dated April 9, 1798. See also Miller, *The Federalist Era,* pp. 215–17.

98. *Ibid.,* p. 211. Samuel Smith to McHenry, dated April 5, 1797.

99. *Annals of Congress,* 5th Congress, 2nd Session, pp. 700, 1402, 1553, 1769–70, 1772, 1868–96, 2068–69.

100. *The Federal Gazette,* July 7 and 20, and September 4, 1798; *Gazette of the United States,* June 9, 1798. The press reported that French armies were being readied for the invasion of the United States, that Philadelphia was to be burned, and that the "French

the enemy without, Americans were warned, but the "French Party" and the "Jacobins" at home which must be suppressed. By the spring of 1798 the atmosphere crackled with rumors of impending invasion and revolution. The moment was ripe for the enactment of extremist legislation to silence French sympathizers and political enemies who voiced opposition to the government and thus to the Federalist Party.[101]

The resulting four acts, generally lumped together as the Alien and Sedition Acts, which were pushed through Congress during June and July of 1798, imposed curbs upon freedom of speech and of press and curtailed the liberty of foreigners in the United States.[102] Although none of these laws were inspired by Adams or represented the policy of his administration, the President tacitly approved of them and contributed materially to the atmosphere which produced them. In his replies to the addresses sent him by various groups, Adams indulged in intemperate, almost violent, language serving no other purpose than to place him in agreement with those High Federalists who favored the Alien and Sedition Acts. To the citizens of Caroline county Adams warned that there could be no peace until "the impulses of passion, the insinuations of foreign influence," and "the intrigues of factions" were destroyed by uniting behind the government; while to the citizens of Baltimore he declared:

Republics are always divided in opinion concerning forms of governments, and plans and details of administration—

Party" was trying to effect a revolution to deliver the country into the arms of a foreign power.

101. James Morton Smith, *Freedom's Fetters: The Alien and Sedition Laws and American Civil Liberties* (Ithaca, N.Y.: Cornell University Press, 1956), pp. 16ff. See also John C. Miller, *Crisis in Freedom: The Alien and Sedition Acts* (Boston; Little, Brown & Co., Inc., 1951), *passim*.

102. These acts were the Naturalization Act (June 18, 1798); the Act Concerning Aliens (June 27, 1798); the Act Respecting Alien Enemies (July 6, 1798); and the Act for the Punishment of Certain Crimes (July 14, 1798). Smith, *Freedom's Fetters*, pp. 150–51.

these divisions are generally harmless, often salutary, and seldom very hurtful, except when foreign nations interfere and by their arts and agents excite and ferment them into parties and factions: such interference and influence must be resisted and exterminated or it will end in America, as it did anciently in Greece, and in our own time in Europe, in our total destruction as a republican government, and independent power.[103]

The Federalists were certain, moreover, that foreign-born residents and newly arrived immigrants were foremost among those "parties and factions" of which Adams spoke. By 1798 it was disturbingly clear that the great majority of these people, once they became citizens and voters by virtue of lenient state naturalization laws, were swelling the ranks of the Republican Party and thereby contesting the Federalists' control of the eastern seaboard. This was particularly true of the tremendous numbers of Irish immigrants, estimated by the Federalists at forty thousand men—"a force sufficient to form an imperium in imperio." No lovers of Great Britain, the United Irishmen were alternately feared and admired as the "most God-provoking Democrats on this side of Hell!"[104]

At the outset Maryland supported the discriminatory legislation. The Naturalization Act, which raised the probationary residence qualification for citizenship from five to fourteen years, had been antedated by a resolution passed by the General Assembly proposing that no one be eligible for membership in Congress unless he were a natural-born citizen or a resident of the United States at the time of the signing of

---

103. *Gazette of the United States,* May 4, June 30, and July 1, 1798. The *Gazette* also ran articles urging an immediate declaration of war.

104. Cited in Miller, *The Federalist Era,* p. 229, and Smith, *Freedom's Fetters,* p. 24. See also William Cobbett, *Detection of a Conspiracy Formed by the United Irishmen, With the Evident Intention of Aiding the Tyrants of France in Subverting the Government of the United States of America* (Philadelphia, 1798), *passim.*

the Declaration of Independence.[105] In Congress, both the Naturalization Act and the Alien Enemies Act[106] received the support of Maryland's representatives, with only Federalist George Dent and Republican Samuel Smith abstaining on the latter measure.[107] Likewise, the Federalist press in Maryland expressed emphatic approval of these measures, asserting that it was about time rebellious foreigners were "crushed with indignation and driven from influence."[108]

The Alien Enemies Act, however, would not go into effect unless there were a declaration of war. This left most foreigners untouched by its provisions, a situation which the Federalists proposed to remedy by the more stringent Alien Friends Act, which gave the President authority to order deported at any time, in peace or war, those aliens whom he deemed dangerous to the country's peace and safety. The response to this measure was immediate.[109]

Of the Maryland delegation only Samuel Smith spoke in opposition to the Alien Bill. Challenging the measure's constitutionality, he observed that its chief victims would be the German, Irish, and English immigrants who were obviously not covered under the Alien Enemies Act. A large number of these people, notably the Germans and Irish, had settled in Maryland, where they were in the process of becoming naturalized, useful citizens. It would be most unjust, Smith concluded, now to subject them to deportation without trial on the basis of mere hearsay. Despite these objections the measure passed the House by a close party vote of forty-six to forty. Only three of Maryland's representatives, all Federalists,

---

105. *Votes and Proceedings,* Senate and House of Delegates, November Session, 1798.
106. This act defined enemy aliens as those citizens of a foreign power resident in the United States upon the declaration of war between that foreign power and the United States. As enemy aliens they were liable to be apprehended and deported.
107. *Annals of Congress,* 5th Congress, 2nd Session, p. 1796.
108. *The Federal Gazette,* July 13, October 6, and September 27, 1798.
109. Dauer, *The Adams Federalists,* pp. 165–66. The Alien Friends Act was also known as simply the Alien Act.

voted in the affirmative.[110] In the Senate Federalists James Lloyd and John Eager Howard supported the bill.[111]

The Act for the Punishment of Certain Crimes, popularly known as the Sedition Act, was the next measure brought forth in the so-called American Reign of Terror. With foreigners effectively silenced by the two Alien Acts, Federalists in Congress began to discuss the necessity of an accompanying sedition law for those who were already citizens. Before the House could do so, however, the Senate acted on its own initiative through the introduction of a bill by Maryland's James Lloyd "to define and punish the crime of sedition." In its original form the bill declared the people and government of France to be enemies of the United States, and the death penalty was to be meted out to any citizen found guilty of adhering to them by giving them aid and comfort. During debate this passage was stricken from the measure and a new section was added making the printing of a seditious libel in any paper competent evidence as to the guilt of the editor, publisher, or printer of the paper. In this form the bill passed the Senate on July 3 with both Lloyd and Howard voting in the affirmative.[112]

On the 10th it was sent to the House, where further refinements were made. The first and second sections were again modified so that combinations against the law were prohibited, as well as libelous or false statements against any part of the government or any of its officers. Conspiracies were punishable by five years imprisonment or a fine up to $5000, and libel against the government by two years imprisonment or a fine up to $2000. The operation of the law was limited to March 3,

---

110. *Annals of Congress,* 5th Congress, 2nd Session, pp. 2020–29. French aliens, of course, would be covered by the Alien Enemies Act should war with France be declared. The Federalists voting in the affirmative were Baer, Craik, and Hindman.

111. *Ibid.,* p. 2171.

112. *Annals of Congress,* 5th Congress, 2nd Session, p. 588. See also Dauer, *The Adams Federalists,* pp. 160–64.

1801.[113] Again, Samuel Smith led the fight to shear the bill of some of its more repressive features. Although they were powerless to prevent passage, much of the credit toward softening the restrictions on individual liberties belonged to the Baltimore congressman. On July 10 the act passed the House by a vote of forty-four to forty-one, with but two Maryland representatives voting in the affirmative.[114]

In the ensuing uproar over the Alien and Sedition Acts, Republicans resorted to the only agencies of expression now left open to them in protest against the extreme course taken by the Federalists—the state legislatures. Two such bodies, those of Virginia and Kentucky, passed resolutions in 1798 and 1799 declaring the aforementioned acts unconstitutional and expressing confidence that the other states would concur in maintaining "the authorities, rights, and liberties reserved to the states respectively, or to the people." The Kentucky Resolutions, moreover, asserted that the states had the right to judge the constitutionality of acts passed by the general government and to nullify those considered to be unconstitutional.[115]

The Kentucky Resolutions reached the Maryland legislature in November 1798, and were referred to a committee of the House of Delegates. In December this committee reported that "the said resolutions contain sentiments and opinions unwarranted by the Constitution of the United States and the several acts of Congress to which they refer." They were, furthermore, "highly improper and ought not be acceded to by the Legislature of this State." An amendment was then proposed declaring that the General Assembly had the "right

---

113. Smith, *Freedom's Fetters*, pp. 440–42; Miller, *The Federalist Era*, p. 231.
114. *Annals of Congress*, 5th Congress, 2nd Session, p. 2171. The two Federalists supporting the Sedition Act were Hindman and Baer.
115. William MacDonald, ed., *Select Documents Illustrative of the History of the United States 1776–1861* (New York: The Macmillan Company, 1930), pp. 149–57. The Alien and Sedition Acts were held to be unconstitutional under the meaning of the First Amendment.

to express its opinions on all acts of the General Government and request an appeal thereof if they deem the same unconstitutional or impolitic." This was defeated by a vote of twenty-seven to eighteen, following which the committee's original report was passed by the House and concurred in by the Senate.[116]

The story was much the same with the Virginia Resolutions, which were considered by the General Assembly in January, 1799. After giving the resolutions "serious consideration," the committee to which they were referred reported that it was "their decided opinion that no state government, by Legislative act is competent to declare an act of the Federal government void, it being an improper interference with that jurisdiction which is decisively vested in the Courts of the United States." In view of "the present crisis of affairs," the committee concluded, "a recommendation to repeal the Alien and Sedition Acts would be unwise and impolitic." The House adopted this report in the form of a resolution by a vote of forty-two to twenty-five. The Senate again concurred, unanimously. Maryland's Federalist lawmakers were clearly not disposed to jeopardize their own party by coming to the aid of the "servile minions of France."[117]

As the Congressional elections drew near, debate raged in the public prints over the wisdom and constitutionality of the Alien and Sedition Acts. Washington county's *Maryland Herald* asserted that the Constitution was a compact among the states and that the latter alone could judge when that compact had been violated or broken.[118] By giving the President power to banish aliens, alleged "Rights of Man," the functions of

---

116. *Votes and Proceedings*, House of Delegates and Senate, November Session, 1798.

117. *Votes and Proceedings*, House of Delegates and Senate, November Session, 1798. See also Miller, *The Federalist Era*, pp. 238–42, and *Gazette of the United States*, November 7, 1795. See also Robert Goodloe Harper to his Constituents, dated February 10, 1799, in Bayard Papers, M.H.S.

118. *Maryland Herald*, Elizabeth Town, Washington County, June 31, 1799.

the legislative, executive, and judiciary were unconstitutionally united[119]—a charge which brought forth the proposal that citizens of Washington county should assemble at Hagerstown to protest the encroachment of their "blood-bought liberties."[120] The Federalists, on their part, contended that the Alien and Sedition Acts were necessary to silence the "restless and indefatigable French party."[121] Should this faction continue fomenting rebellion, it would be punished according to its deserts.[122] But while Federalists such as Luther Martin declared that the laws in question were consistent with the Constitution and necessary for the safety and preservation of the country,[123] there were those of more moderate thought who maintained that they went too far in denying freedom of speech and press.[124] This feeling was perhaps best expressed in a letter from Baltimore Federalist James Ash to Secretary of War McHenry:

> I can see no reason . . . to *exterminate* every one who had been of the *Democratic side*. . . . The doctrine of extermination would be a delightful way to introduce a *civil war*, while, on the other hand, changing the deluded people by degrees from past error . . . will nerve our *union, Country*, and *Government* stronger than at any former period. . . . If *extermination* be Mr. Martin's policy, I shall never agree with him, because it is much better to *reform*, than to *destroy*. The one is a leading feature in *genuine christianity*, and good *Government*, the other the demon of anarchy and confusion.[125]

---

119. Bartgis's *Federal Gazette,* Frederick Town, August 1, 1798, September 13, 1798.
120. *Maryland Herald,* Elizabeth Town, January 31, 1799.
121. *The Federal Gazette,* Baltimore, September 1, 1798.
122. *Ibid.,* July 13, 1798.
123. *Ibid.,* January 9, 1799. See also Steiner, *James McHenry,* pp. 333–34. James Ash to McHenry, dated August 24, 1798.
124. *The Federal Gazette,* Baltimore, October 2, 1798.
125. Steiner, *James McHenry,* pp. 333–34. James Ash to McHenry, dated August 24, 1798.

Underscoring Ash's comments, residents of Baltimore reminded Adams that he was "the chief magistrate of *a free people* and not *the despotic ruler of slaves.*" At the same time Jefferson was upheld as "a patriot dishonoured by unmerited suspicion."[126]

Although there was no dearth of issues in the 1798 election,[127] the contest in Maryland turned almost entirely on the struggle with France and the resultant Federalist legislation. In Baltimore, where party spirit raged "with great violence . . . beyond anything ever before known,"[128] Federalist leaders declared they would secure "a free importation of arms, and a general exportation of French democrats."[129] Samuel Smith was bitterly attacked in what would become the most difficult fight in his career. Of this fact he was early apprised by his friend, Governor Henry:

I hope you know, that an attempt will be made to turn you out at the next Election; and that you are prepared to enter the list with any champion that can be produced—even if it was reduced to a certainty that they would succeed, still I am desirous that [you] should stand. It will be to your interest and honor to stand by your friends until you are rightfully driven from your post. In such a conjuncture of public affairs a defeat may be more honorable to you, than the victory to your Enemies. The temper of the times is extremely unfriendly to a fair discussion of any question of public moment, and a desultory conversation, hastily intro-

---

126. *The Federal Gazette,* July 9 and 23, 1798.
127. The passage of a direct tax on houses, lands, and slaves, for which every Maryland congressman voted, was practically forgotten during the campaign, although it worked a hardship on many planters. See *Annals of Congress,* 5th Congress, 2nd Session, p. 1925. During the summer and fall a yellow fever epidemic swept southward from Philadelphia to Baltimore, leading to a general business stagnation in the city. See O. H. Williams Papers, Vol. 10, for many extant letters on this crisis.
128. George Salmon to James McHenry, dated September 25, 1798. MS in McHenry Papers, M.H.S.
129. *The Federal Gazette,* July 5, 1798.

duced and loosely conducted, can seldom be precisely stated
or fairly interpreted. The passions which guide each side,
the political course of a man's opinions, will give a cast to
his decisions, unperceived by himself and without a deliberate exercise of his judgement.[130]

Henry's letter was indicative of the plight in which many
moderate Federalists now found themselves. Unwilling to
support the policies of the High Federalists, as embodied in
the Alien and Sedition Acts, their only alternative lay in
backing candidates such as Smith or George Dent, whose
politics were practically bi-partisan.[131]

Smith's opponents, however, ignored his moderate voting
record in Congress and concentrated instead on his sympathies
toward France. As a merchant, Smith was accused of carrying
on trade with that country although his ships were supposed
to be destined for England; as a Congressman, he was censured for voting against abrogating the treaty of friendship
with France; and as a militia leader he was imputed to have
declared that if the French invaded the United States he would
not oppose them but accept them as friends. Significantly, the
Federalists avoided the glaring fact that he had also attacked
and voted against the Alien and Sedition Acts. Apparently
this would not help them garner votes, as only one reference
was made to Smith's opposition to these laws.[132]

Although Smith was successfully able to defend himself
against the pro-French stigma with which he was chal-

---

130. John Henry to Samuel Smith, dated August 9, 1798. MS in Vertical
File, No. 78, M.H.S.
131. Dauer, *The Adams Federalists*, pp. 170–71, lists but twelve congressmen "who fall under the classification of moderates." Republican Samuel Smith and Half-Federalist George Dent are included
among these twelve.
132. *The Federal Gazette*, August 22, September 4 and 27, 1798; *The
Telegraph and Daily Advertiser*, Baltimore, September 5, 1798; "To
the Voters of the City and County of Baltimore," broadside in
Samuel Smith MSS, Library of Congress.

lenged,[133] he had a more difficult time refuting Federalist charges that he had advised Adams to pay the tribute demanded by the Directory in the XYZ negotiations. This accusation was made by Federalist Senator John Eager Howard, who secured his information from South Carolina Federalist Robert Goodloe Harper and from Delaware Federalist James Bayard. Both of these men heard Smith say that it would have been "good policy . . . to yield to the proposals of Mr. Talleyrand." But Harper also added that Smith "did not say so expressly," and advised Howard beforehand that "for my own part, I should not . . . think . . . the publication of it . . . likely to be useful."[134] Nevertheless, Howard proceeded to gather more evidence and a broadside was published complete with charges and affidavits against Smith.[135] Bayard eventually bailed the Republican out by publicly acknowledging that Smith had uttered the remark in jest.[136]

Baltimore's Federalist candidate faced almost as difficult a contest as Smith. James Winchester was accused by members of his own party of being "an improper choice," a man having neither character nor political principles who wandered from one party to another with uncommon ease. He was thus appraised by James Ash in a letter to McHenry:

Let us compare his *professions* with his *actions,* and trace the corresponding analogy. In the Day of *Democratic* Societies, Mr. Winchester was not only a member, but a violent one; and I have been lately informed . . . that he offered some resolutions at a meeting, which went to the subversion

133. *The Federal Gazette,* August 28, 1798, September 5, 1798.
134. Robert Goodloe Harper to John Eager Howard, dated August 7, 1798. MS in Bayard Papers, M.H.S.
135. "To the Voters of the City and County of Baltimore," Broadside, M.H.S.
136. James Bayard to Samuel Smith, dated August 29, 1798. MS in Samuel Smith Papers, Library of Congress. See also John Henry to Samuel Smith, dated August 9, 1798. MS in Vertical File, No. 78, M.H.S.

of all government. And when Electors were last chosen to elect a President, he voted and declared himself for Mr. Jefferson, and now he is to be the Supporter of the administration. Let no such man be trusted. . . . The whimsical and capricious character is little to be relied on.[137]

The electorate evidently agreed. Observing that Winchester "now abhors democracy as much as his friend Luther Martin does water," the Republicans returned Smith to Congress with a four hundred vote plurality out of 2,224 votes cast.[138]

From the Eastern Shore, Federalist candidate William Hindman gloomily reported that the Republicans were waging a fiercely successful battle which kept their candidate, Joshua Seney, "in perpetual motion":

He and his friends are unceasing in their Exertions; innumerable Lies which have not the shadow of foundation are in Circulation to destroy me in the good Opinion of the People. The Sedition Bill, by them called the Gag Law, they build much upon, & I fear with too much truth, as the basest misrepresentations are made of that law, which have made such unfavorable impressions upon the Minds of the People that it will be impossible to remove them in time. This I foresaw when I voted for the Bill. . . . From what I have been able to collect I am of opinion Seney will be elected.[139]

Day and night, Hindman concluded, Seney's riders were out "trying to poison the minds of the People, & representing me as their worst Enemy. You can have no idea of the violence and virulence of the Jacobins here, & wonderful to relate, their numbers are increasing beyond calculation. I have for some time observed that their insolence keeps Pace with the

---

137. Steiner, *James McHenry,* pp. 333–34. James Ash to McHenry, dated August 24, 1798.
138. *The Telegraph and Daily Advertiser,* Baltimore, September 1, 1798; *The Federal Gazette,* October 2 and 8, 1798.
139. William Hindman to James McHenry, dated August 12, 1798. MS in McHenry Papers, M.H.S.

Deviltry of the French." Nor were matters helped when Hindman slipped on a lady's fan and fell while dancing at a local wedding, thereby preventing the Federalist candidate from moving about among his constituents.[140]

Other than the Sedition Act, the Eastern Shore Republicans relied on personal attacks against both Hindman and John Adams to stir up the electorate. Hindman was accused of often being either drunk or asleep when in Congress, and it was asserted that his election would result in the creation of a monarchy, since it was well known that both Adams and the Federalist Party harbored such designs upon the unsuspecting people.[141] On their part, the Federalists maintained that "there are two parties in the country—the one for supporting the wise measures of the administration, the other opposed to them." Seney was held not only to oppose the government, but to be against the very man who did most to establish it—George Washington. In this respect he was accused of avowing "the Sentiment that Mr. Jefferson & Mr. Madison would have done better at the Helm of Affairs than Washington & Adams. . . . What Cheats & Imposters these Jacobins are. From Them, good Lord, Forever deliver us."[142]

But the Lord and the electorate had other plans, and rather ironic ones at that. Seney easily won the race (bets were $3000 to $130 that he would do so), but the effort literally killed him and he died within two weeks of his victory. Republican Joseph Nicholson was elected to take his place in Congress.[143] The Eastern Shore's eighth district, in utter contrast to the seventh, returned Federalist John Dennis with little opposition.[144]

---

140. Same to Same, dated August 29, 1798. MS in McHenry Papers, Series II, Library of Congress.
141. William Hindman to James McHenry, dated September 8, 1798. MS in McHenry Papers, Series II, Library of Congress.
142. *The Maryland Herald,* Easton, September 4, 1798; Steiner, *James McHenry,* pp. 334–36. Hindman to McHenry, dated August 29, 1798.
143. *The Maryland Herald,* Easton, October 8 and 24, 1798.
144. *Ibid.*

Elsewhere in the State, Federalists had little cause for jubilation. The Chesapeake-oriented sixth district dumped Federalist William Matthews in favor of Republican candidate Gabriel Christie, while Southern Maryland's first district returned moderate Federalist George Dent—an accomplishment which party leaders accepted with a minimum of distaste. In Western Maryland's third and fourth districts the Republican upswing was alarmingly noticeable by even the most optimistic Federalists. Although incumbents William Craik and George Baer were returned, the Alien and Sedition Acts and the direct tax of 1798 (the latter bringing echoes of the unpopular whiskey tax) nearly cost them the election. The only glimmer of light in an otherwise darkening future was seen in the returns for Maryland's maverick second district, composed of Anne Arundel and Prince George's counties, where Republican Richard Sprigg, Jr., was defeated by High Federalist John Hanson Thomas.[145]

Before the election—as if clairvoyant—Eastern Shore pessimist William Hindman advised James McHenry that "none but decidedly federal men ought to be appointed to office in the present critical & alarming state of our affairs."[146] The implication by Hindman was clear: with the Federalists in Maryland steadily losing ground as Republican strength increased, the party could rely only upon McHenry's position as Secretary of War to maintain its strength and unity through the latter's distribution of patronage. Even this source of support was to be denied, however, when a split in Adams's cabinet forced McHenry to resign.

The President's suspicions of McHenry's loyalty had ripened into outright distrust following the Secretary's intrigue in

145. *The Maryland Herald*, Elizabeth Town, August 23 and 30, 1798, September 20, 1798, and October 12, 1798. Bartgis' *Federal Gazette*, Frederick Town, September 13 and October 9, 1798. See also Dauer, *The Adams Federalists*, p. 318.
146. William Hindman to James McHenry, dated August 12, 1798. MS in McHenry Papers, M.H.S.

1798 to place Hamilton as second in command to Washington upon the enlargement of the army in the wake of the French crisis.[147] Early in 1799 Adams and McHenry drifted further apart when the President prepared a measure which marked the definite end of his connection with the High Federalists. This was the nomination of a new mission to France, it having become apparent that such a delegation would be honorably received. The danger of a French invasion, moreover, had passed; Nelson's smashing victory over the French fleet at the Battle of the Nile not only ended this threat but was in large part responsible for the Directory's desire to patch up its quarrel with the United States. Although the cabinet was completely opposed to the idea of a new mission, since this would obviously mean the end of Federalist drum-beating, Adams proceeded to nominate Maryland Federalist William Vans Murray as minister plenipotentiary to the French Republic. Murray's nomination was not accepted by the Federalist Senators, but when the President threatened to resign should the mission be blocked, a compromise ensued whereby a commission of three Federalists was agreed upon and Murray's candidacy was set aside.[148]

Despite this compromise, the proposed mission created a deep rift within the Federalist Party and within the cabinet itself. Its most immediate result was to precipitate the resignations of McHenry and Pickering in May, 1800—a result, one might suspect, which Adams intended from the very beginning. The entire proceeding, complained McHenry, was carried out by Adams "without any consultation, or giving the least indication of his intention" to any of his secretaries. Even if such a course were necessary, he concluded, it was "such a departure from established practice as could not fail to

---

147. Steiner, *James McHenry*, pp. 309–431, unravels the entire long, involved intrigue. See also Dauer, *The Adams Federalists*, pp. 212–13.

148. Dauer, *The Adams Federalists*, pp. 225–37. See also Miller, *The Federalist Era*, pp. 242–46.

excite considerable sensibility."[149] McHenry's subsequent letter-writing defending his case did not help the Federalist cause.[150]

Divided, and lacking patronage after McHenry's resignation, the Maryland Federalists faced the elections of 1800 with an attitude of imminent defeat. French belligerency had been on the decline since 1799, and Adams's move to reestablish friendly relations with that Republic had not only divided the High Federalists from the party moderates, thereby wrecking what tenuous solidarity there was, but had left the excessive Alien and Sedition Acts dangling nakedly with absolutely no justification. Describing the dilemma which the Federalists now faced, McHenry wrote: "I see rocks and quicksands on all sides and the administration in the attitude of a sinking ship."[151]

149. Steiner, *James McHenry*, p. 419. McHenry to Washington, dated November 10, 1799. See also *ibid.*, pp. 452ff. See also William Vans Murray to Henry Maynadier, dated June 13, 1801, MS in Murray Papers, M.H.S. William Cooke to Charles Carroll of Carrollton, dated February 28, 1799, MS in Carroll Papers, 1781–1833, Vol. 8, M.H.S., and Robert Goodloe Harper to James McHenry, dated August 2, 1799, MS in Harper Letters, M.H.S.
150. Steiner, *James McHenry*, pp. 452ff.
151. *Ibid.*, p. 420. McHenry to Washington, n.d.

5

The Republicans' Triumph:
1800-1806

FEDERALISTS in Maryland and the country at large
viewed the approaching elections in 1800 with feelings
ranging from anxiety to downright gloom. The heavy expense
of waging the undeclared war with France, the new taxes the
war had made necessary, the large increase in the national
debt, the fear of "monarchism," and the overwhelming un-
popularity of the Alien and Sedition Acts played into the
hands of the Republicans. Above all, the party was handi-
capped by the fact that the dispute with France failed to
erupt into open war. By 1800 peace was in the air, and the
Federalists were finding themselves discredited as warmongers
and initiators of the most repressive legislation ever passed.

Worse, the party was shot through with division. Soon
after the mission to France sailed, the Hamiltonian Federalists began to take the position that Adams should not be
supported in the coming presidential contest. Accordingly
when the party caucus in May 1800 selected Adams and
Charles Cotesworth Pinckney as its standard-bearers, Hamilton undertook to elevate Pinckney to the Presidency and to
relegate Adams to the Vice-Presidency by manipulating the

vote in the electoral college. The plot was the same as in 1796, the only difference being a slight change in characters. For a time it appeared that some semblance of unity might be maintained between the two factions, but this was not to be. Shortly after the caucus pledged the party's equal support to both candidates, Adams precipitated an open rupture by demanding McHenry's resignation. Pickering's dismissal followed almost at once. The breach in the ranks of Federalism was thus unveiled for all to see, and the opposition entered the gap with relative ease. In the ensuing months the Federalist campaign turned into a donnybrook, with the two wings of the party more bitter in their denunciations of each other than of the Republicans themselves.[1]

For Maryland Federalists the election of 1800 presented the most serious challenge since the ratification of the Constitution. Their problems were twofold. First, in order to forestall a Republican victory, the state's entire electoral vote must somehow be salvaged for Adams and Pinckney. Second, party unity in Maryland had to be maintained at all costs,

---

1. Dauer, *The Adams Federalists*, pp. 246–50. There is evidence that a coalition was attempted early in 1800 between the moderate Republicans, whose chances to carry the election appeared uncertain, and the Adams faction of the Federalists. This would have been one method of preventing the influence of Hamilton from continuing. Dauer points out that Samuel Smith approached Secretary of the Navy and fellow Marylander Benjamin Stoddert on this question, Smith declaring that except for some administration measures, for which Adams was not responsible, he approved of the course which had been followed. But Republican successes in New York and Pennsylvania so buoyed up the hopes of that party that there was no further mention of the plan. The evidence of a Federalist split also might have influenced the Republicans not to proceed with this plan. Stoddert felt that the basis of such a coalition would have been the reorganization of the cabinet, plus an agreement from Adams that he would step aside after his second term in favor of Jefferson. See also Steiner, *James McHenry*, pp. 452–66. Hamilton's desire was that Federalist electors support Adams and Pinckney equally, thus enabling the election to be thrown into the House in the event of a Federalist victory. He expected, however, the detached South Carolina vote to give a greater number for their favorite son; in any case Pinckney would come out as president.

regardless of the split between the Hamilton and Adams factions. In their effort to solve the first problem, the Federalists attempted to change the method of selecting electors from the district system to legislative choice. Little could be done about the second situation, however, and for the most part Federalists in the state tried to make the rupture go away by ignoring its existence as much as possible and concentrating instead on the horrors of a Republican victory.

The Maryland Federalists were not alone in their desire to abandon the district system of choosing electors, for dominant parties in other states were also making changes in the method of choice. In each case the reasons for doing so were the same—to secure some degree of partisan advantage over the opposition. Thus in 1799, when the congressional elections demonstrated that at least five districts in Virginia would choose Federalist electors, the legislature's Republican majority abolished the district system and provided for election by a general ticket—a method certain to favor the Republican candidates. In Massachusetts the Federalist-controlled legislature abandoned the district method, which was certain to give the Republican candidates at least two votes, in favor of election by the legislature. And in Pennsylvania, Republicans and Federalists were deadlocked between the choice of a general ticket as against the Federalist-favored district system then in force. Should the district system be maintained in Maryland, Charles Carroll predicted that at least three of the state's electors would be Republican; a Federalist victory in the state could be best secured by taking the election from the people and bestowing it upon the Federalist-controlled legislature.[2]

This is precisely what Alexander Hamilton was urging Maryland leaders to do[3] and, following his advice plus the

---

2. Steiner, *James McHenry*, pp. 468–69. Carroll to Alexander Hamilton, n.d. See also Dauer, *The Adams Federalists*, pp. 250–51.

3. *Ibid.*, p. 466. Hamilton to McHenry, dated August 27, 1800. Again, Hamilton declared that the election must be thrown into the House of Representatives.

dictates of party survival, Federalists requested Governor Benjamin Ogle to call a special session of the General Assembly for this purpose. But just as Governor John Jay of New York refused to "propose a measure for party purposes which it would not become me to adopt," Ogle consistently declined to sanction a move that could be defended only on the ground that the end justified the means. Since the Federalists in Maryland had deliberately chosen the method of selecting electors that was now leading to their downfall, they could not legitimately change the rules when they were losing the game.[4]

Nevertheless, Federalist demands that the district system be abandoned deluged the public prints throughout the summer of 1800. "Bystander" argued that legislative choice was necessary "to prevent a President from being elected by the Minority of the Nation,"[5] while "Fair Play" elaborated that the district system would have to be abandoned unless and until every state in the Union adopted it to insure complete equality in the selection of electors.[6] Losing patience, another correspondent fulminated that "the people of Maryland have become too saucy and are really beginning to fancy themselves equal to their superiors."[7] With this Charles Carroll agreed. Writing his son he agonized: "The more I reflect on the present crisis, the more I am persuaded of an approaching revolution which will subvert our . . . social order and the rights of property."[8]

The Republicans, however, were not in the least receptive to overtures exchanging the district system for legislative choice. Lashing back in a three-pronged attack, they scored the Federalists as the party of the Alien and Sedition Acts, as

4. Dauer, *The Adams Federalists*, p. 250. See also Steiner, *James McHenry*, p. 470. McHenry to Oliver Wolcott, dated October 12, 1800.
5. *The Federal Gazette*, August 13, 1800.
6. *Ibid.*, August 8, 1800.
7. *Ibid.*, August 9, 1800.
8. Charles Carroll of Carrollton to Charles Carroll, Jr., dated November 3, 1800. Henry O. Thompson Papers, M.H.S. See also *The Federal Gazette*, Aug. 9 and Sept. 18, 1800.

the party which prevented suffrage reform in Maryland,[9] and
as the party which was now trying to take the presidential
election out of the people's hands. Voters were warned that
the Federalists had no other motive in their wish to abandon
the district system than the simple desire for naked power.

9. Chilton Williamson, *American Suffrage: From Property to Democracy, 1760–1860* (Princeton, N.J.: Princeton University Press, 1960), pp. 120–50. The Republicans were both right and wrong on the controversial issue of suffrage reform. The man chiefly responsible for reviving the movement in Maryland was Federalist Delegate Michael Taney, who introduced a bill to establish universal manhood suffrage on December 5, 1797. Because the distinction between Federalist and Republican had been drawn more in national than in state politics, the Taney Bill created considerable confusion and embarrassment within the ranks of each party. Taney had previously taken the "popular" side in politics by voting for paper money, but he had also voted against efforts to prohibit the practice of primogeniture. He was considered a Federalist because he supported John Adams and the foreign policies of his administration. It is possible, therefore, that Taney introduced his bill in belief that the threat of American involvement in war against France made it just and necessary to appease militiamen, some of whose fathers in '76 refused to fight unless given the right to vote. Although personal reasons might also explain his support for suffrage reform, Taney's intervention is difficult to explain thoroughly on the basis of the meager evidence available. His bill was defeated in the House by a vote of 30 to 21. This was not a clear-cut party vote, however, as leading Republicans Robert Smith and Joseph Nicholson joined with ultraconservative Philip Barton Key to kill the measure. Nevertheless, it was the Federalists in the House, together with the Federalist-dominated Senate, who defeated the suffrage bills of 1797 and 1799, thereby gaining the opprobrium of Maryland's citizens. After 1799 the Republicans, sensing the political atmosphere, attempted to seize the initiative by sponsoring reform legislation in the state. See also *Votes and Proceedings,* House of Delegates and Senate, November Session, 1797, 1798, and 1799; Scharf, *Maryland,* 2:609–11; Frederic Emory, *Queen Anne's County, Maryland: Its Early History and Development* (Baltimore: Maryland Historical Society, 1950), pp. 367ff; and Samuel Tyler, *Memoir of Roger Brooke Taney* (Baltimore: J. Murphy and Company, 1876), p. 80. For an excellent statistical study of the Maryland suffrage, see J. R. Pole, "Suffrage and Representation in Maryland from 1776 to 1810: A Statistical Note and Some Reflections," *The Journal of Southern History* 24 (1958):218–25.

This, declared one writer, was in keeping with the oligarchy's contention that "man is a being formed only to be ruled by the will of others and not his own." Unless that oligarchy were overthrown, added "A Practical Mechanic," poor but honest men who had shed their blood in the Revolution would remain enslaved forever.[10]

Attacks of this nature, especially Republican condemnation of the Alien and Sedition Acts, placed the Federalists on the defensive in both the General Assembly race and the more important electoral contest. Replies upholding the Alien and Sedition Acts were generally ineffective, and most Federalists agreed with one correspondent who questioned the constitutionality of the acts but defended their enactment on the basis of necessity and expediency. Those candidates such as Jeremiah Townley Chase, who defended the excessive Federalist measures to the bitter end, paid the penalty when the votes were counted. An electoral candidate pledged to support John Adams, Chase published a lengthy broadside in which he not only upheld the constitutionality of the two acts but declared them to be "just, reasonable, and proper." They were, he asserted, "a terror to none but evil doers," and Adams—"a tried, firm, and decided patriot"—assented to them under "the impulse of duty . . . to restrain practices which are abhorred by every good man and friend to truth and justice."[11]

While Chase boldly defended Federalist policies regardless of the consequences, thereby losing the electoral race to Republican Gabriel Duvall, the General Assembly contest in the very same district nearly resulted in the death of Republican candidate John Francis Mercer. Becoming involved in a news-

---

10. *The Baltimore Telegraph and Daily Advertiser,* August 16, July 28, November 8, and December 24, 1800; *The Federal Gazette,* July 7, 1800; *Maryland Gazette* (Annapolis), July 1800, *passim,* and August 14, 1800; "A Plain History of the Federalist Party in the Legislature," by "A Practical Mechanic," broadside, M.H.S.

11. *The Federal Gazette,* July 23, 1800; "To the Citizens and Free Voters of the Fifth District," by Jeremiah Townley Chase. Broadside, dated September 2, 1800, M.H.S.

paper clash with former South Carolinian, Robert Goodloe Harper, over an article written by the latter under the name of "Civis," Mercer descended to personal stone-throwing and found himself challenged to a duel. After his election as delegate from Anne Arundel and Prince George's counties, Mercer took temporary refuge at his estate in Stafford county, Virginia, from which spot he accused Harper of being "peculiarly indelicate & cruel." Friends hastened to intervene, and three months after the affair began, Mercer apologized to Harper, both men admitting that in "the furor of the moment" they had acted in a manner "unworthy of us both."[12]

The result of the elections of 1800 in Maryland was substantial gains for Republicanism in both the legislative and electoral contests. The House of Delegates was divided forty to thirty-seven in favor of the Republicans, and although three delegates were declared to be "no party" men, James McHenry was forced to concede that "an anti-Federalist majority" had been swept into office. But the Republicans were not assured of legislative control, for despite McHenry's pessimism, the presence of three independents did make a difference. Thus, while it was possible to defeat Federalist plans to choose electors by the legislature, the Republicans were unable to prevent the reelection of Federalist Governor Benjamin Ogle by the Assembly or the election of Federalist William Hindman to the United States Senate.[13]

Nor did the Federalists fare as well as they hoped in the electoral race. McHenry had expected at least seven Federalist votes in this contest and he was sadly disillusioned at the resultant five-to-five division between the two parties. La-

---

12. *The Federal Gazette*, October 15, 1800. Correspondence discussing this affair began on October 21 and extended to December 19, 1800. It involved letters between Mercer, Harper, John Eager Howard, Robert Smith, and John Ross Key, located in the Harper-Pennington Papers, M.H.S.

13. *The Federal Gazette*, October 25, 1800; Steiner, *James McHenry*, p. 470. McHenry to Wolcott, dated October 12, 1800; *Votes and Proceedings*, House of Delegates, November Session, 1800.

menting the outcome in a letter to his friend Oliver Wolcott,
the former Secretary of War placed the blame for such a miserable showing on the "languor & inactivity . . . among the
well informed federalists." But, as events proved, McHenry
himself shared much of the responsibility for this languor.[14]

An analysis of the electoral vote pattern is significant. The
Republicans carried the Chesapeake-oriented counties of the
second, fifth, and sixth districts, composed of Prince George's
and Anne Arundel (including Annapolis), Baltimore town
and county, and Harford, Cecil, and Kent. In addition to the
loss of these perennially anti-Federalist districts skirting Chesapeake Bay, Western Maryland's fourth district was also lost
by the Federalists. Composed of Frederick county west of
the Monocacy River, Washington, and Allegany counties, this
area had been gradually slipping away from Federalist control since the enactment of Hamilton's whiskey tax. The direct
land tax of Adams's administration, together with the Alien
and Sedition Acts, completed the chain of events which ultimately brought this agricultural, heavily German area into
the Republican camp. Federalists were returned, however,
from the remaining areas of Southern and central Maryland
and the lower Eastern Shore. Baltimore went Republican by
an overwhelming majority, the city masses expressing their
preference for Jefferson by 1,497 votes as against 438 votes in
favor of the Adams elector.[15]

If the Federalists were bitter in their hour of defeat, they
had no one to reproach but themselves. Thoroughly divided
throughout the campaign, their energy was sapped by Hamilton's intrigues to place Pinckney in the presidency. Adams
was aware that a "damned faction" was working against him,

---

14. Steiner, *James McHenry*, p. 470. McHenry to Wolcott, dated October
    12, 1800; Scharf, *Maryland*, 2:601–2.
15. Charles O. Paullin, *Atlas of the Historical Geography of the United
    States* (Carnegie Institution of Washington, 1932), plate 102D;
    Beard, *Jeffersonian Democracy*, pp. 389–401; Scharf, *Maryland*, 2:
    602; and Scharf, *Chronicles of Baltimore*, pp. 281ff. See also *The
    Federal Gazette*, November 11, 1800.

and early in the contest he had denounced Hamilton as its leader. The New Yorker responded by gathering evidence purporting to prove that Adams was totally unfit to hold the nation's highest office. Circulated at the height of the campaign, the "Letter from Alexander Hamilton Concerning the Public Conduct and Character of John Adams" accused the President of "disgusting egotism," "distempered jealousy," "ungovernable indiscretion," and "vanity without bounds." Although the letter was intended for circulation only among the leaders of the Federalist Party (a restriction to which Hamilton had reluctantly consented), it soon appeared in the public prints, where its effect served to increase the already growing sense of futility among Federalists everywhere.[16]

In Maryland Charles Carroll, James McHenry, and Robert Goodloe Harper led the movement against Adams. Asserting that he feared Adams's reelection more than Jefferson's, Carroll at once gave his approval to the now public letter. "Surely it must be admitted," he wrote McHenry, "that Mr. Adams is not fit to be President, and his unfitness should be made known to the Electors & ye Publick; I conceive it a species of treason to conceal from the Publick his incapacity."[17] McHenry agreed that the President possessed "foibles, passions, & prejudices" which "must expose him incessantly to the intrigues of foreigners & the unprincipled & wickedly ambitious men of either party," but he felt nevertheless that Hamilton had gone too far in publicly washing the party's soiled linen. An open breach was more than the Maryland leader bargained for and apparently more than he could handle. Responding to Hamilton's request for "new facts," McHenry declared that he was "not pleased with the facts attached to

16. Miller, *The Federalist Era,* pp. 262–64; Dauer, *The Adams Federalists,* pp. 252–56; Steiner, *James McHenry,* pp. 466–77. Hamilton to McHenry, dated August 27, 1800; Carroll to McHenry, dated November 4, 1800.
17. Steiner, *James McHenry,* pp. 473–76. Carroll to McHenry, dated November 4, 1800; Hamilton to Carroll, dated July 1, 1800; Charles Cotesworth Pinckney to McHenry, dated June 19, 1800.

my name . . . having been brought into public view" without his consent. Continuing, he observed:

> Those among the federalists in this State, I mean those within my observation, the most anxious for the election of Mr. Adams, consider the publication of your letter rather calculated to distract than to do good. . . . The chief will destroy himself fast enough without such exposures. Can it happen otherwise to a man . . . who . . . is almost always in the wrong place to the wrong persons. My great fear is that while he is destroying himself, he will destroy the government also.[18]

Robert Goodloe Harper did not share McHenry's feeling respecting the efficacy of Hamilton's letter. With his father-in-law, Charles Carroll, he confidently predicted throughout the contest that Maryland's electoral votes would all go to Pinckney.[19]

The influence of Maryland's Pinckney supporters, however, was more than offset by those pledged to back Adams. In this group were such men as Samuel and Jeremiah Chase, Benjamin Stoddert, William Craik, and William Vans Murray. Two others, Republican Samuel Smith and former Federalist George Dent, also made known their determination to thwart Hamilton's plot. Though supporting Jefferson, both men were in a position to prevent attempts to deflect votes from Adams in the state.[20] Hoping to overcome Hamilton's blow to party

18. Steiner, *James McHenry*, pp. 452-84. McHenry to Wolcott, dated July 22, 1800; Hamilton to McHenry, dated November 13, 1800; McHenry to Hamilton, dated November, 1800; Hamilton to McHenry, dated November 22, 1800; McHenry to Wolcott, dated December 2, 1800; McHenry to Philemon Dickinson, dated September 3, 1800.

19. Steiner, *James McHenry*, pp. 458-64. Harper to Hamilton, June 5 and August 9, 1800.

20. *Ibid.*, p. 463. John Rutledge, Jr., to Hamilton, dated July 17, 1800. See also Dauer, *The Adams Federalists*, pp. 254-56; *The Federal Gazette*, November 11, 1800; and *The Maryland Herald*, Elizabeth Town, November 6, 1800.

unity, the Adams Federalists ignored factional differences as much as possible by concentrating instead on the disaster of a Republican victory. "The present crisis portents your ruin," correspondents declared. "The enemies of your country and its government are plotting your destruction; it becomes you to defeat their machinations or the fruits of your independence will be wrested from you."[21] Jefferson was held to be an atheist, an anarchist, and a slanderer of men,[22] but at the same time the Federalists took pains to point out that "he could with great truth pronounce Mr. Adams to be as *firm* and *decided* a republican as ever lived."[23] A letter written by Washington in 1798 defending Adams's administration was highly publicized. In it the Father of His Country castigated the "French Party" as the curse of America "and the source of the expenses we have to encounter," while praising the measures taken by Adams to put the country in a posture of defense.[24] Moreover, Federalists declared, it was not Jefferson alone who had been responsible for the Declaration of Independence. Citizens were reminded—none too subtly—that Adams "was among the first who suggested the idea of the Independence of America, and was one of the principal promoters of the famous resolution of the fourth of July."[25]

Federalist division in Maryland surely contributed to the party's defeat in 1800, despite concerted efforts by many leaders to gloss over the fracture by uniting behind Adams. The prevalent atmosphere appears to have been one of imminent defeat. This feeling was succinctly expressed by James Mc-Henry, who wrote Wolcott on the eve of the election that

21. *The Federal Gazette*, August 22, 1800.
22. *The Federal Gazette*, August 4 and September 3 and 25, 1800.
23. "To the Citizens and Free Voters of the Fifth District," by Jeremiah Townley Chase. Broadside, September 2, 1800, M.H.S.
24. *Ibid*. Ironically enough, this letter of August 2, 1798, was written to Pinckney supporter Charles Carroll. It was cited at length in Chase's broadside.
25. *Ibid*. See also broadside "To the Citizens and Voters of the Fifth District," dated September 27, 1800, M.H.S.

"we shall make little or no exertions for the federal candidate; not from any indifference to the good old cause, but from a kind of conviction that our labour would be lost."[26] "So much for the consequences of diplomatic skill," Wolcott snorted, upon hearing that the Federalists had failed.[27]

Unity for the Federalists did not come with defeat, however. The election resulted in a 73-73 tie between Jefferson and Aaron Burr of New York, the latter running as the Republican vice-presidential candidate. It was thus necessary for the House of Representatives to determine the outcome, and in this situation Federalist divisions over Adams and Pinckney now changed to a difference of opinion over the choice of Jefferson or Burr.[28] Hamilton at once wrote McHenry to urge the Maryland Federalists in Congress to support Jefferson at all costs.[29] He then followed this with another letter containing a scathing denunciation of Burr:

He is in every sense a profligate; a voluptuary in the extreme, with uncommon habits of expence; in his profession extortionate to a proverb. . . . His very friends do not insist upon his integrity. . . . No Mortal can tell what his political principles are. He has talked all around the compass. At times, he has dealt in all the *Jargon* of Jacobinism; at other times, he has proclaimed decidedly the total insufficiency of the Federal Government & the necessity of changes to one far more energetic. The truth seems to be that he has no plan but that of Getting Power by *any* means and keeping it by *all* means. It is probable that, if he has any theory, 'tis that of a simple despotism.[30]

But though McHenry noted that one "as well might be ex-

26. Steiner, *James McHenry*, pp. 476–82. McHenry to Wolcott, dated November 9, 1800; Wolcott to McHenry, dated December 12, 1800.
27. *Ibid.*, p. 482. Wolcott to McHenry, dated December 12, 1800.
28. *Ibid.*, pp. 483–84. Uriah Tracy to McHenry, dated December 30, 1800.
29. *Ibid.*, pp. 484–85. Hamilton to McHenry, dated January 4, 1801.
30. Steiner, *James McHenry*, pp. 485–88. Hamilton to McHenry, n.d.

pected to measure a strait line with a crooked rule as to find public virtue in the private profligate," he was at first inclined to favor Burr.[31] Other Federalists were more outspoken in upholding Burr's selection. Senator William Hindman best presented their side of the story:

> The Federalists, almost with one Mind from every Quarter of the Union, say elect Burr. . . . The Federalists will tell You that They must be disgraced in the Estimation of the People, if They vote for Jefferson, having told Them that He was a Man without Religion, the Writer of the Letter to Mazzei, a Coward &c &c. Burr is but little known to the People, the Antis can say Nothing against Him, as their votes have placed Him where He is. . . . He is a Soldier & a Man of Energy & Decision, & as Europe is now plunged into a dreadful War, of which We may perhaps participate, I will ask you whether it would not be wise to have such a Character at the Head of our Affairs. I believe, moreover, that He would support the Federal Cause, as the Jeffersonians would become his bitter implacable Enemies. I lament that there should be any Diversity of Sentiment among the Federalists on this Subject.[32]

McHenry was soon convinced by Hamilton that the "Federal Troy" would be utterly destroyed unless Burr were defeated, and he thereupon seconded Hamilton's efforts to swing the votes of Maryland's delegates to Jefferson. This did not prove to be an easy task, for in addition to Hindman's influence with the state's four Federalist representatives, former South Carolinian Robert Goodloe Harper exerted his talents to support Burr. Connected with Maryland politics through his position in the Carroll family, Harper probably had more than a minor

---

31. *Ibid.*, p. 485. Notation by McHenry on the cover of Hamilton's letter of January 4, 1801. See also pp. 488–89, Uriah Tracy to McHenry, dated January 15, 1801.
32. Steiner, *James McHenry*, pp. 489–90. Hindman to McHenry, dated January 17, 1801.

role in the maneuvering and bargaining which centered upon Maryland's votes.[33]

Hamilton's adjurations upon the Federalist members of Congress thus appeared to have had little effect, and during most of the balloting his party stood firmly for Burr as though its life depended on it. There was in the House, however, one key representative whose inclination to keep supporting Burr was rapidly lessening. This man was James A. Bayard. The sole representative of the state of Delaware, Bayard had it in his power to shift the vote of his state from Burr to Jefferson, thereby giving the latter candidate the nine states requisite to election. Although Bayard preferred Burr, the New Yorker refused to give the Federalists "any assurances respecting his future intentions and conduct, saying that to do it might injure him with his friends, and prevent their co-operation."[34] Actually, Burr saw no reason to open negotiations with the Federalists, who were already, so to speak, in his bag. As the deadlock in Congress continued, with no hope of receiving the necessary promises and assurances from the wily Burr, Bayard became alarmed for the Constitution and the security of the government. Since he had gotten nowhere with Burr, the Delaware Federalist now attempted to strike a bargain with Jefferson whereby, in exchange for the requisite votes, the Virginian would promise not to inaugurate a wholesale removal of Federalist officeholders. The intermediary in these "negotiations" was Samuel Smith. Smith, however, had

---

33. *Ibid.*, pp. 490–92. McHenry to Wolcott, dated January 22, 1800. See also Robert Goodloe Harper to his Constituents, a printed letter dated February 24, 1801, in Bayard Papers, M.H.S.; Aaron Burr to Pierpont Edwards, dated July 15, 1802, and Aaron Burr to Harper, dated December 19, 1803, MS correspondence of Aaron Burr, M.H.S. All of these deal with the events of 1801 in varying degrees. Harper maintained that he "was one of the last to yield" in giving up Burr. Burr's Federalist proclivities formed the subject of discussion in a letter from Richard Dallam to Francis J. Dallam, dated April 4, 1807, MS in Dallam Papers, 1792–1866, M.H.S.

34. Cited in Miller, *The Federalist Era*, p. 271.

been active in negotiations of another sort long before Bayard approached him.[35]

In December, when it appeared likely that a tie might result, Smith had sought and received the following assurances from Burr:

> It is highly improbable that I shall have an equal number of votes with Mr. Jefferson; but, if such should be the result, every man who knows me ought to know that I would utterly disdain all competition. Be assured that the Federal party can entertain no wish for such an exchange. . . . And I now constitute you my proxy to declare these sentiments if the occasion should require.[36]

But when the tie did occur, Burr made absolutely no move to implement his promises. Alarmed, Smith journeyed to Philadelphia on January 4 to meet with Burr personally and make further pleas that he remove himself from the race. According to Smith, Burr declared at this meeting that "the House could and ought to make a choice, meaning if they could not get Mr. Jefferson they could take him (Burr)." Smith informed Burr that this could not be done, that the Republicans would have to support Jefferson, but he nevertheless failed to get Burr to declare that he would not serve if elected President.[37]

Having failed to effect Burr's withdrawal, Smith was next approached by Bayard during the week of balloting, which began on February 11. Bayard assured Smith that his vote, together with his influence over the votes of Maryland's four Federalists and Vermont's Lewis Morris, could turn the election for Jefferson. Smith promised to speak with the Virginian concerning Federalist fears over patronage. As reported by

---

35. Miller, *The Federalist Era*, pp. 270–74.
36. Aaron Burr to Samuel Smith, dated December 16, 1800. Deposition of Smith, April 15, 1806, to New York Supreme Court in case of *Gillespie* vs. *Abraham Smith*. Samuel Smith Papers, Library of Congress.
37. Gabriel Christie to Samuel Smith, dated December 19, 1803. MS in Samuel Smith Papers, Library of Congress.

Bayard, Smith's "discussion" with Jefferson resulted in the following:

> The next day, upon our meeting, General Smith informed
> me that he had seen Mr. Jefferson, and stated to him the
> points mentioned, and was authorized by him to say that
> they corresponded with his views and intentions, and that
> we might confide in him accordingly.[38]

Satisfied with Smith's response, Bayard expressed his determination to abandon the struggle. On February 16, after thirty-five ballots had failed to break the impasse, he informed his Federalist colleagues that he had decided to support Jefferson. Although the clamor "was prodigious, the reproaches vehement," an arrangement was at length worked out whereby Jefferson was elected without a single Federalist vote being cast in his favor.[39]

Maryland's votes throughout the balloting were decisive. Republican Congressman Joseph Nicholson left his sickbed and traveled through a snow storm to prevent the state from going to Burr. A bed was prepared for him in a room adjoining the House chambers where he remained during the voting, writing Jefferson's name with difficulty each time the ballot box was sent. The wife of Federalist Congressman William Craik threatened to institute divorce proceedings should her husband not vote for Jefferson. But Craik's marriage was saved when he and Maryland's three other Federalist repre-

---

38. Deposition of James Bayard in *Gillespie* vs. *Abraham Smith*, Samuel
Smith Papers, Library of Congress. Jefferson denied in 1806 that such
a conversation had ever taken place. Smith later admitted that he
had not approached Jefferson directly, but conversed with him on his
general appointment policies without expressly telling him of Bayard's
demands for assurances. This satisfied Smith, and he gave the opinion
to Bayard as if it were Jefferson's own statement.

39. Stevens T. Mason to General Joseph Martin, dated February 17, 1801.
MS correspondence of Stevens T. Mason, M.H.S. See also Steiner,
James McHenry, pp. 492–93; Beard, *Jeffersonian Democracy*, pp.
401–14; Scharf, *Maryland*, 2: 602–3; and Miller, *The Federalist Era*,
p. 273.

sentatives followed Bayard's lead by casting blank ballots on February 17. This arrangement left their reputations untarnished by absolving them of all responsibility for the horrors they confidently expected would occur upon Jefferson's victory. Sam Smith, Nicholson, Gabriel Christie, and George Dent then carried Maryland into the Republican camp.[40]

From the standpoint of the Federalists the worst had happened: their party had been ousted from the national government and a "Jacobin" was now in the presidency. Politically bankrupt, the Federalists would never again produce a serious presidential candidate. Nor would their distrust of the people, and their ideal of government by the rich, the wise, and the good ever again be openly espoused by an American political party. For the downfall of Federalism was due not merely to its self-defeating political philosophy or the ineptness of its leaders, but to the vindictiveness with which it condemned all opposition and its disdain of the popular intelligence. Although Federalism had forged the Constitution into a workable instrument of government, the party's contempt for the untutored masses condemned it to defeat in 1800 and to ultimate extinction as a political force. After 1800 the Republican Party became a national party, but the philosophy of Federalism became increasingly sectional and in the end it became a party in search of a section.[41]

The remnants of the Federalist Party now took refuge in the states. There the light of Federalism continued to shine, but its rays were the long ones of an approaching sunset.

In Maryland, Republican ascendency increased steadily from 1800 to 1806, with the Federalists waging little more than a rearguard action to stop their enemy's growth. Successes there were, but these were the exception and not the rule. The Congressional elections of 1801 showed Republicans that the Federalists were not going to give up the ghost with-

40. Scharf, *Maryland*, 2: 602–3; Miller, *The Federalist Era*, p. 271.
41. Miller, *The Federalist Era*, pp. 272–77; Beard, *Jeffersonian Democracy*, pp. 464–67; Dauer, *The Adams Federalists*, pp. 260–65.

out a struggle, but it is significant that the three Federalist candidates elected to Congress were returned from the traditionally conservative Southern and Potomac-oriented counties where the party had always been strongest. Central and Western Maryland, together with the Eastern counties of the upper Chesapeake, returned five Republicans from districts where the Federalists were steadily losing ground. In several districts Federalist opposition would cease completely by 1806.[42]

The Republicans moved at once to consolidate their positions both in Congress and in the states. Parts of the Sedition Act were repealed by Congress in February, 1801, as a general reform movement got underway giving meaning to the "revolution" of which Jefferson had spoken.[43] In Maryland the Republicans pushed a suffrage bill through the House of Delegates in December, 1800, by a vote of 57 to 11, after efforts had been repulsed to amend it so as to confine the franchise to the owners of property valuated at thirty pounds.[44] The bill, ironically, was introduced by Delegate Edward Lloyd, the son of former Senator James Lloyd who had co-authored the Sedition Act of 1798. It allowed all free white adult males, if twelve months resident in a county, to vote by ballot in elections for sheriffs, delegates, and other state officials.[45]

The Senate refused to accept the bill, countering it with a revised version imposing property qualifications. When the delegates declared that the Senate's proposals would disfranchise many persons entitled to vote under the constitution, the upper house replied that suffrage without restrictions would be disastrous, for the time would come—as it had before in history—when a large number of people would be

---

42. Dauer, *The Adams Federalists*, pp. 323–28, appendix.
43. *Annals of Congress*, Sixth Congress, 2nd Session, pp. 975, 1038, 1049.
44. *Votes and Proceedings*, House of Delegates, November Session, 1800.
45. *Ibid.* The terms of the original bill were sufficiently confusing to require amendments in 1810 removing all ambiguity. The original bill failed to make clear that voters in state elections could also vote in congressional and presidential elections. See *Maryland Gazette*, November 14, 1810.

without property, virtue, or knowledge to resist the siren call of the demagogue. Moreover, the Senate concluded, the state of natural liberty did not necessarily include the liberty to vote.[46]

But the House would not let the matter rest, for by allowing the Senate to delay it would not be possible to secure the bill's passage in two successive legislatures, which was the only way of amending the constitution. In December of 1801, therefore, the Delegates played their trump card by threatening to demand the calling of a constitutional convention to make the Senate an elective body. This stratagem, which had been held in reserve until all other means of persuasion had failed, was sufficient to force the Senate's capitulation. The august and conservative upper house, horrified at the mere thought of being thrown open to direct balloting by the people, tacitly and quickly agreed to accept universal white suffrage in return for its continued election by indirect means. Since the Senate was chosen by electoral districts, where Eastern and Southern sections predominated, its acceptance of suffrage reform meant the uninterrupted domination of those areas in state affairs.[47]

The suffrage bill was confirmed in the 1802 session of the General Assembly, with the Senate concurring unanimously. This victory did not exhaust democratic sentiment in the state, however, for in following years efforts were made to secure popular election of the Governor, Senate, and Justices of the Levy Courts; to increase the representation of Baltimore; to abolish religious qualifications for office; to repeal other property tests; and to do away with a tax for the support of the Christian religion. Although the Republicans were the most active in this respect, Federalists such as Delegate John

---

46. *Votes and Proceedings*, Senate, December 19, 1800.
47. *Ibid.*, House of Delegates and Senate, November Session, 1801. See also Scharf, *Maryland*, 2: 608–12; J. R. Pole, *Journal of Southern History* 24: 1958, 218–28; and Williamson, *American Suffrage*, pp. 134ff.

Hanson Thomas of Frederick county also led in the movement for reform. Whether such Federalist efforts stemmed from genuine democratic beliefs or simply from a desire to garner support at the polls can only be surmised.[48]

Reform legislation both in Congress and in the state provided the keynote for the elections of 1802. Republican Congressmen Samuel Smith, Stevenson Archer, and Joseph Nicholson had led the Maryland floor fight to repeal the Judiciary Bill of 1801—a bone in the throat for Republicans—and to reduce the time necessary for naturalization. Federalist representatives John Dennis and Thomas Plater, on the other hand, vigorously defended the acts and accused the Republicans of undermining the foundation of constitutional government by removing officials for purely personal reasons. In the voting which followed, including that on the bill to repeal internal taxes, Federalists Dennis, Campbell, and Plater balloted in the negative while Maryland's five Republicans solidly backed the administration.[49] In the Senate, Republican Robert Wright supported the administration on all counts (including the vote on the Louisiana Purchase), while Federalist holdover John Eager Howard sided with his party.[50]

The ensuing contest put the Federalists squarely on the record against reform. Most of the party was easily in agreement with Charles Carroll's assertion that Jefferson was "too theoretical and fanciful a statesman" to direct the growing nation with "steadiness and prudence." Better that he "try

48. Scharf, *Maryland*, 2: 610–11; Williamson, *American Suffrage*, pp. 150–51; John Hanson Thomas to William Potts, Jr., dated February 12, 1800. MS in Edwin Thomas Papers, M.H.S. In 1804 a bill passed the House of Delegates providing for the direct election of Senators, but the Senate refused to adopt it unless the House would agree to redistrict the state so that counties would be represented in proportion to their population. The House refused to accept this qualification, and the issue was dropped.

49. *Annals of Congress*, Seventh Congress, First Session, pp. 798–846, 934, 982–1074. See also *Ibid.*, Eighth Congress, First Session, pp. 548–50.

50. *Ibid.*, Senate, pp. 250–84.

his experiments . . . in the little republic of San Marino," Carroll concluded, for "his fantastic tricks would dissolve this Union."[51] The *Frederick Town Herald* declared that Jefferson alone had been responsible for unleashing the "Demon of Discord" upon the country,[52] and Samuel Chase added that it had been Jefferson's influence upon Maryland's most "degenerate sons" which was responsible for the recent destructive reform measures passed by the legislature.[53] Another correspondent accused the President of being a "hypocrite and enemy of the people," for did not everyone know that the Virginian had nothing in common with the poor?[54] "I am astonished," wrote one Federalist, "at the popular delusion and madness that possesses men of property when I see them assent to a change in our Constitution, and give men without any property the vote."[55] Republicans of Franklin county admitted that, while not all Federalists opposed reform, the passage of the suffrage bill had been "a blow against Federalism in their county, at least, if not in the state as a whole."[56]

Every effort was made by the Federalists to damn Jefferson personally, in hopes that Marylanders would repudiate those who supported him. "Arouse! Arouse from your slumbers," they warned the voters in a series of accusations that reached an all-time low in political defamation. Jefferson was castigated as a coward and a cheat, as a man who loathed the common sort, and as an atheist who was responsible for bringing back the anti-Christ Thomas Paine to the United States on a government ship. It was well known, the Federalists de-

51. Charles Carroll to Alexander Hamilton, dated April 18, 1800. Cited in Kate Mason Rowland, *The Life of Charles Carroll of Carrollton, 1737–1832* (New York: G. P. Putnam and Sons, 1898), 2: 235–36.
52. *Frederick Town Herald*, June 19 and 26, 1802; September 18, 1802.
53. Cited in Williamson, *American Suffrage*, p. 145.
54. *The American and Commercial Daily Advertiser*, Baltimore, June 13, 1802.
55. *The Republican, or Anti-Democrat*, Baltimore, September 29, 1802.
56. *The Republican Advocate*, Frederick Town, December 6, 1802.

clared, that the Virginian had not authored the Declaration of Independence, but did the people not know that he had fathered a mulatto son who bore an amazing resemblance to the Chief Executive? And now the Republicans were planning on giving over the entire state to the colossus across the Potomac by electing the "Virginian" John Francis Mercer to be governor, "as if the people of Maryland had not sense enough to govern themselves."[57]

If having "sense" meant electing Federalists, then the people had none, for the election resulted in a seven-to-two Republican majority for Congress and an estimated forty to fourteen Republican majority for the General Assembly. The returns were evidence enough that politicians who had been opposed to reform were neither forgiven nor forgotten. Most of the Republican campaign devolved on smoking out those who had been against such reform, with a notable amount of success. In Frederick, Washington, and Cumberland counties, newspaper campaigns were organized forcing candidates to state unequivocally whether or not they would vote in favor of the suffrage bill's second passage. Elsewhere, meetings were held protesting the votes of delegates in the legislature who had refused to support the bill. Although the Federalists argued that their opponents were resorting to intrigue and misrepresentation to gain ascendancy over the people, it was the appeal of the Republicans' program together with their unsurpassable organization which brought them victory in 1802.[58]

But for differences in degree, much the same can be said for the elections of 1804 and 1806. In the contest of 1804 the Federalists sank to their lowest ebb on both the state and

---

57. *The Maryland Herald,* Easton, September 28, 1802; *The Federal Gazette,* July 28, 1802; *Frederick Town Herald,* August 14 and 21; September 11, 18, and 25, 1802; Charles Carroll to Robert Goodloe Harper, dated March 13, 1802 and December 14, 1802, MSS in Harper-Pennington Papers, M.H.S.

58. *The Republican, or Anti-Democrat,* Baltimore, September 29, 1802; *The Maryland Herald,* Easton, October 12, 1802; *The Federal Gazette,* Baltimore, October 12, 1802; *The Maryland Gazette* (Annapolis), October 14, 1802. See also Williamson, *American Suffrage,* pp. 148–50.

national levels. Opposition was almost totally absent in the General Assembly election. The same was true of the Congressional election, in which six of the seven Republicans returned to the House of Representatives were unopposed. Moreover, the Republicans nearly succeeded in snatching away the traditionally Federalist eighth district on the lower Eastern Shore. Had they been successful, only Southern Maryland's first district would have remained to the once-dominant Federalists, who themselves faced no competition there. The electoral contest was even less exciting, and it came as no surprise when Maryland cast nine of its eleven votes for Jefferson and Clinton, with but two going to Pinckney and King.[59]

Although the elections of 1806 found the Federalists more than ever resigned to a Republican sweep, their prospects were brighter than at any time in the preceding four years. Republican prosperity had leveled off, the international situation was becoming more critical in its effect upon the United States,[60] and a split in Republican ranks within the state presaged growing factional animosity. This perceptible crack occurred in the wake of Governor Mercer's break with Republican leaders in the House of Delegates. A bitter personal rival, Republican Edward Hall, had been elevated by them to a seat on the Governor's Council, and Mercer met the re-

59. Charles Carroll to Robert Goodloe Harper, dated May 5, 1804. MS in Harper-Pennington Papers, M.H.S.; James McHenry to John Caldwell, dated July 16, 1804. MS in McHenry Papers, M.H.S.; *The Federal Gazette*, September 22 and October 2, 1804; *Frederick Town Herald*, October 6, 1804 and November 17, 1804; *The Maryland Gazette* (Annapolis), September 20 and October 16, 1804. See also Scharf, *Maryland*, 2: 613.

60. See letters of Charles Carroll to Robert Goodloe Harper and to Charles Carroll, Jr., dated February 1806, to December, 1806. Cited in Rowland, *Charles Carroll*, 2: 260–70. In 1806 Maryland merchants adopted a memorial which was sent to the President and to Congress, containing a lengthy review of existing conditions and demanding a strong defense of America's neutral rights. See Matthew Page Andrews, *History of Maryland: Province and State* (New York: Doubleday and Co., Inc., 1929), p. 418.

buff by forming a new alignment in the General Assembly composed of moderates of both parties.[61]

But while the Federalist challenge was relatively stronger in 1806, it had no appreciable effect on the composition of the General Assembly. Shortly after the election, that body adopted a resolution expressing hope that soon "we . . . may be able to annihilate the demon of conspiracy, the offspring of desperate and abandoned men. . . ."[62]

In the Congressional contest, however, the Federalists were able to retrieve Maryland's third district. This was composed of Potomac-oriented Montgomery county and that part of Frederick county east of the Monocacy River. Traditionally conservative, the third district had remained in Federalist hands until the elections of 1802, at which time it sent Republican Patrick Magruder to Congress. Its return to the Federalist fold under the leadership of arch-conservative Philip Barton Key upset the ratio in Congress from 7–2 to 6–3, the only loss sustained by the Republicans in 1806.[63]

Without doubt the most outstanding event affecting the Maryland Federalists during this period was the impeachment trial of Supreme Court Justice Samuel Chase. While this took place in the United States Senate, and was of little effect upon Maryland's political development, still its origins lay within the state and it did arouse considerable concern among Chase's fellow Federalists back home. For these reasons the reactions to the impeachment trial warrant attention.

---

61. Charles Carroll to Charles Carroll, Jr. Dated September 4, 1803. Typescript copy of Carroll correspondence, in Henry O. Thompson Papers, M.H.S. See also William Pinckney to John Francis Mercer, dated May 6, 1804. MS in Chase Papers, M.H.S., and John Francis Mercer to Samuel Chase, dated May 26, 1803. MS in Chase Papers, M.H.S.

62. *Votes and Proceedings*, Senate and House of Delegates, November Session, 1806.

63. Charles Carroll to his son, Charles Carroll, Jr., dated January 16, 1806, October 7, 1806, and January 23, 1807. Typescript copies of Carroll correspondence, in Henry O. Thompson Papers, M.H.S.; Robert Goodloe Harper to Harrison Gray Otis, dated May 27, 1806. MS in Harper-Pennington Papers, M.H.S. See also *Maryland Gazette* (Annapolis), August 23, 1806.

Maryland politics had been considerably embittered by the Republicans' success in securing confirmation of the suffrage bill in 1802, and Samuel Chase was foremost among those conservatives in the state who were bitterly aroused by the reform measure. In May of 1803, while holding Circuit Court in Baltimore, the Supreme Court Justice took advantage of the opportunity to excoriate both the Maryland suffrage bill and the repeal of the Judiciary Act by Congress in his following charge to the grand jury:

Our state and national Institutions were framed to secure to every member of . . . society *equal liberty* and *equal rights*, but the late alteration of the federal Judiciary . . . and the *recent* change in our State Constitution, by the establishing *universal suffrage;* and the further alteration that is contemplated in our State Judiciary (if adopted) will, in my judgement, *take away all security for property and personal liberty.* The independence of the National Judiciary is already shaken to its foundation; and the virtue of the people alone can restore it. . . . The change of the State Constitution, by allowing *universal* suffrage, will, in my opinion, certainly and rapidly destroy all protection to property, and all security to personal liberty; and our Republican Constitution will sink into a *mobocracy,* the worst of all possible Governments. . . . Will liberty or property be protected by laws made by representatives chosen by electors who have no property in a *common interest* with, or *attachment* to the Community?[64]

Eight months later, on January 7, 1804, the Republican Party responded to the gauntlet thrown by Chase when John Randolph of Roanoke introduced a motion in the House of Representatives for the Justice's impeachment. The motion passed the House on March 12, by a vote of 73 to 32, with Maryland's delegation splitting on straight party lines.[65]

---

64. "Instructions to the Grand Jury," by Samuel Chase, Undated MS in Chase Papers, M.H.S. See also Notebook of Samuel Chase, MSS notes in Chase Papers, M.H.S., and "Notes on the Life of Samuel Chase," Aldine Papers, M.H.S.

65. *Annals of Congress,* Eighth Congress, First Session, pp. 1180–82.

Chase was immediately bombarded with letters offering encouragement and help from Federalists throughout Maryland. The motion for impeachment was considered by them "as the entering wedge to the compleat anihilation [sic] of our wise and independent judiciary," an act of arbitrary *"vengeance,"* a "daring," "disgraceful," "extraordinary" attempt at personal punishment, and as "the most terrible engine which faction can employ." Chase was warned to keep his well-known temper in check by preserving "a coolness and dignity commensurate with this all important case," for it would be but the first of Republican attempts to "familiarize impeachments" by using "trivial causes of complaint" as pretext for being brought to trial. A battery of lawyers, meanwhile, offered their services in Chase's defense. Ultimately Maryland Federalists Luther Martin, Robert Goodloe Harper, and Philip Barton Key were selected. Their powerful arguments before the Senate secured the Justice's acquittal two months after the trial began in January, 1805, the final vote being taken only a few days before Jefferson's second inauguration. Republican failure to convict thus defeated a move which history has judged as distinctly partisan. "I consider it a triumph," wrote Charles Carroll to his son-in-law Harper, for "this day has determined whether a sense of justice has overcome the blindness and bitterness of party zeal. When I reflect on the baseness of the measures which has given the ascendancy to the ruling faction, their abuse of power obtained, and violations of the Constitution to perpetuate it, I despaired of Mr. Chase's having even a third of the Senators in his favor."[66]

J. Stephenson to Col. Moses Rawlings, dated January 6, 1804. MS in Rawlings Papers, M.H.S.

66. Luke Wheeler to Samuel Chase, dated January 24, 1804, and James Winchester to Samuel Chase, dated January 26, 1804. MSS in Chase Papers, M.H.S. David Randolph to Chase, dated December 25, 1804, and Samuel Stringer to Samuel Chase, Jr., dated March 21, 1805. MSS in Chase Papers, M.H.S. Thomas Chase to Ann Chase, dated April 14, 1804. MS in Chase "Homebook," M.H.S. Benjamin Latrobe to Aaron Burr, dated January 6, 1805, to John Lenthall, dated Janu-

All the same, it is interesting to note that it was now the Federalists who were loudly proclaiming themselves to be the friends of liberty and justice against the abuses of power by "the ruling faction." When they had held that position, at the time of the Alien and Sedition Acts, it was the same Justice Samuel Chase who had proclaimed:

There can be no government without subordination, which implies submission; and submission implies that the *minority* surrender up their judgement and will to the Decision of a *Majority*. . . . It cannot be credited that Congress will *intentionally* violate the federal Constitution contrary to their sacred trust; or *wilfully* impose unreasonable and unjust burthens in which *they must participate*. . . . *A false patriot professes himself a friend to liberty*, and yet *wilfully misrepresents* his Government, and the conduct of . . . *the Legislature* . . . and *openly* opposes, or *secretly* foments and encourages, *opposition* to the execution of the Laws. . . . You have *no right* to decide on the *justice* or the *validity* of the *law;* and if you should exercise *the power* . . . you would thereby usurp the authority entrusted by the Federal Constitution to the *Legislature*.[67]

Had Chase and the Federalists been guilty of only the one abuse for which they now damned the Republicans, their party would probably have still been in power. But history is not recorded in rejected alternatives.

ary 7 and 26, 1805, to Thomas Jefferson, dated January 26, 1805. MSS in Latrobe Letterbooks, 1804–1817, Vol. I for 1805, Benjamin H. Latrobe Collection, M.H.S. James Bayard to Robert Goodloe Harper, dated January 7, 1805. MS in Bayard Papers, M.H.S. Robert Goodloe Harper to Robert Walsh, Jr., dated May 29, 1804, and Walsh to Harper dated February 14, 1805. MSS in Harper-Pennington Papers, M.H.S. Benjamin Stoddert to James McHenry, dated February 16, 1805. MS in Oliver Papers, M.H.S. Charles Carroll to Robert Goodloe Harper, dated January 12, February 28, and March 2, 1805. MSS in Harper-Pennington Papers, M.H.S. Samuel Chase, Jr., to Eliza Chase, dated 1841. MS in Chase Papers, M.H.S.

67. "Instructions to the Grand Jury," by Samuel Chase. Undated MS in Chase Papers, M.H.S.

6

The Ebbtide of
Maryland Federalism

THERE was never a more auspicious atmosphere for the resurrection of Federalist political fortunes than the growing international crisis darkening the days of Jefferson's second administration. England and France had been embroiled in the Napoleonic Wars since 1803, and by 1807 the struggle had taken on the character of a massive trade conflict with profound effects for the United States. For American neutral rights went by the board as each belligerent built up a structure of retaliatory measures aimed at destroying the other's trade. The result was increased interference with American commerce by both protagonists and the repeated seizure of cargoes bound from the United States to Europe.[1]

It is difficult to state precisely whether France or Great Britain was more to blame for violations of American neutral rights. However, while France confined its actions to mere confiscation of cargoes, England took goods and men as well, in implementation of both the Rule of 1756 and the traditional doctrine of impressment.[2]

---

1. Bemis, *Diplomatic History,* pp. 138–58.
2. *Ibid.,* p. 39. The Rule of 1756 declared that a belligerent which had

Impressment was the most corrosive issue ever existing between Great Britain and the United States, despite repeated attempts made as early as 1791 to settle it. For England, which never asserted the right to impress American natural-born citizens, this practice was a means of procuring desperately needed manpower during the present crisis. For the United States, it was a threat to its national sovereignty and to the liberty of its own citizens, be they natural-born Americans or naturalized immigrants. Estimations of the number of Americans impressed since 1791 went as high as 14,000, and petitions demanding redress of the evil continually flowed into Congress from all parts of the country. Thus, while England and France were alike guilty of depredations on American commerce and infringements on its neutral rights, in American eyes Great Britain was the more heinous offender.[3]

The culmination of insults to the American flag by England occurred on June 22, 1807, when the United States ship of war *Chesapeake* was hailed by the British man-of-war *Leopard* ten miles off Chesapeake Bay for search. When Commodore Barron of the *Chesapeake* refused to submit, the *Leopard* attacked; after a brief battle in which twenty-one Americans were killed or wounded, the *Chesapeake* struck its colors and was searched for British deserters. Four men were taken off, only one of whom was a genuine deserter. In humiliation the *Chesapeake* limped back to port.[4]

Americans everywhere were electrified by the news. In Maryland public meetings were held throughout the state, and for a brief period of time unity of sentiment between Fed-

---

prohibited its colonial trade to foreign nations in time of peace could not reverse the practice in time of war in order to take advantage of the immunity of neutral carriage.

3. Clement C. Sawtell, "Impressment of American Seamen by the British," *Essex Institute Historical Collections* 76 (Salem, Massachusetts, 1940): 325–28; *American State Papers, Foreign Relations* 4 (Washington, 1834): 57–95; *Annals of Congress,* 9th Congress, 1st Session, House of Representatives, p. 451; *Ibid.,* Senate, p. 57.

4. Bemis, *Diplomatic History,* pp. 145–46.

eralists and Republicans was achieved at a stroke. Citizens meeting at Annapolis on June 29 pledged their "lives and property in support of such measures as may be adopted by the Government for avenging the present sanguinary insult," and promised to cease trading with Britain until the administration had secured redress. A similar meeting adopting resolutions of the same character was held in Baltimore under the chairmanship of Republican Sam Smith. The House of Delegates passed a resolution pledging full support to the President over "this flagrant and unprecedented outrage upon our national character," and assured Jefferson of Maryland's "patriotic determination to brave all the calamities of war rather than tamely submit to the tryranny and insolence of any nation." A Federalist-sponsored amendment to tone the resolution down was overwhelmingly defeated.[5]

An immediate declaration of war was expected and in many instances demanded. Indeed, so positive was Charles Carroll of impending hostilities that he took hasty steps to call in all loans and advised his son-in-law to do the same before business ceased and debtors began to default.[6] But the President determined upon the use of economic coercion instead, a method that he assumed would be especially effective against a nation so dependent on trade as Great Britain. Allowing angry passions to cool during the summer of 1807, he finally called Congress into special fall session, and after learning that England had enacted a yet stronger order-in-council, he recommended an embargo on all American shipping in hopes of bringing both belligerents to a proper line of con-

5. Elihu S. Riley, *The Ancient City A History of Annapolis in Maryland* (Annapolis: Annapolis Printing Office, 1887), p. 226; Andrews, *History of Maryland*, pp. 420–22; *Votes and Proceedings*, House of Delegates, November Session, 1807.
6. Charles Carroll to Robert Goodloe Harper, dated July 4, 1807. MS in Harper-Pennington Papers, M.H.S. See also Harper to Harrison Gray Otis, dated May 27, 1806. MS in Harper-Pennington Papers, M.H.S.; and Charles Carroll to Charles Carroll, Jr., dated January 16, 1806, to March 13, 1807. MSS in typescript copies of Carroll correspondence, in Henry O. Thompson Papers, M.H.S.

duct. The 82–44 vote in the House found Maryland's representatives divided, with Federalists Philip Barton Key and John Campbell, together with Anne Arundel Republican Archibald Van Horne, voting in the negative. Republican Senator Samuel Smith supported the measure which passed the upper house by a vote of 22–6, while Eastern Shore Republican Philip Reed did not vote.[7]

At the outset the embargo was popular in Maryland, and it received warm support from merchants in the commercial and exporting sections of the state although evasions took place regularly.[8] The Baltimore *American,* believing that the measure might well be a prelude to war with England, declared that "if an appeal is made to arms, they will find the flame of '76 not to be extinct. The mere remembrance of the bloody scenes of former days, will inspire Americans with a renovated hatred against the merciless marauder of the seas."[9] Three months later the Baltimore *Evening Post* reported:

> Though all lamented the necessity which imposed it, there were few, very few, reflecting men who do not approbate (the Embargo); and for the honor of the people of Baltimore and the information of the *Federalists of Boston,* who presume that every man, formerly of *their* party, MUST be opposed to every measure of the present administration, we feel free to declare, that the late proceedings of the government . . . have met the most general and cordial support—not only from republicans, but from those commonly called Federalists.[10]

Still voicing unity, residents of Baltimore assembled in town

---

7. *Annals of Congress,* 10th Congress, 1st Session, pp. 1220–22; *Ibid.,* Senate, p. 51.
8. John S. Pancake, "Baltimore and the Embargo, 1807–1809," *Maryland Historical Magazine* 47 (September, 1952), 176–77. See also Louis M. Sears, *Jefferson and the Embargo* (Durham: Duke University Press, 1927), pp. 56ff.
9. *American and Commercial Daily Advertiser,* Baltimore, December 24, 1807.
10. *Evening Post,* Baltimore, March 23, 1808.

meeting at the Centre Market and commended the embargo as "the wisest measure" the administration could have passed. Of the thirteen resolutions adopted, one declared that "we should view with horror, and resist to extremity, any attempt to dissolve the union of these States, the basis of our unrivalled prosperity."[11] While directed toward New England, from whence protests were already emanating as the economic pinch began to hurt, Baltimore's touted prosperity was also daily becoming more figurative than real. With trade drastically curtailed, efforts were channeled into the development of domestic manufacturing. The General Assembly passed resolutions encouraging home industries, and shortly thereafter the Athenian Society was incorporated in Baltimore to establish a warehouse for the storage and sale of such articles as might be produced in the state. Annual premiums were offered for the best domestic productions in hopes of stimulating enthusiasm among the people to appear clothed in fabrics made at home. The keynote in this respect was set by the President himself, who was reported to have been seen wearing "a neat suit of homespun" as a "patriotic example . . . worthy of general imitation." Federalists also commended the efforts to promote local industry, which were already being forced upon the country.[12]

---

11. Scharf, *Maryland*, 2:622–30.
12. Jacob Bouldin to Nicholas Ruxton Moore, dated February 14, 1807. MS in Bouldin Papers, M.H.S. See also letter of Walter Rutherford, dated September 23, 1791. MS in Bordley-Calvert Manuscripts, 1720–1828, M.H.S.; Benjamin Latrobe to F. C. Graff, and to Charles Gwynn, dated August 20 and December 9, 1812. MSS in Latrobe Letterbooks, Vol. II for 1812, Benjamin H. Latrobe Collection, M.H.S.; Thomas Jefferson to D. B. Warden, dated December 29, 1813. MS correspondence (photostat) of Thomas Jefferson, M.H.S.; and Richard Caton to Robert Goodloe Harper, dated February 22, 1816. MS in Harper-Pennington Papers, M.H.S. For developments of 1808, see *Votes and Proceedings*, Senate, November Session, 1808; *American State Papers, Commerce and Navigation*, Vol. I, Class IV, 725–39, 816; *Maryland Gazette* (Annapolis), July 14, 1808, and June 13, 1810; and *Federal Gazette*, August 26,

But the political honeymoon—such as it was—came to an end by the summer of 1808. As Maryland began feeling the embargo's full effects, the benign attitude of unity and good will between the two parties rapidly deteriorated. Federalists throughout the state became violently vocal, and merchants who had at first wished the experiment success began violating the measure shamelessly.[13] The press woefully predicted that "the political intelligence from the great Atlantic States, if it do not warrant entire confidence that the golden principles of FEDERALISM have revived in full vigor and health, at last instructs us that the fatal *Embargo Law* threatens fearful ruin to the tottering cause of democracy." Continuing, the same editorial asserted:

The good and powerful portion of the people are prepared constitutionally to rise up in their strength against the destructive policy of our rulers. Let *democracy* and her treacherous handmaiden, *French Influence,* stand aghast.

1808. In 1810 the *Maryland Gazette* published the report of the Committee of Inquiry of the Maryland Association for the Encouragement of Domestic Manufactures. This stated that Baltimore's spinning and weaving establishments were "making a rapid progress." Approximately 14,000 spindles, in three establishments, were soon to go into operation. In addition, there were over fifty looms in the Baltimore area that were privately owned and operated. Articles being manufactured in Maryland included paper, gunpowder, spades and shovels, iron, nails, steel, and glass, while the following articles manufactured in various parts of the country were available in Baltimore warehouses: flaxen and tow linen, cotton sheeting and skirting, printed calicoes, shawls, handkerchiefs, cotton and linsey stripes, shambrays, Virginia cloth, bedticking and coverlids, yarn and thread of various kinds and colors, sewing silk and cotton, coarse and fine clothes, buckskin breeches, morocco hats, and even cashmeres. "Upon the whole," the Committee of Inquiry concluded, "the laudable design of the *Maryland Association* is likely to be realized beyond the most sanguine expectations; perseverance being all that is necessary to accomplish the end."

13. Pancake, *Maryland Historical Magazine* 48: 176–79; Sears, *Jefferson and the Embargo,* pp. 222–28; Scharf, *Maryland,* 2:628–30; *Federal Gazette,* September 13 and 14, 1808.

. . . The guilty may escape retributive vengeance for a while, but Justice will overtake them yet.[14]

Although the embargo hurt Baltimore as much as Boston or New York (the loss in the total value of exports exceeded eighty percent in the first year alone[15]), it was the farmers rather than the merchants or the city masses who complained first and loudest. According to one report, farmers from the wheat country in the Monocacy Valley area found the lack of markets and the high cost of manufactured goods to be the chief cause of their suffering.[16] Seizing upon this, the arch-conservative *Federal Republican* cried that "the Farmer is nearly ruined by Mr. Jefferson's experiments, who cannot sell his crop for half price, and whose grain is rotting upon his hands."[17] Statistics published by the same paper in the winter of 1808 showed that market prices of imported goods had climbed to record highs—lemons were up 168 percent, high-grade brandy up 33 and ⅓ percent, low-grade brandy up 50 percent, and shoes were up 15 to 33 percent. "The only way for the people to save themselves from ruin," declared editor Alexander Contee Hanson, "is to turn such unworthy servants out of office and elect men who they know will vote against the embargo and all such measures as are intended to destroy commerce and injure agriculture which is her hand-maid."[18] "An American" added that the government had arbitrarily condemned both ships and crops to rot when it passed the embargo against the wishes of the people.[19] "Soon," volunteered another, "the flour will begin to spoil, . . . the salt in the coun-

---

14. *North American and Mercantile Daily Advertiser*, Baltimore, May 22, 1808.
15. *American State Papers, Commerce and Navigation*, Vol. I, Class IV, 725–40. *Federal Gazette*, August 16, 1808.
16. *Evening Post*, Baltimore, June 11, 1808.
17. *Federal Republican and Commercial Advertiser*, Baltimore, August 22 and September 2, 1808.
18. *Ibid.*, August 28 and December 12, 1808.
19. *Federal Gazette*, September 14, 1808.

try will be engrossed and sold out at high prices, coarse cloths
and linens must inevitably be very dear; in short, the people
will have to contend against every difficulty without being
permitted to use the means they have within their power to
relieve themselves."[20]

The Republican press agreed with the Federalists that "it
is the height of folly to assert . . . the restrictions of the embargo are not hard to be bourne—it is the summit of
ignorance to believe that the people do not and will not suffer
much." But it felt nevertheless that the majority of Americans
were still in favor of the measure as the best means of coercing
England and France into making concessions. This was the
view, declared the *Evening Post,* "among some of the greatest
shipowners of this port," and Marylanders could do no better
than follow their example and "bravely . . . meet the throes
and convulsions of the day."[21] When Robert Goodloe Harper
refused to drill his militia company during the Fourth of July
celebrations in protest over the embargo, the Republicans
pointed out that "toasts given by MERCHANTS of this city
. . . generally countenance and support the EMBARGO, while
toasts drunk by LAWYERS . . . generally reprehended the
measure."[22] Not the least vociferous of these "lawyers" was
Luther Martin, currently in financial straits because of "the
most weak or wicked measure that was ever adopted by the
most weak or wicked administration." Having written a vitri-
olic pamphlet entitled "The Honest Politician," in which he
asserted that "there are few men, indeed, who in jesuitical
cunning, exceed Mr. Jefferson," Martin was himself under-
going scornful denunciation by the opposition press as a

20. *Federal Gazette,* August 19, 1808; Charles Carroll to Charles Car-
    roll, Jr., dated March 13, 1807, February 1, 1808, February 12,
    1808, and February 19, 1808. MSS in typescript copies of Carroll
    correspondence, Henry O. Thompson Papers, M.H.S.
21. *Evening Post,* August 14, 1808. As noted, merchants met the
    "throes and convulsions of the day" by a good deal of smuggling.
22. *Ibid.,* July 6, 1808; *Federal Republican,* July 11, 1808.

drunkard and a reprobate—"Luther, Lord of Slander Hall."[23]

As the elections of 1808 approached, Federalists in Maryland were determined to take advantage of the growing anti-embargo sentiment to win back the State. In July, Robert Goodloe Harper tried to bring order out of party chaos by creating a statewide political organization to provide centralized direction throughout the campaign. A printed letter was circulated among local Federalist leaders calling for a meeting in Baltimore on the fourth Monday of July—"to be attended, if possible, by one or two persons from each county." Declared Harper:

> A FEW additional counties would give us the majority in the House of Delegates; and even enable us, notwithstanding the weight of the Senate, to appoint the Governor and Council, and a Senator of the United States. The effect of such an event on the politics of this state and of the whole Union, is as obvious as it is important. It would swell the tide of public sentiment, now beginning to turn into the right direction, appal [sic] our opponents, and greatly strengthen the hands of our friends.[24]

In addition, Harper informed party leaders of the creation of Federalist committees in Massachusetts and Philadelphia "to correspond throughout the Union . . . in relation to the

---

23. *Federal Gazette*, September 16, 1808; *Evening Post*, July 13, 1808; "The Honest Politician," 1808. Pamphlet written by Luther Martin, in Maryland Department, Enoch Pratt Free Library, Baltimore. Martin was involved in a bitter controversy with Jefferson over the latter's alleged slander of Mrs. Luther Martin's father (Indian fighter, Michael Cresap), in the *Notes on Virginia*. See also Martin to Jefferson, dated December 11, 1797. MS in Jefferson Papers, Library of Congress; Henry P. Goddard, *Luther Martin: The Federal Bull-Dog* (Baltimore: J. Murphy and Company, 1887), pp. 16ff; Brant, *Madison*, 1:288ff; and William Peden, ed., *Notes on the State of Virginia* (Chapel Hill: University of North Carolina Press, 1954), pp. 62ff, 253, 298–301.

24. Robert Goodloe Harper to John Hanson Thomas, dated July, 1808. A printed circular letter signed by Harper, in Harper-Pennington Papers, M.H.S.

PRESIDENTIAL ELECTION." The Massachusetts Committee proposed a gathering in New York "of one or two delegates from each state north of Virginia" in order to determine the expediency of nominating a Federalist candidate for President—"and what course it will be wise to pursue upon the presumption that it is impossible to elect one."[25] As events turned out, no standard-bearer was chosen, and the Federalists threw their support instead to Republican vice-presidential nominee George Clinton. By so doing, they hoped not only to split the Republican Party but to secure the election of one who was regarded by Federalists as sympathetic to their interests.[26]

Opposition to the embargo set the keynote for the Federalist campaign. The measure was held to have been originated by "His Gallic Majesty," and citizens were warned that unless they wished "the bloody scenes of the French revolution . . . to be acted over here, it becomes us to be on our guard and to look steadily and closely to those who are preparing the way for a despotic usurper."[27] *Federal Republican* editor Alexander Contee Hanson declared Jefferson to be a hypocrite of the first order, for the embargo had nothing to do with the

25. Harper to Thomas, dated July 1808. Harper-Pennington Papers, M.H.S.
26. Governor Robert Wright to Samuel Smith, dated June 13 and 24, 1808. MSS in Wright Collection, M.H.S. See also *Federal Republican*, July 18, 1808; *Votes and Proceedings*, House of Delegates and Senate, November Session, 1807; and Scharf, *Maryland*, 2:630–31. There was evidently little unity among the Republicans themselves, judging from the intra-party conflict which took place after Jefferson announced his decision not to seek reelection for a third term. The *Federal Republican* noted with glee the epithets hurled at either Madison or Clinton by the Republican press, leading Republican Governor Robert Wright to declare that "our cause cannot be injured but by republican Editors." Wright, however, made known his disgust with the party caucus for taking away the nomination from the people, and went on to express his hope that Clinton would be elected over Madison, as Virginia was becoming "omnipotent." "Can any man be of opinion that Mr. Madison is better qualified than Clinton?" he asked.
27. *Federal Republican*, July 8 and 11, 1808.

British orders-in-council but was instead one of the most "artful productions ever to flow from a democratic pen . . . in order to inflame the people of this country against G. Britain."[28] It was a law, Hanson continued, "which is to be enforced at the point of a bayonet and will bring on a struggle which may terminate in the overthrow of the government."[29] As the contest wore on, the paper's attacks became so vituperative that a group of "humane, mob-courting democrats" offered two hundred dollars to anyone who would tar and feather Hanson.[30]

The Republicans, on their part, insisted more than ever that American honor was at stake in the nation's determination to force England to respect neutral rights. "A RIGHT ROYAL FEDERALIST," who was clearly a Republican, declared that a Federalist victory would result in "a separation of the States, and resisting all Laws, especially such as will not permit the English King to seize all American property he can find on the ocean; and impress every seaman into his service. For say they, is not the ocean his, does not America belong to him, and has he not a right to the services of his subjects?"[31] After reminding the voters that the Federalists believed Americans were unfit to govern themselves, "TRUTH" gave the residents of Talbot county the following appraisal:

> The leaders of the federal party, or their fathers before them, tasted the sweets of the old British government and grew rich—but under this elective government they are

---

28. "Speech", by Alexander Contee Hanson. Undated MS in A. C. Hanson Collection, M.H.S.
29. *Federal Republican*, September 2, 1808.
30. *Federal Republican*, July 18, August 10, and October 19, 1808. Hanson was the son of Alexander Contee Hanson, Chancellor of Maryland and leading exponent of the ratification of the Constitution, for which he wrote his celebrated "Aristides" articles. The younger Hanson was one of the most extreme, conservative Federalists in Maryland.
31. "TO FEDERALISTS," by "A RIGHT ROYAL FEDERALIST," broadside, dated 1808, M.H.S.

obliged to work for a living, which goes hard with them.
They want you, as well as their negroes, to work for them,
and to pull off your hats as of old. . . . They want the British
government to enslave you again, and make them your taskmasters as in England, and in days of old. . . . May they not
prefer a KING to a President?[32]

Despite Republican appeals to patriotism, honor, Anglophobia, and the maintenance of America's neutral rights, the
Federalists' Anti-Embargo Ticket successfully carried the
state in the election of 1808. But while the Federalists secured
a 43–37 majority in the House of Delegates, Maryland's congressional representation remained unchanged from the 6–3
ratio in favor of the Republicans. Nor were the Federalists
successful in the contest for Presidential electors. With the
exception of the traditionally conservative first and eighth
districts, comprising Southern Maryland and the lower Eastern
Shore, Republican electors were returned in a solid block.
Nine votes were thus cast for Madison and Clinton, while but
two were cast for Federalists C. C. Pinckney and Rufus King.[33]

The results in Baltimore were the most significant of the
election. Here, the Federalists concentrated their major efforts
on snatching the district away from the Republicans by aggravating the already-existing friction between the agricul-
turally dominated county and the commercially dominated
city. Under the leadership of Federalist candidate William
Winder, the party took a strong stand against the embargo and

---

32. "TO THE PEOPLE OF TALBOT COUNTY," by "TRUTH,"
    Broadside, dated September 26, 1808, M.H.S.
33. *North American and Mercantile Daily Advertiser,* Baltimore, Oc-
    tober 7, 1808; *Federal Gazette,* September 7, and November 6 and
    7, 1808; *Federal Republican,* October 10, 1808; Charles Carroll to
    Charles Carroll, Jr., dated September 30, 1808. Typescript copy of
    Carroll correspondence in Henry O. Thompson Papers, M.H.S.; and
    Benjamin Henry Latrobe to Samuel Hazlehurst, dated November 20,
    1808. MSS in Benjamin Latrobe Letterbooks, Vol. I for 1808,
    Benjamin H. Latrobe Collection, M.H.S. See also Scharf, *Maryland,*
    2:631.

the resultant plight of the "suffering husbandman." Winder
challenged the county farmers to overthrow the yoke of city
domination by merchants who were growing rich from evading
the embargo.[34] Little attention, it appears, was given to winning votes in the city where the Republican political organization was virtually unassailable. When the votes were counted,
Republican candidates Alexander McKim and Nicholas Moore
accumulated a total of 6500 in comparison to the 1828 ballots
cast for Winder.[35]

Since most of the Federalist vote was amassed in the county,
one can only surmise that there existed in Baltimore a considerable number of merchant Republicans who, the embargo
notwithstanding, saw no future for themselves either within
the Federalist Party or the Federalist business community. In
this respect the Jeffersonians, to some extent, represented
mercantile capital as well as productive capital. Nor must the
appeal of Jeffersonian Republicanism to the city masses be
forgotten. This was directed specifically toward the "mechanic" or laboring groups who were sufficiently numerous to
carry elections, especially when politically organized in Baltimore's strong Democratic Society. Conversely, while the basis
of Republican strength throughout the country was agrarian,
it was the agrarian sections of Maryland, such as heavily agricultural Frederick county, which returned a Federalist ma-

---

34. *Federal Gazette,* August 24, 1808; *Federal Republican,* September
    9 and 21, 1808. Winder's charge contained much truth. John Ran-
    dolph of Roanoke announced on the floor of the House of Repre-
    sentatives that 100,000 barrels of flour had been smuggled out of
    Baltimore in 1808, and Secretary of the Treasury Albert Gallatin
    declared that Baltimore was guilty of heavy violations of the em-
    bargo. See the *Federal Gazette,* September 13, 1808; *Annals of
    Congress,* 10th Congress, 2nd Session, p. 2239; Pancake, *The Mary-
    land Historical Magazine* 47:177ff; and Sears, *Jefferson and the
    Embargo,* pp. 222ff.
35. *Federal Gazette,* August 24 and September 22, 1808; November 7,
    1808; *North American and Mercantile Daily Advertiser,* October 7,
    1808; *Federal Republican,* November 8, 1808.

jority to the House of Delegates in 1808. One might conclude that while Federalist and Republican policy favored different economic groups, yet each party derived its support from a broader basis of the population that resists categorization.[36]

No sooner did the General Assembly convene in Annapolis than debate began on a Federalist-sponsored resolution condemning both the embargo and the overall policies of Jefferson's administration. The Republican-controlled Senate, which had not been up for reelection in 1808, opposed the resolution by pointing out that the Presidential election and the Congressional election in Maryland resulted in Republican victories. But though the Senate accused the Delegates of misconstruing the actual will of the people, the House proceeded to pass a strong condemnation of the embargo. The resolution was supported by delegates from all counties except those along the upper Chesapeake Bay.[37]

The embargo's days were numbered, however, and on February 27, 1809, it was repealed by Congress, with Maryland's entire delegation voting in the affirmative. The nonintercourse plan, which was substituted in its place, also received the approval of all but one of the state's representatives.[38] To Jefferson's chagrin, March 4, the date of his retirement from office, was set as the time for the repeal to go into effect.

36. *Frederick Town Herald,* October 8 and November 6, 1808; *Federal Republican,* October 10, 1808. Miller, *The Federalist Era,* maintains that the defection of the business community from Federalism originated in their disgust "with the narrow and exclusive policies pursued by Federalist banks and the Federalist-dominated state legislatures." See p. 174. See also Dauer, *The Adams Federalists,* pp. 3–17, 261–82; and Beard, *Jeffersonian Democracy,* pp. 268–83. Fear of Baltimore's Democratic Society was openly voiced by the *Federal Gazette,* September 27, 1808.

37. *Votes and Proceedings,* House of Delegates and Senate, November Session, 1808. The Senate did not concur in the resolution. See also *Maryland Gazette* (Annapolis), December 8, 1808.

38. *Annals of Congress,* 10th Congress, 2nd Session, pp. 1254–58, 1502, 1541; *Ibid.,* Senate, pp. 138–40, 409.

Gloating, the *Federal Republican* declared that "the indignation of an injured people will follow their betrayer to his retreat."[39]

Although the embargo was not a complete failure, politically it had served only to revive the Federalist Party and give it a new lease on life. That Federalist success in 1808 was an aberration—a political protest by Maryland's farmers based on genuine economic discontent—appears to be borne out by the election results of 1809. For while the injury to agriculture was not immediately alleviated by the embargo's repeal, the alliance between Southern and Western Maryland which had carried the state for Federalism the year before crumbled in the wake of gradual economic recovery. The Republicans "gained a majority of 10 or 12" in the House of Delegates which, together with the Republican-controlled Senate, enabled the party to return Samuel Smith to the United States Senate and elect Edward Lloyd as Governor.[40] By 1810 these gains were solidified through the spurt given the economy upon the passage of Macon's Bill Number 2. With rising agricultural prices and a resurgence of trade, bringing real prosperity to Maryland for the first time since the embargo,[41] the Republicans reasserted their hold on the state by again capturing the House of Delegates and returning six Congressmen

---

39. *Federal Republican*, March 3, 1809.
40. William Smith to William Elie Williams, dated October 13, 1809. MS in O. H. Williams Papers, Vol. 9, M.H.S. and Same to Same, dated January 1, May 29, and June 20, 1809; "TO THE GOOD PEOPLE OF FREDERICK COUNTY," unsigned broadside, dated September 18, 1809, M.H.S.; "TO THE FREEMEN OF MARYLAND," by "AN OLD SOLDIER OF PRINCE GEORGE'S COUNTY," broadside dated 1809, M.H.S.; *Votes and Proceedings,* House of Delegates, November Session, 1809.
41. Charles Carroll to Charles Carroll, Jr., dated December 5, 1809, March 19, April 29, and November 26, 1810. MSS in typescript copies of Carroll correspondence, Henry O. Thompson Papers, M.H.S. See also *Annals of Congress,* 11th Congress, 2nd Session, pp. 1192–96; and *Maryland Republican,* Annapolis, July 7, 1810.

to the House of Representatives.[42] Consoling themselves by

---

42. The campaign oratory changed not a bit in this contest in comparison with earlier campaigns. The Federalist press again accused the
Republicans of being the friends of France and the leaders of mobs
and riots. See *Federal Republican*, July 7, September 14, and September 21, 1810. There were two highlights, however, which are
worthy of notice. The first concerned "a libel . . . in the highest
degree atrocious," made upon Robert Goodloe Harper by Baptis
Irvine, editor of the Republican *Whig*. Purely personal, the attack
nevertheless united Federalists throughout the state against "the
abuse and calumny of jacobin editors." Although urged to vindicate
himself by either challenging Irvine or responding to the charges in
print, as Federalists "residing at a distance . . . have no means of
knowing your character but through the medium of newspapers,"
Harper appears to have remained silent and let his friends come
to his defense. See Robert Walsh to Harper, dated February 19
and 22, 1810; Christopher Hughes to Harper, dated February 20,
1810; and Virgil Maxcy to Harper, dated February 29 and March 5,
1810. MSS in Harper-Pennington Papers, M.H.S. The second incident concerned an altercation which took place at the Fourth of
July celebrations by Baltimore's Federalist-sponsored Washington
Society. Republicans invaded the hall during an oration being delivered by Harper and created a riot in the building, which was
jammed with about 3,000 people. The scuffle was put down and
order was restored, but fighting continued outside in the streets.
See Alexander Contee Hanson to Harper, dated June 18, 1810, and
June 26, 1810 (in which it was decided not to parade through the
streets), and Catherine Carroll Harper to Harper, dated March 5,
1810. MSS in Harper-Pennington Papers, M.H.S. See also *Federal
Gazette*, July 5, 1810, and *Federal Republican*, July 5 and 7, 1810.
For the campaign of 1810 itself, see the *Maryland Republican*,
September 8 and 22, 1810; *Federal Republican*, August 7, Septem-
ber 11, and October 9, 1810; and Thomas Jefferson to W. D. G.
Worthington, dated February 24, 1810. MS correspondence of
Thomas Jefferson held at M.H.S. Discussing the Federalists in this
letter, Jefferson declared: "I bear them no malice. Contented with
our government, elective as it is in three of its principal branches,
I wish not, on Hamilton's plan, to see two of them for life, & still
less hereditary as others desire. I think that the yeomanry of the
Federalists think on this subject with me. They are substantially
republican. But some of their leaders, who get into the public
councils, would prefer Hamilton's government, & still more the
hereditary one. *Hinc illae lachrymae.* I wish them no harm, but
that they may never get into power: & that, not *for their harm*,
but for the good of our country. I hope the friends of republican
government will keep strict watch over them. . . ."

predicting imminent catastrophe, Federalists warned the people that "France never represented so august, so pleasing and so tranquil a spectacle, as the day before the commencement of the revolution."[43]

Meanwhile, Federalist hopes were pinned on securing victory in 1811, at which time both the House of Delegates and the Senatorial electors would be chosen. Although there would seem to be little reason for such hopes, the Republican split in Maryland occasioned by Robert Smith's clash with Madison and Gallatin and his subsequent resignation as Secretary of State, provided Federalists with the opportunity to fragment the hitherto solid party organization of their opponents.[44]

Scarcely had the announcement of Smith's resignation been made than the ex-secretary supplied the Maryland press with a "brief unvarnished statement of facts" in an "Address to the People of the United States."[45] Proclaiming that he would vindicate himself and his policies in spite of Madison's offer of the diplomatic post at St. Petersburg, which was intended to keep him quiet and salve his ego at the same time, Smith proceeded to relate the disagreements that existed between himself and the President over "certain *measures* and certain *nominations* . . . touching our foreign relations." He maintained that the reason for his dismissal lay in his handling of the negotiations with British Minister David Erskine in 1809, together with his well-known opposition to the Macon Bills and Madison's nonintercourse policy in general. Napoleon, Smith declared, had not really revoked the Berlin and Milan decrees, and it was his correspondence with French envoy M. Serrurier and with General Turreau questioning

---

43. *Federal Republican*, July 31, 1810; *Maryland Gazette* (Annapolis), June 13, 1810.
44. Charles Carroll to Robert Goodloe Harper, dated July 4, 1811. MS in Harper-Pennington Papers, M.H.S. Robert Smith was the brother of Baltimore Republican leader and merchant, Samuel Smith. For a history of the Smith-Madison dispute, see Brant, *Madison*, 5, *passim*.
45. *Maryland Gazette* (Annapolis), July 3 and 11, 1811.

France's sincerity that Madison resented most. Aside from a more personal note introduced,[46] the entire import of Smith's "Address" implied that the President had a conscious and premeditated determination to lead the country into war with England in order to secure reelection in 1812. The Federalists did not fail to seize upon these accusations. At last, they felt, the truth was coming out.[47]

The administration's reply was swift and sharp. Given through a letter written by J. B. Colvin, a clerk in the State Department, it might just as well have been written by the President himself. Smith was accused of perverting the facts and employing them for an improper purpose, Colvin concluding that "the inferences presented to public view in Mr. Smith's address are fabricated, misrepresented or strained, calculated more to ferment the passions of party than to develop the truth. . . . Mr. Smith does not himself seriously believe what he insinuates."[48] But the damage had already been done, and the passions of party were aroused. "He has painted Madison in his true colors," Charles Carroll declared. "I have no doubt that . . . the Washington Cabinet . . . is determined on a war with England and an alliance with France."[49]

---

46. Smith accused Madison of holding a grudge against him because he failed to get a member of Congress to introduce a bill that the President particularly desired.

47. Jefferson had written to Smith earlier of his "sincere concern" at the misunderstanding, "some intimations of which had been quoted from federal papers, which I supposed false as usual." Upon realizing that the misunderstanding was indeed "serious," he placed his "confidence in the candor and liberality of both parties," trusting that it "will not be permitted to lead to any sinister effects . . . . No one feels more painfully than I do the separation of friends, & especially when their sensibilities are to be daily harrowed up by cannibal newspapers." Jefferson to Robert Smith, dated April 30, 1811. MS correspondence of Thomas Jefferson, M.H.S. See also Benjamin Latrobe to Bradford and Inskeep, and to Louis Mark, dated March 22, 1811. MS in Benjamin Latrobe Letterbooks, Vol. I for 1811, Benjamin H. Latrobe Collection, M.H.S.

48. *Maryland Gazette* (Annapolis), July 31, 1811.

49. Charles Carroll to Charles Carroll, Jr., dated June 28, 1811. Cited

The Federalist response to Smith's exposure of his party's skeletons took the form of a conference in Baltimore to publicize the government's "criminal connivance" with the "contemptuous perfidy of France." Party strategy for the election of 1811 was worked out, candidates for the General Assembly were suggested, and the people were deluged with prayers "that the angel which presides over the destinies of Maryland may permit the voters to choose suitable electors."[50] For all their belated efforts at structural organization, however, the Federalists were unsuccessful in destroying Republican solidarity. In the only power shift that took place, the Federalists captured normally Republican Kent county while the Republicans won normally Federalist Dorchester county. A Republican Senate was returned, and in the House of Delegates the Republicans secured a preponderance of 44-36. Needless to say, it was also a Republican, Robert Bowie, who was elected governor in 1811.[51] No sooner was this victory confirmed than the Assembly adopted a series of resolutions asserting that "the measures of the administration, with respect to Great Britain, have been honorable, impartial and just," while "the measures of Great Britain have been, and

---

in Rowland, *Charles Carroll* 2:287–88; Robert Goodloe Harper to Robert Walsh, Jr., dated March 7, 1811. MS in Harper-Pennington Papers, M.H.S.; Same to Same, dated February 22, 1811; Speech of Charles F. Mercer, dated 1811, in Harper-Pennington Papers, M.H.S.

50. Harper to Walsh, dated March 7, 1811, in Harper-Pennington Papers, M.H.S.; Robert and John Goldsborough, *et al.*, to Harper, and James McHenry, *et al.*, dated June 1, 1811. MS in McHenry Papers, M.H.S. See also Alexander C. Hanson to ? ? ? Dated May 11, 1811, in Aldine Papers, M.H.S., and the following broadsides at M.H.S.: "TO THE PEOPLE," by William Clemm, dated 1811; "TO THE PEOPLE OF MARYLAND," unsigned, dated September 2, 1811; and "FEDERAL CALUMNY REFUTED," signed by William Pinkney, dated August 13, 1811. See also *Maryland Gazette* (Annapolis), September 4 and 19, 1811; October 10 and 24, 1811; and June 5 and 12, 1811. See also Steiner, *James McHenry*, pp. 572–73.

51. *Maryland Gazette,* September 12, 1811; Scharf, *Maryland,* 2:632.

still are destructive of our best and dearest rights, and . . .
can be supported only by force. Therefore, if persisted in, by
force should be resisted."[52]

Federalist beliefs that war with England would soon take
place[53] were heightened by the tenor of Madison's message
to Congress in November, 1811. This asserted that American
relations with Great Britain had deteriorated almost to the
breaking point because of her refusal to repeal the orders-in-
council.[54] On the day following the President's message, the
House of Delegates requested that the Governor and Council
furnish it with information "as to the quantity of arms and
military stores belonging to the state, and their respective
places of deposit, or where and to whom distributed."[55] Two
days later a bill was introduced providing for more effectual
regulation and discipline of the militia.[56] On the 19th the
House of Delegates considered and adopted by a vote of
34-23 the Senate's resolution that "the President's message,

52. *Votes and Proceedings*, Senate and House of Delegates, November
    Session, 1811; *Maryland Gazette* (Annapolis), November 14 and
    December 12, 1811; January 2, 1812.
53. Robert Goodloe Harper to Augustus John Foster, dated June 1812,
    and Alexander C. Hanson to Harper, dated June 8, 1812. MSS in
    Harper-Pennington Papers, M.H.S. "There can be no doubt," wrote
    Harper, "that the war into which the government of the United
    States seems about to enter, is contrary to the opinions, the feelings
    and wishes of a great majority of the people. This is attested . . .
    by all the recent elections. This the war party probably knows.
    Indeed it is difficult to suppose them ignorant of it. But their ex-
    pectation no doubt is that . . . the passions of the nation will be
    roused and inflamed against Great Britain. On these passions they
    rely for the continuance of their power, and for the means of carry-
    ing on the war. Whether the event will assure their expectations
    and their hopes depends much, perhaps entirely, on the conduct of
    Great Britain herself . . . on her manner of carrying on the war."
    See also Charles Carroll to Charles Carroll, Jr., dated May 28, 1812.
    Typescript copy of Carroll correspondence, Henry O. Thompson
    Papers, M.H.S.
54. *Maryland Gazette* (Annapolis) November 7, 1811.
55. *Ibid.*, November 14, 1811. See also *Votes and Proceedings,* House of
    Delegates, November Session, 1811.
56. *Ibid.*

temperate, impartial and decisive, deserves *all our praise and support*. . . . The independence established by the aid and valour of our fathers will not tamely be yielded by their sons. The same spirit which led the freemen of Maryland to battle, still exists in the State and waits only for its country's call."[57] In the voting only one Federalist decided in favor of passing the resolution.[58]

As the country moved closer to war, Maryland's Federalist representatives in Congress became more outspoken in their criticism of the administration. The *Maryland Gazette* reported that on January 15 Philip Barton Key spoke with "uncommon animation and ability" against allowing the militia to be marched outside the United States. Key declared that the states could not give their assent to this, volunteers could not offer it, and Congress could not accept it. The militia, he held, could be constitutionally called out in only three cases: to repel invasion, to suppress insurrection, and to execute the laws. No state-commissioned officer, Key concluded, could exercise command outside the country. Although but fourteen Congressmen supported the bill which Key had condemned, two days later a measure authorizing the President to accept and organize a volunteer corps was passed by a vote of 87–23 after the proviso binding the militia to do duty "within or out of the United States" was withdrawn.[59] In the Senate, Republicans Smith and Reed voted in the negative on a bill to raise additional military forces. Passing the Senate by a vote of 14–7, this act empowered Madison to call up 15,000 men, when "he may deem expedient," for a period of eighteen months.[60]

While Congress thus prepared for conflict, petitions flowed in seeking to prevent a declaration of war. The majority of

---

57. *Votes and Proceedings,* Senate and House of Delegates, November Session, 1811.
58. *Ibid.* See also *Maryland Gazette* (Annapolis), January 2, 1812.
59. *Maryland Gazette* (Annapolis), January 23, 1812.
60. *Ibid.,* April 16, 1812.

these petitions emanated from Boston, but they were also received from New York, Philadelphia, and Baltimore.[61] Presented by both Federalists and Republicans, who put forth a variety of reasons why war was economically not feasible at this time, the petitions were in some instances referred to the Committee of the Whole House for discussion. This, the *Maryland Gazette* sarcastically commented, was "only a delicate way of giving them the go-by."[62]

The Federalist press, meanwhile, did not fail to publicize French confiscations that were taking place after the Berlin and Milan Decrees had supposedly been revoked. The owner of a tobacco plantation in Anne Arundel county declared that of forty-two hogsheads of tobacco shipped from Baltimore, twenty-four had been confiscated by French decree in April of 1811.[63] The *Maryland Gazette* pointed out that the French were impressing American seamen as well as confiscating American cargoes. In an article entitled "Unparalleled Aggressions," the *Gazette's* editor reported that the American ship *Catherine*, "on a fair and legal voyage with ample documents," was captured by a French privateer, taken into Danzig, condemned with its cargo by a decree issued in Paris, and twenty-one members of its crew were impressed into the French navy. In proof, the editor published an affidavit signed by Frederick Soper recounting his seven months' impressment and subsequent escape.[64] This was soon followed by a similar affidavit written by one Jacob Smith of Plymouth, Massachusetts, detailing the capture of his ship, the *Gershom*, by two French frigates. The captain of one of the frigates, said Smith, told him his orders were to burn, sink, or destroy all American vessels bound to enemy ports, and that this was to be done under the decrees of Napoleon which had not been repealed.[65]

---

61. *Ibid.*, November 21, 1811, and December 19, 1811.
62. *Ibid.*, April 23, 1812, and May 7, 1812; *Annals of Congress,* Senate, 12th Congress, 1st Session, p. 262.
63. *Maryland Gazette* (Annapolis), February 13, 1812.
64. *Ibid.*, March 26, 1812.
65. *Ibid.*, April 2, 1812.

On April 23 two crew members of the late brig *Three Friends* certified that their ship had been captured and burned by French frigates under the command of Commodore Raoul. The seamen produced a written statement signed by Raoul in which he said his orders were to "destroy all American vessels bound to or from enemy's ports."[66] The editor of the *Federal Gazette* also furnished conclusive evidence, "beyond the possibility of doubt," that the French were still destroying American ships engaged in trade with the British, Spanish, or Portuguese.[67]

Such determined efforts on the part of the Federalist press to publicize French aggressions did not go unnoticed. In May, citizens meeting at Baltimore's Fountain Inn adopted a series of Resolutions condemning both belligerents. The fourth resolution expressed the following sentiment:

> That the conduct of France, and of other powers in alliance with her and under her immediate influence, towards the United States has been scarcely less atrocious than that of England; and if the pending negotiations should terminate without an honorable adjustment of existing differences, we have full confidence that our government will direct the most active hostilities to be commenced against her for a redress of our grievances and the maintenance of our rights.[68]

At a meeting held in McCoy's Tavern at Elk Ridge, residents of Anne Arundel county—"utterly disclaiming all party views" —declared that both England and France were equally guilty of aggressions on American shipping. In a proclamation submitted to Congress they resolved that it "is premature and impolitic at the *present crisis* to declare war against Great Britain, because the country is not in a sufficient state of

66. *Maryland Gazette* (Annapolis), April 23, 1812.
67. *Ibid.* Cited in the *Federal Gazette,* Baltimore.
68. Scharf, *Maryland,* 2:633–34.

preparation to afford reasonable calculations upon success—
because we view the conduct of France as equally offensive
and hostile in *principle*, & because, by selecting G. Britain
singly, as an enemy, this country . . . may hereafter be in-
sensibly driven into an entangling alliance with France, with
whom no nation hath hitherto allied without the *loss of its
liberty and independence.*" The proclamation suggested that
the millions of dollars needed to win a war might just as well
be put into naval equipment and maritime defense for the
protection of American ships and soil, for it was the government's duty, it concluded, to "extend its protecting arm with
equal care over the *commercial* and *agricultural* interests of
the nation. . . . *Maritime* rights . . . can only be maintained
by *maritime* means."[69]

But the petitions, memorials, and proclamations went for
naught. On June 25 the *Maryland Gazette* published the report
of the Committee on Foreign Relations which, "relying on
the patriotism of the nation, and confidently trusting that
the Lord of Hosts will go with us to battle in a righteous
cause and crown our efforts with success," recommended "an
immediate appeal to ARMS." The vote in Congress found
Maryland's delegation split along party lines, with but one
Federalist voting in favor of war. In the Senate, Smith voted
in the affirmative while Reed voted against.[70]

No sooner was war declared than the Federalists began
denouncing the machinations of the "French Party" for unleashing such a "stupid and villainous" contest against Europe's sole defender of liberty and freedom.[71] Benjamin Stoddert declared that England had all the right in the world to
impress her "suffering subjects . . . who have left their

---

69. *Maryland Gazette* (Annapolis), June 11, 1812.
70. *Maryland Gazette* (Annapolis), June 18 and 25, 1812.
71. Robert Goodloe Harper to John A. Foster, dated June, 1812. MS
in Harper-Pennington Papers, M.H.S. See also Benjamin Stoddert
to Harper, dated September 4, 1812. MS in Harper-Pennington
Papers, M.H.S.

Country . . . tho they may have naturalized themselves a thousand times in the U. S."[72] "Z" announced that he would not stop condemning the Republicans even though anyone declaring himself a Federalist was open to the charge of being a Tory and a traitor. "In these modern days," "Z" continued, "to be a tory is to be a man obnoxious to violent demagogues of the ruling party who will, on every possible occasion, studiously direct the popular resentments against him." Conversely, the only rights enjoyed under Republican government were the "equal rights to pay salaries."[73] "Pacificus" added that the war, being fought solely for the acquisition of Canada, would but hasten the collapse of the already unwieldy Union if, indeed, the United States could even conquer that vast province.[74] And when the American expedition to take Canada did fail, "Confirmation" declared that the Republicans could not figure out why "two thousand men employed to distribute *proclamations* up and down Canada should have failed to overturn the country!"[75]

By far the most consistent Federalist accusation was that Madison desired war not to defend American honor, but to secure his own reelection by winning the support of the War Hawks.[76] This brought a retort from Benjamin Latrobe that "no man in his senses believes . . . France has the most distant influence on the measures of our government. As a dose of Party Cantharides the accusation may be administered, but no well informed man believes it."[77] Ironically, High Federalist Philip Barton Key agreed. Almost alone among the Mary-

---

72. Benjamin Stoddert to Robert Goodloe Harper, dated November 16, 1812. MS in Harper-Pennington Papers, M.H.S.
73. *Maryland Gazette* (Annapolis), June 11, 1812.
74. *Federal Republican,* November 4, 1812.
75. *Federal Gazette,* August 31, 1812.
76. Stoddert to James McHenry, dated November 24, 1812. MS in McHenry Papers, M.H.S.
77. Benjamin Latrobe to A. Binney, dated June 29, 1812; to Eric Bollman, dated August 23, 1812; and to Robert Goodloe Harper, dated August 28, 1812. MSS in Latrobe Letterbooks, Vol. II for 1812, Benjamin H. Latrobe Collection, M.H.S.

land Federalists, Key publicly announced that "whatever differences of opinion may exist among ourselves, there can be none as to the propriety of supporting the integrity of the Union."[78]

That Key's sentiments were not shared by others in Maryland became abundantly clear during the following weeks. On June 20, two days after the formal declaration of war, Baltimore's *Federal Republican* set the keynote of Federalist opposition for party extremists by launching a vituperative attack upon Madison and the administration. Published as an editorial entitled *"Thou hast done a deed whereat valour will weep,"* the criticism hurled by editor Alexander C. Hanson was as follows:

Without funds, without taxes, without a navy, or adequate fortifications—with one hundred and fifty millions of our property in the hands of the declared enemy, without any of his in our power, and with a vast commerce afloat, our rulers have promulgated a war against the clear and decided sentiments of a vast majority of the nation. As the consequences will soon be felt, there is no need of pointing them out to the few who have not sagacity enough to apprehend them. Instead of employing our pen in this dreadful detail, we think it more apposite to delineate the course we are determined to pursue as long as the war shall last. We mean to represent in as strong colors as we are capable, that it is unnecessary, inexpedient, and entered into from a partial, personal, and, as we believe, motives bearing upon their front, marks of undisguised foreign influence which cannot be mistaken. We mean to use every constitutional argument and every legal means to render as odious and suspicious to the American people, as they deserve to be, the patrons and contrivers of this highly impolitic and destructive war, in the fullest persuasion that we shall be supported and ultimately applauded by nine-tenths of our countrymen, and that our silence would be treason to them. . . . We are

78. *Annals of Congress,* 12th Congress, 1st Session, pp. 1190–92.

avowedly opposed to the presidency of James Madison, and we never will breathe under the dominion, direct or derivative, of Bonaparte, let it be acknowledged when it may. Let those who cannot openly adopt this confession abandon us; and those who can, we shall cherish as friends and patriots worthy of the name.[79]

But while Hanson's position was applauded by a small core of party diehards, there were few moderate Federalists who would "openly adopt this confession." This latter group not only disapproved of Hanson's extreme attitude, but felt that his newspaper tended to inflame party passions and urge otherwise law-abiding men to commit some act of violence.[80] The moderates could not have been more right. For several days following the appearance of the editorial, public meetings were held throughout Baltimore to consider the expediency of suppressing the paper. The Republican press denounced Hanson with a bitterness well adapted to rouse the already-excited populace. By June 22, rumors of impending mob violence led co-editor Jacob Wagner to take the precaution of removing important papers and books from the *Federal Republican* office, then located at the northwest corner of Gay and Second Streets. At about nine o'clock that evening a crowd of from three to four hundred persons, armed with axes, hooks, ropes, and other paraphernalia of destruction, gathered in front of the building and proceeded to break into the office. Presses, type, paper, and other equipment were thrown into the street and destroyed. The frame building itself was leveled to the ground, during which process a man trying to force out a window fell with it into the street and was killed. Unwilling to disperse, the rioters went next to Wagner's home and searched it. Wagner and

---

79. *Federal Republican*, June 20, 1812.
80. Alexander C. Hanson to John E. Hall, dated August 22, 1812, and October 22, 1813. MSS in Hanson Family Papers, M.H.S. See also Robert Goodloe Harper to John Hanson Thomas, dated July 7, 1812. MS in Harper-Pennington Papers, M.H.S.

Hanson, however, had wisely left the city, which by then was in possession of the rioters. With the two principal Federalists gone, the mob attempted to wreak its vengeance upon various other persons. Prominent Federalists James and Samuel Sterett were assaulted, while one Mr. Hutchins narrowly escaped a coat of tar and feathers for alleged remarks defaming George Washington, only because he managed to secret himself.[81]

In the ensuing weeks the mob continued to roam the streets at will. Several vessels lying at the docks, bound for Portugal and Spain, were dismantled because they were suspected of sailing under British licenses. The Negroes, who had long been suspected of holding secret meetings and making threats, were attacked, their homes were sacked, and at least two houses were pulled down completely. Numbers of respectable Federalists found it wise to leave Baltimore. Departing for Allegany county, James McHenry demanded a Federalist "union of force, to discountenance and put down every attempt against the laws and the public peace." Continuing, McHenry advised:

Let them . . . face the evil as soon as it appears. If they shrink from it they will quickly be made sensible that they walk the streets at the mercy of the secret instigators of misrule; that the air of Baltimore is the air of a prison; that houses are no places of safety; that there is a mine under them ready to explode, the moment they shall either by word or by look give offence to their masters. I lament that I am obliged to leave the City.[82]

Considerable damage had been done before Baltimore's

---

81. John Hanson Thomas to Alexander C. Hanson, dated June 22, 1812; and Hanson to Thomas, dated June 28, 1812. Cited from *Portrait of the Evils of Democracy* (Baltimore, 1816), pp. 85–87, M.H.S.
82. McHenry to Robert Oliver, dated June 24, 1812. Cited in Steiner, *James McHenry*, p. 580. Oliver, a Baltimore merchant, owned the building in which the *Federal Republican* was housed.

Republican mayor, Edward Johnson, together with the militia, managed to restore order throughout the city. But the mob had nevertheless succeeded in its end results: the *Federal Republican* was driven from Baltimore. It was immediately reestablished in Georgetown, where, despite threats from both Baltimore and Washington, it continued regular publication until the end of July. To Hanson, however, the enforced move was an indication of the weakness and lack of unity among Maryland's Federalists. He remained determined to return to Baltimore, and to meet any future violence by that town's mobocracy with strong resistance. Force would be repelled by force if necessary.[83]

Opposition to the war continued in Maryland, meanwhile, but although the Federalists were as determined as Hanson to voice their opinions, the tenor of their criticism was distinctly less incendiary and abusive. The Federalist minority in the House of Delegates—"impelled by a sense of duty to their constituents and in justification of their own political conduct"—issued a "UNANIMOUS ADDRESS . . . TO THEIR CONSTITUENTS" accusing the Madison administration of "infatuated determination" in its foreign policy to select Great Britain as the enemy so that the United States might play the fool for France. The address declared that "attachment to France has been the bane of our national happiness. It is . . . the efficient cause of all the evils which have accumulated upon us as to the disastrous moment, when it is about to commit us in a war with G. Britain, and its more dreadful concomitant, an alliance with France." The machinations of the Irish and French elements in the country were accused of bringing on war with England because of their inveterate hatred for the British, while the country's depressed economy, exhausted treasury, and expiring commerce were blamed solely on Jefferson and Madison. The address closed with a charge that Madison's administration

---

83. *Federal Republican,* June 24, 1812. See also Hanson to Harper, dated July 24, 1812. MS in Harper-Pennington Papers, M.H.S.

had bribed the British-Canadian agent John Henry with
$50,000 on the eve of a national election in order to discredit
the Federalist Party. All those wishing to uphold national
honor, peace, and prosperity were encouraged to vote Federalist on "the first Monday in October next."[84]

Nor were the Federalist legislators in the Assembly content
to rest on the laurels of one address that was mainly an
appeal to public opinion. A resolution by them had already
been introduced in the House of Delegates calling war with
England "inexpedient" and "destructive of the true interest
of our constituents . . . at the present period." War against
one of the belligerents, the resolution concluded, "would be
submission to the other." When this was defeated by a vote
of 35-32, the Federalists attempted to kill a Republican-
sponsored bill authorizing Maryland banks to lend money to
the United States government. Worcester county Federalist
Ephraim K. Wilson introduced an amendment forbidding
any such loans until "after a new election of directors." An
amendment was also introduced by Somerset county Federalist William Jackson requiring the assent of a majority
of the stockholders holding more than one-half of the capital
in any given bank before loans could be made to the federal
government. Both amendments were defeated by strict party
votes of 34-31. Undaunted, the Federalists turned their attention to preserving their control over the state militia. Section
thirteen of the new militia bill, then under consideration by
the House, revoked the commissions of all cavalry officers.
New commissions were to be issued in their place. Federalists
feared that these would favor Republicans—that many Federalists would lose their present commissions and not receive
new ones. Jackson, presenting a petition from the members
of the First Baltimore Troop, asked that Section Thirteen be
stricken out of the proposed bill. But the Federalists again
lost—this time by a vote of 36-30—and they finally resigned
themselves to insinuations that two Republican delegates

---

84. *Maryland Gazette* (Annapolis), July 2, 1812.

were "accessary to the pretended Plot of Henry." The two Republicans so accused were asked to lay all their correspondence with John Henry before the House. After submitting this correspondence for examination they were immediately cleared of all charges, and thus the Federalists experienced their last rebuff for that term in the General Assembly.[85]

While the Federalists were recuperating from the effects of the late but not uneventful legislative session, the partisan press managed to keep the otherwise quiet summer of 1812 alive with expressions of controversial opinions. Next to critical attacks upon the Republican Party and President Madison, France continued to enjoy the odium of receiving the most acid condemnations that Federalist pens could bestow. "Is it not a subject of bitter lamentation," asked "THE PEOPLE'S FRIEND," "that there should still exist a blind partiality in our national councils for a nation whose aggressions have multiplied in a geometrical series, who is wilfully deaf to the calls of justice, and treats our demands with derision and contempt?" Americans, he declared, were "kneeling as suppliants at the footstool of a French usurper," and soliciting an alliance "with a government whose fraternal hug would be more deadly than the grasp of a serpent."[86] "A CITIZEN" felt that "we are, or very soon shall be, entangled in a strict union with France," and condemned Jefferson and Madison for "ruining our navy, which was rapidly advancing to maturity under the administrations of Washington and Adams." It was absurd, he wrote, to entirely abandon a commerce "which even in its abridged state we found profitable; and to the number of seamen already confined in British ships to add a number ten times greater, by using, for the protection of both, means not adapted to the object. To wage war on land for rights which can be enjoyed only on the ocean, must strike every mind as ridicu-

---

85. *Maryland Gazette* (Annapolis), July 2, 9, and 16, 1812.
86. *Ibid.*, July 9, 1812.

lous."[87] "ONE OF THE PEOPLE AND A FRIEND TO GOV-
ERNMENT," however, felt that both "rivals in iniquity,"
Britain and France, should be taken to task by the United
States. Adopting a moderate view, the writer warned Americans never to forget their privileges, and added that even
though Federalists disagreed with Republicans over the war,
they should support the majority will "*within its constitutional
boundaries.*"[88]

The stand taken by "ONE OF THE PEOPLE" provides an
insight into the disunity prevailing within Federalist ranks
at this time. It hints at the growing factionalism between
staunch oppositionists and moderate cooperationists—a factionalism that was eventually to split the Federalist Party on
both the state and national levels and render it politically
powerless. Perhaps the general opinion of most Maryland
Federalists was expressed by a group gathered at Cool Spring
Cove, near Annapolis, on July 4, 1812. Among the eighteen
toasts drunk in celebration of the nation's thirty-sixth anni-
versary was one to "the Federalists of Maryland—Ever ready
to support the government of their country, though they may
disapprove the measures of the administration." This was
followed by a toast to "the object of every just War—A speedy
and honourable peace."[89] But the Federalists would not have
gone so far as their Republican neighbors who, not to be
outdone, met on the Annapolis College Green the same day
and also consumed eighteen toasts that were exceedingly
favorable to the government. The conduct of Congress, the
President, and the "constituted authorities" were particularly
commended, while the sixteenth toast noted the following:

The declaration of war against Great Britain—'tis right;
negotiation was finally exhausted, it remained to submit or
to fight, the former course inglorious, the latter glorious—

87. *Maryland Gazette* (Annapolis), July 16, 1812.
88. *Ibid.*, July 23 and August 13, 1812.
89. *Maryland Gazette* (Annapolis), July 9, 1812.

the standard is hoisted, and all our good citizens rally to it—may it be substantially nailed, to be lowered only by the hands of the enemy.[90]

However, if Maryland Federalists were unwilling to accept the laudatory opinions put forth by the Republicans, neither were most of them willing to accept the angry denunciations hurled at the government by their fellow Federalists in the northeast. The *Portsmouth Oracle*'s statement that *"the minions and tools of power* are attempting to establish *Tyranny* by *intimidation* and *menace"*[91] would have been considered much too strong—incendiary words fit only for Hanson's *Federal Republican.* Federalist opinion in New England, moreover, continued to wax bitter as the summer wore on.[92] The legislature of Massachusetts declared that "the war . . . is a wanton sacrifice of your best interests. A war begun upon principles so outrageous to public opinion, to the feelings and interests of this people, can be supported only by the violence which destroys the freedom of speech, and endangers the liberty of the citizen."[93] The "ADDRESS OF THE TOWN OF NEWBURYPORT," reprinted in the *Maryland Gazette,* stated that "a ruinous, an unexpected, a mad war, has been declared by the general government . . . a war without object, without hope; a war for which the nation is not prepared, but which has been prepared for the nation . . . a war in which is jeopardized all that is dear to man, all that is the birthright of freemen."[94] Federalist opinion in New York, while much milder than that of New England, also held that Madison was "not possessed of, or did not

90. *Ibid.*
91. Cited in *Maryland Gazette* (Annapolis), August 6, 1812.
92. For a discussion and comparison of Federalist political sentiment in New England with that of Maryland, the author has relied on press opinions drawn from his "The Extent of Rhode Island's Participation in the War of 1812" (Master's thesis, University of Rhode Island, 1958), pp. 27–64.
93. Cited in *Maryland Gazette* (Annapolis), July 23, 1812.
94. Cited in *Maryland Gazette* (Annapolis), July 30, 1812.

exercise, a sound political discretion."⁹⁵ Thus, even in Federalist opposition, there was more division than agreement. How much support, if any, should be given by Federalists toward winning the war was the most divisive question of the day. It was clear that some degree of unity in both sentiment and action was sorely needed.

There were several Federalist arguments, however, that were common to the party as a whole in both the North and the South. All Federalists agreed that the country was unprepared to fight a war with England. Another common belief concerned the revocation of the British orders-in-council, news of which arrived in the United States shortly after war had been declared. As expressed by "AMICUS POPULI ET PACIS" in a letter "TO THE PEOPLE OF THE UNITED STATES," such revocation afforded "the most favourable opportunity" for President Madison to restore peace between the two countries. The substitution of "conciliation" for war, the writer felt, "would cover the president with glory, entitle him to the honest applause of his countrymen, and remove all impediments to his re-election." He therefore proposed that Madison appoint a minister, holding "the olive branch in one hand and the sword in the other," with power to end the conflict at once.⁹⁶ The administration's failure to heed this advice led to a third argument heartily accepted by most Federalists. If the Republicans persisted in carrying on the war once the causative factor had been removed by England, then they must certainly have ulterior motives. To the Federalists these motives were entirely clear: the war was really an aggressive one that was being fought as an excuse to take Canada. Such being the case, declared the *Maryland Gazette*, the war "is not the war of the PEOPLE, inasmuch as they have EVERYTHING TO LOSE AND NOTHING TO GAIN

95. Resolutions drawn up by John Jay, Rufus King, Richard Harrison, and Matthew Clarkson, August 18, 1812. Cited in *Maryland Gazette* (Annapolis), September 3, 1812.
96. *Maryland Gazette* (Annapolis), August 20, 1812.

BY IT." The paper held that if "Canada, this promised land, shall be taken, it must be done by the usual means of war—MEN AND MONEY." Referring to the recent misfortunes of General Hull, it added that "Proclamations, we have seen, won't do the business," and estimated it would take at least 30,000 men and $180,000,000 to subdue Canada. Since the money necessary to support the war could not come from America's crippled trade, the *Gazette* continued, "it must come from the hands and mouth of Labour; from the FARMER AND MECHANIC." And once Canada was taken, "the President and his friends and parasites" would be the only ones to gain—through "EXECUTIVE PATRONAGE."[97] In a critical article entitled, "But—WE OUGHT TO VOLUNTEER," the *Washingtonian* held that no Americans except those who wished to carry on a foreign war were obliged to volunteer "to march to Quebec." The rulers and national legislators should not volunteer, said the author, for they must "guide the vessel of state through the storm they have ventured to meet. They must remain snug within the walls of the Capitol." No man was *"in duty bound to volunteer,"* the *Washingtonian* concluded, but the author predicted all the same that the "laboring poor . . . who have the least to defend" would end up making all the sacrifices while others grew rich and fat "upon the sins and miseries of the people."[98]

Throughout this period the *Federal Republican* had continued publication from Georgetown, but Hanson's determination to reestablish the paper in Baltimore did not abate during his forced exile.[99] Friends urged Hanson to return as soon as possible, for "unless the people are immediately roused, and the Federalists are immediately rallied, all opposition

97. *Maryland Gazette* (Annapolis), October 15, 1812. The editor based his figures on the administration's own calculation of $30,000,000 for each of the six years that the war would probably last if Canada were to be taken.

98. Cited in *Ibid.*, August 13, 1812.

99. Hanson to Robert Goodloe Harper, dated July 24, 1812. MS in Harper-Pennington Papers, M.H.S.

to the ruling policy will be unnerved, and the influence of
these satanic outrages in Baltimore will spread throughout
the State." Until the paper's return, wrote John Hanson
Thomas, "we have no press in Maryland. God grant it a
speedy, permanent, and honourable resurrection."[100]

In July, Hanson sent co-editor Jacob Wagner to Baltimore
to select a new headquarters for the *Federal Republican*.
Wagner carefully chose a sturdily built brick house at 45
South Charles Street, which he leased from a Mrs. White. On
July 22 he assigned his lease on the house to Hanson for one
dollar, and wrote him that "from all I can learn, a wonderful
apathy prevails among the Federalists respecting the *Federal
Republican*, and some have contracted an aversion to its
publication, lest they may be involved in inconvenience or
broils. This is a state of things radically different from what
was impressed on me ever before." The following day, however, Wagner wrote again, assuring Hanson that "the croaking
is confined to democrats and a few federalists, who by means
of jobs and dependence upon the executive, are labouring in
the promotion of its views."[101] Meanwhile, Thomas heard of
the plans afoot and wrote Hanson from Cumberland, Maryland, that "nothing in this world at present would afford me
more real pleasure than to assist in the noble undertaking."[102]
Another Federalist, John Lynn, proposed that the house on
South Charles Street be well fortified with arms and ammunition, plus a "full quantity of gallant men," and advised that
"a store of tomahawks and hatchets, with dirks for every
man, be provided. Lathing hatchets would be a good substitute for tomahawks," Lynn added in a postscript, "if they

---

100. Thomas to Hanson, dated June 22 and 28, and July 20, 1812. Cited
in *Portrait of the Evils of Democracy*, pamphlet dated 1816, M.H.S.
See also *Maryland Gazette* (Annapolis), August 13 and 20, 1812.
101. Wagner to Hanson, dated July 22 and 23, 1812. Cited in *Portrait
of the Evils of Democracy, passim*. See also *Maryland Gazette*,
August 20, 1812.
102. Thomas to Hanson, dated July 20, 1812. Cited in *Portrait of the
Evils of Democracy*, M.H.S.

cannot be had."[103] As events turned out, Thomas was unable to take part in the enterprise, which was indeed fortunate for him. His last letter to Hanson, expressing his "regret . . . and mortification" at having to withdraw his offer of assistance, warned him not to use force, "that is deadly force, until the attempts of the assailants will justify you in the eye of the law."[104] This letter probably did not reach Hanson in time to forestall the damage that occurred, but it is indicative of what the Federalists expected when they attempted to reestablish themselves in the city. As General "Lighthorse Harry" Lee informed Hanson, in a letter offering his services, Republicanism "must not be allowed to take root in our land, or soon will our tall trees be abrupted from their foundation." This time, Lee concluded, the Federalists would "die or conquer."[105]

Accompanied by eight friends, Hanson returned to Baltimore on July 26 and took possession of the South Charles Street residence. On the morning of the 27th, with no previous notice or fanfare, the *Federal Republican* issued forth from its new office. The paper's lead editorial castigated the town, the police, and especially the mayor for conspiring to destroy Federalism by methods as violent as the French Revolution. It argued, moreover, that the paper's destruction had been plotted long in advance, and that the stimulus had come from Washington. The editorial concluded with a special attack on the Governor, who had "taken no steps to check or discountenance the continued disorders in the emporium of the State," and who knew "the real authors of the riot and the political motives by which they were actuated. . . . The *Federal Republican*, which this day ascends from the tomb

---

103. John Lynn to Thomas, dated July 19, 1812. Cited in *Ibid.*
104. Thomas to Hanson, dated July 27, 1812. Cited in *Ibid.*
105. Henry Lee to Hanson, dated July 20, 1812. Cited in *Portrait of the Evils of Democracy.* See also Otho Luckett to Hanson, dated July 24, 1812, and Augustus Taney to Hanson, dated July 24, 1812. Cited in *Ibid.* See also *Maryland Gazette* (Annapolis), August 13 and 20, 1812.

of its 'martyred sire,' will steadily pursue the course dictated
with its latest accents."[106]

Hanson's vigorous attack upon the public authorities again
aroused the Republicans of the town, and by nightfall mobs
began to gather. The Federalists, however, felt they were
capable of handling any riots that might occur. During the
day over twenty-five men had assembled at the house on
South Charles Street. Together with the large quantity of
arms and ammunition they had brought with them, the paper's
new headquarters had been transformed into a veritable for-
tress. Inside the house, in addition to Revolutionary heroes
Henry Lee and James Lingan, were representatives of Maryland's proudest families, including Warfields, Winchesters,
Murrays, Gwinns, Gaithers, and Pringles.[107]

For a while it appeared as if the efforts of a local magistrate to disperse the gathering crowds would meet with
success, for most of those who had been making all the noise
were only young boys seeking excitement. At eight o'clock
a carriage loaded with muskets and other arms pulled up; it
was unloaded and the arms were conveyed through an armed
guard into the house. It was at this point that the crowds
returned, shouting in abusive language and throwing stones
at the windows. Two guns, loaded with blank cartridges,
were fired from the second story of the house in hopes of
dispersing the growing mob. This served only to increase
the violence. An attempt was made to gain entry by rushing
the door, more stones were thrown and windows broken, and
general firing began within the house that resulted in wound-
ing several people and killing one man. A Judge Scott, the
only civil officer present, tried fruitlessly to get the mob to

---

106. *Federal Republican,* July 27, 1812; see also *Portrait of the Evils of
Democracy,* M.H.S., and Owens, *Baltimore on the Chesapeake,* pp.
163–64.

107. *Portrait of the Evils of Democracy,* M.H.S. See also Hanson to
John E. Hall, dated December 16, 1813. MS in Hanson Family
Papers, M.H.S., and Hanson to Edward Coale, n.d. MS in A. C.
Hanson Letterbook, Hanson Family Papers, M.H.S.

leave, but the crowd secured a field piece instead and was preparing to fire it when a troop of cavalry arrived under the command of Major John Barney. Order was temporarily restored; when groups began to form again, Barney stood in front of the field piece and declared that if it were fired he would be the first to die.[108]

This sort of thing went on all night. At six o'clock the next morning Mayor Johnson appeared, accompanied by more militia under the command of General Stricker. A parley then ensued between the Mayor and the Federalists. Hanson was against any kind of surrender, but the long assault had worn down the spirits of his little band, and there had already been some outright defections among them. The remaining men—one of whom had been wounded—prevailed upon him to accept the safe-conduct to the city jail which the Mayor and General Stricker offered. Assurances were given that a military guard would be furnished and every effort made to ensure their safety. Hanson finally agreed, and between eight and nine o'clock the entire party, now numbering twenty, was escorted to the jail by the militia. Federalist resistance had completely collapsed.

But the worst was yet to come. Once the prisoners were safely in jail, Mayor Johnson, believing that the real danger was over, allowed most of the militia to disperse. The mob reformed several times throughout the day, but was broken up with little difficulty. The more sober citizens of the town also organized for their own protection, but even they were led to believe, by General Stricker's reassurances, that there was no possibility of more disorder. The prisoners, meanwhile, had been confined to one large cell,[109] the door of

---

108. *Portrait of the Evils of Democracy*, M.H.S. See also *Joint Committee to Inquire into the Causes and Extent of the Late Commotions in the City of Baltimore*, 1812. Peabody Institute, Baltimore.

109. In the excitement and confusion surrounding the commitment of the Federalists to jail, an innocent clerk employed by a nearby counting house had been locked in with them. His release was not effected until shortly before nightfall. See *Portrait of the Evils of Democracy*, M.H.S.

which was composed of thick iron bars fastened together so as to make a grate. This enabled the Federalists to see what was going on outside, and to hear threats shouted by the milling people of the fate awaiting them come evening. Hanson requested the jailer to lock the door of the cell and give them the key, which the latter agreed to do at first but then neglected to keep his promise. During the afternoon the prisoners were visited by Mayor Johnson and other leading citizens, who informed them of the efforts being made for their protection. According to a later report by Federalist prisoner John Thompson, "a butcher by the name of Mumma, and two others, understood to be prominent in the mob, entered the room in company with the Mayor and remained after him. While the interview . . . continued, this butcher was employed in observing and most attentively remarking their countenances and their dress. As many of them were strangers in Baltimore, his object . . . was to . . . identify them, and point them out to his associates when the massacre should commence."[110]

Sometime in the night, by obvious prearrangement, the mob formed again and began a furious attack on the front door of the jail. Upon hearing of this, Mayor Johnson rushed to the scene and attempted to intervene, but it was a fruitless effort and he was immediately dragged away while the attack was renewed. A passer-by, meanwhile, hastened to General Stricker's house, but was told by a servant that he "could not be seen; and that if he could, it would be unavailing, for he had already done all he could or *would* do." From this point on there were no further attempts to stop the mob's fury, and within the next two hours it succeeded in gaining

---

110. The prisoners included: Hanson, Henry Lee, James Lingan, John Thompson, Otho Sprigg, Robert Kilgour, Henry Nelson, George Richards, Jacob Schley, Peregrine Warfield, William Schroeder, Henry Kennedy, John E. Hall, Beroge Winchester, David Hoffman, Ephraim Gaither, Mark Pringle, William Gaither, William Bend, Horatio Bigelow, and Edward Gwinn. See *Portrait of the Evils of Democracy*, M.H.S.

possession of the prison's main entrance. Two very strong doors remained to be forced before the Federalists could be reached, but within half an hour these too had been disposed of. The prisoners had about four pistols among them and one or two dirks, which were passed out; then, following Hanson's advice, the men extinguished the lights, created as much confusion as possible, and attempted to escape by rushing out among the mob *en masse*. About nine or ten Federalists were able to escape by thus melting into the crowd.

Mumma, however, managed to catch the rest. The gigantic butcher posted himself at the cell's entrance to mark each of the victims as he came out. He signaled each man's arrival at the door by delivering a mighty blow with his fist, whereupon the crowd rushed upon the unfortunates and either rolled or threw them down the high flight of stairs in front of the jail. Once at the bottom the Federalists were mercilessly beaten, kicked, and trampled on until no sign of life was apparent.[111]

One by one the victims were thrown upon a growing pile, where they lay in a heap for nearly three hours. If an arm twitched or a leg moved it was the signal for another attack, knives being stuck into the hands and faces of the senseless men. One of the rioters tried to cut off General Lee's nose, but missing his aim he managed to slice it nearly in two while another thrust a knife into the still-conscious Virginian's eye. This, too, fortunately missed its mark. General Lingan, almost infirm with age, was beaten to death while he pleaded for his life. He reminded the crazed mob he once fought for their liberties in the Revolution, that he had a large family dependent on him for support, but these remarks only served to spur them on. "Every supplication was answered by fresh insults and blows. At length, while he was still endeavoring to speak . . . one of the assassins stamped upon his breast, struck him many blows in rapid succession, crying, 'the

---

111. *Federal Republican*, August 12, 1812. See also *Portrait of the Evils of Democracy*, M.H.S.

damned old rascal is hardest dying of all of them,' and re-
peating the opprobrious epithet of Tory!" Several of the
younger men, including Hanson, retained their senses but
managed to feign death so that they would not receive the
same fate as Lingan. They sustained the tortures inflicted on
them without a groan or a murmur, and listened to the mob's
deliberations about disposing the bodies without showing
the least sign of emotion. Many suggestions were put forth
as to the best way to conclude the massacre:

> At one time it was proposed to throw them all into the
> sink of the jail. Others thought it best to dig a hole and
> bury them all together immediately. Some advised that they
> should be thrown into Jones' Falls, a stream which runs
> in front of the jail. Some that they should be castrated.
> Others again were for tarring and feathering them, and
> directed a cart to be brought for that purpose to carry them
> about town. Others insisted upon cutting all their throats
> upon the spot, to make sure of them. And lastly, it was re-
> solved to hang them next morning, and have them dissected.
> Pointing to Hanson, and jabbing him severely with a stick
> on the privates, one exclaimed, 'this fellow shall be dis-
> sected.'[112]

Luckily for Hanson, he was so thoroughly hacked about and
covered with blood that the mob was unable to identify him,
and he was therefore saved from death and dissection. As
dawn neared the mob's blood lust became satiated and they
tired of the sport. Whatever spirit gave unity to the monster
was dissipated and, bit by bit, it fell apart, the shamefaced
individuals who had composed it slinking off to their homes.
Some of the crowd remained to attend to the victims, ban-
daging and dressing their wounds and providing carriages
for their escape from the city. Those that were too injured

112. *Portrait of the Evils of Democracy,* M.H.S.; *Federal Republican,*
     August 3 and 7, 1812; *Maryland Gazette* (Annapolis), August 13,
     20, and 27, 1812.

to be moved were hidden in nearby homes until they could
be secreted into the countryside. One unfortunate was hustled
off in a cart, beaten, tarred and feathered, and set on fire so
that his abductors could have the sadistic pleasure of watching
him roll on the ground in agony as he tried to extinguish
the flames.[113]

Although most of the violence had been concentrated upon
the Federalists at the city jail, other parts of Baltimore had
not been spared by the mob during that dreadful night. The
house on South Charles Street had been almost completely
pulled down. One group threatened to demolish the post
office, where copies of the *Federal Republican* had been deposited for circulation in the mails. The postmaster refused
to deliver up the newspapers, and managed to delay an
assault on the building until the arrival of a troop of horse
which dispersed the mob by charging into it. Threats were
also made against the *Federal Gazette*, but these were not
carried out and its office was saved from destruction.[114]

---

113. *Portrait of the Evils of Democracy*, M.H.S.
114. There is a host of material at the Maryland Historical Society on
the Riot of 1812. The most pertinent information is the following:
Alexander Hanson to John E. Hall, dated August, 1812, August 22,
1812, October, 1812, October 22, 1812, October 23, 1812, Novem-
ber 10, 1813, December 16, 1813, and February 11, 1815. MSS in
Alexander Contee Hanson Collection, M.H.S.; Hanson to his wife,
Priscilla Hanson, all undated, in Alexander C. Hanson Letterbook,
Hanson Family Papers, M.H.S.; Hanson to Edward Coale, dated
December 28, 1812 and April, ? ? ?, in Hanson Letterbook, M.H.S.
See also Robert Goodloe Harper to John Hanson Thomas, dated
July 7, 1812, Harper to Hanson, dated August 26, 1812, Benjamin
Stoddert to Harper, dated August 31, 1812, and Same to Same
dated September 1, 1812. MSS in Harper-Pennington Papers,
M.H.S. See also Alexander Contee Hanson, *et al.*, against the State
of Maryland, July term, 1812. MS in Harper-Pennington Papers,
M.H.S.; Benjamin Latrobe to F. C. Graff, dated August 14, 1812,
MS in Latrobe Letterbooks, Volume II for 1812, Benjamin H.
Latrobe Collection, M.H.S.; Henry Lee, Jr., to William Elie Wil-
liams, dated August 4, 1812, MS in O. H. Williams Papers, Vol. 9,
M.H.S.; William Wirt to Daniel Bryan, dated February 26, 1814,
MS in William Wirt Letterbooks, 1806–1816, M.H.S.; Charles Car-
roll to Charles Carroll, Jr., dated August 5, 1812, in typescript

The immediate result of the July 27 riot was a pronounced swing in public sentiment toward Federalism. The savage attack on a group of men who had done nothing but criticize their government provided the Federalist Party with a full-blown set of martyrs and the golden key to success at the polls in the coming elections. Eulogies, letters, accounts, and protests at once appeared in Maryland's public prints as the issue developed into a *cause célèbre* that gave rise to more copy than could be remembered in a long, long time. Numerous public meetings were held, indignantly denouncing the mob whose action had left such a stigma on Baltimore that it was rapidly becoming known as "mobtown." Demands were made for a "candid, impartial, and minute investigation of the business" by the City Council, in the interest "of the honor . . . and future prosperity of Baltimore." Mayor Johnson replied by entreating all "good men to remain quiet at home, unless called upon to support the civil authority." Measures had been adopted, he reported, "to suppress every species of disorder, and at a concerted signal thousands will rush forth to maintain the majesty of the laws."[115] In a eulogy of Generals Lingan and Lee (the latter was at first believed to be dead), "A SOLDIER OF '76" declared that the men were attacked merely because they were Federalists and thus in favor of peace. "Oh Maryland! How art thou fallen and degraded!" he cried, as he compared the soldiers' deaths to the slaying of Abner by Joab.[116] Leading Federalists, such as Robert Goodloe Harper, Philip Barton Key, Walter Dorsey, and Thomas Buchanan, published a joint

---

copies of Carroll correspondence, Henry O. Thompson Papers, M.H.S.; Reverend John Hargrove to Robert Goodloe Harper, dated July, 1815, MS in Vertical File, M.H.S.; Thomas Chase to Samuel Chase, Jr., dated August 21, 1812, photostat of MS letter in Chase Papers, M.H.S.; and *Portrait of the Evils of Democracy*, 1816, M.H.S.

115. *Maryland Gazette* (Annapolis), August 6 and 13, 1812. See also *Federal Republican*, Georgetown, August 3, 1812.

116. *Maryland Gazette* (Annapolis), August 13 and 20, 1812.

statement protesting the innocence of their colleagues. Hanson and his followers, they held, had acted in self defense, and should not be under presentment or indictment for any crime whatsoever.[117]

Resolutions condemning the riot were passed in almost every county of the state. Citizens of Charles county met on August 11 and adopted fourteen resolutions upholding freedom of the press and the right "to investigate the measures of the General Government." The action—or rather inaction—of Mayor Johnson and General Stricker merited "the abhorrence of all honourable minds" for their "deliberate and perfidious abandonment" of the besieged Federalists. Lastly, the mob assault was held to have "disgraced our national character, weakened our confidence in the power of the law," and ruined the prospects of future emigration to Maryland by causing the banishment of mercantile capital, thus producing serious injury "to the agriculturalist." As evidence of their respect for General Lingan, the citizens resolved to wear crepe on their left arms for one month.[118] Residents of Montgomery, Frederick, Saint Mary's, and Prince George's counties also expressed their "horror and indignation . . . on the lawless proceedings . . . against the Liberty of the Press, the Security of Person and Property, and every privilege which is assured by the social compact."[119] Montgomery county citizens instructed their delegate to the next General Assembly to promote an investigation into the cause of the riot, and stated their determination to erect a monument in memory of General Lingan. A poem entitled "ON THE DEATH OF GENERAL LINGAN," signed by "X", followed their resolves.[120]

Governor Bowie's reply to the stream of criticism stressed

---

117. *Ibid.*, August 20 and 27, 1812, and September 17, 1812. See also *Frederick Town Herald*, August 1 and 6, 1812.
118. *Maryland Gazette* (Annapolis), August 20 and 27, 1812.
119. *Ibid.*, August 27, 1812.
120. *Maryland Gazette* (Annapolis), August 20 and 27, 1812.

the impropriety of forming opinions and making resolutions
while the matter was still under judicial investigation. "To
the courts of justice," the Republican Governor declared,
"belongs the important power of enquiring into the circumstances of the case, and of pronouncing the sentence of the
law." Instead of keeping the issue alive through constant
publicity, he added, "it is the part of patriotism—it is the
duty of every good citizen . . . to cultivate a spirit of harmony and concord, to avoid all internal broils and domestic
disturbances, and thereby the more effectually concentrate
the public force against the common enemy." The charges of
"perfidy" and "cowardice" made against Johnson and Stricker
were dismissed by Bowie as unfounded. He concluded his
rather weak stand by promising the people to "lose no time
in adopting every measure which may be called for by the
occasion."[121]

But neither the publicity nor the criticism ceased upon
Governor Bowie's appeal. "Let the Executive of Maryland
do its duty," raged the *Federal Republican,* for "the yeomanry
of the state are ready, nay anxious, to discharge their own."[122]
Charles Carroll wrote his son that "the late occurrences in
Baltimore, and the temper of this Government render a
residence insecure in this State, and I may want all the sums
I can command . . . to move out of it if the state of politics
does not grow better, and men be suffered to speak their
sentiments on the measures of the present rulers of our country and to take what newspapers they please."[123] "A Federalist of Kent" urged fellow members of his party—an honorable
party "formed on the purest models of Grecian and Roman
virtues"—to take a militant stand against the war. "The spirit
of Washington breathes in you," he declared. "Remember

---

121. *Ibid.,* September 3, 1812.
122. *Federal Republican,* Georgetown, August 19, 1812.
123. Charles Carroll to Charles Carroll, Jr., dated August 5, 1812. Type-
    script copy of Carroll correspondence, in Henry O. Thompson Pa-
    pers, M.H.S.

who you are, and rise with the magnitude of the crisis. . . .
Having withstood the fury of a long train of persecutions
and oppressions, undismayed by perils and uncontaminated
by the sordid suggestions of interest, you have passed an
ordeal that has purified and confirmed your virtue." He concluded with an optimistic prediction that "the day fast ap-
proaches when the rays of the Sun of Federalism, which
already illuminate the land of Pickering and Otis, Griswold
and Quincy, will penetrate the Alleghany, dispersing the
mists of democracy, and purifying the political atmosphere
with the beams of virtue, truth, and liberty."[124] "HISTORI-
CUS" pointed out that the riot proved Republicans "are now
driven to the last resort." In a letter entitled "Drowning Men
Will Catch at Straws," he asserted that the Republicans "have
turned all their talents to misrepresentation, and with greater
avidity than ever betoken themselves to 'right down hard'
lying."[125]

But all this was as nothing in comparison to the publicity
given General Lingan's funeral by the Federalists. Celebrated
"with the most awful solemnity and perfect order," the newspapers reported of the great effect produced "by the presence
of the VETERAN BAND OF THE REVOLUTION, who
flocked from all quarters to assist at the obsequies of their
departed brother in arms." The *Federal Republican* commended the "manly firmness of the military, who notwithstanding the *request* (backed by *threats* to issue an *order*
were the *request disregarded*) of the PRESIDENT, that they
would NOT APPEAR ON THIS OCCASION, paraded with
promptitude and imparted the most imposing grandeur to
the scene." According to Hanson, the throng of mourners
gathered to hear the oration by George Washington Custis
was so great that the church originally selected for the service
was not large enough to contain the crowds, and "a shady

124. *Maryland Gazette* (Annapolis), September 3, 1812.
125. *Maryland Gazette* (Annapolis), September 10, 1812.

eminence in the suburbs of the town was substituted in its place."[126]

Late in July, Hanson and the other Federalists who participated in defending the house on South Charles Street were indicted and bound over for trial. Hanson was specifically charged with the murder of Dr. Thadeus Gale, who had been killed in trying to storm the house, while the others —"being moved and seduced by the instigation of the devil"— were indicted as accomplices. The charges were later reduced to manslaughter, but when the trial took place at Annapolis the following October there were no convictions. With Hanson being defended by Luther Martin, Philip Barton Key, and Robert Goodloe Harper, the acquittal verdict was practically a foregone conclusion. The Federalists celebrated the event with a banquet in Hanson's honor, at which eighteen toasts were consumed by the "true disciples of Washington." The first toast honored the state of Maryland—"Subdued to the dominion of faction, whose deeds are marked with blood, her regeneration is great, her salvation has been achieved."[127] Others honored freedom of the press, General Lingan, and Timothy Pickering—"a man most inflexibly just . . . devoted to liberty." President Madison, however, was not forgotten: he was wished a speedy retreat to Montpelier, "that his country may be released from French bondage." Toasts in favor of "a speedy and honourable termination to a wasteful and

126. *Federal Republican*, August 3 and 9, 1812; *Maryland Gazette* (Annapolis), September 10, 1812; Benjamin Stoddert to Robert Goodloe Harper, dated September 1, 1812, MS in Harper-Pennington Papers, M.H.S.; Same to Same, dated August 31, 1812; Alexander C. Hanson to Edward Coale and John E. Hall, n.d., MSS in Alexander Contee Hanson Collection, and A. C. Hanson Letterbook, Hanson Family Papers, M.H.S. See also *Portrait of the Evils of Democracy*, for the oration delivered by George Washington Custis.

127. The "regeneration" and "salvation" spoken of referred to the Federalist victory in the October, 1812, elections for the House of Delegates. Hanson himself was a successful candidate for Congress from the third district, even though he was on trial at the time.

unnecessary war" concluded the evening's festivities.[128]

If the immediate result of the Baltimore Riot was a swing in public sentiment toward Federalism, the more tangible result was a political upset that put Maryland in the Federalist camp for the next several years. This was accomplished by a resurgence of Federalism in the counties, which, alarmed and indignant because of the excesses of the Republicans, and fearful that Baltimore was wielding too much influence in state affairs, combined their strength to push the Republicans out of the legislature in the elections of 1812.[129] The change represented both economic discontent on the part of the agrarian areas, due to the war and the consequent loss of grain markets, plus an intrastate town-versus-country conflict which Alexander C. Hanson correctly foresaw as a part of the greater struggle between the propertied classes and the city masses.[130] "As humanity abhors massacres," he declared, "so will the next election . . . witness the abhorrence of our farmers and planters" toward the Republican organization in Baltimore.[131]

Not since the embargo had Federalist chances for victory been so strong. In a letter to the *Maryland Gazette*, a Talbot-county Federalist enthused that the Republicans were "much chopfallen at their war measures having made so many converts. Talbot is about being born again . . . beyond a doubt. Caroline has come to her senses and will be Federal. Dorset I can say but little about. There is so great a change on this shore, that there is little doubt if things are managed with

128. *Federal Republican,* September 7, 1812; *Maryland Gazette* (Annapolis), October 22, 1812; Alexander Hanson *et. al.* against the State of Maryland, July Term, 1812. MS in Harper-Pennington Papers, M.H.S.; and Hanson to Priscilla Hanson, n.d. MS in A. C. Hanson Letterbook, Hanson Family Papers, M.H.S.
129. Benjamin Stoddert to Robert Goodloe Harper, dated September 4, 1812. MS in Harper-Pennington Papers, M.H.S.
130. *Federal Republican,* August 7, 1812. See also Hanson to Harper, dated August 22, 1812. MS in Harper-Pennington Papers, M.H.S.
131. *Federal Republican,* August 3 and 11, 1812.

proper resolution that we shall be Federal."[132] "OURTIUS" declared that no sensible person could be in doubt about whom to support at the polls. "Resolve to support only those who will endeavour . . . to restore tranquillity again in the country," he cautioned. "Some no doubt will approach you with Peace, Peace, in their lips; cry out Commerce, Prosperity, and Trade; but at the same time harbour quite different sentiments in their hearts. Be not deceived, lest they should disguise their real intentions under the garb of hypocrisy, and delude you by the semblance of patriotism. . . . Inquire for the real advocates of peace," "OURTIUS" concluded, "and on them only bestow your suffrages."[133] As the hustings drew near, meetings of "Friends of Peace, Commerce, and Good Order" were held throughout the state, and the "Peace and Free Trade Ticket" appeared everywhere.[134]

But the Federalists had little to fear, for the change in Maryland's political sentiment was borne out by the election results. Although the Congressional alignment remained unchanged at a 6–3 Republican-Federalist ratio,[135] the House of Delegates was wrested from Republican control by a 54–26 majority. Four Republicans each were returned from the Chesapeake counties of Baltimore, Harford, Anne Arundel, and Queen Anne's, while Kent returned two Republicans and two Federalists, and the cities of Baltimore and Annapolis returned two Republicans each. Every other county in the state went Federalist except Washington, which remained in Republican hands by a narrow margin of 360 votes. The

132. *Maryland Gazette* (Annapolis), August 27, 1812.
133. *Maryland Gazette* (Annapolis), October 1, 1812.
134. *Ibid.* See also *Federal Republican*, October 12, 1812.
135. Hanson, who was elected to Congress from the third district, did not defeat a Republican but replaced fellow Federalist Philip Barton Key. See Hanson to Harper, dated August 22, 1812, and Harper to Hanson, dated August 26, 1812. MSS in Harper-Pennington Papers, M.H.S. See also Charles Carroll to Charles Carroll, Jr., dated May 28, 1812. Typescript copy of Carroll correspondence, Henry O. Thompson Papers, M.H.S.

Senate, which had been chosen in 1811 for a five-year term, was controlled by the Republicans. Nevertheless, with a secure majority in the lower house, the Federalists easily elected Levin Winder to the governorship together with a Federalist-dominated Council to serve with him.[136]

While the Federalists were thoroughly united in their campaign to capture the state, the choice of a Presidential ticket found them as divided as before. The majority appeared to favor anti-war Republican George Clinton, although Robert Goodloe Harper did so reluctantly. Writing former Secretary of the Navy Benjamin Stoddert, he declared:

> If I could be satisfied that the Union could be kept together four years more, under Madison's administration, and a french alliance and the consequent introduction of french troops be avoided, I would consent to endure for that time all the other evils of the present system in the hope of getting completely rid of it afterward, and restoring the government to the hands of men of sense, honour, and correct principles. But I greatly fear that the despair which must be produced in the Eastern States by the reelection of Madison, would produce some violent convulsion there.[137]

Stoddert agreed. "Clinton," he wrote, "is not a character that the country can confide in. . . . He is violent & cruel without being firm and consistent. He has always been a decided, & even a rancorous opponent of the Federalists."[138] Harper was

---

136. *Maryland Gazette* (Annapolis), October 8, 15, and 22, 1812, and November 12, 1812; *Frederick Town Herald*, September 12, 1812, and October 3, 1812; *Maryland Republican* (Annapolis), September 2 and 16, 1812, November 8, 1812; and *Federal Republican*, October 12, 1812. Ironically, while the Federalists did not win Baltimore, they did elect the sheriff there. The Federalists almost captured Frederick county in the Congressional campaign.
137. Harper to Stoddert, dated September 10, 1812. MS in Harper-Pennington Papers, M.H.S.
138. Stoddert to Harper, dated September 4, 1812. MS in Harper-Pennington Papers, M.H.S.

urged, therefore, to support the nomination of John Marshall as the Federalist standard-bearer when he attended the New York gathering of party leaders in the fall. "A northern Fed. cannot carry an opposition ticket," Stoddert advised, and went on to show that the only way Madison could be "dethroned" was by "breaking in upon his stronghold, the Country south and west of Potomac." No Federalist ticket, he concluded, could "be carried against Madison which does not qualify Virginia's sterling pride—and which has not the sterling worth and popularity of Marshall to aid it."[139]

Although Stoddert continued to drum up support for Marshall throughout Maryland,[140] the Federalists decided against a national ticket and instead encouraged passive support for Clinton. At least, Harper wrote, "he would bear a great deal from G.B. rather than throw the least weight into the scale of France"; it was known, moreover, that Clinton thought the war was begun by a "corrupt administration, against the commerce of the country."[141] Stoddert reconciled himself to the party's choice, realizing "it was too much to expect that Eastern men, who by the bye, are very much governed by prejudice, could be prevailed on to surrender up their strong prejudices against Southern Presidents."[142]

Even so, the Maryland Federalists were more successful in securing Presidential electors than at any time since 1800. Of the five electors pledged for Clinton, three were from the Potomac-oriented Southern counties and the lower Eastern

139. Stoddert to Harper, dated August 31, September 4, and September 14, 1812. MSS in Harper-Pennington Papers, M.H.S.
140. Harper to John Hanson Thomas, dated September 10, 1812. MS in Harper-Pennington Papers, M.H.S.
141. Harper to Stoddert, dated September 10, 1812. MS in Harper-Pennington Papers, M.H.S.
142. Stoddert to Harper, dated November 16, 1812. MS in Harper-Pennington Papers, M.H.S. See also Benjamin Latrobe to Archibald Binney, dated August 5 and September 15, 1812. MSS in Latrobe Letterbooks, Vol. II for 1812, Benjamin H. Latrobe Collection, M.H.S.

shore, while two were from the fourth district of Frederick, Allegany, and Washington counties. The upper Chesapeake area, however, remained solidly Republican.[143]

Having been returned to power in Maryland largely on the basis of intrastate conflict between town and county, the Federalists moved to confirm their victory by flatly refusing additional representation to Baltimore's 35,000 inhabitants when the General Assembly convened in November.[144] This was followed by a resolution introduced in the House of Delegates creating a "Committee of Grievances and Courts of Justice" to "inquire into the late unhappy disturbances in the city of Baltimore," with a view to preventing "a recurrence of similar mischiefs." The Committee issued its lengthy report in December, and it came as no surprise that residents of Baltimore were castigated for their "general spirit of intolerance" and their "turbulent and vindictive" attitude towards the Federalist Party. Mayor Johnson's refusal to forcefully disperse the mob was taken as evidence that "he connived at and approbated their excesses." He was also found guilty "of a most reprehensible indiscretion" for using "intemperate" language against the *Federal Republican*—"the inevitable effect of which was to sanction and excite . . . the popular excesses against the same." General Stricker was accused of failing "to gratify the spirit of the requisition made on him by the civil power, when he issued . . . orders not calculated to ensure the return

143. *Maryland Gazette* (Annapolis), August 27, 1812; *Federal Republican,* October 12, 1812; *Federal Gazette,* October 8, 1812; and Scharf, *Maryland,* 3:25–26. For information touching on the election, see Benjamin Latrobe to Joel Barlow, dated August 12, 1812; Latrobe to Eric Bollman, dated January 8, 1813; and Latrobe to H. Latrobe, dated January 14, 1813. MSS in Latrobe Letterbooks, Vol. II for 1812, Benjamin H. Latrobe Collection, M.H.S. See also Benjamin Chew to John Eager Howard, dated July 25, 1812. MS in Bayard Papers, M.H.S., and Robert and John Goldsborough *et. al.,* to Robert Goodloe Harper, James McHenry, *et. al.,* dated June, 1811. MS in McHenry Papers, M.H.S. See also Steiner, *James McHenry,* pp. 582–86.

144. *Votes and Proceedings,* House of Delegates, November Session, 1812.

of order." Major Barney was held to have erred when, "instead
of preserving a dignified stand . . . he so conducted himself
as to banish that awe and apprehension which the presence
of an armed cavalry naturally inspires." Barney's "pledge to
the Mob," that none in the house would escape, served only to
confirm their opinion that they—the mob—were justified in
their "horrid outrages." The Committee reserved its most bitter
denunciations, however, for Tobias E. Stansbury, Republican
delegate from Baltimore and a Brigadier General in the state
militia at the time of the riot. Stansbury, it declared, "frequently used violent and inflammatory expressions, intended
and calculated to excite the mob to break the gaol, and to
murder Mr. Hanson and his friends who had confided themselves to the protection of the law."[145]

The Republicans immediately challenged the Committee's
report, Delegate Donaldson predicting that a full investigation would cost the state between $10,000 and $15,000. When
a bill was rendered, therefore, in the amount of $784.60, the
Maryland Gazette was led to comment that Donaldson's estimate was "only a new year's trick he wishes to play upon
you."[146] Although the Republicans felt the Committee's report
was "unfaithful and unsupported by evidence," it nevertheless
passed the House by a party vote of 36–20. The Federalists
were unsuccessful, however, in securing the passage of an act

145. *Votes and Proceedings,* House of Delegates, November Session,
     1812; *Maryland Gazette* (Annapolis), November 26, 1812; Decem-
     ber 31, 1812.
146. *Maryland Gazette* (Annapolis), January 7 and 13, 1813. The *Ga-
     zette* also reported the final demise of the Baltimore mob, which
     occurred not in Baltimore, but in Buffalo, New York. In a letter to
     his brother in Baltimore, cited in the *Gazette,* Abel Grosvenor re-
     ported that on November 25, 1812, a mob known as the "Volunteers
     from Baltimore," and led by the editor of the Baltimore *Whig,*
     traveled to Buffalo where they "became outrageous, and swore that
     they would tear down the house of every federalist in the village—
     that they would kill all the federalists and damn'd tories." The local
     militia was called out to put down the riot, in the course of which
     the writer sustained several bayonet wounds, but succeeded in escap-
     ing from the mob. See *Ibid.,* December 17, 1812.

providing for the "administration of justice . . . in the city and county of Baltimore."[147] Nor were they able to secure passage of a resolution ordering Stansbury's arrest by the sergeant at arms and his deliverance to the Anne Arundel county jail, there to await trial for his part in the riot. Instead, a more watered-down resolution was passed, by a vote of 29–27, empowering the Attorney General of Maryland to issue subpoenas to a number of witnesses so that they could testify before the Baltimore grand jury concerning Stansbury's actions on July 27. For different reasons, neither party was satisfied with this measure. The Federalists rightfully believed Stansbury guilty, and did not wish to give him the benefit of the doubt before a grand jury.[148]

The year had indeed wrought a distinct change in Maryland. War discontent and the fear of growing urban preponderance had again swept the Federalists into office. They had presented no positive program to the electorate, however, and although this fact was perhaps ignored in the immediate thrill of victory, it boded ill for the future. Their success at the polls, Federalists declared, meant that Maryland wished a speedy conclusion to an ignoble and unnecessary war. The party could now take its stand on this issue knowing that a majority of the voters agreed. This attitude was best expressed in the decision of the editor of the *Maryland Gazette* to give his paper a *"decided political character,"* starting with the issue of January 1, 1813. Perhaps thinking of the *Federal Republican's* martyrdom, the editor added that "he is not unmindful of the difficulties of the undertaking; he is well aware

---

147. *Votes and Proceedings,* House of Delegates, November Session, 1812. It was pushed through the House of Delegates, but failed of passage in the Senate.

148. *Votes and Proceedings,* House of Delegates, November Session, 1812. Although the House failed in getting its original measures passed, it took this opportunity to blame Baltimore as "the ardent advocate of every measure of the general government leading to the war." See also, in this respect, Judge Richard T. Earle's "Charge to the Grand Jury," November Term, 1812. MS in Bordley Papers, 1784–1955, M.H.S.

that they who do not bow down to the Golden Image must
be contented to be charged with heresies—to have their motives misrepresented—their faith doubted, and themselves
threatened with Fire and Faggots. . ."[149] But he was also
aware, as were the majority of Federalists, that there was
nothing like the shedding of a little blood to give moral sanction to one's political stand. However unconvinced of Federalist righteousness before the Baltimore Riot, there were few
in Maryland who had doubts after that affair.

---

149. *Maryland Gazette* (Annapolis), December 17, 1812.

7

Divided We Fall: The "Blue Lights" and the "Coodies"

THE Federalists who gathered in Annapolis for the 1812–1813 session of the General Assembly were anxious to bring the war to an end as quickly as possible. Shortly after the House of Delegates met, resolutions were introduced condemning offensive war. The preamble to these resolutions stated that the avowed causes of the war were Great Britain's orders-in-council and her impressment of American seamen. "The first of these causes is removed," it declared, "and it may reasonably be inferred . . . that the latter might be adjusted to the satisfaction of both nations." The six resolves that followed affirmed Maryland's willingness to support and prosecute "a defensive war . . . at all hazards," but held that "offensive war is incompatible with the principles of republicanism." The declaration of war "by a small majority of the Congress of the United States" was condemned as "unwise and impolitic," while the stand taken by the governors of Massachusetts, Connecticut, and Rhode Island, respecting the militia quota demanded by the Secretary of War, was upheld as entirely "constitutional" and meriting the legislature's "decided approbation." The resolves concluded with a plea to build up the navy, which the Delegates felt was "the kind of national defence least dangerous to liberty, and most compatible with the genius, habits, and interests of the people of the United States." The six resolutions were then adopted by a vote of 41-21 and passed on to the Senate.[1] Within two weeks the Republican-dominated upper house responded, upholding the war as "just, necessary, and politic," and asserting its full confidence in President Madison's leadership.[2] Party differences thus remained as polarized as before.[3]

Of the Federalist resolutions passed in the House of Delegates, the last two were clearly the most important. The fifth —approbating the conduct of the New England states—was the strongest censure yet put forward by Maryland's Federalist Party, which, not condoning the war, had nevertheless remained sourly loyal to its prosecution.[4] The resolve, therefore, was indicative of the growing strength of the party's extreme oppositionist wing—a group which admired the leadership of Timothy Pickering and the Essex Junto, and which desired to emulate the position being taken by the northeastern states.[5]

---

1. *Votes and Proceedings,* Senate and House of Delegates, November Session, 1812. See also *Maryland Gazette* (Annapolis), December 24, 1812, and January 7, 1813.
2. *Votes and Proceedings,* Senate, November Session, 1812.
3. See Charles Carroll to Charles Carroll, Jr., dated December 30, 1812. Typescript copies of Carroll correspondence, Henry O. Thompson Papers, M.H.S. See also Carroll to Robert Goodloe Harper, dated March 1 and 9, 1813, and December 16, 1813. MSS in Harper-Pennington Papers, M.H.S.
4. Charles Carroll to Charles Carroll, Jr., dated December 5, March 12, and April 27, 1813. Typescript copies of Carroll correspondence, Henry O. Thompson Papers, M.H.S.
5. Alexander C. Hanson to Edward Coale, n.d. "Col. Pickering shows towards me the tenderness of a father. I love him, and will fight by his side while I can stand." See also Hanson to Coale, dated June 11, n.d., in Alexander C. Hanson Letterbook, Hanson Family Papers, M.H.S. See also Josiah Quincy to Horace Morison, dated June 6, 1851, and Quincy to John Hanson Thomas, dated April 18, 1852. Typewritten copies of MSS letters of Josiah Quincy, Tiffany Papers, M.H.S.

Although Federalists throughout the country were as one in opposing the war, the only area which backed up its words by action (albeit negative action) was New England. Opposition was manifested there by flat refusal to render financial and military support to the war. The government loans of 1812–1814 were utter failures in New England. The response of moneyed interests to the loan of 1812, for instance, was typical of that region's reaction to all the war loans. Whereas New York and Philadelphia each subscribed more than $1,500,000, the loans from all of New England totaled less than $1,000,000. Boston's subscription of $75,000 to the loan of 1813 presented a marked contrast to the more than $3,000,000 taken in Baltimore, or the $7,000,000 offered in Pennsylvania.[6] Effective military support was equally refused. Use of the state militia outside their respective state boundaries was withheld as long as possible, and on the day Washington was invaded Connecticut recalled her militia home.[7] It was this staunch attitude which appealed to such men as John Hanson Thomas and Alexander Contee Hanson, Maryland's acknowledged High Federalist leaders. They were encouraged by Pickering himself, who paid a visit to his Maryland colleagues during the summer of 1813. A Republican newspaper described the grand Federalist gathering held on that occasion as a "kissing scene," which was probably not far from wrong.[8] But for all their vigorous and dynamic plans of opposition in the New England manner, the High Federalists in Maryland were neither in control of their party nor representative of its majority. As

6. *American State Papers, Finance*, 2:590. See also Henry Adams, *History of the United States* (New York: Charles Scribner's Sons, 1891), 6:309.
7. Renzulli, "Extent of Rhode Island's Participation in the War of 1812," pp. 33–34.
8. Cited in Carl Brent Swisher, *Roger B. Taney* (New York: The Macmillan Company, 1935), pp. 62–63. See also Hanson to Harper, dated June 11, 1813. MS in Harper-Pennington Papers, M.H.S., and Hanson to Coale, dated December 23, n.d., and December, 1813; and Same to Same, dated January 17, 1813. MS in Alexander Contee Hanson Collection, M.H.S.

the war progressed, a growing antagonism developed between this group and the moderate Federalists, eventually splitting the party into two irreconcilable factions, to the intense delight of the Republicans.[9]

The sixth resolution passed by the House of Delegates—the plea to build up the American navy—was as notable as the resolve preceding it. It expressed a belief common to the Federalist Party in all sections of the country, for advocacy of a large, strong navy was a consistent Federalist policy accepted and supported by even the New England stalwarts. Commenting on the victory of the *Hornet* over the *Peacock*, a Rhode Island Federalist paper summed up northeastern opinion when it declared that "as Federalists we deprecate the war, but we are full of pride and pleasure at the honor which this affair, brilliant without precedent, has reflected upon the national character."[10] In the same vein, the Maryland House of Delegates ordered a "golden medal" struck in honor of Lieutenant William S. Bush, who had lost his life while serving on the *Constitution* in its victorious battle with the *Guerriere*. The Federalist House, moreover, requested Governor Winder to present a sword, suitably engraved, "in testimony of the very high sense entertained of the cool, intrepid gallantry, good conduct, and services, of Captain Hull, of the officers and crew of the frigate *Constitution*, in the attack, defeat, and capture of the British frigate *Guerriere*."[11] Several months later the *Maryland Gazette* reported the victory of the *Constitution* over the *Java* in front page headlines proclaiming "ANOTHER SPLENDID NAVAL VICTORY," while a Federalist correspondent to that paper, discussing "the splendid actions of

---

9. See letters of Hanson to Edward Coale, and to John Hanson Thomas, all undated. MSS in Alexander Contee Hanson Collection and A. C. Hanson Letterbook, Hanson Family Papers, M.H.S. These provide the best information on the growing split within Maryland Federalist ranks.

10. *Newport Mercury*, April 3, 1813. Cited in Renzulli, "Extent of Rhode Island's Participation in War of 1812," p. 118.

11. *Maryland Gazette* (Annapolis), November 19, 1812.

our heroic marine band," declared that "we have seen enough
to convince us that we are not inferior to that nation [Great
Britain] in naval tactics, of which she herself must be fully
satisfied."[12]

Despite such commendation of American naval prowess,
the Maryland Federalists continued to criticize Madison's conduct of the war along the lines laid down by New England.
A resolution condemning the President, who "by perverted
and strained interpretations" had abused his emergency power
of calling out the militia, passed the House of Delegates by a
vote of 45–21. It further declared that such use of the militia
when no emergency existed was "an open and dangerous assumption of power." The legislature also proposed an amendment to the Constitution limiting the President's eligibility for
reelection "until the expiration of five years after he shall have
been out of that office." Governor Winder was ordered to forward this proposal, aimed at thwarting another Republican
victory in 1816, to the executives of the other states.[13]

The tenor of Federalist criticism grew stronger and more
bitter during 1813. Perhaps the primary reason for this was
the administration's refusal to give Maryland the assistance for
which she asked. This had been freely granted to other states,
notably Virginia, and its denial to Maryland was indignantly
looked upon as a piece of political vengeance meted out by
Madison. Anxious to place the blame in its proper place, "A
CITIZEN" asserted that the "executive of Maryland have not
been guilty of any neglect of duty, whatever may have been
said by some men who pretend to more wisdom than they
really possess. That we have not received the protection to
which we are entitled, no person can deny." But, "A CITI-
ZEN" added, let it be remembered that this is the fault of
our good president, and let those who think proper to complain of the want of protection, learn to place the blame upon

12. *Maryland Gazette* (Annapolis), January 14 and February 25, 1813.
13. *Votes and Proceedings,* House of Delegates, November Session, 1812.
   See also *Maryland Gazette,* December 17 and 31, 1812.

the proper person."[14] Alarmed at the increasing severity of Federalist reproaches, and declaring that "we are now assailed . . . by traitorous combinations and conspiracies within," the Maryland Senate urged the revival of the Revolutionary act against tories. The "dark and criminal designs" of the opposition, it warned, were intent on aiding the British in conquering the country.[15] Uniquely reversing their former role, the Federalists now came forward in defense of liberty of expression and the right to criticize the government. The Delegates, in rejecting the Republican-sponsored measure which would have suspended the rights of habeas corpus, remarked that "it would be painful for us to perceive the authors of any penal statute . . . liable . . . to become the first among its victims."[16]

Federalist Maryland's anger against the government grew in direct proportion to the threat of enemy invasion. Since Virginia had received substantial protection from the government, without having loaned it as much money as Maryland, the Federalists lost no opportunity in pointing this out and in rubbing salt into the wounds—even though the wounds were clearly their own. "Virginia," a correspondent declared, "has but to ask and she receives; but Maryland, for her late political disobedience, is denied those means of defence which she has a right . . . to demand." Although Maryland is "far more critically situated" than Virginia, the writer pointed out, the state "is told that she has too many vulnerable points to expect complete protection, and therefore she must take care of herself in the best manner she can."[17] The Virginia legislature's pledge of their *lives, fortunes, and sacred honour,* was the subject of a lampoon in the *Maryland Gazette* which sneered that "either the Virginia legislature were merely gasconading when they pledged their fortunes and the other

14. *Maryland Gazette* (Annapolis), March 18, 1813.
15. *Votes and Proceedings,* Senate, November Session, 1813.
16. *Ibid.,* House of Delegates, November Session, 1813. The Senate's bill further provided for a person's arrest on mere suspicion of aiding the enemy or actively opposing the government.
17. Cited in Scharf, *Maryland,* 3:36–38.

marketable commodities mentioned, and intended to take no other share in the controversy than a liberal participation in the honours and emoluments; or else they have since become disgusted with the feeble and miserable manner in which the business has been conducted, and have, in consequence resolved to withhold any *gratuitous* aid." For until the present time, concluded the *Gazette*, Virginia has "utterly refused to aid their favorite Madison with the *loan* of a single dollar."[18]

Neither was the opportunity lost among Federalists to poke fun at the government's miserable financial condition. "A FRIEND" advised Republicans to return to the old-time practice of holding "numerous and respectable meetings" in order to raise money and men with which to support the war, for Federalists should not be expected to contribute.[19] In a more serious vein, "A STOCKHOLDER" declared that Gallatin's continual requests upon the banks for loans with which to carry on the war were grounds for depositors to withdraw their money. The directors, after all, were appointed by the stockholders to employ their money in the way authorized by the original charter, and "without the consent of the stockholders could no more lend it to the administration than to pocket it themselves."[20] Such controversy over loans and finances frightened "ABSALOM," who asked that "if all this money is to be borrowed, and such a heavy debt incurred, may we venture to hope that it will be at a low interest?"[21]

---

18. *Maryland Gazette* (Annapolis), February 18, 1813.
19. *Ibid.*, February 25, 1813. See also Benjamin Chew to John Eager Howard, dated July 25, 1812. MS in Bayard Papers, M.H.S.
20. *Maryland Gazette* (Annapolis), March 11, 1813. Charles Carroll declared that "if this has been done without consulting a majority of the stockholders and obtaining their consent, I think the procedure a scandalous breach of trust." Charles Carroll to Harper, dated February 28, 1814. MS in Harper-Pennington Papers, M.H.S. See also R. L. Colt to Carroll, dated September 21, 1814. MS in Carroll Papers, Lot No. IV, M.H.S., and Ann Crawford to Cornelius Howard, dated November 28, 1814. MS in Cornelius Howard Papers, 1727–1844, M.H.S. Also see Theodorick Bland to Sophia Bland, dated September 24, 1815. MS in Bland Papers, 1757–1846, M.H.S.
21. *Maryland Gazette* (Annapolis), March 18, 1813.

Plans for a second invasion of Canada, after Hull's disaster at Detroit the year before, brought forth another barrage of Federalist denunciations.[22] The government's incomprehensible decision encouraged "General Jonathan Windmill" to issue a call from his camp near "Proclamation Green" to the "MEN OF FREDONIA." Describing himself as a man who "snuffs a battle in every western breeze" and who "glories in the tented field," General Windmill called for "volunteers in "halves, quarters and eighths" to help him conquer Canada. "I will put you together as you arrive," he declared, "and organize you for a short tour. But remember that every man who accompanies us places himself under *my* command, and shall submit to the *salutary* restraints of being killed in bloody battle."[23] "A SIMPLE ONE" offered the government his solution for the manpower shortage: more Republicans should serve in the ranks than hang around and wait for commissions. "We have officers enough in all conscience," he held, "and many more who are willing to wear epaulets."[24] Even if the government had enough soldiers to take Canada, "A COUNTRYMAN" asserted, "where are our *generals* to command them? One of them has been pronounced a traitor, and a second proclaimed a poltroon. None of them have given evidence of either skill or bravery. Are we to endure the expenses and loss of another campaign, merely to ascertain how many poltroons and treacherous generals we have in our army?"[25]

22. "We were very late in getting into motion for the main object, that of possessing ourselves of the Canadas," Jefferson wrote D. B. Warden on December 29, 1813. At the war's end, he wrote: We have recently heard that peace is concluded. It is well . . . but we were just getting forward a set of officers, who having already redeemed the honor we lost under the traitors, cowards and fools of the first year, would very soon have planted our banners on the walls of Quebec and Halifax." Jefferson to Warden, dated February 27, 1815. Photostats of MSS correspondence of Thomas Jefferson, M.H.S.

23. *Maryland Gazette* (Annapolis), January 14, 1813.

24. *Ibid.*, February 25, 1813.

25. *Maryland Gazette* (Annapolis), January 28, 1813.

"Men of no principle . . . whiskey pot orators . . . the scum
and refuse of mankind who were vomited on our shores by
the terrible eruptions of Europe"—such were the violent
epithets hurled at the administration by the uncompromising
group within Maryland's Federalist Party.[26] "AN AMERI-
CAN," overlooking Madison, chose instead to vilify Jefferson
—the man who did away with the country's "dull monotonous
prosperity" because he believed it only "a specious dream."
The blame for the war was placed squarely on his shoulders,
and the Sage of Monticello was denounced as "the curse and
scum of the nation."[27] "The names of Jefferson and Madison
will long be held in recollection," Federalists declared, "and
future historians will do them ample justice by a minute
recital of their indifferent acts—Years after the commotions
which now agitate the republic shall have subsided, and the
tranquillity, if ever, of former times restored, those acts will
be remembered only to be execrated."[28]

The split in Republican ranks, occasioned by the Committee
on Foreign Relations' proposal partially to suspend the non-
importation law, was gleefully pounced upon by Federalists
as evidence of growing discord within the "Jacobin" party.
The more they "wrangle among themselves," observed the
Maryland Gazette, "and quarrel about the tendency of mea-

---

26. *Ibid.,* January 14, 1813. See also Robert Walsh to Harper, dated
    December 2, 1813. MS in Harper-Pennington Papers, M.H.S. See also
    the following letters to Harper: General J. Devereux to Harper, dated
    January 3, 1814; Samuel Stanhope Smith to Harper, dated January
    9, 1814; and Charles Carroll to Harper, dated January 16 and Feb-
    ruary 26, 1814. MSS in Harper-Pennington Papers, M.H.S. These
    letters discuss "the most base, insidious, deceitful, & stupid govern-
    ment with which it has ever pleased God to curse a simple and con-
    fiding people. But they are pushing to a crisis a system introduced
    by Jefferson, which subjects the country to the low passions of the
    populace; and I look forward, I fear too surely, to the anarchy . . .
    and party frenzy which is destined to burst in pieces this recent and
    once happy republic." (Smith to Harper).
27. *Maryland Gazette* (Annapolis), January 21, 1813.
28. *Maryland Gazette* (Annapolis), February 25, 1813, and March 18,
    1813.

sures which the combined agency of the whole party has produced, in that proportion does the political prospect of the country brighten around us."[29] But by the summer of 1813 the "political prospect" had still not brightened; if anything, the situation was a good deal darker. Continuation of the war, a Federalist moaned, is "day after day plunging us deeper into disgrace and rendering us ten-fold more contemptible in the eyes of all foreign nations. . . . Mr. Madison may well call this 'a season of trial and calamity.'" However, added the writer, could not this state of things be easily traced to the "imprudence of our own rulers . . . notwithstanding all the arts made use of to cloak their designs? Could it for a moment be supposed that this state of things proceeded from measures which were unavoidable? It may, indeed, be well to set apart days of humiliation, fasting, and prayer."[30]

Maryland's most active Federalist during this period was Alexander Contee Hanson. As former editor of the *Federal Republican*,[31] Hanson had never let slip an opportunity to rain abuse upon Madison and the administration. One of his most characteristic shafts declared that "there is scarcely an act of tyranny and oppression complained of against George

---

29. *Ibid.*, Februaary 25, 1813.

30. *Maryland Gazette* (Annapolis), July 29, 1813.

31. Following the Baltimore Riot, Hanson gave up his editorship to go into politics. Circulation of the *Federal Republican* increased greatly, however, and Hanson wrote that for the first time it was beginning to yield a profit. "But for the *Fed. Republican*," he declared in an undated letter to Edward Coale, "I should now have been a pettifogging attorney without practice, and in point of note & respectability barely upon a level with your Ridgely's" Hanson to Coale, n.d., MS in A. C. Hanson Letterbook, Hanson Family Papers, M.H.S. In another letter, Hanson wrote that "the paper was never in greater demand than at present in Baltimore." Same to Same, dated February 11, 1813. MS in A. C. Hanson Collection, M.H.S. In 1815 the *Federal Republican* returned to Baltimore. See Hanson to Harper, September 22, 1815, and Harper to Hanson, September 28, 1815. MSS in Harper-Pennington Papers, M.H.S. See also Cornelius Howard to Robert Read, dated December 30, 1815. MS in Cornelius Howard Papers, 1727–1844, M.H.S.

the Third which has not been committed by Jefferson and his political pimp . . . whiffling Jemmy."[32] As third-district representative to the Thirteenth Congress, Hanson was able to continue his fulminations against the Republicans in general and the War Hawks in particular. Hammering against the pro-French policy of the administration, he declared from the floor of the House that "no matter what is done, still will the rays of truth pierce solid walls and shed its light on the land." When Republican Robert Wright, also of Maryland, accused both Hanson and his paper of being in the pay of Great Britain, Hanson replied by challenging him to a duel. Two weeks later he launched an attack on Henry Clay and "that damn Felix Grundy," and was called to order by the Speaker of the House when he branded Grundy as "the apologist of France." He then pointedly remarked that Grundy could set an example in and out of Congress which would require a very stout heart to follow.[33] Hanson also managed, by some undisclosed means, to obtain a letter supposedly written by the French Minister to Secretary of State Smith before the war began. The letter was said to be of a most insulting nature, in that it practically dictated the terms which the United States would have to meet before France would negotiate a treaty of commerce. Federalists accused the administration of trying to conceal the letter's existence, and Hanson did his utmost to force a Congressional investigation of the matter. Every resolution along these lines was defeated, however, and the Federalists at length contented themselves with having the letter read into the records.[34]

---

32. *Federal Republican*, July 4, 1811.
33. Hanson to Coale, dated January 17 and 27, 1813, and Same to Same, n.d.; Hanson to John E. Hall, n.d.; Hanson to Robert Goodloe Harper, dated May 31, 1813; Hanson to Coale, dated June, 1813; and L. C. Carpenter to ???, dated July 7, 1813. MSS in Alexander C. Hanson Collection, and A. C. Hanson Letterbook, Hanson Family Papers, M.H.S. See also *Annals of Congress*, 13th Congress, 1st Session, pp. 113–18, 251, and *Ibid.*, 2nd Session, pp. 1204, 1228.
34. See Hanson to Coale, dated January 17, 1813, and Same to Same, n.d., MSS in Alexander C. Hanson Collection, M.H.S. See also

But Hanson's High Federalist faction—becoming known throughout Maryland as the "Blue Lights"[35]—was not supported by Maryland's moderate Federalists in its extreme attacks upon the government. This group was also opposed to the war, but felt that party differences should be temporarily put aside in the interest of terminating the war speedily and honorably. Opposition of the Hanson variety, felt the moderates, would not end the conflict any sooner. The leadership of this group was provided, almost by accident, by Roger Brooke Taney of Frederick county.

Taney had already achieved prominence in Maryland as one of the younger lights of the Federalist Party. The son of Michael Taney, who had first introduced the bill for suffrage reform in the Maryland legislature, he worked loyally with other leaders and enjoyed a growing influence in the party's councils. At the same time, Taney had refrained from participating in the process by which some of his associates worked themselves into a frenzy from 1808 onward. Once war was declared, the young Frederick lawyer found it necessary to make a choice between his convictions and his friendship with such men as Hanson and John Hanson Thomas, who had taken him in and given him position and prestige in the Federalist Party. The first breach—a minor one—occurred when Taney made known in a letter to his younger brother Augustus that he disapproved of Hanson's plan to reestablish the *Federal Republican* in Baltimore. Augustus Taney had agreed to join the group defending the South Charles Street headquarters, but his elder brother warned him that forcible reestablishment of the paper in Baltimore might legitimately

---

Hanson to John E. Hall, dated October 15, 1813. MS in A. C. Hanson Collection, M.H.S. For a good account of Hanson's activities in Congress, including the affair of the letter, see Joseph H. Schauinger, "Alexander Contee Hanson, Federalist Partisan," *Maryland Historical Magazine* 35 (Baltimore: 1940):354–64.

35. Called "Blue Lights" after the name given New England Federalists who were accused of sending up rocket signals, or blue flares, from the mainland to British ships hovering off the coast.

result in serious criminal charges, including murder or man-slaughter should violence occur. The letter subsequently fell into Republican hands and was published in the newspapers, considerably embarrassing the Federalists involved in the expedition, and discrediting Roger Taney in their eyes.[36]

Nevertheless, the party leaders supported Taney as the Federalist candidate for Congress from the Fourth District in the October 1812 elections. His nomination had probably been decided upon before it was known how fully he disagreed with his party in its opposition to the war, or perhaps the nomination was made in the hope of securing his support thereby. His name was announced beneath the slogan, "AN HONORABLE PEACE, UNION, AND FREE TRADE," and while Taney was declared to be opposed to an unnecessary war, a saving clause was included in his platform to the effect that if peace could not be obtained on honorable terms the war was to be prosecuted with foresight, energy, and vigor. An attempt was made to show that Taney's letter to his brother had been perverted by the Republicans for purely partisan ends, but it was still disconcerting to have published an indirect statement by the Federalist candidate that the Baltimore martyrs—whose martyrdom was to bring success to the party —had been little more than criminals. Taney lost the election to Republican incumbent Samuel Ringold. He also lost the friendship of the High Federalists, including his former close associate, John Hanson Thomas. Shortly afterwards, Taney and a substantial bloc of the party membership broke away from the Hanson faction.[37]

On the surface this split was caused by Taney's refusal to

---

36. Augustus Taney to Alexander Contee Hanson, dated July 24, 1812. Cited in *Portrait of the Evils of Democracy*, M.H.S. See also Swisher, *Taney*, pp. 56–58.
37. Hanson to Edward Coale, n.d., but written about 1813. MSS in A.C. Hanson Collection, M.H.S. In these letters Taney is referred to as a "jackall." See also Swisher, *Taney*, pp. 58–62; and Swisher, "Roger B. Taney and the Tenets of Democracy," *Maryland Historical Magazine* 34 (Baltimore, 1939):207–22.

support Clinton in the presidential contest. The underlying cause, however, was the moderates' insistence that whatever the right or wrong of the conflict, the country was at war and must put aside internal strife in order to defend itself. It was at this time that the moderates came to be known as "Coodies," because of their opposition to Clinton, and Taney—being the leader of this group in Maryland—was nicknamed "King Coody" by the extremists.[38] Both the name and the party division continued throughout the war and for a number of years thereafter. The breach was smoothed over to some extent, but was never really healed after 1812.[39]

The result of the Federalist split was noticeable in ensuing elections. The Federalists barely carried the autumn election of 1813, which saw considerable Republican gains in the legislature. Talbot county, which had returned four Federalists in the last election, now returned four Republicans. Caroline county sent only one Federalist instead of the four returned in 1812. In Allegany county, three Republicans and one Federalist were elected by a close vote of 596 to 593, but through a technical interpretation of the law, residents of the county's fourth precinct were deprived of their votes. The four Federalist candidates were thereupon declared legally elected by

38. The title was coined from the name of Abimelech Coody, a fictitious character created by Gulian C. Verplanck, one of Clinton's sharp-tongued enemies in New York. Articles attacking Clinton appeared under Coody's name, declaring "that the good sense of the real American people is blinded, while their passions are heated, till at length . . . they find themselves arrayed under the banners of opposing factions, and contend with all the rancorous and deep-rooted hostility of rival nations." These articles attacking Clinton as a demagogue made Coody a prominent political character. Those who stood with him were called "Coodies." See Swisher, *Taney,* pp. 60–61.

39. Hanson to John E. Hall, October 19, n.d.; Hanson to Coale, n.d.; and Hanson to Priscilla Hanson, n.d. MSS in Alexander C. Hanson Collection, M.H.S. See also Hanson to Coale, dated October 11, 1813, and Same to Same, n.d. MSS in A. C. Hanson Collection, M.H.S. See also Robert Goodloe Harper's "Address to the Voters of the Congressional District of Baltimore," n.d. MS in Harper-Pennington Papers, M.H.S.

a returning board composed of four Federalist judges. Since
the possession by either party of the three contested delegates
would determine whether the Governor would be Federalist
or Republican, the contest aroused intense interest. When the
House of Delegates convened in December, Republicans hotly
objected to the admission of the Allegany county Federalists.[40]

Determined to maintain their slim majority in the lower
house, the Federalists contended that the certificates of election furnished by the returning board, while noting irregulari-
ties, were at least *prima facie* evidence that the Federalist candidates were duly elected. The House had no constitutional
right, they declared, to decide on the legality of a contested
election until after the legislature had been organized. In the
course of the debate the Republicans made several unsuccessful attempts to organize the House before admitting the
Allegany delegates. Five stormy days later, the Committee
on Elections reported in favor of the Federalists. The House,
by a strict party vote, adopted the report and proceeded to
get on with the business of choosing a Governor.[41]

But the Republicans refused to give in. The Senate threatened to secede unless the Allegany Federalists were turned
out, while the more vociferous Republicans in both houses
threatened to resort to arms unless the Federalists yielded.
The issue was finally settled when the Senate (which had to
meet with the House in joint convention to elect the Governor) decided that each house should be the judge of its own
elections. At the same time the Senate unanimously resolved
that the whole affair had been a sacrifice of the people's rights
to a mere form. Although Federalist Levin Winder was reelected Governor, seventeen Republican holdouts refused to

---

40. *A PLAIN HISTORY of the Conduct of the Federal Party in Our
STATE LEGISLATURE on the Subject of GENERAL SUFFRAGE,
the ALLEGHANY FRAUD, and the Claims of Poor Men to the
PRIVILEGE OF VOTING*, undated pamphlet, Maryland Department, Enoch Pratt Free Library, Baltimore. See also Scharf, *Maryland*, 3:55–57.
41. *Votes and Proceedings*, House of Delegates, November Session, 1813.

vote. Throughout the state, party bitterness had reached new heights. The *Maryland Gazette*, which had maintained a dignified silence under the numerous attacks by the *Maryland Republican*, finally broke under the strain. In an editorial it declared that "every third word . . . in that contemptible chronicle . . . is a lie duer paid than the Turk's tribute." Jehu Chandler, the *Republican's* editor, was held to be a "vulgar scoundrel . . . a puffed up, conceited, swollen fool. . . . We strongly suspect him to be a member of the Jacobin Club."[42]

While the Federalists had not done so well as they expected in the elections of 1813, their success at the polls in 1814 more than made up the difference. This success was in large part due to Maryland's invasion by the British, which, coupled with the inability of the federal government to stem the tide of aggression, again threw many voters into the Federalist camp on a protest basis. It was reported that "in Calvert county absolute ruin has so suddenly overwhelmed its citizens, that 'like men without hope' they have become incurious to passing events, and in the torpor of despair can only sigh over their blasted prospects and ruined fortunes." Further reports declared that "a retaliatory system of plunder and conflagration, long since predicted, has laid the dwellings of the people bordering on the Patuxent in ashes; has driven them from their homes, and has almost made them beggars and outcasts."[43] Although the Federalists certainly did not

---

42. *A PLAIN HISTORY*, Enoch Pratt Free Library; *Votes and Proceedings*, Senate and House of Delegates, November Session, 1813; A. C. Hanson to Edward Coale, dated October 11, 1813, MS in A. C. Hanson Collection, M.H.S.; *Maryland Gazette* (Annapolis), January 26, 1814, and June 30, 1814. See also Scharf, *Maryland*, 3:55–57.

43. *Maryland Gazette* (Annapolis), June 30, 1814. See also John Stull Williams to William Elie Williams, dated June 20, 1814; and William Cooke to William Elie Williams, July 17 and August 22, 1814. MSS in O. H. Williams Papers, Vol. 9, M.H.S.; John H. Mercer to Governor Levin Winder, dated August 30, 1814. MS in Vertical File, No. 80, M.H.S.; Charles Carroll to Robert Goodloe Harper, dated August 30, 1814. MS in Harper-Pennington Papers, M.H.S.; and Francis Scott Key to John Randolph of Roanoke, dated October 5, 1814. MS in Howard Papers, M.H.S.

rejoice in the misery being visited upon the state, it was, nevertheless, political grist for their party. "King Coody" Taney correctly grasped the state of affairs when he wrote General William Winder in August, 1814, that "the two great parties who divide the country are too busy quarreling with one another and preparing for the ensuing elections to bestow much thought on defending the country against the common enemy. . . . If those who are in authority at Washington, will give themselves a little trouble they might easily make their political friends ashamed of abandoning them in the midst of the perils into which they have encouraged them to go." Taney's letter expressed, either directly or by implication, the full position of the Coodies. It left aside all opinions of the administration, of the Republican Party, and of the merits of the war itself. These matters were irrelevant at the moment. What was essential was that partisanship of every sort be put aside so that the Union might be saved.[44]

But the elections of 1814 revealed greater partisanship between Federalists and Republicans in Maryland than at any time prior to the war. Pounding vigorously on "the disgrace of abandoning the seat of government & acknowledging that the Conquerors of Canada cannot defend their own Capital," and on the hardships being suffered by Maryland because of inept Republican rule, the Federalists won a resounding 59–21 victory in the General Assembly. Levin Winder was easily reelected to his third term as Governor, defeating Republican nominee Robert Bowie by a vote of 48–23. In the Congressional contest the Federalists fared equally as well, five representatives being returned from Southern Maryland, the lower Eastern Shore, and the Western counties of Frederick, Washington, and Allegany. The upper Chesapeake area remained solidly Republican, however.[45]

---

44. Taney to William Winder, cited in Swisher, *Taney*, p. 66.
45. Francis Scott Key to John Randolph of Roanoke, dated October 5, 1814. MS in Howard Papers, M.H.S. On the campaign of 1814, see the following letters: Robert Goodloe Harper to John Hanson Thomas, dated July 18, 1814, MS in Harper-Pennington Papers, M.H.S.; Alex-

Early in 1815 the war blundered its way to an inglorious close, thereby removing the main Federalist contention that it would result in the Union's dissolution. The war's end, ironically, was a misfortune for the Maryland Federalists, for it deprived them of their most valuable issue on the state level and left the party without a platform, while on the national level the Hartford Convention—in what it did and what it was suspected of doing—struck a fatal blow at the Federalist Party as a nationwide organization.[46] "It will readily be imagined," Roger Brooke Taney wrote many years later, "that after this the federalists of Maryland would hardly desire to continue the party association and continue the lead in hands which appeared to be not only indifferent to the sufferings of our citizens, but ready to take advantage of the peril in which the State was placed to extort from it the surrender of a portion of its legitimate power." Continuing, Taney declared:

---

ander Contee Hanson to Harper, dated September 29, 1814, MS in Harper-Pennington Papers, M.H.S.; Same to Same, dated October 9 and 11, and November 7, 1814, MSS in Harper-Pennington Papers, M.H.S.; Hanson to Harper, dated December 28, 1814, MS in Vertical File, M.H.S.; William Cooke to William Elie Williams, dated October 10, 1814, MS in O. H. Williams Papers, Vol. IX, M.H.S.; and Joseph Brevitt to Zachariah Spottiswood, dated April 29, 1814, MS in Brevitt Letterbook, 1798–1815, M.H.S. See also the following broadsides, all at M.H.S.: "Don't Give Up the Ship, Freemen of Maryland," by "Lawrence," dated 1814; "TO THE PEOPLE OF TALBOT," by "A FRIEND TO FREE VOTING," dated September 26, 1814; and "TO THE CITIZENS OF TALBOT," by "A FRIEND OF JUSTICE," dated September 21, 1814. See also Scharf, *Maryland*, III, 129–139.

46. On Maryland's opposition to the Hartford Convention, see Robert Goodloe Harper to Josiah Quincy, dated January 17, 1814, MS in Vertical File, M.H.S., and Harper to William Sullivan, dated November 2, 1814, MS in Harper-Pennington Papers, M.H.S. In these letters, Harper makes known his "regret and apprehension" at the plans for a New England Convention, declaring: "We dread its going too far and ending in the destruction of that which it is intended merely to controul." Although Maryland suffered as much or more than New England, Harper pointed out, the entire state fought back when invaded. See also *Votes and Proceedings*, Senate and House of Delegates, November Session, 1814, for details regarding Federalist activity in defense of the state prior to the British invasion.

While the enemy was in the midst of us assailing our cities, and burning our houses, and plundering our property; and the citizens of the State, without distinction of party, were putting forth their whole strength and blending in its defense, those with whom the Maryland Federalists had been associated as political friends in the Eastern States, and whom they had regarded and treated as the leaders of the party, were holding the Hartford Convention, talking about disunion, conferring with one another in secret conclave; demanding from us, one of the Southern States, a surrender of a portion of the political weight secured to us by the Constitution; making this demand, too, in the hour of our distress, when the enemy was upon us. They were, moreover, using every exertion in their power to destroy the credit and cripple the resources of the general Government, feeble as it then was, and leaving us to defend ourselves as we could by our own resources.[47]

In the face of such "treason," concluded Taney, "we thought it time that the party connection should be dissolved."[48]

Soon afterward the Maryland Federalists suffered other misfortunes and embarrassments. Alexander Hanson began to drift away from the party, and by 1815 he was in sharp conflict with his former colleagues. Unable to control the new orientation and direction which Federalists in the state were trying to adopt, and angry that they would not support the extremist *Federal Republican* as the party organ in Maryland, Hanson went into semi-seclusion at his estate, "Belmont," from whence he vented his wrath against the betrayal of Federalist principles in occasional letters to Robert Goodloe Harper.[49] John Hanson Thomas, whom the party had planned

---

47. Cited in Tyler, *Memoir of Roger Brooke Taney*, pp. 158–60.
48. *Ibid.* See also Scharf, *Maryland*, 3:129–30.
49. Schauinger, *Maryland Historical Magazine* 35:362. See also Hanson to Harper, dated January 13, 1815, and September 22, 1815. MS in Harper-Pennington Papers, M.H.S. See also letters of Hanson to Edward Coale, n.d., MSS in Alexander Contee Hanson Collection, M.H.S.

to send to the United States Senate, died. Realizing that the end was near, Thomas disconcerted the "Blue Light" Federalists by calling Taney to his bedside and effecting a belated reconciliation with the king of the "Coodies." This dramatic episode led Hanson to remark caustically that it was "given to none to know with certainty, who may not be impelled by ambition, jealousy or envy to abandon and betray a friend," the implication being that Taney had used Thomas to win prestige and position for himself, and had then abandoned him over the war issue.[50]

Hanson's disaffection and Thomas's death established Robert Goodloe Harper as the leader of the Maryland Federalists. In 1815 he was put forward by the party as the Federalist choice for the United States Senate,[51] filling the seat recently vacated by Baltimore Republican Samuel Smith. But Harper's candidacy was no sooner announced than a letter written by him in 1814, and accidentally misplaced by the recipient, was published by the Republicans in the *Baltimore Patriot*. This letter declared that the British were right on the most important issues over which the United States had gone to war. "It

50. *Maryland Gazette* (Annapolis), May 18, 1815.
51. Catherine Carroll Harper to Harper, dated March 1, 1814; Hanson to Harper, dated April 3 and June 6, 1814. MSS in Harper-Pennington Papers, M.H.S. Robert Oliver to Harper, dated October 18, 1814, MS in Oliver Papers, M.H.S. Roger B. Taney to Harper, dated October 18, 1815, and Harper to Taney, dated October 20, 1815, MSS in Taney Papers, M.H.S. Taney supported Harper in the latter's bid for the Senate, writing:

> It has been my lot to differ from the prominent men of the party to which I belong, as to some of the principles asserted by them during the war—and as to the temper and feeling with which it was proper at that time to conduct the opposition. I fear I must include you among those with whom I have thus differed. Yet my regard and respect for you has not been diminished. I hold in grateful remembrance your example and your efforts in the most dark and ill-omened hour of the war; and with pleasure acknowledge that your claim to the vacant honour ought to be without rival. . . . I am not willing to be suspected for a moment of consenting to become your competitor—especially in the peculiar circumstances in which you are now placed.

will be a bitter pill for Mr. Madison," Harper had written, "to acknowledge the British right of impressment, and their doctrine of perpetual allegiance; but he must swallow it. He will squall and kick and make wry faces but down it must go. The thing is right in itself."[52] Although many Federalists privately agreed with Harper's sentiments, they felt that the party had too often been labeled as disloyal and pro-British, and steps were immediately taken to disavow the letter as just another Republican perversion to trick the people. Nor were the Federalists pleased when Hanson wrote at this time that "experience has shown . . . that the shades of difference between the two parties are but slight, with some few distinguished exceptions among the prominent men on both sides." Federalism, declared the embittered Hanson, was not all "that was pure, disinterested and exalted."[53] Nevertheless, Harper was returned to the Senate.[54]

Other aspects of the election of 1815, however, were not so heartening. There was an increase of eleven Republican members in the House of Delegates, and while the Federalists still held a majority in that house, the combined membership of both Senate and Delegates reduced their overall majority to one vote on joint ballots. Although Hampton Federalist Charles C. Ridgely was elected Governor by a narrow margin of two votes, receiving forty-seven ballots to Robert Bowie's forty-five, it was all too clear that the Federalists must make

52. Harper to George Baer, dated October 10, 1814. Cited in *Maryland Gazette* (Annapolis), September 14, 1815. See also Hanson to Harper, dated September 22, 1815, and September 28, 1815, MSS in Harper-Pennington Papers, M.H.S. R. R. Wormley to Harper, dated October 28, 1815, MS in Harper Letters, M.H.S. Statement of William Harden, dated October 16, 1815. MS in Harper-Pennington Papers, M.H.S.

53. Hanson to Harper, dated September 22, 1815. MS in Harper-Pennington Papers, M.H.S.

54. Richard Caton to Harper, dated January 8, 10, and 12, 1815; William Wilson to Harper, dated October 3, 1815; and Robert Walsh, Jr., to Harper, dated November 30, 1815. MSS in Harper-Pennington Papers, M.H.S.

a better showing in 1816. In order to do this, two things were essential. First, party harmony must be restored between the "Blue Lights" and the "Coodies." Secondly, the state Senate must be swept clean of the Republicans who had dominated it for the past five years.[55]

The Senate, which had been chosen in 1811, before the issues of the war had become the dominant factor in Maryland politics, effectively checked Federalist measures in the House of Delegates throughout the entire war. In 1814, for instance, when the lower house passed a resolution condemning the administration, the Senate retaliated by passing a resolution warmly approbating both the President and Congress.[56] The Federalists were determined to end inconsistencies such as this. If they could capture both houses in 1816 they would be in a position to dominate the General Assembly without restraint.

The contest of 1816, therefore, assumed a stature of greater importance to Maryland Federalists than any election since 1812. The result would determine not only which party would rule, but—should the Federalists win—which faction of their party would rule. So important was victory in this election that the Federalists resorted to various types of strategy to guarantee their winning the Senate. It was certain, for example, that there would be an extremely close battle over the one senatorial elector to be chosen by the normally Republican city of Annapolis. Thus, five months before the election, the Federalists "colonized" Annapolis with about forty men—mostly laborers—who ostensibly claimed to be in search of

---

55. Scharf, *Maryland,* 3:140. See also "The Dying Groans of Democracy," undated broadside, M.H.S. Edward G. Williams to William Elie Williams, dated September 29, 1815. MS in O. H. Williams Papers, Vol. IX, M.H.S. John Marshall to Harper, dated April 20, 1815. MS in Leakin Papers, M.H.S. Hanson to Harper, dated January 13, 1815, and September 22, 1815. MSS in Harper-Pennington Papers, M.H.S.
56. *Votes and Proceedings,* Senate and House of Delegates, November Session, 1814.

work. Although no work was found, they continued to dwell contentedly in taverns throughout the city. An investigation by suspicious Republican leaders led to the discovery that the men had been hired for twenty dollars a month and board to establish legal residence in Annapolis and vote the Federalist ticket. Republican meetings were immediately held to expose the scheme, and party animosity ran so high that when one Mr. Bassford, a teacher, changed his party affiliation from Republican to Federalist, "his school became so reduced in numbers he had to quit the town."[57]

The Federalists were also forced to compromise with the "Coodies," and the results indicate that the latter exacted a high price for their support. Several "Coodies" were chosen as Federalist candidates for the House of Delegates, and Taney himself was nominated by the party for the state Senate. When the votes were counted it was found that more than half of the senatorial electors chosen were Federalists. Federalist papers compared the victory second in importance only with the Battle of Waterloo, but it soon turned to ashes in the mouths of the "Blue Lights." Not only did the "Coodies" successfully elect a large number of Senators from within their own ranks, but they created a permanent party split by carrying factional warfare into the contest for the election of members to the lower house. This was to be held the following month.[58]

---

57. Riley, *The Ancient City*, p. 253.
58. "To the Citizens of Cecil County," by "CECIL," broadside, dated 1816, M.H.S. *EXTRACT from a LONG TALK Delivered by Dr. Leib*, pamphlet dated May 13, 1816, M.H.S. Richard Caton to Robert Goodloe Harper, dated August 22, 1816, and Charles Carroll to Harper, dated September 11, 1816. MSS in Harper-Pennington Papers, M.H.S. Alexander C. Hanson to Edward Coale, dated September 20, n.d., and Hanson to R. Rabb, dated September 23, n.d. MSS in A. C. Hanson Collection, M.H.S. Although undated, both of the latter letters discuss the senatorial election of 1816. See also Deposition of Solomon Davis, and reply by Otho Sprigg, dated July 11, 1816. MSS in Vertical File, M.H.S.; Edward G. Williams to William Elie Williams, dated September 27, 1816. MS in Williams

Taney's group was mainly opposed to the election of Alexander Contee Hanson, who had rejoined the party in its hour of victory. Hanson had already been selected as the Federalist candidate to the House of Delegates from Montgomery county, the "Coodies" not having been strong enough in that traditionally Federalist district to prevent his nomination. However, rather than designate a candidate of their own on an independent ticket, and being unwilling to permit Hanson's victory, the moderates determined to throw the election to Republican candidate Robert Magruder. By so doing they divided the Federalist vote and brought about Hanson's defeat.[59]

Holding the balance of power as they did, "Coody" strength emerged as a force to be reckoned with in Federalist Party councils. The "Blue Lights" were prevented from completely enjoying the victory for which they had worked so hard, and in the next few years found themselves more and more on the defensive. During this time Taney filled a vacancy in the United States Senate, caused by Harper's resignation, with one of his own supporters. He also successfully blocked the removal from office of a large number of Republican judges, took a decisive role in the selection of candidates for the

Papers, Vol. IX, M.H.S.; and Benjamin Latrobe to Harper, dated December 16, 1816. MS in Benjamin H. Latrobe Papers, M.H.S. See also Swisher, *Taney*, pp. 72–74.

59. Hanson to Edward Coale, dated September 20, n.d. MS in A. C. Hanson Collection, M.H.S. Upon hearing of Magruder's election, Hanson wrote: "For myself, I considered all connection between me and the federal party dissolved, and I was disposed to curse the hour when first I attached myself to so base a party." This was just histrionics, however, although shortly afterwards Hanson became so ill over his defeat that he suffered a hemorrhage of the lungs. Taney lived to regret his friendship with the Magruder family, for it was a Magruder who insulted his father, Michael Taney, resulting in a duel in 1819. Taney killed John Magruder in the duel, but died himself a year later in exile in Virginia. When his body was returned to the family estate in Maryland, several Magruders broke open the casket and smashed the face of the corpse with stones. See Statement of Washington Perine, dated July 30, 1938. MS in Perine Papers. M.H.S.

House of Delegates, and ousted the "Blue Lights" (or "Big Bugs" as they were now called) from the Governor's Council. As "Coody" power grew, Taney and his followers became the objects of constant vilification from the Hanson wing of the Federalist Party. This anger was perhaps best expressed in the following letter from Thomas Grosvenor to Alexander C. Hanson upon the latter's defeat in 1816:

> The Torrent of *Moderation* is now rushing with such fury through the state, that I question whether it can be stemmed. Let it spend its force—it will leave the federal party divided . . . . if not ruined, and it will leave the state in jeopardy, if not in the very clutches of Democracy. It will have its course—In the meantime aloof from its influence, your time will pass more pleasantly than heretofore, and in . . . a few years hence, times more propitious, less corrupt and dastardly will afford you ample opportunity to reap honourable fame. That Democracy *will*, for a time, triumph in the event there can be no doubt. That every sound federalist in the state will groan is equally true. . . . Federalists will very soon understand what Coodyism is in its nature & detest it more than they ever detested Democracy, I am sure.[60]

But the rule of "King Coody"—and the "Blue Lights" too— was fast drawing to its close. By 1818 Federalist representation in the House of Delegates had dropped to an insignificant minority.[61] Federalist control of the Senate, however, remained

---

60. Thomas Grosvenor to Alexander Hanson, undated MS letter in A. C. Hanson Collection, M.H.S. See also Swisher, *Taney*, pp. 72–78. Attacks on Taney became so malignant that he was at last forced to answer them publicly, which he did in a twelve page "Address" to his constituents in Frederick County.

61. George Baer to Ignatious Davis, dated January 8, 1817. MS in Aldine Papers, M.H.S. Hanson to Edward Coale, dated March 22, n.d., and March 27, 1817. MSS in A. C. Hanson Collection and Hanson Family Papers, M.H.S. Hanson to George Corbin Washington, dated November 27, 1817. MS in Hanson Family Papers, M.H.S. See also Same to Same, dated December 16 and December 30, 1817. MSS in Hanson Family Papers, M.H.S.

until 1821—unwanted, moribund, by virtue of circumstances rather than by the people's will. Although the party continued to nominate candidates up to this date,[62] lingering on bereft of national leadership, for all intents and purposes Federalism in Maryland died in 1819.[63] Taney and the "Coodies" soon drifted into the Jacksonian Democracy that was beginning to take form in the new era.

Well before 1819, however, the term "Blue Light" had become an opprobrious epithet reserved only for the most intransigent Federalists. When Jehu Chandler, editor of the *Maryland Republican*—that "puffed up, conceited, swollen fool"—implied that a certain Mr. Watkins was to be the subject of a forthcoming article entitled "BLUE LIGHT VS. BLUE LIGHT," he was accosted on the street by the gentleman in question and severely beaten with his own walking stick.[64] The Federalist resurgence which had begun so magnificently with a riot in Baltimore thus ended ignobly on a street in Annapolis.

The Federalist Party's downfall in Maryland, as on the

---

62. The last broadside which the author encountered, concerning Federalism, was dated August, 1821, and entitled "To the People," by "A POOR MAN," at M.H.S. See also Thomas Jefferson to David B. Warden, dated December 26, 1820. MS correspondence of Thomas Jefferson, M.H.S.

63. The attitude of gloom among the Federalists is best reflected in the following correspondence: Alexander Hanson to George C. Washington, dated January 8, 12, 14, and 27, 1818; February 6, 1818; November 18, 1818; and December, 1818 (about 20 letters in all), MSS in Hanson Family Papers, M.H.S. See also Charles Carroll to Robert Goodloe Harper, dated February 26, 1818, MS in Harper-Pennington Papers, M.H.S.; John Eager Howard to William Elie Williams, dated August 20, 1818; Christopher Hughes to Williams, dated August 25, 1818; and Edward Greene Williams to Williams, dated October 9, 1818, MSS in O. H. Williams Papers, Vol. 10, M.H.S.; George M. Dallas to Benjamin Chew Howard dated April 25, 1818, MS in Howard Papers, M.H.S.; Robert Walsh to Harper, dated March 26, 1818, MS in Harper-Pennington Papers, M.H.S.; and "TO THE VOTERS OF FREDERICK COUNTY," by William Elie Williams, dated September 30, 1819. Broadside, M.H.S.

64. *Maryland Republican*, June 22, 1816.

national level, was owing primarily to its self-defeating political philosophy. It was a party of the status quo, which more often than not degenerated into a protest movement of the counties and rural areas of the state against the growing preponderance of Baltimore, Annapolis, and the urbanized section along the upper Chesapeake Bay. As such it ceased offering a positive program to the electorate, for which it publicly professed distrust. Neither were the Federalists willing to wed Hamiltonian economic theories to the more popular and dynamic philosophy of Jeffersonian Republicanism. Possessed with fears of mobocracy should the political balance of power rest with the propertyless class, Federalism refused to recruit its leaders from beyond the narrow oligarchic circle of Maryland's aristocratic families, nor would it adopt the devices of mass political organization so successfully used by the Republican opposition. Above all, the party was characterized by fear—fear of change and fear of the people who would be the instruments of change. This was clearly recognized by the "Coodies," who strove to create a moderate, middle-of-the-road program appealing to both urban and country sections of the state. The conservatives would not accept this, for it meant broadening their social concepts to a point inconsistent with their fundamental belief. This belief, one might say, was rule by the aristocracy only—not by a Jeffersonian aristocracy of talent.

From the viewpoint of the conservatives, the American experiment of government by the rich and the well-born had ended in tragedy. And yet this group wrought better than they knew. They saved Maryland from the chaos of paper money and economic ruin; they successfully weathered the struggle to prevent ratification in the state; they helped make a parchment into a workable instrument of government, thereby proving that republicanism was compatible with stability and the rights of property; they encouraged commerce and financial probity; and they showed that a party could function without appeals to demagoguery. The Federalists functioned best, moreover, when Maryland was weak, discontented, and practically insolvent. Ironically, their support was always strongest in the state's agrarian areas while their appeal was generally directed toward Maryland's commercial elements. Had their philosophy not been so strictly conservative, one wonders whether rural Maryland would still have gone into the Jeffersonian camp.

But the party's conservative policies did not change, did not broaden to meet the new era ushered in by the French Revolution and the American Revolution before that. The Federalists remained the party of the Alien and Sedition Acts, in 1819 as in 1798. No attempt was made to win the masses by organizing around policies which served their interests. Refusing to move forward, they succumbed to panic instead. In the end, still searching for a program, the Federalist Party went down to defeat with its anti-democratic flags flying.

Bibliography

Manuscripts

Aldine Papers. (MS 7) Maryland Historical Society. (Hereafter cited as M.H.S.)

Bayard Papers. (MS 109) M.H.S.

Paul Bentalou Journal, 1784–1813. (MS 125) M.H.S.

Bland Papers, 1757–1846. (MS 134) M.H.S.

Bordley Papers, 1784–1955. (MS 64) M.H.S.

Bordley-Calvert Manuscripts, 1720–1828. (MS 82) M.H.S.

Bouldin Papers. (MS 1212) M.H.S.

Bourne Papers. (MS 1213) M.H.S.

Brevitt Letterbook, 1798–1815. (MS 137) M.H.S.

Carroll Papers, Vol. 8, 1781–1833. (MS 206) M.H.S.

Carroll-Harper Papers, 1753–1880. (MS 1225) M.H.S.

Carroll-McTavish Papers. (MS 220) M.H.S.

Carter Papers. (MS 1228) M.H.S.

Samuel Chase Check Book. (MS 275) M.H.S.

Samuel Chase "Homebook." (MS 969) M.H.S.

Samuel Chase Letters. (MS 1234) M.H.S.

Chase Papers. (MS 1235) M.H.S.

Corner Collection, 1678–1883. (MS 1242) M.H.S.

Dallam Papers, 1792–1866. (MS 1250) M.H.S.

Dulany Papers, 1659–1799. (MS 1265) M.H.S.

Dulany-Lines Papers, 1764–1809. (MS 1562) M.H.S.

Robert Gilmor, Jr. Papers, Vol. 3, Division III. (MS 387) M.H.S.

Alexander Contee Hanson Collection. (MS 408) M.H.S.

Hanson Family Papers. (MS 408) M.H.S.

Harper Letters. (MS 1304) M.H.S.

Harper-Pennington Papers. (MS 431) M.H.S.

Howard Papers. (MS 469) M.H.S.

Charles Howard Papers. (MS 469.4) M.H.S.

Cornelius Howard Papers, 1727–1844. (MS 469.5) M.H.S.

Jefferson Papers, Vol. 63. Library of Congress.

Benjamin H. Latrobe Collection. (MS 2009) M.H.S.

Mrs. Gamble Latrobe Collection. (MS 1638) M.H.S.

Benjamin H. Latrobe Papers. (MS 2009) M.H.S.

Leakin Papers. (MS 1349) M.H.S.

Mackubin Papers. (MS 551) M.H.S.

Madison Papers, Vol. 8. Library of Congress.

James McHenry Papers, Series II. Library of Congress.

James McHenry Papers. (MS 1476) M.H.S.

McHenry Family Papers. (MS 647) M.H.S.

McHenry Journals. (MS 544.1) M.H.S.

McHenry Letters. (MS 1509) M.H.S.

McHenry Papers. (MS 544) M.H.S.

Miscellaneous Collection. (MS 1118) M.H.S.

    Correspondence of: Aaron Burr
                       Solomon Davis
                       Thomas Jefferson
                       Henry Knox
                       Stevens T. Mason
                       Robert Wright
                       Engelhard Yeiser

Murray Papers. (MS 1376) M.H.S.

Oliver Papers. (MS 626) M.H.S.

Pearce Papers. (MS 1384) M.H.S.
Perine Papers. (MS 645) M.H.S.
Pinkney Letterbooks. (MS 661) M.H.S.
Pinkney Papers. (MS 1388) M.H.S.
Potts Papers, 1774–1803). (MS 1392) M.H.S.
Rawlings Papers. (MS 1399) M.H.S.
Ridgely Family Papers. (MS 1127) M.H.S.
Ridgely Papers. (MS 692 and 692.1) M.H.S.
Ridgely-Pue Papers. (MS 693) M.H.S.
Scharf Papers. (MS 1999) M.H.S.
Samuel Smith Collection. (MS 1424) M.H.S.
Smith Letterbooks, 1783–1784. (MS 1152) M.H.S.
Smith Letterbook, 1811–1824. (MS 1152) M.H.S.
Samuel Smith Papers. Library of Congress.
Taney Papers. (MS 800) M.H.S.
Edwin Thomas Papers. (MS 1520) M.H.S.
Henry O. Thompson Papers. (MS 821) M.H.S.
Tiffany Papers. (MS 1443) M.H.S.
Tench Tilghman Papers, 1731–1808. (MS 1445) M.H.S.
Vertical File. M.H.S.
Otho Holland Williams Papers, Vols. 3–10. (MS 908) M.H.S.
William Wirt Letterbooks, 1806–1816. (MS 1014) M.H.S.

Broadsides

"Address of the House of Delegates of Maryland to their Constituents," January 16, 1787. M.H.S.
"Address of the Maryland House of Delegates to their Constituents," 1787. Broadside Collection, Portfolio 28, no. 24. Rare Books Division, Library of Congress.
"An Address of the House of Delegates of Maryland to their Constituents." Ridgely Papers, Box II. M.H.S.
"A plain History of the Federalist Party in the Legislature," by "A Practical Mechanic." M.H.S.

"A Plan of the New Federal Government." Ridgely Collection, Box II, M.H.S.

"Don't Give Up The Ship, Freemen of Maryland," by "Lawrence." 1814. M.H.S.

"FEDERAL CALUMNY REFUTED," by William Pinkney. August 13, 1811. M.H.S.

"Friends to Amendments," 1789. M.H.S.

"Money! Money! Money!" M.H.S.

"No Party," 1789. M.H.S.

"Observations on Infidelity, and the Religious and Political Systems of Europe, Compared with those of the United States," 1807. Peabody Institute, Baltimore.

"Petition of Sundry Inhabitants of Harford County." M.H.S.

"The Dying Groans of Democracy." M.H.S.

"The Federal Ticket," 1789. M.H.S.

"TO FEDERALISTS," by "A RIGHT ROYAL FEDERALIST," 1808. M.H.S.

"To the Citizens and Voters of the Fifth District," September 27, 1800. M.H.S.

"To the Citizens and Free Voters of the Fifth District," by Jeremiah Townley Chase. September 2, 1800. M.H.S.

"To the Citizens of Cecil County," by "CECIL." 1816. M.H.S.

"TO THE CITIZENS OF TALBOT," by "A FRIEND TO JUSTICE." September 21, 1814. M.H.S.

"To the Delegates of Washington County in the Maryland House of Delegates," from the "Inhabitants of Washington County." Otho H. Williams Papers, Vol. 9. M.H.S.

"TO THE GOOD PEOPLE OF FREDERICK COUNTY." September 18, 1809. M.H.S.

"To the Freemen of Baltimore Town and the Fourth District." M.H.S.

"TO THE FREEMEN OF MARYLAND," by "AN OLD SOLDIER OF PRINCE GEORGE'S COUNTY." 1809. M.H.S.

"To the Independent Citizens of Maryland," by Samuel Chase. Chase Collection. M.H.S.

"TO THE PEOPLE," by "A POOR MAN." August 1821. M.H.S.

"TO THE PEOPLE," by William Clemm. 1811. M.H.S.

"To the People of Maryland." M.H.S.

"TO THE PEOPLE OF MARYLAND." September 2, 1811. M.H.S.

"TO THE PEOPLE OF TALBOT COUNTY," by "TRUTH." September 26, 1808. M.H.S.

"TO THE PEOPLE OF TALBOT," by "A FRIEND TO FREE VOTING." September 26, 1814. M.H.S.

"To the Roman Catholic Voters of Baltimore," by Samuel Chase. October 4, 1788. M.H.S.

"To the Voters of Ann-Arundel County." September 23, 1786. M.H.S.

"To the Voters of Baltimore-Town," by Samuel Chase and David McMechen. October 3, 1788. M.H.S.

"To the Voters of the City and County of Baltimore." Samuel Smith Papers. Library of Congress.

"To the Voters of the City and County of Baltimore." 1798. M.H.S.

"TO THE VOTERS OF FREDERICK COUNTY," by William Elie Williams. September 30, 1819. M.H.S.

Untitled Folio Broadside. December 24, 1784. M.H.S.

Pamphlets

A PLAIN HISTORY of the Conduct of the Federal Party in Our STATE LEGISLATURE on the Subject of GENERAL SUFFRAGE, the ALLEGHANY FRAUD, and the CLAIMS OF POOR MEN to the PRIVILEGE OF VOTING. n.d. Maryland Department, Enoch Pratt Free Library, Baltimore.

An Introductory Discourse to an Argument in Support of the Payments Made of the British Debts into the Treasury of Maryland During the Late War. By John Francis Mercer. Annapolis, 1789. M.H.S.

An Oration on the Birth of Washington. By Robert Goodloe Harper. 1810. Peabody Institute, Baltimore.

Bystander, Or, A Series of Letters on the Subject of the "Legislative Choice" of Electors in Maryland. By Robert Goodloe Harper. 1800. Peabody Institute, Baltimore.

Citizens of the State of Maryland. Petition, 1819. Peabody Institute, Baltimore.

Considerations on the Proposed Removal of the SEAT OF GOVERNMENT, Addressed to the Citizens of Maryland. By "Aristides." Annapolis, 1786. M.H.S.

Correspondence Respecting Russia. By Robert Goodloe Harper. 1813. Peabody Institute, Baltimore.

Detection of A Conspiracy Formed by the United Irishmen, With the Evident Intention of Aiding the Tyrants of France in Subverting the Government of the United States of America. By William Cobbett. Philadelphia, 1798.

EXTRACT From A LONG TALK Delivered by Dr. Leib. May 13, 1816. M.H.S.

Hanson's Pamphlets. By Alexander Contee Hanson. Printed and MSS pamphlets, A. C. Hanson Collection, M.H.S.

Joint Committee to Inquire into the Causes and Extent of the Late Commotions in the City of Baltimore. 1812. Peabody Institute, Baltimore.

Outlines for A Plan of Government for the United States, and Amendments to the Constitutions of the Several States of this Union. By Charles Carroll of Carrollton. MSS Pamphlet, Carroll Papers, Vol. 8. M.H.S.

Political Schemes and Calculations, Addressed to the Citizens of Maryland, By A Native Citizen and Servant of the State. Annapolis, 1784. M.H.S.

Portrait of the Evils of Democracy. Baltimore, 1816. M.H.S.

REMARKS on the Proposed Plan of an EMISSION OF PAPER, and on the Means of Effecting It, Addressed to the Citizens of Maryland. By "Aristides." Annapolis, 1786. M.H.S.

REMARKS on the PROPOSED PLAN of A FEDERAL GOVERNMENT, Addressed to the Citizens of the UNITED STATES OF AMERICA, and Particularly to the People of MARYLAND. By "Aristides." Annapolis, 1787. M.H.S.

The Honest Politician. By Luther Martin. 1808. Maryland Department, Enoch Pratt Free Library, Baltimore.

The Opinion of Judge Bland on the Right of the Judiciary to Declare an Act of Assembly Unconstitutional. By Theodorick Bland. 1816. Peabody Institute, Baltimore.

To the General Assembly of Maryland. Annapolis, 1784. M.H.S.

To the Members of the General Assembly of Maryland. Annapolis, 1784. M.H.S.

Newspapers

American and Commercial Daily Advertiser, Baltimore. 1799–1819.

Baltimore Daily Intelligencer. 1794.

Bartgis's *Federal Gazette,* Frederick Town. 1798.

Evening Post, Baltimore. 1808–1810.

Federal Gazette and Baltimore Daily Advertiser. 1796–1812.

Federal Republican, Georgetown. 1812.

Federal Republican and Commercial Advertiser, Baltimore. 1808–1812.

Frederick Town Herald, Frederick Town. 1802–1812.

Gazette of the United States, Philadelphia. 1796–1798.

Maryland Gazette, Baltimore. 1785–1796.

Maryland Gazette, Annapolis. 1781–1815.

Maryland Herald, Easton. 1798–1802.

Maryland Herald, Elizabeth Town. 1798–1800.

Maryland Journal, Baltimore. 1780–1796.

Maryland Republican, Annapolis. 1810–1816.

North American and Mercantile Daily Advertiser, Baltimore. 1808.

Telegraph and Daily Advertiser, Baltimore. 1798–1800.

The Republican, or Anti-Democrat, Baltimore. 1802.

The Republican Advocate, Frederick Town. 1802.

Public Documents

Browne, W. H., ed. *Archives of Maryland.* 57 vols. Baltimore, 1883–1940.

Kilty, William, ed. *The Laws of Maryland.* 7 vols. Annapolis, 1799–1820.

Maryland. Commissioners' Ledger and Journal of Confiscated British Property, 1781–1785. Hall of Records, Annapolis.

Maryland. Executive Letterbook, 1798. Hall of Records, Annapolis.

Maryland. *Laws of Maryland.* 1786–1816.

Maryland. Papers Relative to the Maryland Stock in the Bank of England. "Rainbow Series," Blue Books II and III. Hall of Records, Annapolis.

Maryland. Sale Book of Confiscated British Property, 1781–1785. Hall of Records, Annapolis.

Maryland. State Treasury Ledger A. Hall of Records, Annapolis.

Maryland. *Votes and Proceedings of the General Assembly of the State of Maryland.* Senate and House of Delegates, 1777–1820.

United States. *American State Papers: Documents, Legislative and Executive of the Congress of the United States, 1789–1815. Commerce and Navigation.* Class IV. Vol. 1. March 1789, to March 1815. Washington, 1832.

United States. *American State Papers. Finance.* Class III. Vols. 1 and 2. March 1789, to March 1815. Washington, 1832.

United States. *American State Papers. Foreign Relations.* Class I. Vol. 4. March 1815, to May 1822. Washington, 1834.

United States. *Annals of the Congress of the United States.* 1st to 20th Congress. Washington, 1834–1858.

United States. *State Papers.* 13th Congress, 3rd Session. 1814–1815. Vol. 4.

Articles

Crowl, Philip. "Anti-Federalism in Maryland," *William and Mary Quarterly* 4 (October 1947):446–69.

Ford, W. C., ed. "Letters of William Vans Murray to John Quincy Adams." *Annual Report of the American Historical Association,* 1912. Washington, 1914.

"Maryland Politics in 1796—McHenry Letters." *Publications of the Southern History Association* 9 (September 1905): 374–88.

"Maryland Politics in 1797 Shown in Letters Selected from the Correspondence of James McHenry," *Publications of the Southern History Association* 10 (January 1906): 31–38.

Pancake, John S. "Baltimore and the Embargo: 1807–1809" *Maryland Historical Magazine* 48 (September 1952): 173–87.

Pole, J. R. "Constitutional Reform and Election Statistics in Maryland, 1790–1812," *Maryland Historical Magazine* 55 (December 1960):275–92.

———. "Suffrage and Representation in Maryland from 1776 to 1810: A Statistical Note and Some Reflections," *Journal of Southern History* 24 (May 1958):218–25.

Sawtell, Clement C. "Impressment of American Seamen by the British," *Essex Institute Historical Collections* 76 (1940):314–44.

Schauinger, Joseph H. "Alexander Contee Hanson, Federalist Partisan," *Maryland Historical Magazine* 35 (Baltimore, 1940):354–64.

Smith, Theodore C. "War Guilt in 1812," *Massachusetts Historical Society Proceedings* 64 (1930–32):319–45.

Swisher, Carl B. "Roger B. Taney and the Tenets of Democracy," *Maryland Historical Magazine* 34 (Baltimore, 1939):207–22.

Taylor, George R. "Agrarian Discontent in the Mississippi Valley Preceding the War of 1812," *Journal of Political Economy* 39 (April 1931):491–505.

Tinling, Marion. "Thomas Lloyd's Reports of the First Federal Congress," *William and Mary Quarterly* 18 (October 1961):519–45.

Unpublished Material

Brown, Dorothy. "Party Battles and Beginnings in Maryland." Ph.D. dissertation, Georgetown University, 1962.

Pancake, John S. "General From Baltimore." Ph.D. dissertation, University of Virginia, 1949.

Renzulli, L. M. "The Extent of Rhode Island's Participation in the War of 1812." Master's thesis, University of Rhode Island, 1958.

Books

Abernethy, Thomas P. *The South in the New Nation, 1789–1819*. Baton Rouge: Louisiana State University Press, 1961.

————. *Western Lands and the American Revolution*. New York: Russell & Russell, Inc., 1959.

Adams, Henry. *History of the United States of America*. 9 vols. New York: Charles Scribner's Sons, 1891.

Allen, A. H., ed. *Documentary History of the Constitution of the United States*. 5 vols. Washington: Government Printing Office, 1905.

Andrews, Matthew Page. *History of Maryland*. New York: Doubleday and Co., Inc., 1929.

Babcock, Kendric C. *The Rise of American Nationality, 1811–1819.* New York: Harper and Brothers, 1906.

Barker, Charles A. *The Background of the Revolution in Maryland.* New Haven: Yale University Press, 1940.

Bassett, John S. *The Federalist System, 1789–1801.* vol. 11 of *The American Nation: A History.* Edited by A. B. Hart. New York: Harper and Brothers, 1907.

Beard, Charles A. *An Economic Interpretation of the Constitution of the United States.* New York: The Macmillan Company, 1913.

———. *Economic Origins of Jeffersonian Democracy.* New York: The Macmillan Company, 1915.

Behrens, Kathryn L. *Paper Money in Maryland, 1727–1789.* Baltimore: The Johns Hopkins Press, 1923.

Beirne, Francis. *The War of 1812.* New York: E. P. Dutton & Co., 1949.

Bemis, Samuel Flagg. *A Diplomatic History of the United States.* New York: Henry Holt and Company, 1955.

———. *Jay's Treaty: A Study in Commerce and Diplomacy.* New York: The Macmillan Company, 1923.

Bond, Beverly. *State Government in Maryland.* Baltimore: The Johns Hopkins Press, 1905.

Bowers, Claude. *Jefferson in Power: The Death Struggle of the Federalists.* Boston: Houghton Mifflin Co., 1936.

Bradford, Alden. *History of the Federal Government for Fifty Years, 1789–1839.* Boston: S. G. Simpkins, 1840.

Brant, Irving. *James Madison.* 5 vols. Indianapolis, Ind.: The Bobbs-Merrill Co., 1941–1957.

Buchholz, H. E. *Governors of Maryland from the Revolution to the Year 1908.* Baltimore: Williams & Wilkins Co., 1908.

Bureau of the Census. *A Century of Population Growth, 1790–1900.* Washington: Government Printing Office, 1909.

Carey, Matthew. *The Olive Branch: Or Faults on Both Sides, Federal and Democratic.* Philadelphia: Published by M. Carey, 1815.

Channing, Edward. *A History of the United States.* 6 vols. New York: The Macmillan Company, 1905–1925.

Clark, Charles, ed. *The Eastern Shore of Maryland and Virginia.* 2 vols. New York: Lewis Historical Publishing Co., 1950.

Cole, Arthur. *Wholesale Commodity Prices in the United States, 1700–1861. Statistical Supplement.* Boston: Harvard University Press, 1938.

Craven, Avery. *Soil Exhaustion as a Factor in the Agricultural History of Virginia and Maryland, 1606–1860.* Urbana, Ill.: University of Illinois Press, 1926.

Crowl, Philip A. *Maryland During and After the Revolution.* Baltimore: The Johns Hopkins Press, 1943.

Cunningham, Noble. *The Jeffersonian Republicans: The Formation of Party Organization.* Chapel Hill, N.C.: University of North Carolina Press, 1957.

Cunz, Dieter. *The Maryland Germans.* Princeton, N.J.: Princeton University Press, 1948.

Curti, Merle. *Peace or War, The American Struggle. 1636–1936.* New York: W. W. Norton & Co., Inc., 1936.

Dauer, Manning J. *The Adams Federalists.* Baltimore: The John Hopkins Press, 1953.

Delaplaine, Edward S. *The Life of Thomas Johnson.* New York: F. H. Hitchcock and Company, 1927.

Dewey, Davis R. *Financial History of the United States.* New York: Longmans, Green & Co., Inc., 1934.

Elliott, Jonathan, ed. *The Debates in the Several State Conventions, on the Adoption of the Federal Constitution as Recommended by the General Convention at Philadelphia in 1787.* 5 vols. Philadelphia: J. B. Lippincott Co., 1896.

Emory, Frederick. *Queen Anne's County, Maryland.* Baltimore: Maryland Historical Society, 1950.

Essary, J. Frederick. *Maryland in National Politics.* Baltimore: John Murphy Co., 1932.

Ferguson, E. James. *The Power of the Purse*. Chapel Hill, N.C.: University of North Carolina Press for The Institute of Early American History and Culture, 1961.

Fitzpatrick, John, ed. *The Writings of George Washington From the Original Manuscript Sources, 1745–1799*. 37 vols. Washington: United States Government Printing Office, 1937.

Ford, W. C. *The Writings of George Washington*. 14 vols. New York: G. P. Putnam's Sons, 1891.

Geiger, Sister Mary V. *Daniel Carroll, A Framer of the Constitution*. Washington: The Catholic University of America Press, Inc., 1943.

Goddard, Henry P. *Luther Martin: The Federal Bull-Dog*. Baltimore: J. Murphy & Co., 1887.

Goodman, Warren H. "The Origins of the War of 1812: A Survey of Changing Interpretations," *The Making of American History*. Edited by Donald Sheehan. New York: The Dryden Press, 1954.

Gould, C. P. "The Economic Causes of the Rise of Baltimore," *Essays in Colonial History Presented to Charles McLean Andrews by His Students*. New Haven, Conn.: Yale University Press, 1931.

Gray, Lewis C. *History of Agriculture in the Southern United States to 1860*. 2 vols. Washington: The Carnegie Institute of Washington, 1933.

Gurn, Joseph. *Charles Carroll of Carrollton*. New York: P. J. Kennedy & Sons, 1932.

Harrell, Isaac. *Loyalism in Virginia*. Philadelphia: Duke University Publications, 1926.

Jennings, Walter. *American Embargo*. Iowa City, Iowa: The University of Iowa, 1921.

Jensen, Merrill. *The New Nation. A History of the United States During the Confederation, 1781–1789*. New York: Alfred A. Knopf, Inc., 1950.

Libby, Orin. *The Geographical Distribution of the Vote of the Thirteen States on the Federal Constitution, 1787–88*. Madison, Wis.: The University of Wisconsin, 1894.

Link, Eugene P. *Democratic-Republican Societies, 1790–1800.* New York: Columbia University Press, 1942.

Lipscomb, Andrew, ed. *The Writings of Thomas Jefferson.* 20 vols. Washington: Thomas Jefferson Memorial Association of the United States, 1903.

MacDonald, William, ed. *Select Documents Illustrative of the History of the United States, 1776–1861.* New York: The Macmillan Company, 1930.

Maclay, E. S., ed. *The Journal of William Maclay.* New York: Albert and Charles Boni, Inc., 1927.

Mathews, Edward. *Counties of Maryland, Their Origin, Boundaries and Election Districts.* Baltimore: The Johns Hopkins Press, 1907.

McMaster, John Bach. *A History of the People of the United States.* 8 vols. New York: D. Appleton & Co., 1883–1913.

McSherry, James. *History of Maryland From its First Settlement in 1634 to the Year 1848.* Baltimore: J. Murphy & Co., 1849.

———. *History of Maryland.* Baltimore: The Baltimore Book Co., 1904.

Melville, Annabelle M. *John Carroll of Baltimore.* New York: Charles Scribner's Sons, 1955.

Miller, John C. *The Federalist Era, 1789–1801.* New York: Harper & Brothers, 1960.

———. *Crisis in Freedom: The Alien and Sedition Acts.* Boston: Little, Brown & Co., Inc., 1951.

Mott, Frank L. *Jefferson and the Press.* Baton Rouge, La.: Louisiana State University Press, 1943.

Munroe, John. *Federalist Delaware, 1775–1815.* New Brunswick: Rutgers University Press, 1954.

Owens, Hamilton. *Baltimore on the Chesapeake.* New York: Doubleday, Doran & Co., Inc., 1941.

Paine, Ralph D. *The Fight for A Free Sea.* New Haven, Conn.: Yale University Press, 1921.

Palmer, T. H. *The Historical Register of the United States.* vol. 2. Philadelphia: T. H. Palmer, 1814.

Paullin, Charles O. *Atlas of the Historical Geography of the United States.* Washington: The Carnegie Institution of Washington, 1932.

Peden, William, ed. *Notes on the State of Virginia.* Chapel Hill, N.C.: University of North Carolina Press, 1954.

Pitkin, Timothy. *A Statistical View of the Commerce of the United States of America.* New Haven, Conn.: Durrie & Peck, 1835.

Pratt, Fletcher. *The Heroic Years.* New York: H. Smith & R. Haas, 1934.

Pratt, Julius, *Expansionists of 1812.* New York: P. Smith, 1949.

Preston, Walter W. *History of Harford County.* Baltimore: Press of Sun Book Office, 1901.

Riley, Elihu S. *The Ancient City. A History of Annapolis in Maryland.* Annapolis: Annapolis Printing Office, 1887.

Robert, Joseph C. *The Tobacco Kingdom.* Durham, N.C.: Duke University Press, 1938.

Rowland, Kate M. *The Life of Charles Carroll of Carrollton, 1737–1832.* 2 vols. New York: G. P. Putnam & Sons, 1898.

Scharf, John Thomas. *History of Baltimore City and County.* Philadelphia: L. H. Everts, 1881.

———. *History of Maryland.* 3 vols. Baltimore: J. B. Piet, 1879.

———. *History of Western Maryland.* Philadelphia: L. H. Everts, 1882.

———. *The Chronicles of Baltimore.* Baltimore: Turnbull Brothers, 1874.

Sears, Louis M. *Jefferson and the Embargo.* Durham, N.C.: Duke University Press, 1927.

Seybert, Adam. *Statistical Annals of the United States of America.* Philadelphia: Thomas Dobson & Son, 1818.

Siousset, Anne L. *Old Baltimore.* New York: The Macmillan Co., 1931.

Smith, Ellen H. *Charles Carroll of Carrollton.* Cambridge, Mass.: Harvard University Press, 1942.

Smith, James Morton. *Freedom's Fetters: The Alien and Sedition Laws and American Civil Liberties.* Ithaca, N.Y.: Cornell University Press, 1956.

Steiner, Bernard C. *The Life and Correspondence of James McHenry.* Cleveland, Ohio: Burrows Brothers Co., 1907.

———. *Citizenship and Suffrage in Maryland.* Baltimore: Cushing & Co., 1895.

Sullivan, Kathryn. *Maryland and France, 1774–1789.* Philadelphia: University of Pennsylvania Press, 1936.

Swisher, Carl Brent. *Roger B. Taney.* New York: The Macmillan Co., 1935.

Thorpe, F. N. *Federal and State Constitutions, Colonial Charters, and Other Organic Laws.* 7 vols. Washington: Government Printing Office, 1909.

Tilghman, Oswald. *History of Talbot County Maryland, 1761–1861.* 2 vols. Baltimore: Williams & Wilkins Co., 1915.

Tyler, Samuel. *Memoir of Roger Brooke Taney.* Baltimore: J. Murphy & Co., 1876.

Wheaton, Henry. *Some Account of the Life, Writings, and Speeches of William Pinkney.* New York: E. Bliss & E. White, 1826.

White, Leonard. *The Federalists. A Study in Administrative History.* New York: The Macmillan Company, 1948.

Williamson, Chilton. *American Suffrage From Property to Democracy, 1760–1860.* Princeton, N.J.: Princeton University Press, 1960.

Index